Defiance and Compliance

New Directions in Anthropology

General Editor: **Jacqueline Waldren**, *Institute of Social Anthropology, University of Oxford*

DEFIANCE AND COMPLIANCE

Negotiating Gender in Low-Income Cairo

Heba Aziz El-Kholy

Berghahn Books
New York • Oxford

Published in 2002 by

Berghahn Books

www.berghahnbooks.com

Copyright © 2002 Heba Aziz El-Kholy

Library of Congress Cataloguing-in-Publication Data

El-Kholy, Heba Aziz.
    Defiance and compliance: negotiating gender in low-income Cairo / Heba Aziz El-Kholy.
    p. cm.
    Includes bibliographical references and index.
    ISBN 1-57181-390-X (cloth : alk. paper) -- ISBN 1-57181-391-8 (pbk. : alk. paper)
    1. Women--Egypt--Cairo--Social conditions. 2. Women--Egypt--Cairo--Economic
conditions. 3. Cairo (Egypt)--Social life and customs. 4. Poor-Egypt--Cairo. 5. Sex
role--Egypt--Cairo. 6. Social conflict--Egypt--Cairo. I. Title.

HQ1793.Z9 C353 2002
305.42'0962'16--dc21   2002018272

British Library Cataloguing in Publication Data

A catalogue record for this book is available from the British Library.

Printed in the United States on acid-free paper.

Contents

This book is dedicated to

SEIF KABIL

and
to the memory of my soul mate

MAGDA AL- NOWAIHI

Acknowledgments

This book would not have been possible without the intellectual, practical and emotional support of family, friends and colleagues in Cairo, London and, more recently, in New York. In Cairo, many people made important comments on drafts of papers that eventually became part of this book. I want to thank Soraya Al-Torki, Hoda El-Sadda, Nadia Farah, Nader Fergany, Farha Ghanem, Marlene Nasr, Cynthia Nelson, Malak Roushdy, Shahnaz Rouze, Hania Sholkamy, Malak Zaalouk and Huda Zurayek. Hani Hanna spent late nights formatting the manuscript. My research assistants, Salwa El Zeniny, Karima Said and Mona Ahmed, meticulously transcribed many tapes.

In London, my foremost gratitude goes to Deniz Kandiyoti, who generously shared with me her time and knowledge and always pushed me further intellectually. Peter Lozios and Anne Marie Goetz provided valuable comments. Nadia Taher read an early draft of the book and made incisive comments that improved it. Nadje Al-Ali shared with me her friendship and many insights. My friendships with Nadia Taher, Caren Levy and Emma Playfair sustained me through many dreary winter months.

I am indebted to my parents, Nadia and Aziz, for instilling in me that un-abating desire to learn, to take up new challenges and to pursue my dreams. Without this foundation, this book would never have seen the light of day. I also want to thank my mother for carefully proofreading the manuscript.

A special note of appreciation is due to Amr and Seif Kabil who, without realizing it, taught me much about "negotiating gender". Amr Kabil provided continuous encouragement and support. My son, Seif, has been a constant source of joy throughout our journey to many places in the course of writing this book; his smile always soothed me during periods of pressure.

I am blessed with an intimate network of friends whose love and unconditional support have enabled me to successfully juggle the competing demands of motherhood, a full-time job and the writing of this book. I want to thank Margo Zaki for all those times she picked up Seif from the nursery when I was away.

Sohier Adam spent time with me in London and was a source of comfort and inspiration during many late nights of writing. Magda Al-Nowaihi believed in me more than I dared believe in myself ; in many way it was her own awe-inspiring courage that gave me the strength to complete this book. Iman Bibars supported me throughout the entire process of research and writing in ways that only an intimate friend with whom one has shared a lifetime is capable of. My friendship with Pratihba Metha was critical for maintaining my sanity during difficult months in New York as I was finalizing the book.

I want to thank the British Council in Cairo for supporting part of this work through a Chevening scholarship from 1995-1998 and the Ford Foundation's regional office in Cairo for partly supporting the field work through a MERC award in 1996. My thanks to Carol Bloodworth, copy editor, for her meticulous editorial comments and to Vivian Berghahn, production manager, who has been a pleasure to work with.

Finally, to the courageous women in Cairo's neighborhoods who so generously opened up their homes and hearts to me, no words of thanks are enough. I only hope that I have managed to remain true to their own perspectives, experiences and agendas and that these will eventually find their way into broader debates about gender relations and strategies for advancing women's interests.

A NOTE ON TRANSLITERATION

The system of transliteration used in this volume is a modified version of that recommended by the International Journal of Middle East Studies. The modifications are due to my desire to be faithful to colloquial Egyptian pronunciations and local dialects, rather than classical Arabic pronunciations. Some modifications have also been necessary for ease of printing and to facilitate reading for the non-specialist.

All transliterated words are in italics throughout the volume, except for those which are now part of the English vocabulary and found in standard English dictionaries, such as sheikh or Quran. Arabic names of persons and places are also not in Italics. Only Arabic singulars are used; plurals are denoted by the addition of an (s). The transliteration does not differentiate between emphatic and non-emphatic sounds.

All diacritical marks are deleted with the exception of the letter *ayn* and the glottal stop, the *hamza*, when it appears in the middle of a word. The *ayn* in denoted by the mark ⊂. The *hamza* is denoted by the mark ⊃. The long high back vowel is denoted by the uu. The long high front vowel is denoted by ii. The long low vowel is denoted by aa. The short high front vowel is (*kasra*) is denoted by the letter i; the short vowel (*fat-ha*) by the letter a; and the short high back vowel (*dama*) by the letter u. A dash is placed between two consonants, which are meant to be pronounced seperately but could be confused for another sound if kept adjacent. For example, *fat-ha, nas-ha*.

The modifications made to accommodate the Egyptian dialect are noted below. Where there is more than one transliteration for a letter, this indicates a regional difference in dialect.

il = أكل
G = ج ع ق
D or Z = ظ ذ ع
T or S = ث

INTRODUCTION:
A PERSONAL TRAJECTORY

How do low-income women in Cairo experience, perceive, respond to, and nego-tiate gender relations and hierarchies in their daily lives, both in the household and at the workplace? This is the main question with which this book is con-cerned. The reasons why I felt compelled to seek answers to this question in the first place, however, may be a story worth telling, as it chronicles a personal and intellectual journey of discovery which started over fifteen years ago.

In 1985, I returned to Cairo, the city where I was born and bred, from the United States of America, where I had lived for two years to pursue a master's degree in the sociology of development, eager to apply my recently acquired knowledge and skills. I was particularly interested in finding a job which would allow me to work on a daily basis in poor neighborhoods around Cairo, which I only had glimpses of as I was growing up.

I would not have defined myself as a feminist then. Although I was immersed in the women in development (WID) literature as a graduate student, gender issues were not central to my concerns. Nor was I particularly aware of how gen-der structures poverty and how poverty, in turn, may influence and shape gender relations, gender interests, and gender hierarchies. In fact, my master's thesis con-stituted an excellent example of a rather gender-blind approach to the analysis of the social organization of irrigation in an Egyptian village.

A few weeks after my return to Cairo, I was offered a unique opportunity to fulfill my desire to practice development and deepen my firsthand knowledge and understanding of poverty. Between 1985 and1987, I worked in one of Egypt's poorest and most marginalized communities, the settlement of the traditional garbage collectors, or *zabbaliin,* in Muqattam which lies on the eastern fringes of the city of Cairo.[1] This is an experience I will always treasure as, much more than graduate studies, it has taught me what development is truly about, and what it could and should be about.[2]

I spent the first six months of my assignment participating in the daily lives of men and women in the *zabbaliin* community. This constituted an unstructured and informal research process, in the course of which I sought to understand power relations within the community and different people's concerns, priorities and needs so as to initiate an appropriate programmatic response. The *zabbaliin* had a strict and visible gendered division of labor. Men were responsible for collecting household garbage from around the city and bringing it back to the settlement in their donkey carts. Women were responsible for hand sorting the garbage into organic and inorganic waste. Organic waste was then fed to the pigs which the *zabbaliin* raise, and inorganic waste, such as plastic, glass, and tin, was recycled (Environmental Quality International report 1987).

As my relations with the community deepened, however, I began to realize that the community was also differentiated in more subtle and less visible ways, and that gender was a central axis of this differentiation. Men and women within the same household often had divergent concerns, priorities and expenditure patterns, voiced different needs and interests, and expressed their grievances and concerns through disparate means. Moreover, men's and women's relationships and access to some of the central institutions and networks in the community, such as the church, the community development association, local offices of the ministry of social affairs, informal employment and saving networks, and so forth, varied significantly.

My observations found confirmation in an emerging literature from a number of developing countries which suggested that women and men had differential access to, and control over, social, economic and political resources within their households and communities. Cross-cultural studies documenting how gender influences intrahousehold bargaining and access to resources has multiplied since the mid-eighties (Bruce and Dwyer 1988; Bryceson, 1995; Guyer and Peters 1987; Haddad et al. 1995;Hoodfar 1990; Jones 1986; Roldan 1988; Whitehead 1981; Young et al. 1981).

My attention soon focused on a particular category of *zabbaliin* households, those for whom women were the main breadwinners. My discussions and observations suggested that these households had particularly pressing problems, and constituted some of the poorest and most vulnerable in the settlement. According to local estimates, about 30 percent of all households in the settlement were solely or mainly economically maintained by women. These women were either widowed, married to disabled/sick men, deserted by their husbands, or married to husbands who were not fully providing for the family. Despite their numbers and relative disadvantage, women-headed households, however, were largely disregarded by the other development projects being implemented in the *zabbaliin* community at the time. As elsewhere in the early eighties, women-headed households in Egypt remained an "ignored factor in development planning" (Buvinic and Youssef 1978).

In an attempt to address this issue, I embarked on a participatory planning process[3] in the *zabbaliin* settlement that culminated in the design and implementation of a credit and technical assistance project for women-headed households.[4] The aim of the project was to enable this particular category of women to both improve their earning capacity, as well as enhance their self-confidence and life options. To alleviate some of the gender-specific constraints which poor women faced in accessing credit, the project required no collateral or guarantees, either in the form of the signature of a man, or the possession of an identity card, as was the case with practically all other credit programs in Egypt at that time.[5]

In the mid-eighties in Egypt, there were no national statistics or analyses of women who were financially supporting their households, and there was little public interest in the issue. In fact, I remember being met with skepticism by some researchers, activists and government officials when I tried to argue that women-headed households might indeed be an important issue to study and a potentially vulnerable group in Egyptian society at large. The major obstacle seemed to be a deeply entrenched view of the "traditional" Egyptian family which cast the man as breadwinner, and a prevailing gender ideology that closely linked maleness and masculinity with the ability to provide financial support (Hoodfar 1990; Nadim 1985; Rugh 1984). The existence of large numbers of women-headed households challenged this ideology in a radical way, and called into question a range of state policies and laws-from social security to personal status laws-which are largely based on the ideology of the male breadwinner.

Moreover, the suggestion that these women were particularly vulnerable, and not adequately supported by their wider kin group, threatened idealized images of the solidarity of the extended Egyptian family. This "public transcript" about the family is an item of national pride for many people, and a central feature assumed to distinguish Egyptians from the "West," whose weak familial relations are popularly invoked as the cause of its presumed moral decay. Surely this was an issue which might be of concern to black families in the United States, I was told by several researchers, but it was not a development priority for us in Egypt. I quickly learned, as Eickleman and Piscatori suggest in their discussion of the family in the Middle East, that "the idea of the family is so central that only with difficulties do societies alter its conventional images and public forms. ... Pressures to change the official and often legally endorsed view of family and familial roles is often regarded with great suspicion ... The family provides a powerful idiom for expressing core national and religious values" (1996:83-84).

I was too close to what was going on in the *zabbaliin* community, however, to be swayed by the skepticism that I was encountering. Despite the lack of statistics documenting the phenomenon of female headship at the time, my fieldwork among the *zabbaliin,* and subsequently in other slum areas in Cairo, strengthened my conviction of the existence of a significant number of households supported by women. I also became more aware of how gender relations and family roles may be rapidly changing in response to broader societal transformations. Although ignored in Egypt, recognition of the phenomenon of female supported households was gradually increasing within the international development community in the light of research in a number of developing countries. This provided me with important ammunition, although I was not then aware of all the literature on the subject (see for example, Bolak 1990; Buvinic and Youssef 1978; Chant 1991, 1997; Harris 1993; Merrick and Schmink 1983; Rosenhouse 1989; Shanthi 1996).[6]

Not only were women breadwinners in the communities I was involved in particularly vulnerable and thus deserving of specific development assistance, but exposing their reality also seemed to me an excellent opportunity to challenge patriarchal legal structures in Egypt more broadly, by questioning the basic assumptions on which they are based. For instance, inheritance laws stipulating that a man has the right to inherit twice the amount allowed for a woman, on the basis that men are the main breadwinners, can be seriously put into question by a socioeconomic reality where women may be increasingly becoming the main financial providers for their families.

The seeds of the central issues with which this book is concerned were sown during those early years of working with women-headed households at the *zabbaliin* settlement, and have matured and evolved over the decade that followed. When I left the *zabbaliin* community in 1987, I had become a self-defined feminist, had developed a keen appreciation of the extent to which poverty is gendered, and was skeptical about the conventional image of the Egyptian family that casts men as sole breadwinners. As a response, I became a founding member of the Association for the Development and Enhancement of Women (ADEW), an organization whose aim is to support households in Cairo where women are the main breadwinners. Founding ADEW in 1989 with a group of like-minded professional men and women in many ways provided me with the necessary institutional base and intellectual support to pursue the issues in which I was interested.[7]

As I continued my work as a professional involved in development programs with a number of international agencies in Egypt, I carried out extensive fieldwork and my experiences and knowledge of low-income neighborhoods in both rural and urban areas increased. So did my understanding and awareness of gender issues. As a volunteer board member of ADEW, I became much more involved in the debates among various women's groups in Egypt, and joined, both as an individual and as a representative of a women's nongovernmental organization (NGO), in the various organized activities and campaigns that aimed to challenge gender inequalities. These debates and campaigns had intensified significantly in the early 1990s partly in response to the International United Nations conferences on population and Development held in Cairo in 1994, and the United Nations conference on women held in China in 1995 (see Egyptian NGO platform of action reports, 1994, 1995).

As my involvement in the "women's movement" grew, so did my own awareness of broader issues and debates among feminists. This fuelled my willingness and ability to more radically challenge patriarchal structures and ideas both at a personal and public level. However, I also became increasingly uncomfortable with the often significant discrepancies, that I began to detect between the types of issues, priorities and visions that were shaping the most vocal feminist agendas in Egypt, and the concerns, struggles and priorities of the poorer women that I was working in a variety of development programs. The issue of "political participation" was a particularly nagging one for me.

Increasing women's "political participation" was identified as an important priority by feminists in Egypt (as elsewhere), and campaigns to raise less privileged women's awareness about the importance of participation in formal elections at the parliamentary and local government levels were launched in the 1990's. Registering women, and issuing voting cards for them was an important feminist tactic and a special organization was set up for that purpose in 1994.

For the many poor women I worked with in the *zabbaliin* community, as well as subsequently in other communities, however, politics was not about voting in the elections. Rather, it was partly about negotiating access to resources from a state bureaucracy that was biased against them both as women and as illiterates.[8] The type of card many low-income women in the *zabbaliin* and other communities needed most, and which many were unsuccessfully struggling to obtain due to a host of complicated bureaucratic regulations and ideological constraints, was not a voting registration card, but a more basic personal identity card, *bitaqa shaksia.* For many poor women, significantly more so than for poor men, possessing such a card was literally on the order of an unattainable dream.

Yet identity cards have an important symbolic value for women as a way of asserting their citizenship and identity as responsible and independent human beings. Moreover, an identity card also has a direct practical value for poor women as it provides an important avenue for participation in the politics of survival. An identity card is essential to enable a woman to access state subsidies and pensions, to register her children in schools, or register a complaint at a police station, if beaten up by her husband.[9] The possession of an identity card thus appeared to me at its core to be an issue of equal citizenship between men and women, and represented both a political as well as a pragmatic concern. However, until recently, when ADEW took up the issue in its campaigns, the symbolic, strategic and practical importance of identity cards for low-income women had been completely ignored by activists. Voting cards were on the agenda, but identity cards were not. This clearly pointed to divergent priorities among different categories of women in Egypt.

The research interests behind this book thus partly stem from my dissatisfaction with our ability to formulate a feminist agenda broad and diverse enough to accommodate and reflect the interests and central concerns of women across class boundaries. I started to wonder whether our guiding agendas in the women's movement were perhaps circumscribed by our own class circumstances as middle-class and upper-class educated women, and whether our strategies, visions and assumptions were dependent on our own social locations and lived realities, locations and realities quite different from those of the majority of women in the country.

I also became increasingly uncomfortable with the discourse and assumptions underlying the various policies and programs developed by governments, NGOs and international agencies to "empower" women. I began to realize that these were sometimes based on ahistorical and decontextualized assumptions about women's and men's lives, devoid of a class perspective and thus often not reflecting the lived realities of poor families. Some aspects of my concerns had to do specifically with the policy focus on an "ideal," and I would venture to say quite middle-class, model of the household as one composed of a married couple with a male provider. My early experience in the *zabbaliin* settlement discussed earlier had already suggested that this was often a fallacy.

Other aspects of my concerns had to do with the assumptions underlying some of the more academic work on gender relations in the Middle East. I was dissatisfied with what I saw as the two polarities in academic writing on gender relations and women's agency; some studies depicted women as utterly oppressed and devoid of agency, (see Tapper 1979; Ahmed 1982); while others celebrated their hidden or informal power, strength and solidarity (AlTorki 1986; Aswad 1978; Early 1993a,b). As is discussed in greater detail in the following chapter, these studies seemed to offer polarized theoretical assumptions regarding power, subordination and women's agency.

My years of experience at the grass roots suggested to me that women are often engaged in a complex process of negotiation at a microlevel in their daily lives. The low-income women I worked with seemed neither unqualifiably "passive" objects of oppression, nor were they powerful agents who exercised authority and agency, and who "have it all together" (Early 1993b), as they have been often depicted in those two extremes of the research spectrum. I thus felt compelled to find ways to maneuver between those two images of women. I wanted to contribute to a better understanding of what women's daily struggles and conflicts were about, what they were saying about their lives and priorities, how they were saying it, and how their concerns and responses varied based on their life cycles. This seemed to me a way to better understand how gendered forms of power operate at a microlevel. My questions were multiple but interrelated: To what extent and in what ways were women trying to challenge aspects of their unequal relationships with men? Which aspects were they not contesting, and why?

I had a hunch, fuelled by my earlier observations, which suggested to me that women may indeed be discontented, speak about the desire for change, and challenge at least some aspects of gender relations and ideologies, but in a "coded" language. The only way to verify this hunch was to carry out in-depth and contextualized research using a methodology that would enable me to pay close attention to women's narratives, expressed both in public and in private, and to local expressions and idioms through which they may express daily forms of discontent.

Focusing only on women's narratives and experiences, however, carries the danger of "naturalizing" the concept of experience or taking it at face value, assuming a one-to-one correspondence between words and things, and ignoring the constructed and discursive character of experience itself (Scott 1992). In addition to listening to women's narratives and experiences, I thus realized that I would need to examine closely the often conflicting realities and discourses which inform women's experiences and structure their visions and identities in specific physical, socioeconomic and historical contexts. Moreover, since ideas about gender and power relations are best revealed through concrete daily interactions and specific activities (see Agarwal 1994; Loizos and Papataxiarchis 1991a), I would also need to carefully observe women and men's actual daily practices and social arrangements. This is precisely what I ended up doing over fifteen months between July 1995 and October 1996 in several low-income communities in Cairo. The outcome of this endeavor constitutes the backbone of this book.

The impetus behind the book thus comes from a long journey of discovery about poverty, gender, power, and the possibilities of social change. My general aim is to contribute to a more nuanced understanding of the dynamics of gender relations (as reflected in the daily interactions and concrete social arrangements between men and women) and gender ideologies (beliefs and values about masculinity and femininity) in a low-income "community" in Cairo, Egypt. My focus, however, is primarily on women, and specifically on the ways in which low-income women at different points in their life course experience, cope with, and respond to gender inequalities both in the family and at the workplace.

The specific objectives of the book are fourfold. The first is generating knowledge about the diversity of gender relations in the Egyptian family in the context of relative paucity of information. Despite some recent nuanced studies (Ghanem 1996; Singerman 1995), knowledge based on stereotypes inspired by orientalist notions of the family on the one hand, and ahistorical feminist notions of patriarchy, on the other, remains widespread. Tucker (1993) emphasizes the lack of ethnographic material on the family in the Arab world. "Although the importance of the family and the daily construction of gender roles and relations is not questioned, we actually know very little about the on-going evolution of the family in any specific context. There has been a tendency to assume the existence of a traditional family, a family defined and regulated by Islamic law that has remained unchanged" (Tucker 1993: 12).

Moreover, urban ethnographies in general, and those related to gender in particular, are scarce in Middle Eastern anthropology, in comparison to those dealing with nomadic or rural populations. In Egypt for example, although 50 percent of the population now lives in cities, no more than a handful of urban ethnographies exist addressing gender issues over the past decade; the majority of those have been carried out by American and European anthropologists. In an annotated bibliography of urbanization studies in Egypt produced by the National Centre for Sociological and Criminological Research in 1990, none of the 250 citations addressed gender issues (Fergany 1993). My study is thus set against a context of relative paucity of research.

The second objective is contributing to theoretical debates related to gender and resistance. More specifically, my research aims to inform debates, in both the anthropological and the broader feminist literature, regarding the ways in which women's gender interests are formed, and how their strategies for expressing discontent and negotiating gender-based power relations, are modified and inflected by their specific socioeconomic locations. Despite the growing literature on power relations and resistance strategies, few have specifically addressed gender issues (Abu-Lughod 1990a; Agarwal 1994; O'Hanlon 1991). Moreover, although several studies have carefully documented the life cycle changes in women's lives, and how these affect their relative power positions (Morsy 1978; Rassam 1980; Taylor 1984), unqualified and universal statements casting women as a group, as passive subjects unaware of their oppression, "continue to hold sway" (Agarwal 1994:422; see also Mohanty 1988).

The third objective is contributing to the formulation of a more comprehensive feminist agenda that is more sensitive to differences among women. This agenda should accommodate class differences and cultural diversity, without losing its basic philosophical commitment to human rights and social justice; an agenda that can "avoid the dual pitfalls of ethnocentrism and unprincipled relativism" (Kandiyoti 1995:29). And, I would also add, one that can avoid the pitfall of elitism and class bias as well. Although feminist scholarship in other parts of the world has taken on the issue of class on board (Ramazanglu 1989; Rowbotham 1981), attempting to look specifically at how poverty and patriarchy intersect (Greely 1983), and examining the "crossroads of class and gender" (Beneria and Roldan 1987), the relationships between poverty and gender concerns have not been central to the debates amongst women activists and researchers in Egypt. In the short run, this research thus aims at informing theoretical debates regarding women's rights, interests and demands in Egypt, as well as providing NGOs and women's activists with insights into the perceptions, practices, priorities and organizing mechanisms of low-income women.

The fourth objective is to generate policy-relevant data which may be used to challenge prevailing, unexamined assumptions about gender relations which currently inform policy and programmatic interventions. In Egypt, many such policies appear to have been based either on stereotypical assumptions about women's and men's roles, or on empirical realities uncritically transposed from very different regions or cultural contexts. In a review article on women, work and wellbeing in the Middle East, Papps (1992) concludes that "we are very far from having sufficient knowledge to implement effective policy or even to evaluate existing policies" (1992: 595).

The book is organized along topical themes. The first chapter discusses the theoretical framework that has guided the research. I critically review some of the debates on power, gender and resistance, and argue that a modified and gendered concept of "everyday forms of resistance" provides a way forward to a more nuanced and historically grounded analysis of gender relations. The second chapter provides an overview of some of the macrolevel socioeconomic and political influences that Egypt has witnessed over the past two decades. My purpose in doing so is to contextualize the results of the fieldwork and thus enable the reader to better interpret and understand the more microlevel processes in the chapters that follow. The third chapter provides the Cairo-and community-level contexts of my research. I provide an overview of the historical development of the city of Cairo, followed by a general description of the research setting and a profile of the study community and research sample. The fourth chapter provides a situated and reflective account of fieldwork encounters. I also justify my methodological approach and discuss the specific research tools adopted.

The following five chapters present the results of the fieldwork and analysis of my data. Each chapter deals with a particular set of social arrangements where gender relations and ideologies are explored; some chapters refer to women as members of their families and households, while others deal with work relations and with women as paid workers. Chapter five is concerned with premarital expectations and standards. It explores how girls are prepared to assume their central roles as wives, mothers and sexual partners, and how decisions regarding choice of spouse are negotiated. The chapter highlights several gendering processes such as female circumcision and menstruation.

Chapter six discusses marriage negotiations and transactions. The focus is on specific practices, such as the accumulation of the *gihaaz*, marriage trousseau, and the insistence on writing an *ayma*, marriage inventory, through which women attempt to gain more secure entitlements in marital property and to mitigate their perceived vulnerability in marriage. Chapter seven discusses the role of gender in structuring earnings, conditions of work and women's options in the informal labor market, focusing on two types of female employment: piecework and waged work. The chapter highlights how the convergence of marital trajectories, the phase of a woman's life cycle, supply and demand factors, and the usage of kinship idioms result in different forms of acquiescence, accommodation and overt protest in work relations.

Chapter eight concentrates on negotiations within the conjugal union, and highlights women's responses to their husband's demands for sex. The chapter also illustrates how women voice their grievances and articulate their discontent, sometimes overtly, and sometimes covertly, through the idiom of spirit possession. Chapter nine discusses intrahousehold decision making and analyzes areas of dissent between husbands and wives, such as decisions related to the education of daughters, and how these are resolved. The chapter also discusses the role of extrahousehold networks in enabling women to gain more leverage within the conjugal union.

In their totality, the chapters of this book thus provide insights into the ways in which different groups of low-income Cairene women juggle the contradictions in their daily lives. Such insights aim at enriching theoretical debates regarding how gender inequalities are produced, reproduced and transformed. They also seek to expand the knowledge base regarding low-income women's priorities, practices, and strategies with a view to informing both activist and policy agendas in Egypt. Finally, the insights generated raise a number of questions about poverty, gender, power and social change that merit further investigation.

NOTES

1. This was in the context of an integrated community development program, implemented by Environmental Quality International (EQI), an Egyptian nongovernmental consultancy organization. I remain indebted to EQI's director, Dr. Mounir Neamatalla, who encouraged my keen interest in learning about poverty and provided me with the intellectual support and flexibility to pursue my interests.

2. The concept of "development" has been the subject of increasing controversy and debate over the past decade. There has been an increasing recognition of the limitations of the early conceptualization of development as a linear process, as well as the overly technocratic, apolitical, top-down, and fragmented approaches to improving human welfare through the vehicle of "development project". For a critique of development discourse and practices, see Ferguson 1990; Hobart 1993; Hancock, 1989.

3. Participation, now a central concept in development discourse, was introduced in the late 1970s partly in reaction to the failure of many large-scale, top-down development projects. The emphasis on consultation with local community members, including women, throughout the design, implementation and monitoring of development programs constituted the backbone of this alternative approach to development. However, several studies have shown the huge gap between the rhetoric and the practice of participation, and the inherent tensions in such a concept. Participation is often used as a means to achieve project efficiency and pass on development costs to beneficiaries, rather than as an end in itself aimed at empowering communities to set the agenda and take control over their own lives. For a critique of the concept, highlighting the benefits and misuses of participatory processes in development see Mayoux (1995) and Nelson and Wright (1994). For a discussion of the history of the concept, see Cohen and Uphoff (1980).

4. The potential and limitations of credit as a development tool for alleviating poverty and "empowering" women has been the subject of much debate. For a recent critique see Goetz and Gupta (1996).

5. The project also organized women into "solidarity groups," inspired by the internationally acclaimed Grameen Bank model in Bangladesh, and building on the traditional informal credit and saving associations, *gamᶜiyya(s)*, which were common among women in the community. The project was funded by the Ford Foundation and OXFAM. For details see EQI (1987).

6. Several researchers in Egypt have recently addressed the issue of women-headed households, particularly as it relates to poverty. See for example, Fergany (1994b). Moreover, the issue has received some recent media attention (*El Wafd* newspaper, 15 October 1997; *Sabah el Kheir* magazine, July 1997).

7. ADEW's activities are modeled after the *zabbaliin* project mentioned earlier. ADEW was the first, and remains the only, private voluntary women's group whose sole concern is empowering women supporting their households, primarily through improving their access to financial

and legal services. For a discussion of ADEW's philosophy and activities, see "Women-headed Households in Egypt: a Panel discussion" (1994); El-Kholy (1996b).

8. I am not at all suggesting that political participation and attempts to register women for elections are not important areas of intervention and that efforts in this regard are laudable. My point is only to suggest that it reflects the legitimate priorities of only a certain group of women.

9. Boys are required by law to obtain an identity card at the age of sixteen. Girls, however, are not, and few are encouraged to do so. The underlying assumption is that women do not need a separate identity as theirs is tied to their fathers and later their husbands. Women face many obstacles in obtaining individual cards. The process, if successful, can take up to one year. To own an identity card, you need a birth certificate, which many women do not have and which is difficult to get. You also need access to two government officials who know you in person and who are willing to stamp your papers. You need to have access to a clinic to get a blood test. You need to have access to a police station. All of this requires time, energy, knowledge, and the ability to break through to the gatekeepers of these various bureaucracies, who are usually unsympathetic, and often intimidating, male officials who uphold prevalent gender ideologies regarding women's roles and identities. The process also requires money, in some cases up to two hundred pounds. As a result, in the worst case scenario, and there are many women in this situation, an identity card remains an unattainable dream (see El-Kholy 1996b).

1
RETHINKING APPROACHES TO
RESISTANCE, POWER AND
GENDER RELATIONS: TOWARDS A
THEORETICAL FRAMEWORK

To understand how gender relations and inequalities are negotiated at a micro-level in the daily practices of low-income women and men in Cairo necessitated that I explore the relationship between two key concepts, power and gender. Despite the centrality of both concepts to feminist scholarship, "the precise nature of this relationship remains shadowy" (Oldersma and Davis 1991). I ventured to examine the connections between power and gender by focusing on a third concept, that of resistance, arguing that a focus on how women negotiate unequal power relations both in the family and in the work place offers a promising avenue for better understanding how gender inequalities are produced, reproduced, and transformed. I specifically argue that a modified and gendered version of Scott's (1985, 1986, 1990) notion of "everyday forms of resistance" is a particularly useful tool for analyzing gender relations at the microlevel.

The concept of "everyday forms of resistance", a term coined by Scott in 1985, captures a wide range of behavior and actions of subordinate groups, ranging between open, collective revolt and passive consent (such as foot dragging, evasion, avoidance protest, sabotage, gossip, slander, and feigned ignorance). Such an approach to resistance, which focuses on the daily, often covert, and noncoordinated practices of subordinate groups allows us to view resistance as a shifting continuum of practices, which must be empirically investigated in specific socioeconomic and historical contexts. This approach also promises to significantly further our understanding of both the mechanisms of power as well as the potential agency of those in positions of relative disadvantage.

Women, particularly in the Middle East, have often been portrayed as either passive and unwary victims of oppression, or as strong and powerful actors. I term these two polarized depictions found in much of the anthropological literature on the Middle East the "oppression" and "strength" strands. On the one hand, there is a large body of research influenced by orientalist stereotypes that largely depict women in the Middle East as submissive, oppressed victims (Ahmed 1982; Tapper 1979). On the other hand, and partly in reaction to the former, there is a plethora of studies that present women as active, powerful and resourceful actors (AlTorki 1986; Aswad 1978; Early 1993a; Early 1993b).

The problems with the former approach, and orientalism more generally, have been well rehearsed elsewhere (see, for example, Ahmed, 1982). The problem with the latter type of approach is the common confusion between women's activity and their power or authority (see Okely 1991). Being active is not the same as being of equal value. Women may be economically active and outspoken, and at the same time subordinate, and bound by many constraints which limit their choices. My concern is thus not to reveal women's informal power as some of these latter studies have done so well. Rather, my aim is to render more visible some of their daily acts of resistance against perceived injustices in specific contexts, as well as to achieve a better understanding of their lack of contestation in other contexts. I argue that an approach to resistance based on covert and individual actions has the potential for providing a more complex and textured account of relations between men and women.

Focusing on women's everyday acts of resistance promises to not only further our understanding of gendered forms of power, but is of potential value for developing policies and strategies for social change as well. An understanding of the potentially consequential acts of everyday resistance is an essential complement to the emerging scholarly focus on women's formal organizations as a major site of protest against gender inequalities. Low-income, largely illiterate women, who constitute the majority of women, have neither the time nor the skills to engage with formal women's organizations, and rarely do. Their voices of protest, their daily grievances, struggles and strategies, which should be the essential building blocks for the work of formal women's groups, are thus rarely noticed or taken into account by activists. Low-income women's voices even more rarely inform theories of power and resistance. Ethnographies guided by a theoretical approach that stresses the place of resistance in the construction of everyday gender relations would thus address an important theoretical and political gap.

In my attempt to understand how women experience, articulate, and respond to their relative disadvantage in both the household and the workplace, I emphasize a conceptualization of gender that focuses on the relationship between men and women as well as between masculinity and femininity. This socialrelations approach is the one implicit in much of the gender and development literature. It remains committed to an analysis of how the female/male distinction reproduces inequality in access to, and control over, resources at every institutional level (Kandiyoti 1998; Moser 1993). Based on this conceptualization, the primary task of gender analysis and feminist activism is thus to interrogate the institutionalized inequalities between men and women (Moore 1988; Nicholson 1994). Following the proponents of this concept of gender, and in line with my own commitment to local understandings and priorities, I argue that social categories such as men and women are thus not homogenous, and emphasize in my research approach the multiple, contested and contradictory meanings associated with male/female identities and distinctions. (See Moore 1994b). This approach may not have the theoretically liberating potential of the post- structuralist (see for example Butler and Scott 1992), deconstructionist conceptualization of gender, and may occasionally result in the slippage between the concept of women and that of gender. Despite its possible limitations, however, I concur with others who have argued that dealing with the world as it is constituted by the categories of members of local communities themselves is more desirable than the analytical distortions and political impotence that could result from importing Western conceptual frameworks that are dismissive of local articulations and understandings (Kandiyoti 1998). Having specified how the term gender is used in the book, I now turn to a discussion of the relationship between the concept of gender and that of resistance and power.

The Emerging Concern: "Everyday Forms of Resistance"

Studies of resistance have traditionally been dominated by accounts of open confrontations in the form of largescale rebellions and revolutions, and have largely focused on class conflict as the major cause of struggle (Paige 1975; Wolf 1969 quoted in Abu-Lughod 1991a). Influenced largely by a narrow Marxist paradigm, resistance has been conceptualized mainly as an organized struggle by subordinate groups informed by a coherent oppositional ideology, focusing specifically on the working class, eventually leading to revolutionary confrontation. A critical assumption in Marxist theory regarding resistance is the relationship between positionality and consciousness, a relationship which emphasizes the split between "objective" conditions of oppression and "subjective" consciousness of this oppression, between ideology and behavior, between the economic and the political spheres. (McLellan 1973). This approach to resistance and consciousness is also implicit in the strategies adopted by early feminists in the West. The emphasis on "consciousness raising" as an essential feminist strategy in the 1960s and 1970s was partly based on the premise that a "collective" consciousness must precede agency.

However, I argue in this book that such approaches may be inadequate for a historically and culturally sensitive understanding of the dynamics of power underlying gender relations. The last decade has given way to a more nuanced usage of the concept of resistance largely as a reaction against the economistic,

14

reductionist and gender blind versions, and interpretations, of Marxist theories of power (Abu-Lughod 1990a). The opening up of new possibilities for understanding power and resistance has been influenced by feminist theory and practice as well as by the post- structuralist/modernist critique, with Foucault's work assuming particular importance.[1] The debate regarding false consciousness predates the post-structuralist movement. However, with post-structuralism the boundaries between the objective and the subjective began to fade more rapidly and the concept of false consciousness lost much of its earlier force. Structures of dominance are no longer being viewed as independent and monolithic entities that are challenged only during dramatic instances of revolt, but rather, as more commonly a web of contradictory processes that are continuously being renegotiated and contested (Haynes and Prakash 1991).

Scott's notion of "everyday forms of resistance" captures this conceptual shift. He uses the term to describe a wide range of contestary actions of subordinate groups, from open, collective revolt to passive revolt, tracing his own interest in the concept to his disillusionment with the outcome of socialist revolutions (Scott 1985). Scott does not display a particular concern with gender relations or gender inequalities, and in fact overlooks the gender dimension. Only a limited number of scholars, such as Hart (1991), whose work I discuss in chapter seven, have explicitly attempted to subject Scott's framework to analysis using a gender perspective.

In his work, Scott is concerned primarily with the "peasantry" and focuses mainly on class domination. Within such relations, Scott argues forcefully for the inclusion of everyday resistance as an integral part of the history of agrarian relations and peasant politics. He notes that:

> a history of the peasantry which only focused on uprisings would be much like a history of factory workers devoted entirely to major strikes and riots. Important and diagnostic though these exceptional events may be, they tell us little about the most durable arena of class conflict and resistance: the vital, day to day struggle on the factory floor over the pace of work, over leisure, wages, autonomy, privileges and respect. Resistance of this kind does not throw up the manifestos, demonstrations and pitched battles that normally compel attention, but vital territory is being won and lost here too. (Scott 1986: 6)

While these "weapons of the weak" Scott argues, consist largely of "routine resistance" and do not pose any major threats to agrarian inequalities, they nonetheless represent a continuous process of renegotiations and testing of social relations, and could have important, if unintended, consequences. Arguing along the same lines, Haynes and Prakash note that "the struggles of subordinated peoples need not be dramatic or informed by conscious ideologies of opposition to seriously affect relations of domination" (Haynes and Prakash 1991: 4). A broader definition of resistance, they argue, would allow a fuller understanding of the very processes through which subordinate groups test and undermine power and the ways in which daily struggles can be transformed into large-scale and conscious challenges to sociopolitical structures. The concept of everyday resistance has since triggered much debate. (See the special issue of the Journal of Peasant Studies 1986.) The main arguments within this debate are summarized in the following section.

What Constitutes Everyday Forms of Resistance?

Despite widespread agreement on the need to explore the diverse forms of nonconventional, nonviolent acts of everyday resistance, a debate continues regarding how inclusive or exclusive such a concept should be. The debate seems to center on two related issues. The first question involves the issues of intentions and motivations of the actors: are they "subjective," "self-indulgent," and "self-interested," or are they "objective," "selfless," and "principled"? The second related issue revolves around the consequences of these acts of resistance, with the central argument centering around an attempt to differentiate between acts of resistance and daily survival strategies. The key question seems to be: To what extent do acts of resistance challenge the forces of oppression? For example, could everyday survival strategies, often used interchangeably with "coping strategies," that seek to maximize life options and in fact result in perpetuating the system of domination be considered forms of resistance?

Some scholars, following a narrow Marxist framework, thus emphasize a distinction between "resistance" and real resistance (White 1986). Real resistance is seen as organized and collective, with revolutionary consequences and embodying a form of consciousness that challenges the basis of domination. "Resistance" as elaborated by Scott and his followers, is seen by these scholars as no more than incidental acts that are individualistic, and opportunistic, with no revolutionary consequences, and embodying intentions to accommodate the structures of oppression rather than to challenge them. White argues that such acts of "resistance" are actually dangerous over the longer run because they may simply act as a safety valve for oppressed people, making them unable to see their oppression, and thus contributing to the emergence of false consciousness.

I disagree with attempts to make such clear-cut differentiation because I think they preclude an understanding of the diverse experiences and perceptions of subordinate groups in a given situation of power, and privilege an objectivist, a priori, interpretation. I also think that the term "coping strategies," given the development and economic discourse in which it has evolved, often does not capture the political nature of some of the acts involved. In fact, the distinction between coping or survival strategies as individualist, economic tactics, and "everyday forms of resistance" as more political ones, may be misleading as it suggests too neat a separation between the sphere of economic and political behavior. Particularly in contexts of poverty, scarcity and deprivation, tactics to ensure

16

survival cannot be easily dismissed as apolitical behavior. As Scott elaborates when discussing peasant politics:

> "Bread and butter" issues are the essence of lower-class politics and resistance. ....
> When a peasant hides part of his crop to avoid paying taxes, he is both filling his stomach and depriving the state of grain. (Scott 1985: 295-96)

Another criticism of Scott's work is his overemphasis on the "individual" nature of everyday resistance. By doing so, he seems to have favored one extreme end and thus loses sight of the "middle ground," the various forms of resistance that social networks or informal groups may be involved in. Turton (1986) develops the concept of "patrolling the middle ground" to turn attention precisely to everyday forms of resistance that fall in the middle of the continuum between individual acts and organized collective actions. This criticism is I believe particularly pertinent when attempting to "gender" the concept of everyday forms of resistance and use it to specifically explore power relations between men and women. There are a number of studies which demonstrate the crucial role that women's informal networks play in enabling them to gain power within their marriages and communities (see for example March and Taqqu 1986).

The main critique of Scott, however, and one with which I concur, is that he does not fully appreciate the cultural and ideological aspects of domination and the structural constraints which limit the actions of subordinate groups, and lay down distinct "rules of the game." These rules often determine what can be legitimately resisted and how effective such resistance can be. Scott's overemphasis on the ability of subordinate groups to always penetrate the hegemonic ideologies of the ruling classes, and to develop an unmystified discourse and consciousness, is most clearly captured in his concept of "the hidden transcripts." He defines the hidden transcript as the "discourse that takes place offstage, beyond the direct observation of the dominant groups"(Scott 1990). However, as Prakash and Haynes (1991) have correctly argued, the ability of subordinate groups to break through the walls of hegemony may be constrained by the very nature of existing power structures; every- day acts of resistance take place in the field of power and thus are themselves affected by the nature of hegemony.

Timothy Mitchell (1990), in a detailed critique of Scott's work, takes particular issue with the "contextfree rationality" implicit in Scott's accounts, and his narrow definition of hegemony which does not allow him to appreciate how various forms of domination operate. As a result, Scott relabels and disguises the hegemonic relations evident in the village he studies by giving such relations titles such as "obstacles to resistance." However, Mitchell argues, "kinship is not something 'given' that happens to work as an obstacle to resistance but another of those strategies of euphemization by means of which relations of dependence and exploitation disguise themselves, as they must, in this case in the form of family ties" (Mitchell 1990:557).

Mitchell is particularly critical of the dichotomy between the material and the ideological, between a power that operates at the level of behavior and that which operates in the realm of consciousness, a dichotomy which permeates Scott's work. Mitchell argues that this is a weakness of all contemporary approaches to power and resistance as well. This dichotomy blinds us from seeing power not just as a coercive force that limits people's options and behavior, but also as one that works on controlling the mind and consciousness by creating certain "truths" and "subjects." Drawing on the works of Bourdieu, which will be discussed later, Mitchell uses the example of kinship idioms once more to demonstrate this point.

> Kinship strategies, for example, clearly belong to the 'realms of both behaviour and belief'; a mode of domination that operates by transforming relations of subordination into family ties works upon the physical body, determining how people eat, sleep, work for one another and reproduce and yet these practices are inseparable from the shaping of ideas, being the source of identity, loyalty and emotion. (Mitchell 1990:558)

It is true that Scott's virtual dismissal of the structural and ideological dimension of domination, particularly in his earlier work, weakens his arguments. Nonetheless, I think that the concept of "everyday forms of resistance," reconceptualised, still offers a way forward for a better understanding of the relationships between power and gender and between men and women. The concept needs to be adapted and given more nuance, by taking into account some of the critiques raised above, and by incorporating insights from a number of theories about both power and gender.

Resistance and Power

A discussion of resistance is not possible without a discussion of power. This is no easy task, however, as power is one of the most contentious concepts in the social sciences.[2] I focus my discussion here on notions of power as reflected specifically in the work of three theorists, Steven Lukes, the French post-structuralist scholar, Michael Foucault, and the Italian Marxist scholar Antonio Gramsci. This focus is partly due to their decisive influence in changing our understanding of the complexity and dynamics of power and domination, and partly because, as mentioned earlier, their interest in resistance appears to rest on a pragmatic desire for change and a commitment to social transformation. Despite differences among them, the works of these theorists also offer insights that are particularly relevant to an understanding of "everyday forms of resistance," particularly as they apply to gender relations, by focusing on the more subtle ways in which power shapes perceptions and actions.

Lukes's work on power (1974, 1986) represents one of the early classic attempts to grapple with the inadequacies of both purely structuralist or purely individual and intentional approaches to power. Lukes views power as both a structural phenomenon as well as a personal attribute and in both cases it need not be intentional. Reviewing various attempts to define power, Lukes proposes what he terms a "three-dimensional" approach to power, through which a diverse range of power relations in various contexts can be identified. Each dimension incorporates the one before it, but also incorporates other layers of social phenomena.

In the "one-dimensional" view of power, the interests of the various parties are regarded as equivalent to their preferences, which are articulated during an actual process of decision making. Thus "to exercise power is to prevail over the contrary preference of others with respect to key positions" (Lukes 1986: 9-10). To locate power, a researcher would need to identify the conflicts that occur during a decision-making process and compare the outcomes of the process to the stated preference of the various parties. Conflicts of interest, however, may not necessarily result in a decision-making or negotiating process. The more powerful party may ensure that the conflict does not appear on the agenda in the first place. This is where a "two-dimensional" view of power becomes necessary.

In the "two-dimensional" view, power is seen to be exercised not only in the same manner as in the one dimensional view, but also by "controlling the agenda, mobilizing the bias of the system, determining which issues are key issues, indeed which issues come up for decision and excluding those which threaten the interests of the powerful" (Lukes 1986: 9-10).[3] To reveal this dimension, a researcher would thus need to identify areas of "non-decision making" and to reveal the grievances and complaints of the less powerful party in the relationship that have not made it to the decision-making agenda (Meyer 1991).

The "three-dimensional" view of power identified by Lukes incorporates both the first and second dimensions, but also incorporates another level of social phenomena. Lukes argues that the absence of grievances does not mean that power is not involved, for power can be "latent." This view of power recognizes that power "may operate to shape and modify desires and beliefs in a manner contrary to people's interests. In consequence, neither revealed preferences nor grievances and inchoate demands will always express them" (Lukes 1986: 10). Arguing for an appreciation of this three-dimensional view of power, Lukes poses the question:

> Is it not the supreme and most insidious exercise of power to prevent people, to whatever degree, from having grievances, by shaping their perceptions, cognition and preferences in such a way that they accept their role in the existing order of things, either because they can see or imagine no alternative to it, or because they see it as natural and unchangeable, or because they value it as divinely ordained and beneficial? (Lukes 1974: 24)

All three dimensions are relevant for understanding different layers of gender relations, and Lukes's theory has been applied to marital relations by several researchers (see for example Kompter 1991). I find the two-dimensional and three-dimensional views of power particularly helpful. Since power can be latent, then presumably so can conflicts and grievances. This proposition opens up space for probing more carefully into the nonconventional ways in which such latent conflicts between men and women may be expressed or articulated.

The two-dimensional view of power is also highly relevant for analyzing questions about feminist practice more generally. In many countries, feminist agendas are predominantly set by the most privileged and powerful by virtue of either class position, race, or education. While this is not problematic in and of itself, it does raise questions about power relations within feminism, by asking who it is that sets the agenda for change, and determines which issues are to be debated, and which are to be excluded. Which feminist discourse is hegemonic and why? This in turn prompts the rather uncomfortable suggestion that middle-class and upper-class feminists may themselves be implicated in perpetuating power inequalities, by privileging their own concerns and priorities that are then reflected in feminist discourse. This issue is discussed in greater detail in chapter six.

Foucault's work also offers important insights for an understanding of power, particularly its micromechanisms. Foucault has in fact fundamentally challenged our thinking about power and its exercise by shifting the focus away from an exclusive attention to power as exercised by the state and state apparatuses. Instead, he highlights what he terms the "capillary" actions of power, those diffuse mechanisms by which power circulates in society. Foucault emphasizes the importance of examining power at its "ultimate destinations," that is power as reflected in its local and regional patterns and structures. Power, according to Foucault does not emanate from one source, but is incredibly diffuse, it is created and undermined all the time.

> Power must be analysed as something which circulates or rather as something which only functions in the form of a chain. It is never localised here or there, never in anybody's hands, never appropriated as a commodity or piece of wealth. Power is employed and exercised through a net like organisation and not only do individuals circulate between its threads; they are always in the position of simultaneously undergoing and exercising this power. They are not only its inert or consenting target; they are always the elements of its articulation. In other words, individuals are the vehicles of power, not its points of application. (Foucault 1986: 235)

Tracing how discourses about power have changed over the past century, Foucault argues that by the eighteenth century a new kind of power had emerged. This was not power based on legal obligations to obey state laws and sanctioned by a judiciary discourse of public rights. Rather the new kind of power that emerged in parallel to, and reinforcing, state power, was based on "disciplinary mechanisms", and "disciplinary discourses" which invoked "norms" or natural rules, not laws. Disciplinary discourse, argued Foucault—apparent in institutions such as mental hospitals, the army, schools, families, and factories—aimed at shaping and influencing people's minds and bodies. Techniques of "surveillance," ceaseless observation, and persistent exposure to the "gaze" of others are the means of enforcing this type of power. These techniques lead to internalized restraint, self-scrutiny and assimilation of certain "truths." These disciplinary mechanisms, Foucault argued, are such powerful forms of domination in contemporary societies that "nothing in society will be changed if the mechanisms of power that function outside, below and alongside the state apparatuses on a much more minute and everyday level are not also changed" (Foucault 1980: 60).

Foucault's concepts of disciplinary discourses and regimes of truth provide useful analytical tools for analyzing gender relations. Gender discourses can be conceptualized as one concrete example of such disciplinary discourses. Moreover, the concept of the "gaze" is particularly useful for understanding how some of the restrictions on women, such as on their physical mobility or sexual behavior for example, as will be discussed in later chapters, are enforced. The challenge then becomes trying to understand how this discourse actually operates at the micro-level in everyday life in different contexts.

Gramsci's reflections on power and domination are equally illuminating. Although his conceptualization of power is much less diffuse than that of Foucault's, he similarly highlights how power and resistance are intermeshed, and how power is reproduced and maintained not only through force, but through a slow process in which consensus is forged between dominant and subordinate groups. Gramsci's major contribution is the development of the idea of ideological hegemony, a complex notion which he uses to describe how relations of power unfold, not only during times of change, but also in everyday life (Hoare and Nowell 1971).

Because Gramsci uses the concept of hegemony in conflicting and contradictory ways throughout his works, it has been subject to varied interpretations. Some attempts in Marxist scholarship to explore the complex forms of domination inherent in Gramsci's concept of hegemony allow a broad interpretation of the term that includes cultural, social and political processes, and emphasizes the "interactional" meaning of the concept (Williams 1977). According to this interpretation, which is most relevant for my purposes here, all power is seen as stemming from a relationship between two parties, a "hegemonic interaction," in which both subordinate and dominant actors have roles to play. Hegemony, achieved through generating an acceptable "common-sense" view of the world and one's position in it, does not imply complete or total control. Negotiation is an inherent part of hegemonic relationships. This is because the common-sense understandings of the world are not consistent, but are fragmented, and often contradictory. The consciousness of subordinate groups in such a relationship is a mix of contradictory views and values, some of which reflect the values of the dominant groups, and some of which emerge more directly from practical experience (Eagleton 1991). "It is in the ambiguities and contradictions of common sense that the differentiation in the values of dominant and subordinate groups becomes visible" (Kompter 1991: 59). Macleod (1992a:18) uses this interpretation of Gramsci's thought to explain why middle-class working women in Cairo are taking up the "veil."

Lukes's notion of three-dimensional power is actually quite similar to Gramsci's earlier concept of hegemony. Both allow us to better appreciate how power works in elusive ways to shape people's consciousness. However, Gramsci's notion also allows space for understanding why and how people contest power and domination, and points to the need for identifying the contradictions and inconsistencies in the beliefs of subordinate groups, and thus of possible sources of change as well.

The works influenced by Lukes, Gramsci and Foucault have highlighted the significance of ideological practices in power and resistance and have called for an appreciation of the interconnectedness of "symbolic and instrumental, behavioral and ideological, and cultural, social and political processes" (Abu-Lughod 1990a: 41). As a result, there is now greater understanding of the connections between physical coercion and violence and ideological instruments of domination, between legality and force and more subtle consensual norms.

Debates regarding what constitutes resistance have thus significantly shifted over the past decade. The importance of moving beyond a strictly economistic analysis of resistance that focuses on "material" struggles over wages, rent and land is now acknowledged (Turton 1986). Similarly, Haynes and Prakash (1991) argue for an expanded notion of resistance that incorporates the realm of culture and ideology and point to a relatively unexplored arena for studying everyday resistance, namely, popular culture. "It is in such cultural forms as work, ritual, gossip, oral traditions, dress and entertainment that domination is constantly being forged and fissured" (1991:16). Along the same lines, they have argued that choice of lifestyle can be a form of resistance and that defending certain types of leisure may be seen as contestary behavior.

It is now well established that power and resistance are not autonomous but are intermeshed and continuously shape each other. An unresolved methodological debate, however, has emerged. Does the researcher focus on studying power as a way of understanding resistance or does she or he alternately focus on acts of resistance as a way of illuminating power relations? Turton (1986) argues that speaking of resistance requires a prior attempt to "identify the specific social relations which support, constrain, threaten or exploit the resistor" (1986: 39). This requires a careful examination and account of the relations, processes and structures of power, both formal and informal, and a fine conceptualization of the extent of domination. "The finer our recognition and appreciation of agencies and instruments of domination, the better we may be able to assess whether they are being resisted, or in what ways they are perceived to be capable of being resisted or not, and the better we may recognize certain acts as being forms of resistance" (Turton 1986: 41).

Others, taking a cue from Foucault's line of thinking, argue the reverse; they argue for the use of resistance as a "diagnostic of power," that is, identifying common forms of resistance and using these strategically to inform us about patterns of power and how people are enmeshed in them (Abu-Lughod 1990a). Foucault notes that resistance can act as a "chemical catalyst so as to bring to light power relations, locate their position, find out their points of application and the methods used" (Foucault 1983: 209). Abu-Lughod argues that this approach is more promising for ethnographic studies because it allows one to move from general and abstract theories of power towards concrete methodological strategies for the study of power in specific contexts. Although clearly, the two positions are not mutually exclusive, the methodological implications and points of entry are different. It seems to me that using resistance as an entry point is a more pragmatic and "bottom-up" way of unpacking and revealing the complex mechanisms of historically changing structures of power.

"Everyday Forms of Resistance" and Gender Relations

Despite the current concern with everyday forms of resistance, studies of resistance dealing with gender relations are only just emerging. For the most part, contestation of gender relations has not been part of the ongoing debates on everyday resistance. The early influential plea by Kate Millet (1969) for a more encompassing theory of politics and power which has generated the powerful concept of "sexual politics," has not been paralleled by a plea for a more encompassing and inclusive theory of resistance. Part of the reason, I believe, may be found in the influence that the concept of "patriarchy," as elaborated in the feminist scholarship of the 1960s and early 1970's, has had on shaping much of the writing and thinking about gender relations.[4] This concept has been used as a blanket term to emphasize the existence of a universal system of domination and "failed to convey movement, the complexities of relations between men and women, or the extent of women's resistance to and transformation of male power" (Ramazanglu 1989: 38).

Patriarchy was viewed as a universal static system and a formidable power structure, with little potential for change except through organized international "sisterhood" movements. This has meant that critical questions about the specific reasons and ways in which women and men reinforce, accommodate to, or resist the specific and overlapping forms of oppression that they face in a particular historical and cultural setting were ignored. Instead, scholarship focused primarily on the search for more general answers to questions about the "causes" of women's universal oppression.[5]

Several scholars, however, have challenged this universal, essentialist and stagnant notion of patriarchy and its utility for identifying and understanding the specific forms of women's subordination cross-culturally (see Davis et al. 1991; Kandiyoti 1988; Ramazanglu 1989; Rowbotham 1991). It is now widely acknowledged that gender is constructed alongside a range of other positionalities, such as class, age and ethnicity, which modify, shape and affect both women's interests as well as their perceptions of particular social arrangements. Women perceive their "gender interests" differently depending on their own daily lived experience, which may involve struggle alongside and against men, as well as against other women (see Beneria and Feldman 1992; Ramazanglu 1989)[6]. They also operate within different gender ideologies (Dwyer 1978a), and develop different strategies for passive and active resistance in the face of oppression (Kandiyoti 1988).

The possibilities of using resistance, or the lack of it, as a conceptual entry point for understanding gender relations has thus come about partly as a result of internal feminist critiques of the notion of patriarchy. It has also been inspired by the broader attempts to rethink notions of power and resistance as discussed earlier. Although more concerned with revealing women's "private" power than dealing resistance per se, Nelson (1974) nonetheless provides one of the earliest attempts to question conventional notions of power as it relates to gender. She argues for recognizing power as a kind of social relation in which men and women engage in "negotiating their social order", that is, "negotiating the rules that define and circumscribe that relationship", rather than as a quality institutionalized in particular social structures. She highlights the concept of "reciprocity of influence," whereby men and women control and influence each other with reference to specific spheres of activity and particular situations.

Okely (1991) provides one of the few attempts to apply the concept of everyday resistance to gender issues more explicitly. She argues that to capture women's subordination, we need to redefine resistance to encompass not just sustained collective action, but also the fragmented, less visible, and often isolated "moments" of defiance and resistance expressed by individuals at distinct moments of their life. She rightly notes that: "Putting up a fight, i.e., not being submissive could be interpreted as a momentary resistance to women's fundamental subordination" (Okely 1991: 7).

Women's responses to practices like wage discrimination, sexual harassment, violence, restricted mobility, and lack of economic support, will clearly vary depending partly on their social locations, in terms of class, age, and family structure for example. I argue, however, that there are various reasons why much of women's protest, particularly within familial relations, is often likely to take the form of the uncoordinated, nonviolent, nonconfrontational types of actions that are embodied in Scott's notion of "everyday forms of resistance".

One major reason is the powerful and mutually reinforcing relationship between gender and kinship, and between gender ideology and kinship ideology.[7] Women and men are not just females and males, but they are also fathers and mothers, daughters and sons, wives and husbands, nephews and nieces, and cousins. This social web of relations, determined by both kinship and gender, means that the nature of relations between men and women are not firm and set, but are fluid and varied. Women are enmeshed, both at home and in the workplace, in a complex web of not only exploitative relations, but also relations of solidarity and reciprocity, based on kinship (Joseph 1993; White 1994). Closely related to the power of the kinship idiom, is the corporate orientation that is valued in many parts of the world, which results in fluid boundaries of personhood and a definition of the self that is highly relational. Persons do not necessarily define themselves as individuals with separate rights independent of a larger group, but rather see themselves as part of, and extensions of, significant others. In one of the few studies of the psychoanalytic dynamics of Arab families, Joseph (1993), takes issue with the Western concept of the "self" and argues, on the basis of her study of a lower-income community in Lebanon, that both men and women are "relationally oriented." She develops the term "connectivity" to describe the relationships she observed in her study area, relationships in which "persons expected intimate others to reach each other's minds, anticipate each other's needs, and shape their likes and dislikes in accordance with others" (Joseph 1993: 467). She argues that the pervasiveness of patriarchy coupled with connectivity "produced persons willing and capable of entering into gendered and aged hierarchical relations" (Joseph 1993: 469).

Another reason why women's resistance is likely to take covert, nonconfrontational, and momentary forms is that women's power and status in the family in some parts of the world, is of a cyclical nature and varies significantly with a woman's age and her structural position in the extended family. In such a system, older women, particularly mothers-in-law, have both more autonomy as well as more power over younger women in the household (Doan et al. 1990; Mernissi 1975; Morsi 1978; Rassam 1980). Such a context creates conflict amongst women and results in a situation where women are subordinate not just to men, but to other women as well. Moreover, it creates a situation where women have a stake in existing patriarchal arrangements. The fact that younger women can anticipate and look forward to gaining more power and authority as they go through their life course, undermines their need to directly challenge existing power structures. Women's stake in specific forms of hierarchical arrangements in the household, thus may not be a reflection of their false consciousness, nor of their conscious attempts to be allies of such arrangements, but rather with their actual stake in certain culturally available positions of power (Kandiyoti 1998).

In addition to the above-mentioned factors, and partly as a result of them, the "enemy" who women should resist is not always clear, and it is not always men. Women's unequal positions are also a result of their structural position in the household, their class location, state policies, as well as global inequalities. Thus, while women may be aware of the constraints under which they operate, "the origin of this force remains elusive" (Macleod 1986: 18). The subtle, elusive, overlapping, and diffuse nature of the constraints on women, the intermeshing of exploitation and reciprocity, the fluctuations of their power due to life cycle changes, and the lack of a clear person, group, or class to confront would arguably lead to diffuse, subtle, nonconfrontational, and noncoordinated forms of resistance.

Several researchers have, implicitly or explicitly, accepted that women's resistance is often covert, subtle, and diffuse. Ethnographies dealing with gender relations within this framework fall broadly into two categories. The first category includes studies that focus on negotiation based on public and shared cultural ideas or representations (for example using such terms as "dialogue" (Dwyer 1978b), "accommodating" (Macleod 1992a; 1992b) and "bargaining" (Rosen 1984)). The second category includes those ethnographies that focus on the separate, rarely noticed subordinate discourses of women which are expressed through mediums and activities like special genres of women's poetry (Abu-Lughod 1986), dramatic games played by and for women (Safa-Isfahani 1980, quoted in Messick 1987) and carpet weaving (Messick 1987). I briefly present an example of each genre.

In her study of a small community of Bedouins in Egypt's western desert, Abu-Lughod provides insights into a particular form of women's discourse that complements the more formal and visible discourse on honor and shame in this community. This discourse is expressed through *ghinniwas,* short poems similar to "Japanese haiku in form but more like American blues in content and emotional tone" and sung largely by women and only amongst them. These poems express personal sentiments of love, loss, vulnerability and a wide range of other interpersonal relations that go against the prevalent code of honor. As such, *ghinniwas* represent not only a complementary discourse but also a culturally legitimate and "honorable" way for women to communicate "immodest sentiments." Abu-Lughod concludes that "poetry as a discourse of defiance of the system symbolizes freedom," and "provides a corrective to an obsession with morality and an overzealous adherence to the ideology of honor and maybe the vision is cherished because people sense that the costs of this system of honor ideology in the limits it places on human experience is just too high" (1986: 258-59).

The second "genre" of research on gender and resistance can be illustrated by Rosen's study of how women and men negotiate and "bargain" over reality in a small town in Morocco. He suggests that men and women attempt to understand their relationships with each other through very different conceptual orientations and explanatory schemes; men stress the natural differences between the two sexes, while women emphasize the social aspects of their relationship (Rosen's 1979 described in Eickleman 1989). Thus, when conceptual disagreements occur, they are expressed in a manner that allows men and women to exercise their respective powers by engaging in a bargaining process regarding what is really true about the situation and what to do about it. "What is negotiable, however, is not their different views of reality, but its scope, its impact and its differential importance" (Rosen 1978: 580). Through observing a number of conflicts and arguments surrounding marriage negotiations, Rosen concludes that although "Moroccan men may present their definition of a given situation as the valid one, women possess sufficient means for hedging against the sheer impositions of this male fiat to grant them the capability of disputing the interpretation to be applied in the first place" (Rosen 1978: 581).

In a more recent and very influential book, Agarwal (1994) stresses the need to examine both the implicit and explicit forms of bargaining that occur between people with access to different kinds of socio-economic and political power. The author presents many examples from South Asia which suggest that women's behavior, such as diverting food and crops, or more symbolic forms of contestation through songs and dance, can be better understood in relation to their lack of options rather than their unquestioning acceptance of male dominance.

Insights about resistance and gender relations can also be indirectly gleaned from the work of other researchers who, grappling with both the inadequacy of the concept of patriarchy and ethnocentric notions of women's consciousness, have argued for a more refined analysis of women's strategies in dealing with the specific unequal relations that they face. Kandiyoti (1988) argues that an analysis of women's strategies can help to "capture the nature of patriarchal systems in their cultural, class-specific and temporal concreteness and reveal how men and women resist, accommodate, adapt, and conflict with each other over resources, rights and responsibilities" (1988: 281). She elaborates on the notion of "patriarchal bargains," which she defines as the specific constraints, emerging from class, race and gender inequalities, that significantly affect women's gendered identity, the nature of gender ideology and the potential for, and concrete forms of, women's active or passive resistance. "Patriarchal bargains" are historically situated and changing systems. In the process of their transformation they can open up new areas of struggle and bargaining between men and women, and lead to new notions of femininity and masculinity.

Despite the obvious potential for a study of gender relations based on a framework of power relations and everyday forms of resistance, such a framework is not, however, without major theoretical and methodological difficulties. In fact, "gender power" is difficult to analyze through existing frameworks of power which have been largely developed for analyzing class relations (Abu-Lughod 1990; Kandiyoti 1998; Meyer, 1991; Sen 1990). Unlike other "subordinate" and "dominant" groups, whose universe may only occasionally overlap, men and women usually operate within the same universe, within the same socioeconomic and cultural text. "A worker and a capitalist do not typically live together under the same roof, sharing concerns and experiences and acting jointly. This aspect of "togetherness" gives the gender conflict some very special characteristics" (Sen 1990: 47).

The constitution of the categories dominant and subordinate thus becomes complicated and the lines of demarcation are not as clear, permanent or stable as between other groups, say between "peasants" and "landlords," or "workers" and "capitalists." As Meyer cogently argues, theories of relationships between men and women must make room for love, for positive emotions, and avoid the dichotomy between power and love (Meyer 1991: 21).

In relations characterized by both love and power, the question of what constitutes domination, what "signifiers" a researcher should look for, and how this relates to women's own perceptions and articulation of their situation, become critical. Some forms of behavior, like wearing the "veil," may for instance be taken up by women voluntarily and considered to be a source of self-worth and pride, and not as a sign of domination. On the other hand, such behavior could also be considered as a form of defiance.

In her study of "lower-middle-class" women in Cairo, Macleod (1992a; 1992b) argues that veiling allows women to assert their respectability and adherence to prevalent gender ideologies at the same time as defying such ideologies by working in the government bureaucracy in response to economic pressures, a process which she terms "accommodating protest." This in turn raises the complicated issue of consent and consensus. The critical question here, it seems to me, becomes what constitutes consent, and the need to differentiate between consent based on belief in an existing system, as opposed to a compliance based on a perception of a lack of choice or alternatives. As Fierlbeck argues, consent may be a meaningless concept unless there is a clear context of options and choices (Fierlbeck 1997).

The point that needs stressing is that a framework for understanding women's resistance must be able to deal with power processes that operate from a basis of not only conflict, but also consensus and cooperation. Risseeuw (1991) highlights this point in her study of gender transformations during the British colonial era in Sri Lanka. Drawing on Bourdieu's notions of "habitus," she argues that "acquiescence" rather than consensus may be a more accurate term to describe the lack of conflict that occurred in Sinhalese families as they encountered new forms of commercial land ownership and chances for social mobility, which had some adverse effects on women. Acquiescence refers to "submission with apparent consent or a disposition to submit or yield. It includes (apparently) satisfied passivity or the lack of opposition; discontentment usually after previous opposition, uneasiness or dislike, but with ultimate compliance and submission" (McKechnie 1971 quoted in Risseeuw 1991: 163).

Clearly then, attempts to study gender relations guided by the notion of everyday forms of resistance, while potentially revealing and powerful, are also bound to be quite "messy" as they do not fit neatly in any one theory of power. However, the search for the perfect theory of power and resistance capable of analyzing the multiple forms that gender relations take in different contexts, may itself be an unproductive undertaking. Rather, a more eclectic approach, based on the specific problems and issues which emerge in different contexts being explored, may be what is called for. As Davis (1991) suggests:

> We need theories to help us analyse asymmetrical relations involving power and gender in all areas and at all levels of social life. Considering the dazzling variety and complexity of social life, it seems highly improbable that any one theory regardless of whether its starting point is gender or power, can ever hope to explain it all. (Davis 1991: 85)

A gendered framework of everyday forms of power and resistance has yet to evolve. It will require more theoretical work, grounded in everyday lived realities of actors in various settings, to develop new concepts that can better capture how men and women attempt to reproduce as well as destabilize gender relations and discourses. Foucault's stress on a nonuniversal, decentralized approach to theoretical endeavors is relevant in this context. He argues that:

> The role for theory today seems to me to be just this: not to formulate the global systematic theory which holds everything in place … (but rather) to analyse the specificity of mechanisms of power, to locate the connections and extensions, to build, little by little, a strategic knowledge. (1980: 145)

Methodologically, this means that it is essential for any study of women's resistance to identify, and be particularly sensitive to, the categories, interpretations, and the cultural idioms that women and men in a particular setting themselves use, to denote notions like resistance, domination, subordination and agency. Such a grounded approach promises to historicize the concept of resistance. It also allows us to view it as a dynamic process of immediate, short-term, medium-term and long-term strategies, which may include both passive and active forms of protest, as well as complicity and acquiescence, and various stages and types of consciousness. For, as Strathern (1987b) emphasizes, resistance and consciousness do not simply emerge, but are created through individual and political struggles that are often complex and contradictory. Thus, as Kandiyoti argues:

> A better understanding of the short and medium term strategies of women in different social locations could provide a corrective influence to ethnocentric or class-bound definitions of what constitutes a feminist consciousness. (Kandiyoti 1988: 286)

And, I would add, such an understanding would also provide a corrective influence to what constitutes women's resistance as well.

This chapter presents the theoretical framework guiding my research, discusses the central concepts informing it, and elaborates my main arguments. The next chapter will provide the contextual framework for the research. It will present an analytical description of some of the most salient macrolevel forces affecting Egyptian society which have had, or are expected to have, a bearing on gender relations and ideologies.

NOTES

1. There is an emerging debate about the extent to which Foucault's work does represent a typical example of postmodernism. By focusing on his later works, particularly his work on the self, McNay (1992) questions the extent to which Foucault's work does represent a clear break with Enlightenment thought. She argues that Foucault's notion of the acting self and his emphasis on exploration of identity, while a critique of essentialism, nonetheless is linked to a general political goal of enhancing individual autonomy, and thus keeps intact a crucial notion of agency on which one could build a politics of resistance and freedom.

2. For a discussion of attempts to define power, and how these reflect different people's interest in both the outcomes and locations of power, see Lukes (1986). For one of the few attempts to link theories of power with gender, see Davis et al. (1991).

3. Lukes builds on the view advanced by Peter Batrach and Morton Baratz (1970).

4. For an overview of how the concept of patriarchy developed and how it has been used by different strands of feminism, broadly grouped as liberal feminists, Marxist feminists and socialist feminists, see Beechey (1979).

5. For an overview of the various attempts to provide social explanations for the universality of male dominance (nature/culture, public/private dichotomies), see Moore (1988) and Rosaldo and Lamphere (1974).

6. The often oppressive relationship between mother-in-law and daughter-in-law in extended households in some parts of the world is one of the more striking examples of the complexities and contradictions of gender relations.

7. For an excellent attempt at exploring the linkages between kinship and gender as two mutually reinforcing social categories, see Collier and Yanagisako (1987).

2

THE MACROCONTEXT:
AN OVERVIEW OF
SOCIOPOLITICAL AND ECONOMIC
TRANSFORMATIONS IN EGYPT

Om Samir, a 36-year-old vendor of plastic kitchen utensils and mother of two boys and a girl, reflects on my question as to what the common Arabic proverb, "a man is a man and a woman is a woman '*il ragil ragil wi il sit si,* '"[1] means to her:

> Frankly, in these times I no longer know … We live in confused times, *zaman aghbar* (from *ghubar, ghabra,* which literally means dusty and implies a fogginess and lack of clarity of vision). These are expensive times, *zaman ghila,* where one no longer knows what is a man and what is a woman … Look at me now, I work all day long, just like a man, even better … My husband is a *faa⁽il,* unskilled day laborer. He works in the construction trade as a helper, carrying bricks and so on. He does his best, but he does not find work every day like before. He went to work in Saudi Arabia fifteen years ago. These were good times, he used to send us money regularly and we built this house and bought a television. But, since he came back from Saudi Arabia seven years ago, we now can no longer live on what he makes … Life has become so expensive … So I go to the market every two weeks, buy items wholesale and carry back them back on the bus. I spend the whole day, as you see me trying to attract and bargain with customers, selling, and haggling, *atlaabit* … I have no choice. Three children are still at school and private lessons are so expensive. My daughter will be getting married soon and I have not yet bought any of the items of her *gihaaz,* marriage trousseau. For five years now I have been working and getting money into the house, just like a man. … At night, however, I become a woman again: can I say no if my husband wants to sleep with me, *yi⁾ di maslahtu*?

Om Samir's comments vividly capture some of the major transformations affecting Egyptian society over the past two decades, such as fluctuations in

31

regional migration and increased cost of living and unemployment. Her comments reveal the burden on poorer households in Cairo since the mid-eighties. Om Samir's reflections also point to some of the adjustments people have had to make in their daily lives in order to survive in the face of major socioeconomic upheavals. These upheavals have clearly left their mark on gender roles and expectations, evolving from a state where, in Om Samir's evaluation, "a man was a man and a woman was a woman," to a situation where "one no longer knows what a man and what a woman is," and a context where "a woman may be both a man in the morning and a woman in the evening."

This chapter provides a brief overview of the conjuncture of a complex set of domestic, regional and international socioeconomic, political and cultural forces to which Egypt has been subjected over the past two decades. I have privileged three macro-level influences because of their better-documented impact on local standards and articulations of gender: regional migration, "open door" state policies, and their more recent manifestation in structural adjustment policies, and the increasing influence of "Islamist" discourse.

These are clearly trends of a very different order, and their impact on Egyptian society in general and on gender relations and ideologies, in particular, vary a great deal. Some, such as regional migration to Gulf countries in the 1970s have had a direct impact on increasing consumerism, changing expectations about marriage, and the alteration of the division of labor within households. Domestic economic policies, on the other hand, have had an impact on both increasing the cost of living as well as strengthening oppositional Islamist groups, resulting in contradictory pressures on families. On the one hand, economic pressures are forcing more women to engage in income-earning activities and to contribute financially to their households, characteristics of a conventionally "masculine" role. On the other hand, an increasingly conservative Islamic discourse is casting women as primarily mothers and wives and is posing ideological restrictions on their movements, rights, and roles within society.

Contextualizing Gender Relations

By providing a brief overview of such macrolevel forces, the aim of the chapter is to contextualize microlevel practices and processes, both in the home and at the workplace, which form the focus of the book. As Om Samir's quote above suggests, national, regional and international forces, far removed from the boundaries of specific local communities, may nonetheless exert a powerful influence on shaping local understandings and articulations of gender, and inviting various forms of responses to gender inequalities. Household formations and gender relations take place in specific sociopolitical contexts and are constrained and informed by broader circumstances beyond the control of individuals or local communities.

It is now widely acknowledged within anthropology that despite the discipline's conventional emphasis on bounded entities, one can no longer meaningfully study a community in isolation from national and international forces and structures, "which although invisible, influence the local economy and politics" (Wright 1994:15). Developing ways of linking microlevel ethnography to macro level processes and institutions and of contextualizing single-locale anthropological research within wider contexts now constitutes a widely emphasized approach within anthropology (Fardon 1995; Miller 1995; Wright 1994).

Situating gender relations within a broader socioeconomic and political context also allows one to challenge the depiction of the "timeless" Arab family that emerges from much of the literature on the Arab world (Ayubi 1995; Tucker 1993). One of the reasons why studies of the family in the Middle East have been generally frozen in time is because adequate connections between broader processes of societal change and microlevel behavior are often not made. The ideal typical Arab family is thus often presented as a patrilocal, patrilineal extended family of several generations living in one physical and economic unit, and operating under the authority and control of a patriarch, the oldest male. An overriding assumption is that power in the family resides in the father "who expects respect and unquestioning compliance with his instructions" (Barakat 1993: 10).

This stereotypical image of the "Arab" family, portrayed in much of the literature, is cast as a monolithic, unchanging entity, with certain characteristics that stand in stark opposition to the "Western" family. Tucker (1993) identifies four aspects of this "otherness" that are particularly relevant to power relations in the household: the prevalence of arranged marriages, the focus on women as bearers of family honor, ᶜ*ird,* the preference for endogamous cousin marriages, in particular the father's brother's daughter preference, and women's relative lack of power due to the threat of divorce and the practice of polygyny.

However, more contextualized empirical and historical research that attempts to link household formations and family relations to broader societal transformations reveals that in reality there is a great deal of variability within this ideal model of the "Arab family." Several studies in Arab countries shed light on the complexity of power in the family, the dynamics of same-sex power relations, such as that between the mother in law and the daughter-in-law (Morsy, 1978), and women's active roles in both the private and public spheres (Abu-Lughod 1986; AlTorki 1986; Rassam 1980). Moreover, Tucker (1993) rightly questions whether the ideal model of the Arab family was ever the reality, or even the ideal, of the majority of people in the Arab world. By comparing data from court records concerning marriage and property among upper class and lower class families in Nablus and Cairo in the 19th century, Tucker demonstrates major discrepancies within, as well as divergences from, this ideal family type. For instance, female codes of modesty and the actual practice of associating family honor with female behavior varied significantly across classes.

Some studies in contemporary Egypt have similarly shown that while some households may display characteristics of the ideal "Arab family," there is in fact a great deal of diversity in the types of family and living arrangements that exist. Such diversity reflects different responses and adjustments to various macrolevel socioeconomic and political transformations. The classic extended family arrangement is only one type of family/household configuration in Egypt. In fact, simple nuclear households actually appear to be replacing extended arrangements in urban Egypt. In one of the neighborhoods that I carried out my research in, 80 percent of all households were simple nuclear ones consisting of married couples with or without children or single parents with unmarried children (Shorter et al. 1994). Moreover, households headed by women are now estimated to constitute at least 18 percent of all households in Egypt (Egypt Human Development Report 1997; Fergany 1994b).

A recent anthropological study of gender and family power in a low-income neighborhood in northern Cairo further challenges stereotypes of power as localized in a father figure and attempts to link local practices with broader socioeconomic phenomena (Ghanem 1996). Ghanem argues that men in this community selectively appropriate certain aspects of the "global" while simultaneously repudiating those aspects which may serve to contest their power in the family or disrupt the status quo. For example, a husband may install a telephone line, a symbol of modernity, but use it to more effectively monitor the movements of his wife. Another may purchase a colored television to accommodate his wife's discontent at having to stay at home, but attempts to control when and how it is to be used (Ghanem 1996). Her study is a perceptive portrayal of how in a context of globalization, both men and women attempt to appropriate meanings and practices and to establish new "truths" to either naturalize or contest power relations between them.

Gender relations and practices at a community level are thus not static, but are in continuous flux as they interact with broader societal transformations. Understanding broad societal changes in Egypt is therefore essential for interpreting the microlevel interactions that are the focuses of this book. Before providing an overview of some of the macrolevel trends that are most relevant to the concerns of this book, however, a brief socioeconomic profile of Egypt is provided below.

Egypt: A Socioeconomic Profile

Egypt had an estimated population of 60,236,000[2] in 1996 (El-Zanaty et al. 1996). It had a Gross National Product of $US 660 per capita in 1993 and was accordingly classified as a "low-income" country by the World Bank (World Bank 1995). However, more recent research (Fergany 1997) suggests that the income levels of a sizeable percentage of population are below that average per capita estimate. This is an important finding which highlights the inherent inadequacies of

GNP measures for capturing socioeconomic inequalities within a country, and suggests a greater degree of impoverishment for certain groups in Egyptian society than official estimates indicate (Fergany 1997).

Estimates of the percentage of Egyptians whose income falls below the poverty line varies widely between 25 and 35 percent depending on the methodology adopted (Egypt Human Development Report 1997; World Bank 1995). In 1995, Egypt ranked 107th out of the 174 countries on the Human Development Index. This low ranking is partly related to the high rate of female illiteracy, estimated at 66 percent of the total female population (UNDP Human Development Report 1995).

Egypt's economy has traditionally been based on agriculture. In 1960, agriculture represented 40 percent of the gross domestic product. By 1995, however, the share of agriculture had declined to only 20 percent whereas the industrial sector has expanded from 15 percent to 22 percent (World Bank 1995). It is estimated that 43 percent of all industrial production in the private sector takes place in small firms of less than ten employees, many of which are "informal" in the sense that they are unregulated by law. These constitute part of Egypt's "informal economy" or "informal economic sector," which has only recently become the subject of research.[3] Because most of my respondents were employed in the informal economy which will be discussed in later chapters, a brief description of the sector is provided below.

Estimates of the size of the informal sector in Egypt vary widely. One estimate based on number of employees per firm suggests that Egypt's informal economy has been on the rise over the past two decades. Census results show a significant increase in informal sector employment between 1976 and 1986, indicating that it has been an important force for creating jobs during this period (Handousa 1991). Assuming stable growth rates in the Egyptian economy, informal sector employment is expected to reach 4.5 million by the year 2000 (Rizk 1991). In addition to its exact size, a related controversial issue[4] with regards to the informal economy in Egypt has to do with wages and earnings, as compared to other sectors of the economy. Abdel Fadil shows that employees in the informal sector are engaged in low-wage, low-income and marginal activities that do not provide a minimum standard of living (Abdel Fadil 1983). On the other, hand, Rizk (1991) argues that concepts like "wages of the poor," "survival," "marginality," and so forth, go against the brighter picture provided by most research findings in Egypt. The 1990 CAPMAS survey, the largest empirical one on the informal sector to date, shows that about 75 percent of workers in the informal sector draw a salary above minimum wage level. Of those, 30 percent earn between LE3 and LE7 a day, 20 percent earn between LE5 and LE 7 a day and 3 percent over LE10 a day[5]. As will be discussed in chapter seven, however, my research suggests that these salary levels may reflect only male employment and are a generally misleading depiction of female employment in the informal sector.

Regional and Internal Migration

Egypt has experienced a number of important transformations over the past two decades which have had a direct influence on its economy, both the informal and the formal sectors. One of the most significant has been large-scale migration. Part of this migration has been internal, from rural to urban areas[6]. In fact, Egypt has had one of the fastest rates of urbanization in the world, which has resulted in the urban population doubling in ten years. Population growth has been accompanied by a steady increase in the ratio of the population residing in urban areas, reaching 44 percent of the total population in 1986 (El-Zanaty et al.1996). (See Table 1). Much of this growth has been uncontrolled and has resulted in the rise of a number of spontaneous urban settlements, as will be explained in the following chapter.

In addition to internal migration, Egypt has also witnessed unprecedented levels of regional migration over the course of the past twenty years. Most of this migration has been to the oil-rich Arab countries of the Gulf as well as to Jordan, Iraq and Libya. Successive waves of out-migration since the early 1970s were triggered by a number of national, regional and international developments. These included high levels of population growth in Egypt, a deterioration in the conditions of life in rural areas, the adoption of liberal economic policies by the Egyptian government and the relaxing of controls over out-migration, the 1973 Arab war with Israel and the concomitant rise of a regional petrodollar economy, and the extended war between Iraq and Iran which has led to a dramatic increase in labor demand in Iraq (Amin and Taylor 1984; Hatem 1983; Taylor 1984).

Since the 1960s Egypt had been exporting a labor force of professionals and administrators to a number of countries in the Middle East. This labor force was carefully regulated and controlled by the government and was in line with Egypt's own manpower needs (Taylor 1984). In the 1970s, however, the government sponsored labor migration was surpassed in size by a largely unregulated gush of labor at various skill levels. As a result, Egypt's share of total Arab migrant labor increased significantly, reaching one-third by 1975 (Taylor 1984).

By the mid 1980s, 11.5 percent of Egypt's total labor force was estimated to be working abroad, as compared to 5 percent in the mid 1970s (LaTowsky 1984). However, professionals no longer constituted the majority of migrants. They were overtaken by skilled and unskilled laborers in the construction sector. The demand for construction workers was triggered by the construction and maintenance of huge infrastructure projects in the rich Arab countries in the Gulf during this period. In 1980, 44 percent of those who were issued residence permits for first time employment in Kuwait were employed in the construction sector. In Libya, Saudi Arabia, and other Gulf countries, the same pattern of labor deployment has been observed (LaTowsky 1984). Many men in the study community were part of this semiskilled and unskilled construction labor force (Landor

1994). They have thus been directly affected by the regional migration of the eighties as will be discussed later on when describing the study community.

It is estimated that only about 10 percent of the migrants between 1975 and 1985 were women (Taylor 1984). It was thus predominantly Egyptian men who migrated leaving their families behind. Accordingly, much of the research on regional migration in Egypt has focused on the impact of men's absence on female autonomy and decision making within the household, particularly in rural areas.

Research results have pointed to conflicting tendencies. There is general consensus that male out-migration has increased women's workloads in rural areas and enabled them to assume new roles previously reserved for men, such as dealing with agricultural banks and cooperatives. Nonetheless, there is disagreement over the impact this has had on patterns of authority and power within the rural household. Some studies have concluded that male migration has led to women assuming greater leverage and control over resources and authority which are expected to continue even after husbands or fathers returned (Kattab and El-Daeif 1982; Khafagy 1984). Others have, however, been more cautious in their conclusions, asserting that the changes that did occur have been marginal, and have not fundamentally challenged or affected the existing character of relations between men and women, or significantly altered gender norms and expectations (Hatem 1983; Taylor 1984).

Taylor suggests that the impact of migration on the position of a migrant's wife is closely related to the type of family structure she is left to manage, and on her stage in the reproductive cycle. Thus the position of younger women with children who live in extended households with their mothers-in-law may actually be negatively affected by male migration since they do not control the incoming remittances and their authority and independence is checked by their mothers-in-law. Taylor argues that even for migrant wives in nuclear independent households for whom migration has resulted in more control over their own lives, their power in the household is neither "total" nor "permanent": husbands remain the main decision makers (Taylor 1984). Some studies have further suggested that the feminization of agriculture that occurred with male migration has actually led to a societal devaluation of this entire sphere of activity. As more women engaged in farming and farm-related tasks due to male out-migration, agricultural activity became devalued in comparison with the work that migrant workers assumed abroad (Abaza 1987).

Another important aspect of regional migration of more direct relevance to gender relations in the study community, and which I observed clearly during my research, has been its impact on increasing consumerism. Taylor (1984) documents the rise in demand for largely imported consumer durable goods, such as televisions, refrigerators and electric household equipment in the village she studied. She also vividly illustrates some of the changes in tastes in furniture and home items that have occurred with migration. The inflow of remittances appears to have been accompanied by an increase in demand for novel "modern" items, creating new popular tastes, such as for instance a demand for blond and blue eyed plastic ornamental dolls. As will be discussed in chapter four, the rise of consumerism and changes in patterns of popular consumption that accompanied regional migration have significantly influenced marriage transactions in the study community. The increase in the costs of the marriage trousseau, *gihaaz*, has apparently forced an increasing number of unmarried women to seek employment as wage laborers in the informal sector. Amassing a large *gihaaz* has become an important mechanism through which women may increase their options and leverage in their future marriages, as will be discussed in chapter six.

The Iraqi invasion of Kuwait in 1992 and subsequent international events have led to the involuntary return of massive numbers of migrants to Egypt, estimated at over a million returnees by the early 1990s. This coincided with the decline of the construction boom in the Gulf countries which had attracted much of the regional migration of the 1970s and 1980s, thus inducing the further involuntary return of migrants. The impact of this massive return migration has not been studied systematically. It is nonetheless acknowledged as one of the reasons for the current high rates of male unemployment in Egypt in general, and among semiskilled and unskilled construction workers in particular, who, as mentioned earlier constituted a significant percentage of the male labor force in the study community. As Landor (1994) demonstrates, based on an anthropological study in 1980 of the labor processes underlying an urban peripheral area on the fringes of Cairo, there is a complex interplay between migration (external and internal) and the growth of unplanned urban settlements. Landor argues that the construction trade, in which most of the male labor force in his study community were engaged, is an unstable form of employment as "it creates an urban labor force only trained for construction work which will be laid off during periods of downturn in the industry"(Landor 1994, 449).

Economic Liberalization and Structural Adjustment

A second significant change in Egypt over the past two decades has been the gradual overhaul of the nationalist, socialist policies which marked President Nasser's regime in the 1950s and 1960s (Oncu et al. 1994). President Sadat's accession to power in 1970 marked the beginning of a new era in Egypt with the adoption of more liberal economic policies and closer ties to the West. Known as the "open door" policies, *el infitaah*, these resulted in a deeper integration of the country into the global political economy, a retreat of the state from economic regulation and welfare policies, and a degree of political liberalization signaled by the emergence of multiple political parties (Oncu et al. 1994; Hatem 1994). Accompanying this process of political and economic liberalization has also been a steady decline in what has been termed "state feminism" (Hatem 1992), that is, in the active social policies of the Nasser period which had resulted in many gains for women, particularly in education and employment. Women's labor force participation increased by 31.1% between1961 and1969, and throughout the 1960s women's rates of unemployment were low. Increased liberalization, however, coincided with a significant rise in women's unemployment in the formal sectors of the economy, from a low rate of 4.1 percent in 1966 to 29.8 percent ten years later (Hatem 1994; Morcoss 1988).

The privatization and structural adjustment policies that Egypt began implementing in 1990, under pressure from the World Bank and the International Monetary Fund, are part and parcel of the liberal economic transformation which started in the mid 1970s. The longer-term impact of structural adjustment policies (SAPs) is yet to be evaluated. Such a task is also fraught with methodological problems. Nonetheless, emerging evidence strongly suggests that, at least in the short term, these policies result in increased poverty and widening disparities between the rich and the poor. Men and women are both negatively affected, but evidence suggests that the impact is differential, and that women often bear a disproportionate share of the burden (Afshar and Dennis 1992; Baden 1993; Beneria and Feldman 1992; Elson 1989,1991; Sparr 1994; UNICEF 1989; Vickers 1991).

Cross-cultural evidence indicates that policies associated with economic liberalization have affected many aspects of women's lives, from educational attainments and employment to marital status, working conditions, family relationships, marriage decisions, self-concept, access to information and public services as well as their understanding of their role and possibilities in life. These different effects may sometimes either reinforce or contradict each other (Sparr 1994). As a result of SAPs, more women than men may become unemployed, yet an increasing number of women may look for income-generating work. Moreover, wage differentials between men and women grow, working conditions deteriorate, more women enter the informal sector, women's unpaid work increases, progress in girls' education slows down, food consumption diminishes, girls' health and mortality worsen, family structures change (Sparr 1994; UNICEF 1989; Vickers 1991).

Some studies have even suggested a possible link between increased domestic violence against women and the increased cost of living due to structural adjustment programs. Price increases affect women's ability to both generate and control resources. In her study of a low-income district in Ecuador over a ten-year period (1978-1988), Moser finds that 48 percent of her subsample of women reported an increase in domestic violence during this period. Her interviewees made an explicit link between increases in prices and their lack of access to cash, reporting being physically or emotionally abused by their husbands when forced to ask for more money (Moser, 1989). Although such inferences are hard to make, a lot of marital conflicts in the study community similarly centered on monetary and budgetary disagreements and were often the cause of verbal and physical abuse by a husband.

There are few empirical studies in Egypt which have addressed the impact of SAPs in general or their differential impact on men and women in particular. The evidence that does exist, however, supports some of the international findings discussed above. Fergany, comparing national income and expenditures surveys between 1990 and 1995, shows that conditions of life have deteriorated at an alarming rate during this period. Real family incomes have fallen by 14 percent on average in urban areas and by 20 percent in rural areas, prices have increased by 170 percent in rural areas and by 160 percent in urban areas, and malnutrition among five year old children (as measured by stunted growth) has increased by 5% during this period (Fergany 1997).

Existing research also suggests that the negative impact of structural adjustment policies varies depending on a woman's life cycle, class position and form of employment. The government's policies to contract the public sector have resulted in an unprecedented unemployment rate among women. By 1986, the overall rate of unemployment in Egypt doubled from 7.7 percent in 1976 to 14.7 percent. It is noteworthy, however, that female unemployment was four times that of male unemployment; with 10 percent for men and 40.7 percent for women (Morcoss 1988). This unemployment has mainly affected new university graduates. Hatem suggests that the inability of young female graduates to find jobs has had a regressive impact on the self-perceptions and consciousness of this new generation, increasing their financial dependence on their own families and encouraging many to adopt the traditional role of dependent housewife (Hatem 1994).

In addition to increasing unemployment for certain categories of women, SAPs have also altered the terms of work in public-sector manufacturing industries. Attempts to reduce the cost of labor have resulted in deteriorating conditions as reflected in practices related to hiring, promotions, and child care facilities and maternal leaves (Hatem 1994). In the private sector, unfavorable hiring practices have also been intensified. Private enterprises get around the legal requirement of providing day-care centers for employees, by stopping short of hiring 100 female workers. Open discrimination against women can be detected in the many employment advertisements specifying that only men are eligible to apply. This is a blatant violation of labor laws, but is tolerated by the government as it is congruent with its laissez-faire policies (Hatem 1994).

Despite the lack of research in this area, structural adjustment policies are also believed to result in a deterioration of the conditions and terms of employment in some sectors of the informal economy, where much of the work of less educated women and men is concentrated. This was clearly evident in the study community. As will be shown in chapter seven, an increasing number of women in the study community appear to be engaged in tedious and low paid work as pieceworkers or as wage laborers in small workshops under precarious conditions. Moreover, the highly visible phenomenon of female street sweepers in Cairo illustrates how notions of what constitutes women's "proper" work may be eroding in the face of economic necessity. Public street cleaning, both poorly paid and socially stigmatized, has always been the domain of men. The relatively recent phenomenon of female street sweepers is also testimony to the increasingly precarious livelihoods that women may find themselves forced into in order to survive.[7]

In fact, the feminization of poverty in Egypt may be on the increase (Egypt Human Development Report 1997). Recent studies point to a large number of households solely or mainly supported by women reaching 18 percent nationally (Fergany 1994b). Microlevel research suggests that the figure may be even higher, reaching 30 percent of all households in some low-income urban communities (El-Kholy 1990; EQI 1987; Fergany 1994b). Moreover, the income levels of households headed by women are estimated to be 40 percent less than those of male-headed households (Fergany 1994b).

In the absence of longitudinal data, it is impossible to talk about trends over time. However, it is widely believed that the numbers of households who are de facto or de jure financially supported by women have increased during the past few years, partly as a result of male unemployment and underemployment. This has obvious implications for the material basis of male authority in the family, and creates new arenas of negotiation and contestation within the household. These trends were clearly reflected in the study community. Although there were only twelve de jure women heads of household in my sample, there were many more women who were de facto the main or sole providers for their families. Only three women reported that they did not contribute any cash to the household.

Public-sector cuts have also had a significant impact on the health and education sectors, both of which have specific implications for women in general, and had visible impacts on women in the study community in particular. State support to the public health care system declined significantly from 5 percent in the 1965 five year plan to 1 percent of total spending in the 1988 five year plan (Kandil 1989 quoted in Hatem 1994). Similarly, in the educational sector, economic investment dropped, educational facilities deteriorated and salaries for teachers as a group dropped drastically over the past two decades. Throughout the 1980s the state encouraged entrepreneurs to open private schools, in an attempt to reduce the burden of providing more and higher quality government education. As a result, private entrepreneurs (some Islamist businessmen and some more secularly oriented entrepreneurs who attempted to emulate the Western school system) began to invest in education (Hatem 1994). The increase in the costs of public education has resulted in a de facto move by both parents and teachers to the informal privatization of a theoretically free educational system, partly through an emerging phenomenon of "private lessons." This phenomenon, discussed in some detail in chapter nine, emerged in my research as an area of disagreement between husband and wife vis-a-vis decisions concerning a daughter's access to education.

The Rise of Islamist Discourses

Finally, a third crucial development in Egypt over the past two decades, is a growing and increasingly militant and conservative Islamist movement. This movement is part of a broader Islamization discourse which has been gaining force as an oppositional movement in many Muslim countries since the 1970s (Kepel 1992), and which has often been popularly termed "Islamic fundamentalism." Since the mid-eighties, however, a growing number of scholars have pointed to the inaccuracy of the term Islamic "fundamentalism," exposing it as an essentially Western construct (Campo 1995; Haddad 1987; Kepel 1992). Terms such as "Islamist," or "political Islam" are now more commonly used to broadly describe these fairly new political movements. While scholars agree that there is a multiplicity of voices and practices within such Islamist discourses (Campo 1995), Islamist movements, nonetheless appear to share some features which justify viewing them as part of a broader oppositional movement calling upon Islam as the source of legislation and moral capital.

One common feature of the new Islamist movements is that they commonly locate women, gender relations and family affairs at the center of their discourse (Auybi 1995; Kandiyoti 1991; Mernissi 1987; Sharabi 1992). According to Islamist ideology, women's rightful place is the home and her first obligation is to her husband and the socialization of Muslim children; women can work outside the home only after fulfilling their primary obligations. Islamists insist on the imperative of modesty, protecting women from temptation and believe in the separation of sexes in public places. The "true" Muslim family that they wish to restore is one where "authority and protection flows from the male head of household down to females and the young. Respect and obedience flow in the opposite direction" (S. Ibrahim 1985: 498). As Kandiyoti argues, in the attempts by Islamists to restore the "Islamic" community, *uma*, women represent the "ultimate and inviolable repository of Muslim identity" (Kandiyoti 1991: 7).

It is generally agreed that the current Islamist trend in Egypt was activated and gained particular strength and popular appeal after the humiliation of the Arab defeat in 1967 by Israeli forces with support from the Western world (Ayubi 1985; S. Ibrahim 1985; Shukralla 1989). The movement was nurtured under president Sadat (1970-1981) who attempted to use Islamist groups to counter leftist opposition, particularly within the national universities. It gained impetus under president Mubarak's current regime. This is partly due to the inability of the successive governments of both Sadat and Mubarak to address the country's severe social and economic problems, from housing and unemployment to the increasingly conspicuous disparities between flagrant wealth on the one hand, and abject poverty on the other. Empirical evidence shows that the "highest percentage of members of the militant Islamic movement comes from the newly built and rapidly expanding periphery of the cities, especially Cairo, where social problems and moral issues reach critical levels" (Auybi 1995: 91).

The liberal economic reforms begun under Sadat and continued under Mubarak resulted in short-lived growth in the 1970s. By the early 1980s, however, they had culminated in a severe economic crisis and high rates of external debt. During the past two decades, prices soared, unemployment and inflation grew steadily, subsidies on most basic goods were cancelled, some public sector industries were dismantled and the public health and education sectors declined (Fergany 1997; Hatem 1994; Shukralla 1994).

Finding affordable housing had also became an unattainable dream for the majority of low-income groups during this period. While rents remained quite low for older housing stock due to the rent control laws which prevailed during the Nasserite era, by the early eighties rents on newly constructed apartments had skyrocketed. The early years of the *infitaah*, witnessed a ten to fifteen fold increase in the price of land within the span of a few years (Hanna 1985). Foreign and joint venture firms entered the construction sector, resulting in an oversupply of luxury apartments. At the same time, they drove up the price of land and rents (Hanna 1985). As a result, one estimate suggests that by the early eighties, 30 percent of the income of couples within the lowest quartile of income distribution in Egypt went to pay for rent (Abt Associates et al. 1981). Moreover, the practice of charging so called "key money," whereby landlords ask new tenants for exorbitant amounts of money before renting out a flat, had become rampant. One study shows that both the incidence and the amount of key-money demands have increased at a rate of 30 percent annually (Abt Associates et al. 1981).

Unmatched by a parallel rise in incomes, the dramatic increase in the cost of housing has had a major impact on one of the fundamental institutions of Egyptian society, the family, by increasing the cost of marriage and contributing to raising the average age of marriage for both women and men. Both developments are sources of great anxiety and frustration, particularly in low-income neighborhoods (Auybi 1995; Singerman 1995). These frustrations were evident in the study community as will be discussed in later chapters. In sum, as Shukralla argues, "the fruits of the promised growth (of *infitaah* policies) never reached the large masses of the population who were finding out that the new alliance with the West went to the benefit of the rich and powerful not the poor" (Shukralla 1994: 15). The current strength and popularity of the new Islamist discourse as an "alternative" must thus be understood in the context of the demise of existing state discourse, whether secular, nationalist or socialist (Auybi 1995; Kepel 1992). These discourses are now perceived by a large majority of Egyptians as linked to a political system that is "synonymous with defeat, humiliation and impoverishment" (Shukralla 1994: 16).

The privatization policies discussed earlier also played an important, albeit unintended, role in paving the way for Islamists to gain power and strength at the local level. One consequence of the withdrawal of the state has been the creation of a social and political vacuum that was quickly filled by Islamist groups. These groups have, since the mid-1980s, stressed tactics "from below" which entailed the setting up of extensive networks in poor quarters and extending numerous social services (Kepel 1992). "Recognizing the impasse that existed regarding the immediate capture of power, they fixed as their first objective to act on the level of the individual, in his daily life, so that he should break radically with the manners and customs of the surrounding "impious" society and comport himself strictly on the model of the prophet" (Kepel 1992: 158).

The reduction of government spending on the health sector referred to earlier was partly compensated for by the rise of alternative "Islamic clinics" in both villages and urban areas. Since the early 1980s clinics attached to mosques have played an increasingly important role in the provision of high quality affordable health care thus presenting Islamists as offering a viable alternative to the social services provided by the state (Hatem 1994; Sullivan 1994). Such services constitute one example of what can be termed the "islamization" of every day life, a phenomenon which was evident in the study community and which is discussed in greater detail in chapter eight.

This sketchy overview of the interaction of various macrolevel forces in Egypt highlights the complex changes that the country has been undergoing over the past two decades. These set the broad parameters within which gender relations and practices in specific local contexts can be studied. Under the conditions of rapid change described above, it becomes inevitable to pose questions about sociocultural reproduction and change. How do social groups, in particular families and communities, where early socialization occurs, cope with these emerging realities as they attempt to reproduce themselves? (See Appadurai 1990.)

During such turmoil and confusion, in this era of *ghubar*, lack of clarity, as Om Samir put it, how do men and women negotiate gender roles and relations at a concrete level in their everyday lives? Given the cultural flux and shaky reference points, the increasing socioeconomic stratification, and the decreasing standards of living to what extent and in what ways are constructed standards of ideal behavior, namely the various "traditional" roles, values, images, and discourses about gender, unsettled? How are women managing the contradictory pressures of seeking paid employment while adhering to increasingly conservative interpretations of their roles? To what extent is new space created through which women can gain advantage and challenge perceived injustices in their lives? It is these types of questions that this book attempts to explore in some detail through fieldwork in specific low-income communities in Cairo.

NOTES

1. This common Arabic proverb is used in many contexts to explain or justify particular gender roles. I recall many instances where this saying was invoked by family and friends in discussions about a range of issues, from marriage to traveling to get an education, to working. It was used either at the beginning of a discussion, thus closing the door for further conversation on a topic, or at the end of a conversation as a last resort for making a point. Although a seemingly obvious and self evident phrase, I remember being puzzled by it as it was often used to refer to different things by different people. This proverb remained at the back of my mind and I sometimes used it as a way to trigger discussions during my fieldwork.

2. This figure excludes Egyptians living abroad.

3. The concept, measurement, and economic role of the "informal sector" have been topics of debate internationally over the past twenty five years. Early critiques of the concept, which focused on overstressing duality, ignoring of linkages between sectors and assumptions of sectoral homogeneity have now been addressed (Scott 1991). Most current research on the informal sector assumes polarization of economic activity, with a continuum between opposite poles, rather than dualism, and acknowledges both diversity within the sector as well as connections between informal and formal economic activities. Some debate, however, still exists based on the differential emphasis given by different researchers to the role of certain causal factors such as technology, legislation and labor characteristics (Scott 1991). Another important contested point also relates to whether the sector is seen as a manifestation of exploitation (Castells and Portes 1989), or as a dynamo of future growth and employment (De Soto 1986).

4. Acknowledging the debates and controversies regarding the definition, role and size of the informal sector in Egypt, Rizk nonetheless attempts to tease out several general characteristics of micro and small-scale economic activities in Egypt by reviewing some of the main studies carried out on the topic. She shows that one of the primary characteristics is that the level of skills in such enterprises is relatively high; 43 percent of workers have specialized skills and 31 percent have medium-level skills. Rizk also finds that informal enterprises are characterized by low-capital intensity, high reliance on local raw materials, and a high degree of self and informal financing mechanisms (Rizk 1991).

5. In 1997, one pound sterling was equivalent to 5.6 Egyptian pounds.

6. Rural urban migration, particularly to the capital city of Cairo, is discussed in more detail in the following chapter.

7. See El-Kholy, "The Feminisation of Poverty or Expanding Employment Opportunities for Women? A Case Study of a Street Sweeper in Cairo" (Forthcoming).

3
THE RESEARCH SETTING
AND CHARACTERISTICS OF THE
STUDY COMMUNITY

⚜

The city of Cairo encompasses a mosaic of different lifestyles, social outlooks and standards. At the same time, communities within this huge metropolis are not isolated entities. They are linked to each other, as well as to their rural origins, and often to international cities and markets as well, in intricate and complex ways. The social and economic embeddedment of urban communities within larger structures and the diversity of values and lifestyles within one community make a "community" study in Cairo quite a complex undertaking. I became very aware of this issue during the early days of my fieldwork, which led me to revise my initial fieldwork plan.

My initial proposal was to carry out in-depth research in a single community, largely for practical reasons. Given the size of urban communities, I had intended to focus even more closely on one *haara*[1] within this community, a practice also adopted by other anthropologists (for example, Nadim 1985). The community I had chosen was Manshiet Nasser, a settlement on the fringes of Cairo set up on government- owned land in the 1960s.

I selected this settlement for various reasons. First, it is representative of the spontaneously formed low-income urban settlements in Cairo, *ᶜashwaᵓiyyat*,[2] which have become established outside of formal zoning and building regulations. Like other *ᶜashwaᵓiyyat*, Manshiet Nasser has been affected by the complex interplay of global and national forces of migration, population increase, structural adjustment, and religious extremism, which Egypt has witnessed over the past fifteen years (see previous chapter). Secondly, Manshiet Nasser has a large concentration of small enterprises, estimated at over two thousand in 1984. These include foundries and other workshops which engage in a wide range of produce: items such as soap, leather goods, brass goods, chalk, ready-made clothes, rugs,

46

toys, furniture, upholstery, and mother-of-pearl items goods. Some of these workshops employ women as wage workers. Moreover, my previous exposure to this settlement suggested that industrial subcontracting activities, carried out by women at home, might also be present.

Thirdly, a rich statistical, demographic and qualitative data base on the settlement is available, although now over a decade, which is rarely the case for other informal settlements (see EQI 1987; Landor 1994; Shorter et al. 1994). The availability of such macrolevel material would allow me to better situate and interpret my own findings. The availability of such data also meant that I could spend most of my fieldwork time focusing on specific research issues rather than trying to get a broader understanding of the social history and demographic features of the community. Last, but not least, I was familiar with the neighborhood and had easy access to it due to my previous involvement as a founding board member of an Egyptian non governmental organization that has been working with women-headed households in Manshiet Nasser for the past eight years.

After spending a few months in Manshiet Nasser, however, I decided to change my approach. Although I had based myself in one *haara* and had established strong relationships with various women there, I realized that confining myself physically to Manshiet Nasser, and to this *haara* would compromise my interest in understanding women's lives and extrahousehold networks. Women's lives were closely intertwined and interconnected with activities in other locations and communities around Cairo. Many worked in neighborhoods other than Manshiet Nasser where they had established long-lasting ties and networks, such as spirit possession networks, market networks, or rotating credit and saving association networks (see the next chapter). I thus decided to abandon my initial plan of carrying a total census of women in all households in the *haara* and branched out instead into three other low-income communities where the women I interviewed led me. These are: Sayeda Aisha, Sayeda Zeinab and El Gamaliya. (See Map 1.) In order to better locate Manshiet Nasser and the three other communities in the broader fabric of the city, the next section provides a brief social history of Cairo before moving on to provide more specific descriptions of the neighborhoods in which I carried out my research.

Cairo: A Mosaic of Lifestyles:

With an estimated population of now over fourteen million[3], Cairo is currently the largest metropolis in the Middle East and North Africa region and one of the ten largest cities in the world. Only a hundred years ago, however, the city had only 905,000 inhabitants (Shorter et al. 1994). The major spurt in Cairo's growth occurred in the present century, specifically during and after the Second World War. This was partly a result of large-scale migration from the countryside triggered by both external and indigenous factors. The disruptions in international trade, specifically the allied blockade of Europe, led to a sudden demand for local supplies to meet the needs of the urban populations and allied troops based in Egypt and the Levant. Employment opportunities in the cities emerged in response to this demand and attracted large numbers of migrants to Cairo (Issawi 1982).

The demands of the war economy coincided with the Egyptian government's industrialization and urbanization policies, which resulted in the disproportionate allocation of national investment in favor of cities. Poor living standards in rural areas, the neglect of agriculture in favor of industrialization, and population pressure (partly due to the rapid decline in death rates that occurred during this period) induced large-scale rural urban migration throughout the 1950s and 1960s (Abu-Lughod 1985; Shorter et al. 1984). Most such migration was "first-step migration," that is, migration favoring the largest cities and bypassing the smaller towns (S.Ibrahim 1985). Cairo received the largest share of migrants, and as a result, the percentage of Egypt's population living in Cairo rose from 12 percent before the war to 20 percent in the 1970s (Shorter et al. 1994).[4]

To absorb its growing population, Cairo, which occupied a small physical area to begin with, could only expand by pushing out its boundaries through building on the agricultural and desert land surrounding it. Substantial plots of agricultural land were converted into housing projects during the present century, and large industrial plants established during Nasser's period were located in areas north and south of Cairo. Originally regarded as satellite areas, these have now become an integral part of greater metropolitan Cairo (Shorter et al. 1994).

Over the past two decades, Cairo's growth has been absorbed through several means. Space was created by expanding existing structures through adding floors or using the roofs as temporary dwellings, and by shrinking the size of residential accommodation through subdividing dwellings (Shorter et al. 1994). This has resulted in the overcrowding and high density so characteristic of Cairo, estimated at 29,472 person per square meter (Farah 1996).[5] Most significantly, urban space has also been expanded by setting up new settlements through building on surrounding agricultural lands, desert areas or hillsides. While some of this expansion has been controlled and planned by the government, the great majority of developments have been spontaneous and unregulated, building on either agricultural private land, or uncontrolled squatting on publicly owned land (El-Waly 1993; Oldham et al. 1987; Shorter et al. 1994). Map 1 shows a delineation of the original boundaries of the city of Cairo and the newly built planned and unplanned settlements.

"Informality," in the sense of lack of adherence to zoning regulations, building codes, or city plans, as well as the absence of government-planned infrastructure, and often lack of title to the land as well, characterized much of this process of building in the new settlements. Despite their illegality, however, tactical permission from the authorities has generally been granted for these settlements (Shorter et al. 1994), which are referred to in Arabic as *ᶜashwaᵓiyyat*, which literally means unplanned or spontaneous.

The government has generally maintained a tactical acceptance of *ᶜashwaᵓiyyat*, until the early 1990s, when the appalling conditions in many of the settlements were seen as the breeding ground for the activities of religious extremists.[6] This association was triggered by the highly publicized confrontation that took place between massive police forces and so-called "terrorists", *irhabiyyiin*, in Imbaba, a crowded settlement deprived of most basic services, which was built on agricultural land in the seventies. This area, with an estimated population of almost a million, was largely controlled by Islamic militant forces who provided the residents with a range of health and other basic services over the past twenty years in the absence of any government presence (Kepel 1992).

Since this confrontation, *ᶜashwaiyyat*, which include an estimated 30 percent, of Cairo's population, have been the target of much public debate and discussion (El-Waly 1993). Significant government investment has now been allocated to the upgrading of many such settlements. There is general consensus, however, that budget allocations fall far short of actual needs and that the top-down approach adopted by the government is not sustainable (El-Waly 1993).

The phenomenal growth of Cairo in the present century has drastically altered the historically distinctive features and the cohesiveness of urban quarters of Cairo. Janet Abu-Lughod's classic study of Cairo remains the best source for understanding the historical and administrative development of the city from its earliest beginnings during the Fatimide rule in the tenth century to the 1960s. She notes the homogenous character and the spatial boundaries of urban neighborhoods which prevailed and were enhanced by the guild system whereby each trade operated under a particular organizational structure headed by a sheikh. The original plan of Fatimide quarters was organized into distinct and bounded subsections referred to as *haaraat* (singular *haara*).

> Socially the *haara* is a group of persons usually unified by ethnic and or occupational characteristics as well as by vicinal ties and segregated physically and socially from other subgroups in the city. Politically it is often a unit of administration and control. As the commercial life of Cairo (*al Qahira*) diversified, and as occupational groups came to dominate more and more of the essential loyalties and identification of the non military classes, the original *haaraat*. were adapted to the requirements of craftsmanship and trade. Whereas the nomenclature of the earlier *haaraat* showed a preoccupation with ethnic and tribal affiliations, the names of later *haaraat* sometimes revealed the dominant occupational or commercial functions of the areas (Abu-Lughod 1971: 24-25).

This distinctive nature of urban quarters in Cairo lasted into the seventies and even the eighties as was noted by other later studies. In her study of a *haara* in one of Cairo's oldest and most densely populated quarters, Nadim (1985) suggested that the *haara* constitutes a complete social unit, with a discrete subculture within the larger culture of the city. She argues that members of a *haara*: "have strong identification …, share certain historical, ecological and sociocultural experiences

49

which point to an identifiable style of life .. (and) which generates a type of social behavior which demarcates the *haara* people as distinct" (Nadim 1985: 107-108).

However, more recent research in several popular urban quarters suggests that over the past twenty years Cairo neighborhoods may have lost much of their distinctive character and geographical boundedness, resulting in a city that is far more heterogeneous and less geographically defined (Singerman 1995). Unable to expand easily because they are surrounded by other densely populated areas, residents of central districts in Cairo have moved to newly established settlements on the fringes of the city. As people were forced out of these older neighborhoods in search of employment opportunities or new housing, they took the "*haara* culture" with them which, in time, was integrated into the various subcultures of the new settlements. As Singerman argues: "a *haara* culture ... now defined more by socioeconomic conditions and cultural preferences is less geographically distinct but increasingly pervasive throughout Cairo and other urban areas of Egypt" (Singerman 1995: 22).

Cairene culture is thus currently highly heterogeneous, and Cairo is often referred to as a "mosaic" of subcultures, reflecting the diverse lifestyles and values of the towns and villages of lower and upper Egypt from which migrants were drawn, as well as the lifestyles of the original city dwellers. One early attempt to categorize the various subcultures and lifestyles in Cairo is offered by S. Ibrahim (1985). Drawing on a variety of sources, he notes that Cairo, like other Arab cities which have undergone large-scale internal migration, is characterized by three distinct types of population: "modern urbanites," "traditional urbanites,", and "rural urbanites."

Modern urbanites are highly educated, well to do Cairenes who work in the city's modern economic sector and share similar values and outlooks with their counterparts in other major cities of the world. "Traditional urbanites" are descendants of the longstanding dwellers of the city, usually living in the older quarters, and who have remained "traditional" in their lifestyle. These include skilled craftsmen and traditional vendors. "Rural urbanites," or "urban villagers" are those who have recently migrated to urban centers but who still retain significant aspects of their lifestyles and value system and who tend to live in newly formed "ruralized" squatter areas and slums. It is these two latter "types" which constitute the majority of Cairo's population (S. Ibrahim 1985).

The liberal "open door" economic policies of the 1970s and 1980s, and more recently structural adjustment programs, have further diversified the socioeconomic characteristics and lifestyles of residents of Cairo. Stark disparities in income, educational levels, access to basic services and lifestyles are now firmly established as major features of the city. Conspicuous wealth and consumerism coexist with severe poverty and deprivation; luxury apartment buildings and five-star hotels rub shoulders with run down structures and crumbling buildings, and donkey carts carrying garbage or selling fruit cross paths with the latest-model Mercedes on the crowded streets of the city. It is now estimated that about 30 percent of the city's residents are below the officially established national poverty line (Farah 1996), and that while rural poverty may have slightly decreased over the past two years, urban poverty has been on the rise (Egypt Human Development Report 1997).

The Neighborhoods: An Overview

According to the typology referred to earlier, Manshiet Nasser residents could be categorized as representative of "rural urbanites" whereas the residents of the three other neighborhoods I worked in would be more typical of "traditional urbanites." All four areas could be considered *sha⁻bi*, popular (see Singerman 1995), or *baladi* (see Early 1993a) quarters, as distinguished from the more Westernized, and more affluent quarters of the city. While these typologies may be useful as broad descriptive categories, they are unable to capture the subtler features of differentiation within neighborhoods. An attempt at more detailed description of the specific neighborhoods I worked in is thus provided in this section.

The overview that follows focuses on Manshiet Nasser because it was the main site of my research; about 70 percent of my respondents resided in this neighborhood. It is based largely on secondary data obtained through a major survey of the community carried out in the mid-1980s (Shorter 1994), an anthropological study carried out in 1980 (Landor 1994), as well as on my own observations. Since I did not carry out a geographically focused study that aimed to get a total picture of a particular community, the descriptions that follow are necessarily sketchy.

Manshiet Nasser is located on quarry land on the slopes of the Muqattam hills, east of the city of Cairo. Spread over an area of about 1.5 kilometers long and one kilometer wide, the community is bounded by hills on the one side and a huge cemetery on the other. On the hills themselves lies a small community of about seven thousand, mainly Christian, traditional garbage collectors, known as the *zabbaliin*. The *zabbaliin* and Manshiet Nasser communities are socially and historically distinct, and until the mid-1980s were also physically segregated. The rapid pace of expansion of Manshiet Nasser, however, has resulted in the physical merging of the two communities, and a certain degree of social merging as well.

From the west, Manshiet Nasser faces the northern sections of a huge cemetery dating to Mamluk times, known as Qayet Bey cemetery, in which a significant number of people now also reside. Two kilometers away from Manshiet Nasser, beyond the cemeteries, lies the district of il Gamaliya, one of the oldest and most densely populated commercial neighborhoods of Cairo, dating to medieval times. The famous il-Azhar mosque and the traditional bazaars of Khan il Khalili and il Ghouriyya are located in this neighborhood (EQI 1987; Shorter et al. 1994). Gamaliya is also one of the four neighborhoods where I carried out my research. (See Map 1 for a location of the settlement in relation to other areas in Cairo).

When I returned to Manshiet Nasser in July of 1995, travelling through its main unpaved, steep road and crossing the railway tracks which run parallel to the settlement's main paved street, my first impression was one of familiarity. Although I had not been to the settlement for a few years, the sight and smell of leaking sewage flooding the two main roads of the settlement was a deeply familiar one, and a testimony to the inadequate infrastructure of the community.[7] The bustling, densely populated dirt roads characterized by the mixed use of space, with buzzing small commercial and industrial establishments interlaced with the community's multistoried houses, made mostly of unpainted brick and concrete, were also familiar sights.

Despite this familiarity, there were also some noticeable changes. The most significant was a more visible physical presence of both the ruling party and nongovernmental religious welfare activities. Two huge black-and-white signs, hanging side by side, now meet the eye as soon as one enters the community through its main entrance: one signals the office of the national democratic party, and the other points to the premises of the il ᶜAshira il Muhammadiyya, one of the two largest Islamic private voluntary organizations operating in this settlement.[8]

A small local mosque, built by the community through local contributions about fifteen years ago and located on the main street parallel to the railway tracks, had also become a more elaborate building, with two new floors, a freshly painted exterior and a large new sign advertising its services. These services included an orphans support program, *kafaalit il yatiim* (through which a monthly allocation for the children of widows and divorcees are administered by two fully covered, *munaqqabaat*, women from outside the settlement), religious classes for women, and literacy classes. I later found out that the activities of the mosque are now being overseen by *il Gamᶜiyya il Sharᶜiyya*, one of the oldest Islamic private voluntary organizations (PVOs) which operates nationally and has branches in most governorates and in many neighborhoods in Cairo.[9] The mosque in Manshiet Nasser was being managed through the PVOs branch located in the nearby quarter of Sayeda Aisha, one of the other communities where I carried out some of my fieldwork. The PVO branch in Sayeda Aisha provided other services, such as a polyclinic and illiteracy classes for both men and women.

Manshiet Nasser's population, estimated at 64,000 inhabitants in 1984, is now estimated to be over one million. The community has six primary and preparatory government schools, private and public health clinics, local offices of the ministry of social affairs, and the ruling party (NDP), and a number of Muslim, Christian, secular, and regionally based private voluntary associations which are providing a range of charity and community development services. Observing this crowded and bustling community, it is difficult to imagine that only thirty years ago it consisted of no more than a handful of families squatting on inhospitable government-owned land. A brief history of how the community developed speaks to the resourcefulness of its inhabitants.

Manshiet Nasser was established in the early 1960s by a number of low-income migrants from upper Egypt who were evicted from another area of the city (EQI 1987). These migrants had moved to Cairo during the Second World War and had set up a small community near the historic bazaar in the core of the medieval city and established a specialized business of recycling low-grade steel recovered from used oil drums. The community became known to the government and its neighboring community as Ꜥizbet il safih, the hamlet of steel, and was left undisturbed for a decade (Landor 1994; Shorter et al. 1994).

In the 1960s, however, the Egyptian government announced that it needed the land on which the Ꜥizba was set up to build a school and a hospital and asked Ꜥizba residents to vacate the land. After many months of negotiations between community leaders[10] and government representatives, a deal was struck whereby tacit agreement was given by the government for Ꜥizba residents to occupy public land on the slopes of the Muqattam hills. As they were not granted official title to the land, residents worried about security, and elder members recall that the new settlement was named Manshiet Nasser, in honor of Egypt's president at that time, so as to increase their chances of tenure (Shorter et al. 1994).

The main occupation of recovering and trading in recycled metal sheets continued in Manshiet Nasser. Gradually, families and relatives of the early migrants from upper Egypt joined them, attracted by the availability of housing and new job opportunities, largely in the construction sector. As the community grew in size and the threat of eviction receded, skilled craftsmen working in nearby bazaar areas, taking advantage of the availability of land in Manshiet Nasser and the lack of government regulation, also started to move into the settlement to set up their own enterprises (Landor 1994). The previous links with the traditional bazaar area in Gamaliya enabled Manshiet Nasser residents to capitalize upon the existing production infrastructure there, while availing themselves of more affordable and larger spaces for individual workshops (Landor 1994; Shorter et al. 1994). As more people moved into the settlement, demand for new building grew and the community attracted large numbers of construction workers such as reinforced concrete workers, masons, painters, electricians and plumbers, to service Manshiet Nasser as well as neighboring communities. (Shorter et al. 1994). The demand for construction workers grew significantly due to the boom in large infrastructure and housing projects which was taking place during this period in the Gulf countries. Many settlers from Manshiet Nasser migrated to the Gulf in search of employment opportunities and much of the building in Manshiet Nasser is said to have been built from "gulf money," that is from the remittances that these migrants sent back (Landor 1994).

The pressure from municipal authorities on densely populated quarters like Gamaliya to relocate their foundries further away triggered the setting up of small foundries and aluminum enterprises elsewhere. Manshiet Nasser was an obvious alternative location for these enterprises given its closeness to the markets, the availability of empty tracts of land, and the fact that it received little official attention[11] (Shorter et al. 1994).

Economically, Manshiet Nasser is thus not dependent on public-sector employment, but is much more closely tied to the informal economy. Work in small industrial and commercial establishments, and a range of jobs in the private construction trade, form the main occupations of Manshiet Nasser residents (Landor 1994). In 1984, it was estimated that the community had over two thousand small enterprises. Although a significant percentage of the labor force comes from outside the settlement, at least 20 percent of the resident male labor force works in Manshiet Nasser (Shorter et al. 1994).[12]

According to a 1984 community survey, Manshiet Nasser can be safely characterised overall as a "low-income" community in the socioeconomic hierarchy of Cairene communities. In 1984, the average monthly household income was LE 130, while the average monthly household income at the poverty line for urban Egypt as a whole was estimated at LE 183 (Korayem 1987). The proportion of households falling below the official poverty line in 1984 was thus 64 percent. Another indication of the poverty of the community can be gleaned from data on dwelling units. In 1984, almost 50 percent of the dwelling units in the community had only one room, and only 30 percent had their own toilet. The settlement was connected to main water lines and had several public taps. However, only about 50 percent of households had private water connections, and carrying water from main taps was an important task that consumed the time and energy of women, mainly the younger ones. Access to electricity was more universal. Most households had electricity connections in their homes, often through illegally tapping the main lines (Shorter et al 1994).

My observations ten years after this survey was conducted indicates that although there are some members of the community with significant resources, the area is still fairly impoverished. About half of the households I visited had no toilet, and families of seven or eight members lived in one or two rooms. Population pressure had far outstripped the capacity of the limited sewage facilities in the settlement, posing a serious health and environmental hazard for the entire community. Moreover, disposal of wastewater continues to be an onerous and time-consuming task for women. There is no income data which with which to make a comparison between income levels in 1984, when the survey was conducted, and the present time.

However, given the decline in the construction boom of the 1970s and 1980s, both in Cairo and the Gulf countries as discussed in the previous chapter, it would be safe to assume that the income of a large number of Manshiet Nasser residents, which was directly tied to the construction trades, has also experienced a decline. Moreover, as will be discussed in chapter four, the apparent increase in the numbers of women employed in informal-sector workshops and as piece-workers further suggests that certain segments of the community are economically and socially disadvantaged.[13]

The three other areas I conducted interviews in are located within a distance of two to three kilometers from Manshiet Nasser. These are Sayeda Aisha, Sayeda

Zeinab and Gamaliya. They are all part of what has been termed the medieval quarters of Cairo whose history can be easily detected through the distinctive forms of architecture of buildings and mosques. Apart from their history, a main difference between these three neighborhoods and Manshiet Nasser is that they are less geographically bounded or physically segregated from other neighborhoods. Although, like Manshiet Nasser, they can also be broadly defined as *shaʿbi* communities, casual observation indicates that they are better off from the perspectives of income and educational. Similar to Manshiet Nasser, however, they are generally more dependent on informal-sector workshops and enterprises than on formal-sector government employment, and display the same forms of mixed use of space for housing and workplaces. Singerman (1995) provides a lively visual description of some of these older quarters of Cairo. For a description of Gamaliya, see also Stauth (1991).

The "Study Community": Poverty, Gender, Religion and Regional Identities

As indicated earlier, my research was not confined to a single neighborhood; about 70 percent of my interviews were carried out in Manshiet Nasser and about 30 percent were spread out in the three other neighborhoods mentioned. In total, I carried out repeated visits to forty-six households, and seventeen workshops in those four neighborhoods. I conducted in-depth interviews with eighty-eight women and twelve men. (See Appendix 1 for a detailed description of the study population.)

An explanatory note regarding my use of the term "study community" or "sample" in future chapters is necessary. When I refer to the study community or sample (which I use interchangeably throughout), I am referring to the entire population I interviewed, in all four neighborhoods. I refer to this group of people as a "community" because they are practically all linked through different networks. I refer to them as a "sample," to indicate that the group was purposefully arrived at through a "snowball" approach to encompass certain age groups and occupations.

I also chose to refer to the group of people I interviewed as a "low-income" group throughout the book. My aim is not to homogenize this group, as I am well aware that there are variations in lifestyle, beliefs, and socioeconomic standing between and within the various neighborhoods I visited. There were also some variations along the above lines in my sample. However, there were also many shared characteristics, such as being mostly rural migrants, lacking formal education,[14] being employed in the informal sector of the economy, being deprived of access to some basic services, and having low levels of income, thus lending some justification to my use of the term "low-income community." Moreover, the nature of the study community, consisting largely of women who are working either as subcontractors or as wage laborers, meant that there was also a certain degree of uniformity in the socioeconomic characteristics of the particular people

I interviewed. Because I was specifically interested in working women, I may have missed out on the more affluent members of the community, who did not need to involve themselves in such work.

Nonetheless there were also articulations of multiple identities and local perceptions of differences within the study community. Respondents sometimes emphasised these differences in my interactions with them, as will be illustrated below. During my fieldwork I thus grappled with the difficulties inherent in the use of a term such as "low-income," which implies a uniformity of identity and may not be sensitive to other attributions of difference by interviewees themselves, who may otherwise share similar socioeconomic characteristics. A further problem with concepts such as "low-income groups" or the "urban poor" is that they have conventionally been defined narrowly in economistic terms and thus do not allow for an understanding of rankings people invoke, based on prestige or social status, rather than on wealth and income alone. One of my tasks throughout the fieldwork was thus to problematize and contextualize, rather than discard, the concept of a low-income group. As the following section illustrates, I tried to do so through working out a local ranking system based on the definitions used by my interviewees.

In attempting to do so, the challenge was to link material or observable aspects or descriptions of poverty, such as levels of education, levels of incomes, types of jobs, housing conditions, and access to basic services with more personal, "subjective" aspects that draw on different people's self-perceptions.[15] I attempted to probe into the gender-specific aspects of poverty and to understand the links between poverty, regional identities, and religion as expressed by my study community. As in the rest of my research, my concern was to carefully capture the specific idioms that people used to describe poverty, and probe into what these meant for them.

Five culturally specific categories of poverty and wealth were invoked in my discussions in the various communities. These are not mutually exclusive categories, and some are occupational categories, but they nonetheless form one local ranking system. The categories which emerged are: *aytaam*, literally orphans, *ghalaaba* (sing. *ghalbaan*), a complex term commonly used for the working poor, *urzuʾi*, referring to those working as casual workers or in irregular jobs, *mastuur*, which literally means covered, and connotes a minimum level of security, and, finally *mabsuut*, literally happy but referring in this case to those who have money in excess of their needs.

Aytaam are considered the poorest segments of the community.[16] It is interesting to note, however, that the definition of the term orphan in this context is restricted to boys and girls whose father is dead. This is different from the standard dictionary definition of an orphan as an individual who has lost both his parents to death. The more restricted definition used in this community reveals a gender bias as it is based on conventional local understandings and constructions of gender roles, whereby men are expected to be the main economic providers. Thus a father's death, but not a mother's, signals economic distress and need. In fact, it is noteworthy that the death of a mother does not qualify a child as an orphan, and thus does not entitle him or her to either the ministry of social affairs orphans' pension, nor to the orphans sponsorship program, *kafaalit il yatiim*, run by an Islamic private voluntary organization in several of the neighborhoods.

The term for orphans, *aytaam*, is commonly used to refer not only to the children themselves, but also to their mothers. Widows are thus considered a particularly disadvantaged group by community standards and are the target of local charity networks and support systems. Widows also are often given priority in some forms of employment such as piecework, as will be discussed in chapter six.

Ghalaaba comes from the Arabic term *ghulb*, which connotes fatigue as a result of daily struggles for survival, as well as endurance despite difficult circumstances. As used by community members, *ghalbaan* implies two important characteristics. On the one hand, it denotes toiling to make ends meet due to a lack of security, and on the other, it implies certain favorable moral qualities such as kindness, lack of greed, and lack of deviousness and corruption. This double meaning of the term is significant and suggests a belief that, despite their poverty, *il naas il ghalaaba* are still honest, and that deprivation has not driven them to cheating or stealing. I often heard people use the term *ghalbaan* with pride. *Il ghalaaba* was often used to denote the working poor, that is, those who may have steady jobs but whose incomes are meager and/or whose job conditions are difficult. Some of those who were considered *ghalaaba*, also worked as casual irregular laborers, *urzuᵓi*. Derived from the Arabic word *rizᵓ*, God-given livelihood, the term connotes a lack of security, the precariousness of livelihoods and a certain degree of fatalism. *Urzuᵓi* refers to a wide range of jobs in which employment is of a casual nature with no assurance of a regular or sustained income.

Mastuur literally means covered in Arabic, and suggests a higher degree of security than that of an *urzuᵓi* or a *ghalbaan*. *Mastuur* implies that what comes in as income, goes out in expenditures, and there is little extra to put into substantial savings or to give away to others as charity, which is an important symbol of status and prestige in the community. *ᶜAla aduhum*, "have enough for themselves only", was another way of describing the bottom end of this category. The terms *ghalbaan* and *mastuur* contrasts sharply with *mabsuut*, which literally means happy, a revealing term which suggests that perceptions of happiness are closely tied to material security and well-being. *Mabsuut* is used to refer to those who are financially well-off, often skilled craftsmen, *sanayᶜiyya*, or wholesalers/merchants, *tuggar*. In addition to wealth, the term also implies security due to a regular income and lack of vulnerability. Existence of substantial savings or investments, often in the form of real estate, and public displays of charity such as slaughtering and distributing a sheep in the Muslim feast, *ᶜiid il adha*, are important distinguishing features of this category of people in the community.

If one were to use this local classification system to categorize my respondents, a limited number of my sample would describe themselves, or would be described by others, as *mabsutiin*. The latter would be mainly men who run or own the workshops and a few of the female grocers, middle-women and door-to-door saleswomen. Some respondents would also fall into the category of *mastuuriin* and some would be considered *aytaam*. The overwhelming majority would describe themselves as *ghalaaba*, working hard to generate a steady income and make ends meet, yet honest, kind and uncorrupted. Within this group some would define their occupational category as *urzuᵓi*, unskilled casual laborers.

My respondents generally identified collectively as *naas ghalaaba*, which I translate as the working poor. However, regional origin was sometimes evoked as an additional marker of difference.[17] While Manshiet Nasser is still identified with its original upper Egyptian *saᶜiidi*, regional subculture, generally considered the most socially conservative of subcultures in Egypt, it now has a significant number of residents of various regional origins. Within the three other neighborhoods, strong opinions about regional identities were also voiced in certain contexts. Women sometimes made a point of identifying themselves to me as either *saᶜayyda*, rural migrants from upper Egypt, *fallahiin*, rural migrants originally from lower Egypt, or *masriyyiin*,[18] which literally means Egyptian, and in this specific context implies longer term residence in Cairo. Unlike the *masriyyiin*, who had no links with rural areas, village networks still played an important role in the survival strategies of both the *saᶜayda* and the *fallahiin*. Intermarriage between groups of different regional origin did occur, but was uncommon.

Each group harbored stereotypical views of the other, which usually surfaced in specific conversations or during particular events such as fights or discussions about marriage arrangements. The moral qualities and behavior of women was one of the important qualities that both the *fallahiin* and the *saᶜayda* evoked to distinguish themselves from the *masriyyiin*, whose women were considered loose, *sitat sayᶠaa*. I was continuously struck by how married men accused of having affairs always were alleged to be having them with women who were *masarwa*, from popular areas in Cairo such as il Hussein or Bab el Sheriyya.

On the other hand, original dwellers of Cairo, *il masriyiin* or *masarwa*, sometimes referred to *saᶜayda* as unfriendly, *rimam*, and ugly, *suud* (literally black referring to their relatively darker complexions). They also distinguished themselves from the *fallahiin* women, who did not know how to dress properly. Nawal, born in and bred in Cairo, stressed that she is *masriyya* in her discussions with me. She recalls how beautiful she was when her husband first saw her in front of her father's house twenty years ago:

> I was thirteen and wearing pajamas with small flowers. I had beautiful straight hair, styled in very long braids. Mind you, I always had my braids in the front, not in the back like the *fallahiin* do.

Similarly, during a discussion with some women about a certain Om Hamid, I asked if they meant the one who lived near the public water tap. "Oh no," replied one of the women, "the one we are talking about is white, not black like those people." I later understood that to mean she was a *masriyya*, not a *sa°idiyya*.

Regional identities were mobilized most dramatically during periods of crisis, such as a death, and there are numerous regionally based PVOs in the community whose role is to generate resources for family members of the deceased, and to cover the funeral and burial costs of their members. During some of the violent fights which took place between different families during my fieldwork (one of which necessitated the intervention of the police), community members also often automatically took sides in the fight according to their regional origin. Regional identities sometimes also affected women's access to networks in the community, particularly employment networks. Some of the workshop owners, for example, stressed that they gave priority to women from their own original region or village. Others, however, gave preference to women from the physical neighborhood regardless of their regional origin.

In addition to regional identities, religious affiliation also formed another layer of identity amongst my research sample. I had various discussions about Christian/Muslim relations in the study community and observed the interaction between the two groups in their daily lives. Interfaith marriages were unheard of, but there was otherwise a range of everyday networks and relationships that closely linked Muslims and Copts. Religious identification did not appear to play the same role in access to networks as did regional origin.

Stereotypes of the members of the different religions, however, were rife and often projected contradictory attributes. Copts were regarded by some Muslim women as much friendlier, *°ishariyiin*, and more capable of keeping a secret than Muslims. Copts were also generally perceived as better off financially than Muslims as a group, and their women were regarded as more beautiful. Om Gamal, a Muslim, explains the reasons for this difference in wealth and beauty by relaying the following story. Her comments are interesting because they reveal how historical myths are created and serve as powerful tools for justifying and maintaining differences in status amongst people.

> It is true, they are more beautiful, but it was our choice. You see, with the advent of Islam in Arabia, the Prophet made people choose, *khayyarna*, between wealth, beauty and religion. We, the Muslims, chose religion. They (meaning Christians) chose wealth and beauty. That is why they are better off than us, *halhum ahsan*, and most are pretty.

Notions of superior physical beauty, however, were marred by unpleasant bodily odors that were referred to as one of the distinguishing characteristics of Copts. "*Rihithum zifra*," they smell of grease, "*lihum riiha khaasa*," they have a special smell, and "although we eat with them and everything, there is something in my body that cannot stand them because they smell like fish," were some of the expressions used to convey this characteristic. It was commonly believed among my Muslim respondents that Christian women, unlike Muslims, do not have a proper bath after they have sex with their husbands, which partly explained their unpleasant smell.

On the other hand, members of one of the Coptic families that I became close to repeatedly told me how astonished they were that I am a Muslim, because I do not look or talk or walk "like them." I am polite, they told me, and do not shout or use vulgar language as Muslims do. They also felt that I visited them because I really cared for them and liked them, unlike Muslims, who always have a hidden agenda, ulterior motives, and are only concerned about their own self interest, *maslaha*.

My research sample thus consisted mainly of women in four different low-income neighborhoods of Cairo who collectively identified as poor people, *naas ghalaaba*, and who shared many socioeconomic attributes. Certain characteristics, however, such as religion and regional origin, also served as important markers of identities. It is amongst this group of low-income people with multiple identities that I carried out my research. The next chapter will discuss my research approach and methods. It will also provide a reflective account of the fieldwork process.

NOTES

1. A *haara* now refers to the narrow unpaved alleyways typical of many lower income and traditional quarters of Cairo, in which various household activities, such as food preparation, takes place. As will be discussed later, however, historically a *haara* was not only a spatial division within the city, but more importantly, it constituted a distinct social and political division.

2. In 1992, there were an estimated sixteen such settlements in greater Cairo, which were estimated to accommodate 30 percent of the city's inhabitants, many of whom are first-generation migrants (El-Waly 1993).

3. This figure refers to the greater Cairo region, which includes the governorates of Cairo and Giza, as well as part of the governorate of Qalubiya. See Map 1.

4. Numerically, migration is no longer a significant source of Cairo's growth and most Cairenes were born in the city. The changes in the regional economy triggered by the 1973 war with Israel, and more specifically the opening up of migration opportunities in oil rich states, has checked the flow of Egyptians from the rural areas to Cairo. Since the mid seventies Cairo's population has thus been increasing largely due to internal growth, and it is projected that by the year 2000, the percentage of Egyptians living in Cairo will actually decrease (Shorter 1989).

5. It is important to note that while Cairo overall is a crowded city, wide variations in density exist between neighborhoods. For example, while Shubra, a working class area in the north of the city has a density of 100,000 people per square meter, Heliopolis, a well-to-do district, has a density of only 13,505 people per square meter (Farah 1996).

6. The government's attitude towards these settlements has gone through several phases over the past twenty years ranging from tactical acceptance, to relocation to eviction or threat of eviction.

7. The local network of sewers and pipes set up under a World Bank upgrading project in the 1970s was never fully completed or up to engineering standards. Many residents connected pit latrines illegally to the main lines without expert supervision, and the hilly topography of

Manshiet Nasser exacerbated the poorly installed connections. As a result, breakage of sewage pipes happens frequently and the leakage and flooding of sewage a distinctive feature of the physical environment.

8. The visible presence of the ruling party increased during my fieldwork and was seen through such actions as the operating of a dental clinic, clearly marked as NDP affiliated, and the building of a brick stairway at the entrance of the settlement. This was probably related to the parliamentary elections which took place in November of 1996, and in which the ruling party, the Nasserite party and the Islamic leaning labor party were all competing for the votes. The ruling party won the elections. A few months after the elections, the dental clinic was shut down.

9. See LaTowsky (1995) for a profile of this organization.

10. See Shorter et al. (1994) for a discussion of the informal leadership structure in the community based on the tribal Arab council. The authors argue that the council played a crucial role in negotiations with the government in the 1960's and in arbitrating conflicts as the settlement expanded. By the mid 1980's, however, the death of the chief of the council and the integration of Manshiet Nasser into more formal institutional webs had significantly weakened the power and influence of the council. During the period of my own research, the influence of the council in arbitrating conflicts was insignificant.

11. Initially settlers did not pay for the land. Gradually, however, an intricate market in land and property slowly developed. In the mid 1980's, 54 percent of dwellings were occupied by renters, with landowners living in the same dwelling or nearby.

12. For a detailed description of the construction labor force and the range of economic activities which exist in Manshiet Nasser, based on an anthropological study focusing on the male labor force which was carried out in 1980, see Landor (1994).

13. Although legally Manshiet Nasser residents are still squatters on public land and have no official land tenure, the community is now recognized by the municipal administration. It has been integrated into a newly formed administrative district, *qism,* which has a police station and which incorporates not only Manshiet Nasser but also seven other subdistricts, including Qayet Bey and the *zabbaliin* community. When referring to Manshiet Nasser in this book, however, I am referring to the community as defined by its residents, and not the broader administrative definition adopted recently by the government.

14. A large percentage of my sample consisted of illiterates, although a few of the younger women and men had also received some degree of education and several had high school diplomas. Variations in education were thus not significant enough amongst my sample. Nonetheless, as will be discussed in chapter nine, education, particularly for women, emerged as a marker of status in the community.

15. Attempts by both international organizations and governments to assess poverty has been conventionally based on trans-cultural "objective" criteria. There is an increasing awareness amongst researchers and policy makers, however, that while objective measures are important for certain purposes, subjective assessments are just as crucial, and recommendations for carrying out more qualitative, participatory assessments of poverty that take into account culturally specific perspectives are now being forcefully made. See El-Kholy (1996b).

16. The inability to purchase meat during the religious feast for Muslims, ⁼*iid il adha*, was commonly used by my respondents as a clear, and publicly known, marker of a family's poverty.

17. See Taher (1986) for one of the earliest and most sensitive discussions of the relationship between class and ethnic identities in a low-income Cairo neighborhood. Her analysis shows that members of the community she studied identified much more along the lines of regional origin than along the lines of class.

18. Cairo is commonly referred to by Egyptians as *Masr*, the same term as that for Egypt, which denotes the importance of the city.

Washing Pegs

The materials and tools displayed on a *tablia* in Om Mohammed's apartment

Om Mohammed displaying the assembled pegs

Om Mohammed's daughter packaging the pegs
using a candle to seal the plastic wrapping

The finished product packaged and piled
by the door for pick-up by middle men

Upholstery Tacks

Tools and supplies

Thirteen-year-old Samira assembling
the tacks, a slow and tedious process

Samira's grandmother takes over her
task when Samira is at school

Samira's mother interspersing tack assembly
with child care responsibilities

Hair Pins

The supplies

A family affair: Sanaa and her mother-in-law assembling the
hairpins while Sanaa's son looks on

Stuffed Camels

Materials and tools

Sewing the camels at home:
an exclusively female task

Stuffing the camels in workshops:
an exclusively male task

The finished product

4
ETHNOGRAPHY IN ONE'S NATIVE CITY: RESEARCH APPROACH, METHODS, AND FIELDWORK ENCOUNTERS

᭥᭥᭥

> What we (anthropologists) find depends on the questions which we ask and on the angle of vision from which we approach our material. If we ask different questions at different points in time, we may well get different answers (Caplan 1988:10).

Ethnography, the basis of anthropological knowledge and theory, has been the subject of increasing debate over the past two decades. Central to such debate has been a recognition of the problems of language and translation (Assad 1986). There has been an increased awareness that the absence of the ethnographer from standard anthropological accounts (as well as the political and cultural baggage he or she carried with him or her), has resulted in both lack of self scrutiny (Dwyer 1982), as well as in essentialist and monolithic representations of the "other" (Marcus and Cushman 1982). The conventional image of the anthropologist as a neutral and objective observer has thus been seriously challenged. It is now well recognized that observation is always mediated by the presence of the researcher and his or her interactions with the study community (Rabinow 1977).

Acknowledging positionality in research, that continuously shifting context which shapes our realities and "from which values are interpreted and constructed" (Alcoff 1988 quoted in Geiger 1990: 171), has constituted a significant development in anthropology which gained impetus with the feminist movement. This move towards reflexivity has served to increase our awareness of both standpoint and the power dynamics of self and other, and to debunk the myth of the "neutral" researcher (Abu-Lughod 1993; Caplan 1988; Mohanty 1988). As Abu-Lughod argues in her criticism of Bourdieu's notion of the "other": "The outside self never simply stands outside, he or she always stands in a definite relation with the "other of the study. ... he/she is always in a position within a larger political and historical complex" (1993: 41).

Acknowledging such positionality, however, has raised complex problems for (feminist) researchers with regards to how they can write about the "other" without either essentalizing or overlooking the implications of the position from which they speak (Moore 1994b). Feminists have also specifically challenged the androcentric bias of much mainstream anthropological scholarship, and have further problematized the relationship between knowledge and power, arguing for the impossibility of separating epistemology from power relations (Caplan 1988; Harding 1987; Strathern, 1987a; 1987b).

While raising similar concerns, recent critiques by postmodernist anthropologists have specifically questioned the way in which interpretative authority is constituted in ethnographic texts. This has resulted in a call for researchers to experiment with new forms of ethnographic writing which are not "homological, plagiaristic, positivist, essentialist or analogical" (Caplan 1988: 9; Clifford and Marcus 1986; Marcus and Fischer 1986).

This chapter is written in light of these debates. It provides an account of my fieldwork, the methodological approaches informing it, and the limitations and pitfalls of my approach. My aim is to present the "angle of vision" which has influenced my choice of specific research questions, as well as to show how I grappled with the complex issues of positionality, location and representation. The chapter is divided into four sections: the first offers reflections upon my own positioning as an upper-middle-class, Egyptian, feminist woman carrying out research among Egyptian men and women in low-income communities in Cairo, the city where I was born and bred; the second lays out my methodological approach and main research questions; the third delineates methods and tools of inquiry, and the fourth discusses issues of interpretation and ethnographic representation.

Insider/Outsider: Fieldwork Encounters:[1]

What one sees or experiences depends upon who one is, both individually, socially and historically. (Caplan 1988:10)

As mentioned in my introductory chapter, the motivation for my research stemmed from my work experience in Egypt over the past thirteen years as a women's rights activist, a professional in the social development field, and a founding member of a women's association supporting female-headed households in deprived neighborhoods of Cairo. Working closely with women through various development programs, I had become increasingly aware of the tensions and discrepancies between the agendas and priorities that we largely educated upper-middle-class women rights activists were putting forth, and the concerns and priorities of many women in the communities I worked in. I began to wonder about the extent to which the issues we were voicing may have been circumscribed by our own class position and to entertain the possibility that our assumptions, strategies, and visions were largely a function of our specific social locations and lived realities, locations and realities often radically divorced from the majority of Egyptian women. My research was thus fuelled by a desire to develop a more situated understanding of gender relations and women's interests from the perspectives of "the poor" in Egypt. My ultimate aim was to contribute to the formulation of more nuanced and textured feminist analysis, practice and policies which are sensitive to class and other differences amongst women.

I thus began my fieldwork with a keen awareness of my complicated relationship to the study community. I was uncertain as to how that defined me in terms of my relationship to the community. A "native"? A "marginal native"? (See Freilich 1977 quoted in AlTorki and El-Solh 1988.) An "insider"? A "halfie"? (See Abu-Lughod 1991.) An "outsider", due to the social distance created by my educational background and class position?

Anxious to locate myself early on in the fieldwork, I consciously chose to define myself as an insider, an indigenous researcher. However, as I spent more time in the various low-income neighborhoods, the difficulties and ambiguities of finding one identity or "location" became vividly apparent (Geiger 1990). I was continuously shifting positions, and roles, from one context and set of discussions to the next (the good Muslim, the Westernized Egyptian, the women's rights activist, the conservative Egyptian mother, the well-connected upper-class Egyptian, etc.). Moreover, there were also sometimes discrepancies between how I wished and imagined that I would be perceived and how my interviewees actually perceived or positioned me. In the following section, I provide an account of how attempts at self-presentation and perceptions of my identities were played out during fieldwork.

Multiple Roles, Multiple Identities

I began my wanderings in Manshiet Nasser on my own, unaccompanied by local informants or research assistants. These unfocused wanderings aimed at achieving a better feel for a community with which I had had previous contact, but which had changed significantly. I was also interested in finding out the extent to which I would be recognized as an affiliate of the Association for the Development and Enhancement of Women (ADEW), which is active in this community and others and of which, as mentioned in the introduction, I was a founding member. As I walked around, I shopped for tea, soap, and matches at the many small local groceries in the community. This gave me a legitimate and relaxed context to start chatting with the owner, often a woman, or other women who also happened to be shopping there. Gradually I was invited to tea and lunch in some of the houses, and my circle of acquaintances started to expand. I felt a strange mixture of familiarity and strangeness during the first weeks, and was surprised at the extent to which my identity as an ADEW board member seemed irrelevant. Very few people identified me with the association, and to those few who inquired about my current involvement in it, I explained that I had temporarily left the organization to pursue my studies.

I was forthright as to the reasons for my presence in the neighborhood, explaining that I was carrying out research (the topic of which I found myself defining differently depending on who I talked to), for my Ph.D., *duktuura*, in a university in England. Some did not quite understand what this meant or entailed, and their main concern was what type of job such an undertaking would enable me to get. Others likened me to the ministry of health and ministry of social affairs personnel who had just been in the community collecting survey data for some development program. Yet others assumed I was training to be a physician (also *duktuura* in Arabic), and some asked if I could examine their children. It was often younger men and women with some education who came to my rescue, explaining that I was preparing to get a job as a professor in the university, just like the daughter of Om Sanaa in a popular Arabic soap opera.[2]

While I took time to explain to everyone who expressed curiosity about me, that I was a researcher, *baahitha*, I never used the word anthropologist, or ethnographer, which do not even have Arabic translations; sociology, ᶜ*ilm il igtimaaᶜ*, was the closest I could use. I found myself changing the way I defined my topic depending on my mood and who I was talking to. Sometimes I was so tired, I did not want to engage in any lengthy discussions so I selected more banal and concrete topics like "small-scale industries." Other times, when I did want to provoke or engage a person, I used more hazy or controversial titles, such as the relationships between men and women. To those whom I interviewed in greater depth, I explained my research interests in detail.

In general, however, I explained that I was trying to understand how women were coping with their lives in this and other low-income communities in Cairo, both in terms of their family situation and their job conditions. "How is this going to help us," was a common reaction, to which I must admit I found my own attempts at explanation rather lame. I generally articulated the position, suggested by Geiger (1990) that as a researcher I would probably not be able to help them change their conditions in any major way, but that what I hoped I could do was make their voices, experiences, and priorities more visible, and thus perhaps influence the way their livelihoods are interpreted and understood by those who may be in positions to support them.

After a few months of observation and exploration, I began conducting in-depth interviews with several women with whom I had established good rapport and who resided in different parts of the community. These were not women whom I selected, but rather they had selected me in the sense that they were the ones who first invited me to their homes and expressed their willingness to be part of my research. After a few interviews, I subsequently decided to focus my investigations on one *haara*, alley. Although the data I was getting from the interviews was rich, the fact that my interviewees did not know each other made me unable to get a feel for the networks and mutual relationships in the community. The *haara* I selected is one which I happened to come across during my walks through the community, and for several reasons, it seemed like a particularly good place to start.

First, as an unpaved, narrow alley off the main paved road, it seemed physically representative of the smaller alleys and streets of Manshiet Nasser. Second, I was attracted by a charming woman in her sixties, Om Azouz, who later on become one of my key informants, and with whom I have developed a special relationship. When I first met Om Azouz on a hot summer day in July, 1995, she was squatting on the mud floor in front of her house hammering away on upholstery tacks, which I subsequently discovered was a widespread type of subcontracting job, performed solely by women, and sometimes children as well (see chapter seven). Squatting beside her, I started chatting informally, and when I left after a couple of hours I knew I had established one of my most important contacts.

During my repeated visits to this *haara*, Om Azouz embraced me with incredible generosity and warmth, despite her obviously meager resources. When I explained to her my interest in women's employment, she introduced me to several other women in the *haara* who worked both as subcontractors like herself, as well as wage laborers in workshops. The fact that this *haara* included women engaged in the two different types of employment that I was interested in made it even more appealing for me as a research site.

Third, the *haara* was relatively compact, comprising probably around 150 households. While I knew I would not be able to visit them all, I hoped to be able to visit a significant number and thus assure a reasonable coverage of the entire population of the *haara*. Fourth, the *haara* had at least two Christian households, and I thought it would be interesting to look at Christian/Muslim relationships, particularly with regards to female networks, in this predominantly Muslim community.

I spent much of my first few months in this *haara* and conducted many in-depth interviews with *haara* residents. While I was convinced that this grounding in a particular geographical location was extremely useful, it also presented problems that I had not anticipated. There appeared to be much jealousy and friction amongst households, and more specifically competition over me (who I visited first, how long I spent with each person, etc.). I had expected that the more people I got to know in the alley, the more comfortable they, and I, would be but instead I had the opposite experience. As long as I was visiting Om Azouz only, people in the street seemed friendlier and less curious. Once I started developing relations with other people and visiting other households, I began to feel less at ease in my dealings, as everyone seemed to have something terrible to say about the others. I had to make an effort not to be drawn into *haara* conflicts, gossip and politics, began to be more self-conscious about who I visited first every day, and tried to ensure that I was not seen to be affiliated with one particular house-hold. This was not easy to do because there were some women who I enjoyed spending time with more than others. When I began visiting one of the Christian households, speculation about my religion surfaced visibly for the first time, and as will be discussed later, religious identification became an important marker of my identity in the field.

My early experiences in the *haara* probably reflected how I think I was perceived by its residents. I initially thought that I had clearly articulated my purpose as a researcher during the first few months. However, it became increasingly clear that community members had their own agenda and consciously cast me in a specific role, that of a resource person, someone who could help solve the many problems they faced. The role and agenda I adopted were in effect being negotiated to accommodate the different agendas of the women I talked to. This attempt to treat me as a resource clearly had something to do with my being an educated, upper-middle class Egyptian, who was assumed to be knowledgeable about the mysterious workings of the bureaucracy in Egypt (which in fact was an accurate perception because of my previous work experience). It was also assumed that I had a network of influential family and friends in Egypt, a network of *wasta*(s), connections, that I could activate to mediate on behalf of the women I spent time with. I was continuously asked questions such as: "Can your husband find my son a job in the textile industry (after I had mentioned that my husband works in textiles)"; "Does he know anybody well connected at the Saudi embassy, to get my brother a visa to Saudi Arabia?" "Do you know anyone in the police station who can help me issue an identity card?"

The perception of my being a possible resource affected my initial contacts and the information I was getting in critical ways. One of my research interests was extrahousehold, female networks. Although I was aware of such networks, both through previous fieldwork as well as the literature, and was prepared to explore extrahousehold forms of cooperation and linkages, my early discussions with women on these topics was met with persistent frustrations. Women often abruptly put an end to my questions, responding that relationships of Cooperation simply did not exist, that the community was fragmented, that there were no forms of mutual help and that people were greedy and selfish. The Arabic saying, "no one wipes your tears but your own hand," was often evoked to emphasize the lack of mutual support systems. As I spent more time in the community, observing the range of networks of mutual help that did actually exist and, more specifically, as I witnessed how the community activated them in response to specific tragedies such as a fire or a death, I realized that I may have been purposefully misled.[3]

It was only upon reflection about the community's possible perception of me as a resource, both economically, but more importantly socially and politically, that I began to understand why I had become the object of intense competition. Individual women were probably purposefully projecting themselves to me as struggling on their own, so as to maximize the individual attention they might command. Given my previous links with the community, as well as my social position, I should have been aware of the possibility of my being perceived as someone with power. I think I probably unconsciously blocked this possibility because of my desire to negate or diminish the social and economic distance between "me" and "them," and to establish a more egalitarian relationship with my interviewees.

This experience, moreover, made me reflect more critically on the findings of one of the earliest studies of poverty in Cairo. In her ethnography of seventeen poor families in a Cairo neighborhood in the early 1970s, Wikan (1980) finds that most social relations in that community were characterized by divisiveness, jealousy, suspicion and infighting, with little sustained cooperation. Wikan concludes that:

> The poor urban neighbourhood reproduces its characteristic social organisation: small divisive coalitions, and enmities in a sea of strangers; unstable scattered circles of acquaintances in spite of limited geographical mobility; a low level of integration. (147)

It would be interesting to consider Wikan's conclusions in the light of whether she may have similarly been perceived as a resource (she mentions several times how she used to regularly distribute gifts of clothes and food in the community, donations which she collected from embassies and well-to-do people in Cairo), and the extent to which this may have influenced her findings and impressions of the community she studied.

Once I became aware of possible perceptions concerning my roles, I began to both discuss the limitations of what I could offer, and to simultaneously act as a resource, openly, when I could. I was generally not approached directly for financial assistance, (I was never asked to lend or give money for example), but instead was asked to act as a *wasta,* connecting and mediating, largely with the local bureaucracies.[4] I also went to great lengths explaining to community members that in fact they were of more use to me than I could ever be to them, since my research depended on my ability to get to know them, interview them, understand their lives and livelihoods, and record it all. After a few more months, when the limitations of what I could do, in fact, became evident and my novelty wore off, I think people realized that I was genuinely there for a specific purpose, and that while I was prepared to act as a *wasta* for anybody to the best of my abilities, there was often little that I could do.

Later on, I was also asked to join several rotating saving associations, *gamᶜiyya*(s), (see the discussion on *gamᶜiyya*(s) in chapter nine) with the provision that I be the last to withdraw my contribution. Thus, in effect I provided economic resources by contributing to the capital of these associations. I was pleased to offer this service, as my main opportunity for reciprocity with people who were so hospitable and generous with their time and energy. I was also aware that this signaled a qualitative shift in my relationships in the community and that I had become more accepted and trusted. However, I must admit, that I was also pleased to be asked to join these associations for purely selfish reasons: being a participant in these networks gave me insights into their dynamics, which I would never have been able to have access to otherwise.

Managing my role as a potential resource was not always easy. In general, I was able to maintain the balance between making myself useful providing advice and health information, connecting people, mediating through the bureaucracy on behalf of women who wanted to receive an identity card or to register a child in school without feeling overwhelmed or overloaded. There were instances, however, where I failed to manage this balance and where I faced the limitations of my role as an individual researcher in a neighborhood deprived of access to many basic services.

I remain haunted by the various situations where I was unable to provide badly needed services for women and their families, and where I stood helpless in the face of a dying infant, a badly beaten wife, or the eviction by the police of various families from their homes. These were situations where I was vividly reminded of the limitations of an academic researcher in terms of changing systems of inequalities. It is these same situations that have made me skeptical of the common claims that feminist methodology, which purports to abolish the object/subject dichotomy, is inherently "empowering," or "liberating," for those being studied (see Reinharz 1992). These claims must be seriously questioned, particularly when research is conducted in situations of extreme poverty and social inequality and where "empowerment" requires much stronger links between research and the commitment and ability to change material conditions and challenge power relations.

Another role that I found myself unconsciously assuming in the course of the field research was that of mediator. The pressure to take sides in fights and quarrels which were sometimes a daily occurrence and to be part of the grapevine of gossip among women was quite strong, particularly at the beginning of my fieldwork. I think in some ways I was being tested, to determine who I would ally myself with. I listened intently to the gossip realizing its power as a form of communication that transmits information about customs, change, and ideas as well as opinions about ideas (Harding 1975 quoted in Cornwall 1996). With some of the women I had become closest to, I took a clear stance and sided with them against other women (and sometimes men) who had wronged them. Most of the time, however, rather than taking sides with one party or the other (because even after fourteen months, I rarely felt secure enough in my interpretations to really evaluate many situations), or at the other extreme, remaining neutral and refusing to get involved in the fights and quarrels, I found myself adopting the role of the mediator.

This role drained me emotionally and was a source of constant stress, although it gave me important insight into community relationships. Unlike my role as a resource person where I felt I was being useful and which I generally enjoyed, I often did not enjoy my role as a mediator. That I was encouraged to play this role by many women, even towards the end of my fieldwork, however, indicates my precarious "insider"/"outsider" status in the community, despite my intimacy with many women. Perhaps I could never be a real "insider." I was considered close enough to be trusted with details of fights and to understand their dynamics, but was without any immediate vested interest, which thus allowed me to be perceived as fair in my arbitration.

Familiarity and Distance

While my nationality, history and fluency in Arabic granted me a degree of instant "insider" status and were significant markers of identity for my interviewees, my religious affiliation which is not clear from my name as is sometimes the case with Arabic names caused confusion initially. Although I was working in predominantly Muslim communities, there was a significant minority of Coptic families. Relations between the groups were complex. Although the groups shared modes of cooperation, a common identity as Egyptians (the main distinction being that of regional origin, i.e.: lower Egypt, upper Egypt, or Cairo as was discussed in chapter three), and formed alliances, there were also tensions and frictions, reflecting increasing tensions along religious lines in the country at large.

In retrospect, it is clear to me that I may not have had the same access and intimacy with women if I had not been identified as a Muslim. While some women asked me directly whether I was a Muslim or a Copt, others did not, but tried to find out indirectly, through probing into the names of my husband, son, or mother. For example, several women asked me why I called my son Seif (a name used by both Muslims and Christians), and not Muhammad (a name solely used by Muslims). I think that, at least for some women, I was only accepted as a real "insider" when they found out, sometimes through subtle means that my husband's name was, Amr, a clearly Muslim name. This established my religious identity, and thus "located" me more neatly and clearly for women and increased my closeness with most of them. It also enabled me to discuss religious issues and participate in religious lessons in the local mosques in a way that may have been difficult had it not been possible to establish my religious identity.

My research encounters clearly challenge the binary categories of insider/outsider and shows that, contrary to conventional usage, these terms are not synonymous with "native" versus "Western" anthropologist. Although a Cairene and an Egyptian, I was sometimes perceived as an "outsider" by the research community and experienced a sense of distance and difference due partly to my class location. The complexity of these categories became even more apparent to me when comparing field experiences with a colleague, Nadje El-Ali, who was carrying out research among upper middle class secular feminists in Egypt at the same time. Nadje is partly German and was neither born nor bred in Egypt or the Arab world. Despite her more "Western" background, I was struck by how she was actually sometimes more of an "insider" than I was, due to the similarities in class and educational levels between her interviewees and herself.

Throughout my fieldwork, I repeatedly confronted these issues of "familiarity" and "distance," long-standing concerns within anthropology. Some scholars have argued for maintaining a "respectful distance" from interviewees to counter the fear of "turning native," or creating "over-rapport" (see Reinharz 1992). For anthropologists who are studying their own society, this is assumed to be a particular danger. (See AlTorki and El-Solh (1988) for a discussion of the presumed advantages and disadvantages of "indigenous" versus "non-indigenous" research.) In a similar vein, the issue of "hybridity" has been addressed by questioning the effects of prolonged exposure to a specific culture. "While culturally enriching, hybridity perhaps induces a half-conscious adoption of the research community's ethos; and this, while enhancing rapport, may block off certain questions and inquiries" (Sayigh 1996: 2-3).

Although born and bred in Cairo, there were several situations where I felt like a "stranger," an "outsider." This was most apparent when I encountered cases of spirit possession in the course of my research. Not only were practices related to it new and unfamiliar to me, but I was also unable to easily decipher the very heavily coded language and symbolism of the spirit possession discourse. This was a totally different communication system, embedded in a subculture that I was unfamiliar with. I was an outsider to the extent that I had initial difficulties believing some of what was going on, particularly when spirits manifested themselves during an interview and started talking to me and to other women in an altered voice. It was not only that I did not believe that this manifestation was genuine which would have been fine, it was more that I even had doubts whether anybody could believe this, including the women involved. I had to nudge myself to let go of my reality and live in the reality of the women I was studying, if I was to proceed any further with my research. (See chapter eight for a discussion of spirit possession.)

Another instance where I was also clearly identified as, and felt like an "outsider" was during my extensive discussions of the *ayma*,[5] discussed in detail in chapter four. The *ayma*, a written inventory of all the furniture, equipment and jewelry brought to the marriage by both the groom and bride with a stipulation that they are to be the sole property of the wife, is not a common practice among upper- class Egyptians. My admission that I did not have an *ayma* drawn up when I married initially provoked reactions of disbelief, pity, shock, and strangeness. These sentiments are summed up well in Om Soad's remarks:

But how is this possible, is there a house without an *ayma* in this country? How can you protect your rights? If you do not have an *ayma*, you must not be really Egyptian then, you must be a *khawagaaya*, foreign woman, or maybe you are married to a *khawaaga*?

There were many other instances, however, where I was clearly appropriated as an insider (although I did not necessarily feel like one in particular situations). One striking episode took place during a heated discussion in a local mosque during a "religious lesson." Some of my questions apparently aggravated the woman who was giving the lesson and she began questioning my identity and rationale for attending. Two of the women whom I had accompanied to the lesson surprised me by immediately standing up to "protect" me, and talk on my behalf. "She is one of us," they said, "an Egyptian and a Muslim, and had a right to pray in the mosque and attend classes if she wanted to." "She is not a *khawagaaya*," they explained, "or a voyeur, *gaya titfarrag*, but a 'real Muslim'." One of the other women, whom I had accompanied to the mosque, also volunteered spontaneously that I was a distant relative who had been working in Libya for many years and was here on a visit. In sum, throughout my fieldwork, I was constantly moving between an "insider/outsider" status; experiencing a constant sense of "shuttling between two or more worlds" (Visweswaran 1994: 119).

Such movement had many unsettling moments. One of the most problematic for me, particularly given my commitment to a feminist methodology, which at it's best requires honesty and openness, was the issue of reciprocity and self-disclosure. I was continuously struck by the various ways in which I felt compelled to dissimulate many aspects of my identity and conceal some of my beliefs. This was sometimes because I felt that certain attitudes were expected of me as an Egyptian, and at other times because I was unwilling to reveal the social gulf that separated me from the women among whom I was conducting research. As a result, I found myself less engaged in self-disclosure and the reciprocal exchange of ideas, experiences and information than I had hoped for or expected.

For instance, I often concealed some of my beliefs, particularly when talking about issues related to sexuality, which formed an important part of my research. It was hard to be truly transparent with personal information, because I assumed that it may have seriously jeopardized my relationship with the women I interviewed. As an Egyptian, my liberal attitudes on these issues may not have been tolerated and I feared being dismissed as a loose, wayward woman. I had purposefully tried to project myself as a "respectable" Egyptian woman, through dressing conservatively, wearing a head scarf occasionally, and "flaunting" my married status and my motherhood (see Morsy's 1988 reflections on a similar strategy).

My five-year-old son sometimes accompanied me to the field (which I think opened many doors and increased my rapport tremendously with women), and I often talked about my husband. Except on a few occasions on bus rides when I accompanied women to their workplaces, I generally experienced no forms of sexual harassment, and I never felt I was considered a sexual threat. I exchanged my views on many marital issues, gave examples from my own marriage, and engaged in arguments about what was a right thing for a woman to do or be (many women expressed sorrow, shock, or surprise that I did not have an *ayma* for example, that I was not circumcised, or that I had only one child and did not plan to have any more). I was much more careful in volunteering and exchanging information about my beliefs concerning sexuality, except in the context of my own marriage and marital relationship. This type of self-censorship may have also resulted in excluding some sensitive issues from the discussion, which women may have responded to had I been more forthright on my views of some issues, such as homosexuality for example.

I think my gender, my marital status and the fact that I was a mother played an extremely important role, not just in having access to women, but in being able to engage with them in intimate discussions about the perils and joys of marriage and motherhood. I am convinced that reaching this level of intimacy would have been less possible had I been a man, or an unmarried woman with no children. Being a woman, particularly a married educated woman, enabled me to gain easy access to men as well, although I doubt if I could have had the same type of intimate discussions that I was able to have with women. Because many interviews focused on marital conflicts where women shared personal, and often embarrassing and troubling details of their relationship, at a certain point my intimacy with women could be maintained only at the expense of engaging in the same level of interaction with men. Given that I often found myself in the role of a "confidante," I felt I had to and was expected to "take sides" and unambiguously "declare my loyalty," which I did, to the women (see Abu-Lughod 1988 for a similar experience).

The result is that I interviewed many fewer men than I had initially intended. Much of the data and analysis in the chapters to follow is thus primarily based on women's perspectives and experiences. Although this may have resulted in a less complete perspective than I had initially aimed for, I think the trade-off of being able to establish deep relationships with many of the women I interviewed and thus generating data and insights on sensitive topics, many of which have not been previously explored in the Egyptian context, was worthwhile.

I also often felt uncomfortable when women started grilling me about my husband's or sister's salaries, the cost of my son's nursery, or the value of my apartment. I dissembled throughout. Of course, women knew that I was more affluent than they were, but it became increasingly clear to me that most had no idea of how large the gap was. Although cognizant that it may have been more "empowering" to make them more aware of the steep class divisions and discrepancies of lifestyles that exist in Egypt, I did not volunteer the necessary information.

As a nonpracticing Muslim, I also felt disingenuous at times. From the moment that I declared that I was a Muslim, women automatically presumed that I was a practicing Muslim who shared their religious framework and beliefs. As mentioned earlier, I was questioned many times about my religion, usually subtly, and sometimes not so subtly. I sensed that saying I was a Muslim gave me more immediate and intimate access to the overwhelming majority of households. I exploited this and never dared to admit that I am a nonpracticing Muslim. I often joined in Friday prayers, particularly during Ramadan. I sometimes felt that this was indeed part of my own self-identity that I could call upon when necessary. At other times, however, I felt I was performing the part of being a Muslim.

It is against this backdrop of multiple identities, perceptions, and roles and in light of this baggage of personal values and convictions that the following chapters analyzing my findings must be read. I am aware that what follows represents only one perspective on gender relations and women's strategies in the study community. This is a perspective arrived at through both who I am and was (both during and after the fieldwork), and who my interviewees were (given their multiple positionalities as well) in their discussions and interviews with me.

Analytical Approach and Research Questions

The aim of my research was to explore the complexity and dynamics of gender relations and gender ideologies in low-income Cairo, with a view to understanding women's daily strategies for responding to what they perceived to be gender inequities. My research, however, focused largely on one specific category of relations between men and women within the household: relations between husbands and wives. I am aware that gender relations are broader than this dyadic relation. However, my choice was partly based on the need to narrow down the field of investigation, and partly influenced by ethnographic research in Egypt, which highlights husband-wife relations as primary ones for the manifestation of male and female identities and roles. For example, in her study of economic and power relations among poor families in a *haara* in Cairo, Nadim (1985) consciously focused on the husband-wife relationship because she found that within this subculture:

> intra-familial relationships could be categorised more meaningfully in terms of males and females. Differences in role playing among members of the same sex is one of degree, rather than one of kind. The son's relationship in the family and his relationship with his mother and sisters is an extension of his father's role. Similarly, the daughter's role is an extension of her mother's. (Nadim 1985: 221-222)

Given the importance of the mother-in law complex in extended families described in chapter one, I had initially planned to investigate the relationships between mothers and daughters-in-law. I was unable to do so thoroughly due to time constraints. I also did not look at parent-child relations, or at sibling relations in as much depth as I would have liked to.

Several general questions, corresponding to the specific and concrete aspects of gender ideologies and gender relations that I chose to focus on, guided my research. Gender ideologies are complex, and often contradictory, composites of beliefs relating to many aspects of masculinities and femininities. To narrow such a broad domain, I focused specifically on local understandings and meanings as they relate to three main arenas: conjugality, breadwinner status and sexuality, all of which are directly related to the various social arrangements that I discuss below.

Gender relations are also extremely broad and are not negotiated in the abstract, but in relation to particular social arrangements. I focused on women's negotiation practices as manifested in two specific, and closely related, arenas or "spheres of activities": the "conjugal contract" (see Roldan 1988; Whitehead 1981), and women's paid work.[6] Within marriage and the conjugal contract, three areas took precedence: premarital standards and marriage negotiations; conjugal relations and sexuality; and, intrahousehold decision making and resource allocation. I also focused on two specific types of women's paid work: waged work in small "informal" sector workshops, and home-based subcontracting.

The decision to focus on these particular arrangements was not arbitrary, but was guided by suggestions from previous research on intrahousehold power relations, both globally and regionally. For example, several earlier studies showed that power and conflict within households are most clearly manifested in the arena of budgetary allocations and decisions regarding spending, savings and investments, and that the control of cashflows within the household is closely related to reinforcing or undermining male dominance (Bruce 1989; Hoodfar 1990, 1997; Nadim 1985; Pahl 1989; Roldan 1988).

Moreover, existing research suggests that provider status and sexuality are two aspects of gender ideologies most directly related to beliefs and expectations about maleness and femaleness, with important consequences for power relations in the family. In her study of the self-images of *bint il Balad*, the traditional low-income urbanite woman, Al-Messiri (1978) shows how women's notions of masculinity center mainly on the ability of the husband to earn money and provide for his family. The close link between notions of masculinity and provider status has also been noted in other ethnographies of Cairo (Hoodfar 1997; Rugh 1984). I was also particularly interested in exploring this link given my experience, as discussed earlier, working with women-headed households.

Three broad sets of issues or questions guided my research. (See Appendix 2). Some of these were formulated prior to my fieldwork and others emerged or were refined during the process of fieldwork itself, through taking cues from the women and following my own intuition and awareness of the issues on which there was a dearth of data. As a result, the balance of questions changed and some received more in-depth investigation than others. I engaged in more discussions related to sex, sexuality, marriage negotiations and subcontracting arrangements, for example, and less than I had intended to in relation to budgetary control and intrahousehold resource allocation.

My starting point, as discussed previously, was to focus on households, both as units of analysis, but just as importantly as springboards for identifying other locations such as the workplace and larger kin and nonkin social networks. While I remain sensitive to the important distinctions between the concept of household and that of family (see Bruce and Dwyer 1988; Netting et al. 1984; Yanagisako

1979),[7] I nonetheless use the two terms interchangeably. My interest was in units of coresidence, which in urban Egypt are primarily composed of kin (Zurayek and Shorter 1988). In this context, the concept of the family, although more encompassing, can thus be approximated to that of household, which lends itself more easily to empirical observation.

Several scholars have highlighted the value of using the household as a site for examining gender relations. Households are the main arena for the expression of gendered roles and expectations and provide a primary material context for the formulation and internalization of gender ideologies (Beneria, 1987). Moreover, as Netting et al. argue, focusing our attention at the household level is particularly useful during times of rapid change as the family/household institution is a sensitive mirror for how people adjust to the shifts in constraints and opportunities that confront them as a result of socioeconomic and political change (Netting et al. 1984). Household studies provide a practical approach to "understanding how global forces are in actuality-rather than by deduction from grand theory-layed out in different local contexts, or in the same locality at different times" (Middletown 1992: 32).

My approach to the study of households, however, was not a static one that concentrates on demographic features and so-called household strategies which presuppose a unitary model of the household. While not negating the existence of various types of intrafamily cooperation, my approach was influenced by feminist critiques that have challenged the idealized, normative view of households as undifferentiated, income-pooling units in pursuit of a common strategy (Bruce and Dwyer 1988; Folbre 1986; Whitehead 1981; Wolf 1990). Therefore, I focused more specifically on processes of negotiation within household units, which may take conflictual forms and may perpetuate domination and hierarchy along gender lines, or may invite resistance.

Feminist research on the family has also highlighted the problems of viewing households in isolation from one other and from the broader context in which they are embedded (Caplan and Bujra 1982; Harris 1981). I thus also examined the ways in which women within different households are linked to each other through broader social relations of cooperation, exchange or conflict, and on the interrelations between women's patterns of negotiation within the household as unpaid family workers, and outside the household as paid workers. With regards to women's paid work, I focused specifically on two types of working women: women who do piecework (subcontracting) at home, and women who receive wages in workshops (largely small, generally unregistered, enterprises employing up to ten workers).

I focused on these two types of work for a variety of reasons. They appeared to be widespread in the study community, they have not been studied in-depth, and they provide two interesting extremes of women's paid work options in terms of flexibility of arrangements, pay levels, skills required, and community acceptance as "proper" women's work. As will be discussed in detail in chapter seven, whereas subcontracting is carried out inside the home and is considered acceptable work for women, wage labor, while more lucrative, is considered shameful and inappropriate. Moreover, as the women engaged in these two activities represented different age groups—single girls predominated in wage labor and married women with children in sub-contracting- they appeared most relevant with respect to my interest in examining life-cycle changes in gender inequalities and patterns of resistance.

Within the specific arenas of gender relations and ideologies mentioned above, I was particularly interested in understanding two types of variations in gender relations: life-cycle changes and generational differences resulting from transformations in gender norms and expectations. To better capture these changes, I focused my investigations on two sorts of families: newly married couples with young children, and families with older children and grandchildren. To analyze changes in marriage practices and forms of paid employment, I adopted a time perspective which enabled me to seek explanations for such changes in terms of broader changes in the socioeconomic and political environment which had taken place concurrently. Such an approach also entailed trying to understand current practices and ideologies "by asking how their connection with the past constrains and shapes their dynamics in the present" (Collier and Yanagisako 1987: 45).

Tools and Methods

During my fieldwork, I lived with my husband and son in my family home in a suburb south of Cairo, about a fifteen to thirty minute drive to the communities I studied. I did not live in any of the communities, as it would have been culturally unacceptable for a married Egyptian woman with her own residence in Cairo to do so, and would have appeared inappropriate and risked jeopardizing my access to the community. I visited the neighborhoods I was interested in, however, on a daily basis throughout these months and spent many of my evenings there.

I used an array of methods of investigations which included: *dardasha* (a common local means of exploration based on informal discussions, chats and conversations); participation in a range of regular livelihood activities (such as peeling garlic and cleaning rice, assembling upholstery tacks and washing pegs, joining rotating credit and saving societies, attending weddings, religious lessons, prayers, funerals, celebration of births, and spirit possession ceremonies); observation of daily activities; and conducting in-depth, open-ended interviews and gathering oral narratives. Only a few of my oral narratives could be described as oral histories, in the sense of being comprehensive accounts of a woman's life story following a life history format (see Geiger 1990). Towards the end of my research I also relied more heavily on focused interviews to probe into specific issues.

My choice of methods stems directly from the nature of my theoretical and methodological concerns outlined earlier. The emphasis on observation and participation in a range of livelihood activities was related to my conviction that theory and interpretations must be grounded in an understanding of the daily material realities and lived practices of men and women, as well as the importance of verifying and identifying the contradictions between beliefs articulated in narratives and actual practices. My use of oral narratives and in-depth, open-ended interviews reflected an interest in "giving voice to women." I was interested in describing and analyzing women's experiences from their perspectives as related to me in specific interactions, and making sense of their place in the world in a way that "is not challenged or outright rejected by the very people whose lives it tries to explain" (Reinharz 1992: 33). And, I might add, often tries to change as well.

Oral narratives and open-ended interviews are invaluable techniques for providing insights about people's experiences of themselves, in their own worlds, and in their own words (Gluck and Patai 1991). Moreover, open-ended interviews are particularly useful for capturing interaction and interconnections between people and events, they allow both the narrator and the researcher maximum flexibility for clarification, and reduce the control and direction of interviewer over interviewee, all qualities which have particular appeal for feminist researchers. Open-ended, in-depth interviews are particularly well suited for an exploratory study such as this one, in which one does not know in advance what types of specific questions to ask. As Anderson and Jack (1991) argue, in-depth interviews represent an important shift from

> information gathering, where the focus is on the right questions, to interaction where the focus is on process, on the dynamic unfolding of the subject's viewpoints. It is the interactive nature of the interview that allows us to ask for clarification, to notice what questions the subject formulates about her own life, to go beyond conventional expected answers to the women's personal construction of her own experience. (1991: 23)

All types of interviews, including open-ended interviews and oral narratives, however, are not without their limitations involving, as they do, two subjectivities, that of the interviewer and that of the narrator. Issues of motives and memory of the narrator, her desire to present herself in a certain way to the interviewer, cannot be ignored. There is a vast literature on biases in interviews (see for example Acker et al. 1983, see Reinharz 1992 for an extended bibliography). It is well recognized that oral narratives always contain a self-serving component and are often shaped according to the narrator's own sense of direction. In other words, they are neither a transparent representation of experience nor a reproduction of reality, but only offer glimpses of different subject positions in specific interactions with the interviewer.

Moreover, discrepancies in power, status, and privilege between narrator and interviewer also pose important challenges to the presumed interactive and non-hierarchical qualities of oral narratives so prized by feminists. While narrators do have some control over the interview process, they are rarely full partners. Their control recedes significantly during the actual transformation of the oral texts into accessible formats for reading, a process which inevitably involves decisions of the selection, framing, editing, and discarding of passages (Borland 1991). As a result, the content of oral narratives may not "contribute to a respectful and non stereo-typical view of those studied, as a social fact, it typically helps recreate a hierarchy of privilege" (Olson and Shopes 1991:198).

I tried to do minimal editing of the transcribed interviews. Nonetheless, I made constant choices about how to translate and present various women's narratives into the context of a written book, what to include and what to leave out, and what to use to support particular arguments, a process in which the women I interviewed had no say. I am aware thus that "their voices" are clearly mediated through this process. I take refuge in the conviction that should the women I interviewed read this book many would recognize their own particular voices in it. I am also aware that the voices that do emerge from my interviews are not static ones that reflect the "real voices" of the women I spoke with. Like myself, my interviewees have multiple and shifting identities and what my interviews captured can be no more than specific subject positions reflecting specific interactions with me at a particular moment in time.

As mentioned earlier, I started my interviews with women at the household level and then traced my way to their work places, and to the locations of the various networks they participate in, which were often in different communities. I also interviewed a limited number of men. These were mainly workshop owners, so as to capture how decisions about pay, hiring, and specific work arrangements are negotiated, male lawyers, to get insight into the legal aspects of marriage negotiations, as well as others who were doctors, religious healers or relatives of the women I interviewed. About 50 percent of my interviews were taped, with the full agreement of the interviewee, and I later transcribed and translated them into English with the help of an assistant.

Along with my observations, participation in livelihood activities, and interviews, I also recorded Arabic proverbs pertaining to gender and family relations. However, I only recorded those that emerged spontaneously in the course of an interview or conversation, and I was careful to record, and later analyze, these proverbs in their "discursive" context, that is, in the context of who used them, when, for what purposes, and for which audience. The importance of such local idioms is not that they provide an accurate description of reality. In fact, the ideas and depictions provided by proverbs may often be contradictory, fragmented, and inconsistent in their ethical judgments or at variance with other cultural beliefs (Webster 1982). However, they nonetheless map out a field of meaning based on local categories, and give people a language to talk about differences, as well as providing local definitions and understandings of concepts like value, status, power, equity, injustice, and domination.

My interest in proverbs and colloquialisms on gender used in a specific context was thus part of my broader conviction of the importance of paying attention to local idioms, forms of expression and usages. As Dwyer notes in her study of gender ideologies in Morocco as conveyed through proverbs and everyday conversations, it is critical for researchers to look at possible conflicts between male and female views of the world as such differences provide insights into possibilities of change (Dwyer 1978a). Since understanding gender ideologies was related to my interest in strategies of resistance and identifying potential sources of change, I was particularly sensitive to variations in beliefs about gender between men and women; proverbs sometimes provided a stark way of articulating such variations.

My main research "sample" on which I based most of the analysis in the chapters to follow, consisted of eighty eight women and twelve men. (See appendix 1 for a more detailed description in terms of age, marital status, education and occupation.) I also had less in-depth conversations and discussions with many other members of the communities. My sample was a purposefully composed one, a theoretical sample, which was not aimed at ensuring statistical representation of women or men in those communities. It was rather intended to select specific categories of individuals using life cycle and employment criteria.

My approach had some inherent limitations. I did not talk to as many men as I had initially planned (see section on fieldwork encounters). The limited number of people I talked to and the fact that this was not a comprehensive study of particular communities mean that issues of comparability and generalization are compromised. However, the advantages of the methods used in this exploratory study, whose purpose was essentially heuristic, is that they enable the generation of the sorts of information that generate both theoretical insights as well as inform policy formulation.

Qualitative methods enable the generation of rich and new information, from the perspectives of people whose voices are rarely heard, and the unearthing of a range of previously unexplored (or unsuspected) relationships on sensitive issues, from which a number of important hypotheses can be derived and more systematically explored. For example, my suggestion in this study that it is mothers who insist on educating their daughters, often despite their husband's disapproval, runs counter to the conventional wisdom in Egypt and elsewhere about the obstacles to girls' education and has important theoretical and policy implications. (See chapter nine for an extensive discussion of this issue.) Moreover, since my aim was to evaluate, critique, complement and contribute to existing feminist and social theories, my methods allowed me to take a "grounded theory perspective" which uses an inductive approach to interpreting data (see Reinharz 1992), thus enabling me to identify new conceptual relationships grounded in actual practices and daily material realities.

Interpretation and Ethnographic Representation

Analysis and presentation of information generated through ethnographic techniques often poses specific challenges of interpretation, and as several scholars have argued, the relationship between ethnography and feminism is an "awkward" one (Strathern 1987b). Issues of representation and the inevitable problem of "speaking about" without "speaking for" (Moore 1994b) occupied me during both the fieldwork and writing process. I recognized early on that some of the questions I had set out to investigate, particularly those related to a concept such as resistance, are interpretative in nature since it is an analytical construct, and is thus less observable than issues such as the division of labor and actual daily practices. In addition to direct observation of conflicts and processes of negotiation, I thus also made inferences about what constituted resistance. However, I attempted to ground these inferences as far as possible as they related to specific events, such as a street argument, a marriage negotiation, or a marital conflict.

I also attempted to resist imposing my own interpretations by engaging in a serious dialogue about meaning with my informants throughout my fieldwork. Borland (1991), giving an example of her experience interviewing her grandmother, cautions us of the possible "interpretative conflicts" that emerge in the process of recording oral narratives. Influenced by feminist concepts of patriarchy and oppression, she had framed her grandmother's racetrack narrative in which her grandmother had recalled how she insisted on betting on a certain horse despite her father's disapproval as a "female struggle for autonomy within a male hostile environment." This interpretation, however, elicited strong disagreement from her grandmother, who accused Borland of projecting her own biases into the narrative and insisting that she herself has never been concerned with female struggles and has never considered herself a feminist. This experience has led Borland to seek ways to "more sensitively negotiate issues of interpretative authority in our research." She suggests that one way to do so is "by extending the conversations we initiate while collecting oral narratives to the later stage of interpretation" (Borland 1991:73).

I have attempted to adopt a similar approach. I shared parts of my analysis and interpretation with some of my respondents, and where there were sharp divergences, I attempted to probe further. My fluency in Arabic and my intimate knowledge of the culture presented me with a distinct advantage in engaging in this type of shared interpretation during fieldwork. My repeated visits to the field during the writing-up process also helped to reduce, or at least made me more aware of the amount of "interpretative conflict" in data analysis.[8] To the greatest extent possible, I have tried to present an analysis that both reflects respondents' perspectives on events and issues, but that is also able to take account of broader socioeconomic phenomena that the women I talked to may not have been aware of.

As the chapters that follow will show in greater detail by juxtaposing my own interpretations against extensive quotes from my interviewees, there are certain areas where the interpretation is clearly a shared one. This is most obvious in my analysis of the practice of the marriage inventory, *ayma*, which women deployed as a damage-control mechanism in the face of a range of potential abuses by their husbands (see chapter six). The analysis is also largely shared with regards to the relationship between public defloration ceremonies and waged work, where respondents also explicitly argued that public defloration ceremonies are more common and more elaborate for women who were known to be working as waged laborers prior to their marriage (see chapter seven).

There were other areas, however, where the interpretations are mine alone, interpretations that I found convincing and compelling in light of other information and theoretical frameworks to which I had access. Some of these interpretations were either contested by the women or were deemed incomprehensible or irrelevant. Examples of such differences were most striking in my discussions of female circumcision (see chapter five). My interpretation of spirit possession as a "discourse of protest" that enabled women to voice their concerns about issues, such as forced sex, which in everyday discourse would be difficult to articulate, also found little local resonance (see chapter eight). My arguments about the "euphemization" of piecework, or the connections between the exploitative relations underlying this pattern of work and international processes of the feminization of labor, were also ones that my respondents could not relate to, for obvious reasons as such interpretation either radically challenges their "doxa," or draws upon information to which they have no access (see chapter seven). While I discussed as much as possible my interpretations with many interviewees, it is important to note, however, that there are also parts of my analysis that I did not share with my interviewees at all. For example, I did not discuss my interpretations regarding the apparent increase in Christian spirits (see chapter eight), nor the role of religious myths in perpetuating power relations and gender hierarchies (see chapter five).

In their conclusion to their study, the Personal Narratives Group (1989) argue that the context and experiences of the women they researched "must be considered from the standpoint of the subject of the personal narrative as well as from the standpoint of the interpreter's analysis of a particular cultural and social system" (1989: 12). Similarly, Gorelick (1991) argues that the "experiential-inductive" perspective has serious limitations for fully understanding "underlying causes of oppression." Cognizant of these limitations, and aware that "giving voice" to women, while absolutely crucial, may not be enough, I have attempted to follow an approach suggested by Acker et al (1983). This entails constructing an account of the lives of the women I researched which highlights and reflects their active voices, perspectives and experiences, accommodates my own analysis, and, very importantly, shows the relationship and the gaps between the two.

This chapter has attempted to provide an account of my fieldwork, the methodological approaches informing it, the "angle of vision" which has influenced my choice of research questions and the specific methods of inquiry I adopted. I have also discussed how I grappled with the complex issues of positionality, location, representation and interpretation. The following five chapters will present the results of my fieldwork and analysis, each exploring a specific set of gender relations and ideologies. The next chapter deals with premarital standards and expectations.

NOTES

1. For a more detailed reflection on identities during fieldwork, see El-Kholy and Al-Ali (1998).
2. Television soap operas are very popular in Egypt. They are watched regularly and are often a subject of discussions and debates. For a discussion of the role of soap operas in Egyptian society see Abu-Lughod (1995).
3. It is of course also possible that community women were not constructing the arrangements I observed as forms of mutual help but as part of their daily realities. In other words, the definition of mutual help may not have been a shared one between my interviewees and myself.
4. This highlights the crucial links between poverty, helplessness, and lack of access to power, thus challenging simplistic, economistic definitions of poverty.
5. The word *ayma* is colloquial, derived from the classical Arabic word for inventory or list, *qaaʾima*.
6. There is cross-cultural evidence of the dovetailing of marital arrangements and women's paid work. Marriage and domestic chores greatly influence the specific forms of paid work that women enter into and the extent and type of women's resistance to perceived inequalities at work. For example, married women may tolerate much lower wages than men in workplaces which provide childcare facilities for their children (see for example, Afshar 1993).
7. Egyptians actually distinguish in Arabic between the family, *ʿeela*, and the household, *maskan* or *beet*.
8. For a discussion of a comparable approach, see Marjorie Mbilinyi (1989).

5
PREMARITAL STANDARDS
AND EXPECTATIONS

"Choose a spouse more carefully for a daughter than for a son." Arabic proverb[1]

Om Gamal and Om Youssef, neighbors for the past twenty years, are shouting at each from their respective windows and gesturing with their hands wildly. In a few minutes, their exchange had escalated from verbal accusations and insults hurled from windows to a physical fight between the two women in the middle of the alley. Although a large crowd, including myself, quickly gathered around the two women and tried to intervene and stop the fight, physical injury had already occurred. Om Gamal had struck Om Youssef with a thick wooden plank. In a few seconds Om Youssef's forehead was bleeding profusely. The sight of blood abruptly stopped the fight, and accompanied by a dozen or so women and men, Om Youssef was rushed off to a nearby public hospital to have her forehead stitched, and to issue a complaint at the police station against Om Gamal.

The fight, I later found out through piecing together bits of information from neighbors, was sparked by Om Gamal's remark to another neighbor that she saw Om Youssef's eighteeen-year-old year old daughter helping her brother put his shoes on, just like a spinster. She thanked God that her own daughter was married at the age of sixteen, and now looks after the needs of her own husband, not her brother, as some of the less fortunate girls in the community were forced to do.[2] The neighbor reported this conversation to Om Youssef, who took it as a serious insult against her daughter, and started insulting Om Gamal. The fight was the topic of conversation among some of the families in my sample for a few days, and everybody, including myself, was expected to take sides.[3]

This chapter discusses premarital standards and preparation for gender roles in adulthood, particularly preparations for marriage. As the incident above shows, marriage is a central aim in the community. Spinsterhood remains one of the worst nightmares for girls and their families, and charges of spinsterhood were often the cause of similar dramatic public, verbal quarrels, *radh*, and sometimes led to physical fights amongst women in the community. The chapter discusses how girls are prepared to assume their roles as future wives, mothers and sexual providers. Within a broader discussion of premarital standards and expectations, the chapter focuses specifically on two premarital "rites of passage" and gendering practices which mark the journey of a girl's transition into womanhood, that of menstruation and female circumcision. The chapter also discusses selection of spouses and how girls attempt to expand their choices in this regard. The chapter aims to set the stage for the chapter following it, which will focus more specifically on marriage negotiations and transactions.

When "Good," *il kheir,* Enters a Girl's Body: Menstruation

Entering a world, *dakhalit dunya*, is an Arabic idiom commonly used to mean getting married and nicely captures how marriage is conceptualized in the study community. Marriage is seen as much more than a partnership, bond or alliance between two people, or even two families. For both men and women, but particularly for women, marriage signifies a qualitative change in their lives. It is the point at which they enter into the "real" world, *dunya*, and experience the true meaning of womanhood, becoming a *sit*, *hurma* or *mara*, which implies becoming both sexually active as well as bearing children, as opposed to remaining in the marginal world of that of a girl, *bint*. Marriage is also the only culturally accepted way for unmarried women to have sex, and bear children.[4]

Once married, women, particularly those who did not engage in paid work outside the house as adolescents, usually enjoy greater freedom of movement. With the birth of their first child, generally expected during the first year of marriage, women move into what is considered their central role, that of motherhood, which enhances their status in their families and the community. Remaining single is a highly undesirable state of affairs, and in the community studied, girls between the ages of twenty and twenty-five who were neither engaged nor married, approached the community's definition of spinsters, *ᶜawaanis*, and were under increasing pressure to get married.[5]

Although women acquire gendered roles and attributes early in childhood, many of those I interviewed recalled realizing a keener awareness of the social consequences of being female between the ages of eight and thirteen.[6] The onset of menarche was sometimes referred to by some of my interviewees, very tellingly, as the point at which "good enters a girls body," *il kheir dakhal gismaha*. This was most often signaled as the point at which girls begin recognizing the full social and community consequences of their identity as female.

It is noteworthy in this context that the Arabic term for femininity, *unuutha*, however, was never used to discuss these changes. Rather women used more generic terms like "grown-up" and physically "ready" for marriage, and more specifically, for motherhood. In fact, unlike the concept of masculinity, *ruguula*, which was conceptualized and articulated in a concrete manner in various contexts, the Arabic term for femininity, *unuutha*, was never articulated to describe female attributes or roles. Unlike the concept of masculinity, there was no local idiom for the concept of femininity different than that of girl or woman. The concept of femininity was much more diffuse and related to a number of attributes such as physical strength and endurance.

With the onset of menstruation, and the bodily changes associated with it, particularly the development of breasts, girls become much more aware of their own bodies as well as of their gendered attributes, expectations and responsibilities. In her pioneering study on women's perceptions of sexuality in a village in Giza, Khattab similarly finds that "menstruation is the first 'rite de passage' which is perceived by most women as directly related to fertility and procreation and consequently to sexuality. Once girls menstruate, they are considered ready for marriage and for intercourse" (Khattab 1996: 6).

Many women reported that these physical changes resulted in significant changes in how they dressed, in their freedom of movement, in their interactions with outsiders, in the types of housework they engaged in—with a more conscious focus on learning specific skills, such as cooking—and sometimes also in their allocation of wages if they were working. Ihsan, who sells tea at a street corner, is twenty-six years old, born and bred in Cairo, did not ever go to school, got married when she was sixteen and now has four children. She comments:

> I think I was about eleven years old when I got my period. From that day I felt, and was treated differently, by everyone around me. My mother talked to me and said that you are now a grown-up girl and have to take care of yourself, and your ᶜ*ard*, honor. My father told me to wear a *tarha* head cover and stop playing outside the house with other children like I was used to. My father also asked my brother, who is one year younger, to monitor my movements. This is what upset me the most, but my parents said we do not have girls who play in the street, it is ᶜ*eeb*, shameful, you are no longer a child. I would let my brother go out and I would escape and go play in the street. When I saw my brother returning, I would run up to our room again, which is on the fourth floor. One day my brother caught me and hit me very hard… I also could no longer go and get the fresh produce from the market near the railroads. The only errands my mother now sent me on were to buy soap and rice from the grocery in front of our house. She would watch me carefully, however, and if she saw me talking to any man, she would tell my brother and he would hit me.

This comment reveals how both girls and boys acquire gendered identities and become aware of male and female role expectations with the onset of menstruation, which in turn influences their behavior. Ihsan's movements were now more restricted and the spaces to which she had access had also changed: the market place became defined as inappropriate for an unmarried[7] girl of her age, whereas a nearby grocery shop was not. Just as significantly, however, Ihsan's brother also acquired a new sense of gender identity in this process. His adolescent "manhood" was in effect to be judged by his ability to monitor and "discipline" his sister. The above example further reveals how power works in subtle ways, through introducing, as Foucault suggests albeit in a different context, "disciplinary mechanisms" which require not just force (Ihsan's brother hitting her), but, just as importantly, constant "surveillance" (Ihsan's mother's watching her carefully).

Fatma, a vegetable vendor married to a baker, talks about her daughter Ibtisam, who is fifteen years old, engaged, and currently working in a small pastry workshop. Fatma reports that in the last year Ibtisam has "grown up," and is no longer a child, *ᶜayyila*. (When probing what she meant by grown-up, she explicitly said that she got her menstrual period). Fatma's comments reveal the implications of "growing up" as well as how girls are prepared for domestic work with more care if they are expected to live with their mothers-in law.

> I am telling Ibtisam she has to be more careful in her interactions with people in the workshop and she now covers her head with a scarf when she goes to work. She is working to complete her *gihaaz*, and she is no longer putting her earnings into household expenses as she used to when she was younger. But I am thinking she also needs to learn how to cook and take care of the house, and bake bread. She will be married to her cousin in the village and will live with her mother-in-law, *dakhla ᶜala beet ᶜeela*. If she does not learn these things, and also get used to staying at home, she will not be able to take it, to adapt to her marital life, *hatitᶜab*. On Sundays, which is her day off, I now teach now her how to cook properly, not just clean the rice and peel the potatoes like she used to.

Once girls begin to be defined as sexual beings, attempts to control that sexuality takes on an increasing importance. Within this context female circumcision emerged as another important premarital practice closely related to constructions of womanhood and manhood. Circumcision is obviously of a different order than menstruation, with different short-and long-term implications. While the bodily changes associated with menstruation are part of a natural process, circumcision is a change that is consciously inflicted on female bodies. Nonetheless, circumcision, as Khattab (1996) argues, emerges as the second most central gendered "rite of passage" for girls. Like other "rites of passage" that signal a girl's transition from childhood to womanhood, it is essentially based on constructions of women as wives and mothers (Khattab 1996).

The history and prevalence of female circumcision has been the subject of an increasing number of studies both in Egypt and internationally (Assad 1980; Dorkenoo 1994; El-Saadawy 1980; Khattab 1996; Toubia 1995). My purpose is not to rehearse the many important points raised by these studies, nor to single out female circumcision as an instance of women's oppression, but rather to elucidate specific theoretical points central to my broader arguments regarding the complexities of power and resistance. Using the example of female circumcision as a gendering practice, I aim to highlight, at least partly how one's apprehension and awareness of certain injustices—and thus one's ability or willingness to contest some aspects of social reality—is very much linked to one's particular social location. Female circumcision is also highlighted because it can further our understanding of how bodies themselves are gendered and how power operates to produce a specific discourse on sex and pleasure.

The reasons for my focus on circumcision as a premarital practice are threefold. The first is the universality of the practice among the women in my sample, both Muslims and Copts: 100 percent of women were circumcised, and 100 percent had either already circumcised their daughters or were planning to circumcise their younger ones when they were a little older. The second is the stark contrast between how circumcision is perceived by the women studied (they referred to as a purification ritual, *tahaara*) and how it is perceived by feminist activists who now refer to it as "genital mutilation."[8] In fact, circumcision (purification or mutilation depending on who you talk to) has been recently defined by middle-and-upper class feminists in Egypt, and much earlier on by Western feminists, as one of the most critical violations of women's human rights in Egypt.[9] The campaign launched against its practice is considered by some as one of the best examples of organized feminist activism in Egypt (see Female Genital Mutilation Task Force position paper 1979).[10]

However, unlike other areas of women's oppression both within marriage, and the labor market, as will be discussed in later chapters, where women often articulated their discontent and evolved strategies to check male power, there was no resistance at all by all the women I interviewed to the practice of circumcision. Rather there was emphatic compliance and complicity[11] with the enforcement of this practice. Circumcision thus provided me with an opportunity for better understanding how power mechanisms could work from a basis of consensus and cooperation rather than conflict.

Third and finally, circumcision is highlighted because of the connections that my interviewees made between the practice and women's sexual appeal and appetite, which relates to my discussions of sexuality in chapter eight. As will be seen later, women's obligations to render sexual services emerged as one of the important arenas for marital disputes and conflicts. Women's discontent with their sexual relations was sometimes vividly articulated through their spirit possession narratives. Some women also manipulated their role as sexual partners in their financial negotiations with their husbands.

"Purification," "Genital Mutilation," or "Gendering the Body"?: Female Circumcision

Circumcision, referred to in classical Arabic as *khafed*, literally decreasing, and known popularly as *tahaara*, purification, denotes the partial or complete removal of the external female genitalia. Excision varies from the removal of the prepuce of the clitoris only to the full excision of the clitoris, the labia minora and the labia majora (Assad 1980). The most commonly practiced type in Egypt is what is known as the first degree where the labia minora are removed and sometimes also the tip of the clitoris (Khattab 1996).[12]

All the women in my sample reported that they are circumcised, and had their daughters circumcised, or would be doing so in the future. Women's ages at circumcision ranged between eight and fourteen years old. Most of the older women in the sample reported that it was performed it at home by a traditional midwife, a *daaya*, whereas most of the younger women in the sample were operated on by a private physician in a clinic. Most women remembered the operation vividly, and were usually willing to talk about their experiences and feelings once I got to know them well.

Om Yehia is a self-employed grocer originally from Sohag in Upper Egypt, but came to Cairo when she was thirteen to get married to her cousin. She recalls being circumcised, at the age of ten, in her village together with two of her relatives of the same age. They knew they would be circumcised and although they were not quite clear what that meant, they realized it was a significant event. Om Yehia recalls how the three of them walked in the village the day the operation was scheduled happily announcing the impending event. A midwife, whom she remembers as a hefty woman, performed it, while her paternal aunt helped her by spreading her legs apart. Three pieces were cut, two on the side and one in the middle, she emphasized, noting that if all three pieces are not removed, the operation would not be considered complete. Om Yehia recalls screaming from the pain and does not remember the use of any anesthesia. To avoid infection and stop the bleeding (which is referred to as ironing the wound, *tikwi il garh*) the *daaya* put rolled henna and lemon juice on the injury. Om Yehia fainted afterwards, and the next thing she recalls is being propped up in bed and being fed soup and rabbit, a special treat.

Om Yehia felt very strongly about the importance of the operation. It makes a woman *hadya*, sexually calm, but, she emphasized, not frigid, *barda*, towards her husband.

> Also, suppose a woman does not get married until she is older. If she was not circumcised she would be itching down there and wanting to play with herself all the time. Although the operation makes a woman colder sexually, *bitbarrad il sit*, a woman can still enjoy sex with her husband, as sexual pleasure is not based on whether a woman is circumcised or not, but rather on her nature, whether she is flirtatious, *shaꞋiyya* or not. I myself used to enjoy sex with my husband very much until he stopped providing for the house eleven years ago, ever since my sixth daughter was born. That is when problems started. He still wants to have sex, but I am no longer interested in it and I refuse. (Chapter eight will deal in more detail with women's perceptions of sex and how they negotiate sexual services.)

Om Yehia confirmed that she has circumcised all her daughters, who are all in school, except the youngest who will undergo the operation when she is old enough. Unlike her, however, all her daughters were circumcised by a private doctor, not a *daaya*. It cost her about LE 15 four years ago; now the cost has risen to LE 50. Her daughters did not object; could not object, she insisted, it was taken for granted, and her husband had nothing to do with the decision. This was a decision within the domain of women, not that of men, unlike decisions regarding choice of husbands where the opinion of their father is more important.

Interestingly, Om Yehia said that she realized that the operation was not an Islamic practice, was not mentioned in the Quran, and was not practiced during the Prophet's time. She emphasized, however, that even during the Prophet's time, people were nonetheless aware of the problem of women's excessive sexual appetite. She then recounted an interesting story (best described as a community myth, since it has no factual religious or historical basis) about Fatma, the daughter of the Prophet who, according to the story, was often sexually aroused, because she was not circumcised.

> She (Fatma) used to sleep with her husband two or three times a day. One day the Prophet came to visit and found them fighting. He asked what was wrong and Fatma complained that her husband does not want to sleep with her. The prophet then looked at the washing jug, *abriꞌ*, that her husband uses to wash with after intercourse and asked it how many times her husband has used it today.[13] The *abriꞌ*, which suddenly started talking, said that her husband has washed himself seven times today (that is, he has had sex with Fatma seven times today). So the Prophet looked disapprovingly at his daughter, patted her and told her: Fatma, be cold, calm down, *kuunni buruud.*

This myth was circulating in the community as a religious fact and is an interesting example of how religious precedents and credentials are creatively invented to grant legitimacy to certain actions.

Another story regarding circumcision that was also recounted to me more than once was that of a woman named Reda. Reda's parents died when she was twelve and she was taken in and raised by one of the well known families in a neighboring community, who were also distant relatives. When she was having a bath once at the age of seventeen, another female member of the family saw her naked and was shocked to find that she was not circumcised and "had an ugly piece of thick skin protruding from her genitals, just like a man's penis." Realizing that her parents must not have circumcised her before they died, but not wanting to publicize this fact fearing that it could jeopardize her reputation and affect her marriageability, her adoptive family decided not to have her circumcised by a *daaya* or a doctor (which would have been a more public event). Instead they tied the "extra piece" protruding from Reda tightly with a piece of thread and left it like that for three months, until it "died," and fell off.

Ragabeya, newly married and now five months pregnant, notes that she was ten years old when she was circumcised by a *daaya*. Details of the event and the pain it entailed remain alive in her mind to this day.

> We went to our neighbors' apartment and there were three other girls waiting to be circumcised. I was the last and it was hard for me to hear the other girls screaming in the next room, but my mother told me they were exaggerating and that it is a very simple operation. The *daaya* made me smell something, but it still hurt very much. It turned out not to be a simple operation after all. I bled heavily, the cut was too deep, so they called the doctor and he stitched me—two stitches in the apartment. I did not go to a hospital or a clinic and was not given any anesthesia. I know now that circumcision is important so that a woman can sleep with her husband with no problems, and so that he can find her appealing. I will also circumcise my daughter when she is about ten, but I will have a doctor do it, in the clinic, to avoid the bleeding and stitching that I underwent. I want to spare her the pain.

Om Sayed, originally from upper Egypt, is married, has five children and a co-wife who lives nearby. She reports that she is circumcised and has circumcised all her daughters (aged twelve to twenty-one). Her comments stress how this tradition is ingrained in the community's value system and is closely tied to conceptions and constructions of female and male bodies.

> The biggest ᶜeeb, shame, is for a woman not to get circumcised. If a woman is not, she is not really a woman. She will have a piece sticking out of her like a man (referring to the penis). Uncircumcised, she would run after men in the street, *timsik il rigalla fil shaariᶜ*, and if fifty men slept with her in one day, she will not be satisfied, *layikfiiha* … You are not circumcised, so what do you do?? … You better not tell anyone here that you are not circumcised. (A strong tone of contempt reverberated in that last remark).

All women reacted with surprise to the fact that I was not circumcised, a clear example of my "otherness," despite many shared values and a common nationality and language. Some tried to casually find excuses for me, "you are not like us, you are really like a foreigner," or used it to explain what they perceived as my frail, unwomanly body, *gismik taᶜbaan, gismik daᶜiif*. Om Sayed, however, was the only one who questioned my sexual behavior, and who also clearly perceived me as a possible threat to her family. The intimacy we had established in previous encounters cooled off significantly after our discussion of circumcision, and my interactions with other household members became more restricted and formal.

While all women reported being circumcised only once as young girls, one woman, Mona, who has finished six years of school, told me that even though she was circumcised by a *daaya* when she was eight, she had to undergo another operation a month before her wedding last month. This was because she discovered that the earlier operation was not done properly and there was still a piece of skin dangling from her. Her husband, a semiskilled carpenter would have found that repulsive and it would have gotten in the way of him enjoying sex, she emphasized, so she had no qualms about removing it.[14]

The universality of circumcision in my sample and women's attitudes towards the practice is confirmed by a recent national study, the results of which were only recently released by the government and were met with much surprise on the part of researchers and activists. The 1995 Egyptian Demographic and Health Survey (EDHS), carried out by the ministry of health, with technical and financial support from USAID, was the first nationally representative survey to measure circumcision among women of reproductive age. The results of the survey of women who had ever been married between the ages of fifteen and forty-nine, revealed that 97 percent reported being circumcised.[15] The majority of respondents, 58 percent, mentioned "good tradition" as the reason for this practice. Thirty-six percent cited "cleanliness" as the reason, and 30 percent said it was required by their religion (these were both Christians and Muslims). Nine percent mentioned "better marriage prospects," 9 percent cited "the preservation of virginity"; 6 percent said that it prevents adultery, and 4 percent gave the possibility of greater sexual pleasure as a reason (El Zanaty et al. 1996).

Female circumcision emerges in my study as a universal premarital practice that cuts across differences in regional origin, religion or form of employment. It is a rite of passage that signals a girl child's transition into her socially ordained roles of future wife, whose role is partly to ensure the sexual pleasure of her husband.[16] The practice results in marked changes in how girls view themselves, but more importantly in how they are viewed and treated by others. Although all my interviewees remembered the pain involved, none voiced any protest and there was no questioning, let alone discernible resistance to the practice. The compliance with this practice contrasts sharply with the organized and vocal protest by more middle—and upper-class feminists (See FGM task force position paper 1997).

This contrast can only be comprehended within the context of what are two very different cultural settings and socioeconomic locations. Such different locations produce, using Bourdieu's term, two very different "habitus," a commonsensical and unquestioned "system of dispositions," which "engender products, thoughts, expressions, actions, whose limits are set by the historically and socially situated conditions of its production" (1977: 73). For the women and men in my study community, circumcision was part of their "doxa," that "practical faith.., undisputed and pre-reflexive compliance with fundamental presuppositions" (Bourdieu 1992, 68).

The practice of circumcision touches upon deeply ingrained constructions of womanhood and manhood and is closely tied to gendered identities and perceptions of women's and men's value and worth. Female circumcision can also be understood with reference to community notions of physical beauty and images of the body. Circumcision illustrates how images of the sexed body are themselves cultural constructs. Ideas about what a female body should look like to men do not include a "piece sticking out", as one of my interviewees put it. A woman's body must be docile and controlled, one that is not too demanding for a man, a body, as one of my interviewees expressed it, that "causes no problems for a man when he sleeps with it," a body that is "calm, *hadya,* but not frigid, *barda,*" as another interviewee put it. Female circumcision is thus both a "rite of passage" for women, and a gendering practice that partly serves to accentuate the difference between both masculine and feminine bodies, and to create certain "truths" about sex, sexual differences, and pleasure.[17]

Foucault's approach to power, discussed in chapter one, particularly the links he makes between sex, power and the body, offers useful insights for understanding the practice of female circumcision in the study community, including women's complicity with it. Although Foucault has been criticized by feminists for not paying particular attention to the gendered nature of the "disciplinary techniques on the body," the relationship that he highlights between sex and power is nonetheless of relevance. Foucault argues that the body is invested directly with relations of domination. The body is "sexed," that is, it becomes a female or a male body, within a discourse of sex that aims at reproducing a specific type of sex, based on heterosexuality as the "norm," the "reality," and the "truth." This type of sex, argues Foucault, is itself an effect of a historically specific organization of power, which produces a specific discourse on bodies and pleasure (Foucault 1981). It is not because we have a body that we have a particular sex, but rather we have a particular kind of notion of sex so that we have a certain type of body (Foucault 1981; Pun 1996: 17). Foucault's analysis provides insights for understanding how circumcision serves to assign masculine and feminine qualities to the body to fit specific power relations.

Situated within this cultural and analytical context of power relations and social identity it becomes easier to understand why the practice of circumcision is so entrenched. It also allows one to appreciate the fact that addressing the practice of female circumcision requires a major shift in women's self-identity and community identity and a shift of both men and women's images of female and male bodies. What is required clearly goes beyond legal measures.[18]

Choice of Marriage Partner: "Choose a Spouse More Carefully for a Daughter than for a Son"

Following these two "gendering processes", menstruation and circumcision, girls begin to be more carefully prepared for wifehood and motherhood, considered as their central roles and identities. In this context, the search for an appropriate spouse becomes a family affair in which much energy and care is invested, particularly by women. This care reflects the fact that an impending marriage affects the social and material position of the family as well as its relationships in the community. The centrality of marriage in low-income neighborhoods of Cairo

has been noted in several other studies (see Hoodfar 1997; Hoodfar and Singerman 1996;Rugh 1984). As Singerman (based on her research in popular quarters
of Cairo) argues:

> Impending marriages affect career choices, education, employment, investment,
> migration, savings and consumption patterns of both men and women ... Parents
> must consider how a marriage will influence their future financial security and mater-
> ial needs. The familial ethos not only emphasises that parents provide for their children
> but also that children support them when they get old. (1995: 84)

Data from the mid-1980s indicate that in Cairo, 32 percent of marriages took
place between relatives (Zurayek and Shorter 1988). An anthropological study in
a low-income area in Cairo in the early 1980s similarly shows that 55 percent of
marriages in that community were between relatives[19] (Rugh 1985). More recent
surveys indicate that the preference for marriages among relatives is still a common national trend. A 1991 survey reveals that 29 percent of currently married
women are married to relatives, often first cousins (Nawar et al. 1995). In my
sample of married women, the majority also reported being married to relatives,
araayib, but only a few to their first cousins.

The majority of married or engaged women in the study community did not
choose, *ikhtaaru*, their spouse. Most marriages were "arranged," with family
members initiating suggestions for a potential groom or bride. This is consistent
with national level data. In a 1991 survey, the majority of currently married
women reported not being primarily responsible for selecting their spouse (Nawar
et al. 1995). It is important, however, to clarify that arranged marriages in the
community studied are not synonymous with "coerced marriages," as is sometimes implied in the literature.

Women's attitudes towards arranged marriages were generally favourable.
While some might object to a particular prospective groom as will be discussed
below, there was no objection to having their parents, particularly their mothers,
closely involved in weighing and assessing various possible spouses, and negotiating with him and his parents on their behalf. Each marriage invariably involves its
own specific dynamics, and suggestions of candidates are discussed at length
informally by the entire family. A suitor's economic ability, level of education,
blood relations, looks, place of residence, demonstrated sense of responsibility
(does he gamble, does he drink, was he financially responsible with his natal family) were the most salient characteristics discussed.

Hoodfar's study of several low-income neighborhoods in Cairo in the mid-
eighties suggests similar findings regarding women's attitudes towards "arranged
marriages" and the involvement of their parents in the choice of spouse. She finds
that women put much emphasis on having their parents participate in their marriage negotiations, including the choice of a spouse. She argues that because
women are "aware of the legal and ideological inequality that rendered them

more vulnerable both within marriage and within society, women increasingly favored the involvement and consent of their parents, often despite their fascination with love marriages" (Hoodfar 1997: 266).

Very few of the marriages I witnessed or was told about took place without this long process of informal discussions and consultations with a prospective bride or actually involved physical coercion. Particularly if a bride explicitly voices her objection to a prospective groom, persuasion and negotiation to seek consent commonly takes place. Physical violence, however, was sometimes used as a last resort. Two women in my sample reported being physically beaten several times by their fathers, and in one case a brother, in order to force them to succumb to a marrying someone to whom they were objecting. In both cases, the groom was a relative. In the parallel cases of a groom not wanting a chosen bride, some pressure is similarly put on him, but I did not witness and was never told of any instances where a man was subjected to physical violence to coerce him into a marriage.

In this context, a girl's level of education emerged as one of the most important variables that significantly increases her ability to choose a spouse. Education allows a girl to be more selective, gives her more legitimate power to say no to a prospective husband, particularly if his educational level is below hers, and enables her and her family to delay marriage until she finishes her education. For most families "finishing education," means completing preparatory or high school. Decisions regarding the education of girls will be discussed in more detail in chapter nine in the context of intramarital negotiations.

The views of men—fathers, older brothers and uncles—often carry more weight in the final official discussions and negotiations regarding choice of a groom than does the opinion of their wives or their daughters. However, mothers play an active role in influencing the opinions of their husbands, by thoroughly investigating, and reporting on, the reputation, employment situation, and the financial and moral qualities of any prospective groom. Although the choice of a prospective husband is a complicated affair, influenced by a variety of factors, a man's financial capabilities, *yiʔdar yikaffi beetu*, his ability to supply a room, or apartment, and to provide for his household after marriage, are often a qualities that take precedence in negotiations.

Om Nasra, a 45-year-old woman whose husband left to work in Libya ten years ago and who rarely sends her money, emphasized the view, voiced by other women, that a mother must take greater care when choosing a spouse for her daughter than when she is choosing a spouse for her son, *istaᶜdil li bintak, la tis-taᶜdil li ibnak*. The essence of this popular idiom is that parents should never rush the marriage of a daughter, but should take time to meticulously investigate the credentials of the prospective spouse, and to carefully negotiate the terms of the marriage. For a son this is less important because if a man marries and his wife turns out to be no good, *mish kiwayyisa*, explained Om Nasra, he can take another wife or divorce her.

If a man turns out to be no good, however, a woman's choices are much more limited. If she asks for a divorce, she may not get it as it is the prerogative of the husband, even though the *ayma* may help in enabling a woman to get a divorce, as will be discussed later. Divorced women are also generally stigmatized, their reputations are often questioned, and it is more difficult for them to access community networks and support systems. As a result, Om Nasra notes bitterly, women, like herself, whose husbands are not "real men," *mafiish marggalla*, often have to tolerate their miserable circumstances rather than seek a divorce:

> I work as a *dallala*, I go from house to house selling clothes and material which I buy at the wholesale markets in other communities. This is how I make a living. If I got divorced, it will be much more difficult for me to move in and out of the community or to go freely into people's houses as I do now. Women here fear for their husbands around divorcees.

Despite the popular advice urging extra care in selecting a daughter's spouse for fear of her divorce given the well-acknowledged social and legal inequalities within marriage, such advice is not always followed. I encountered two cases when marriages to men not well known to the family were rushed in a few months, with practically no protest by the bride or her family. In both cases it was because the groom was financially ready, *gaahiz*, which meant he had secured both an apartment and the required gold wedding present, the *shabka*.

Within the context of these arranged marriages, however, women do attempt to exercise some individual preference. When a prospective bride objects to a marriage proposal, she sometimes articulates her protest overtly to her parents. She is more likely, however, to resort to covert tactics. One such common ploy is that of *tatfiish*, driving the prospective groom away. *Tatfiish*, in this context, rests on the assumption that if you, as the weaker party in the negotiations, cannot say no, you can get the more powerful partner to refuse the match. Nawal, now 42, comments on her attempts at thirteen to drive away a prospective groom.

> My mother told me that they have committed me to a certain man whom I had seen once before in my cousin's wedding, and that we will get engaged in a few months. I cried and said I did not want to get married. My parents insisted and my father beat me up. The man used to visit us a lot and get me presents—perfume, fruit, and once a dress -, but I still felt he was a stranger and I did not want to marry him. I decided to try and drive him away, *ataffisho*. Before he came to visit, I would not take a bath and I would intentionally work in the kitchen and peel garlic so that I did not smell good. Every time he came to the house, I would wear the same dirty and smelly *galabiyya*, and would not braid my hair, but would tie it in a messy bun. Eventually he told my parents that he did not want to go ahead with the engagement, because he felt that I am not yet ready for marriage, that I am too young, am still a child.

Neamat, a 25-year-old unmarried government employee, is also planning to use this tactic as a last resort. Her attempts over the past two years to convince her parents that she is uninterested in marrying a distant relative who has proposed to her, despite the fact that he has secured an apartment, have been futile. This tactic is used carefully, however, because it can have repercussions on a girl's reputation in the community, as well as on that of her siblings and entire family. Nonetheless my discussions suggest that it was considered more acceptable for a prospective groom to withdraw a marriage proposal than for a prospective bride to continue objecting to a particular man.

Sometimes, parents themselves used *tatfiish*, as a diplomatic way of turning away a prospective husband. Om Samira explained how her family drove away Samira's fiancé, who is a not a relative, and to whom she was informally engaged for two years. Unable to afford an apartment or a separate room in Cairo, he had wanted Samira to move to the countryside to live with his family. This was an offer that neither Samira nor her mother found attractive as they recognize the heavy labor that a young bride living in a rural extended household would have to endure. Moreover, proximity to the parental home was a strong preference amongst both mothers and daughters in my sample, and was an important concern during marriage negotiations. Rather than saying no outright, however, Samira's parents did so in a way that would not offend the groom and would not imply that it was Samira herself who was objecting. In their negotiations, they insisted on an engagement present worth seventy grams of gold, which they knew the man would not be able to afford.

When I later discussed this account with one of Samira's neighbors, Magda, who is a little older and not yet married, she mentioned that Samira was in fact lucky. She was a pretty girl with fair skin,[20] and thus could afford to be more selective about who she marries and where she wants to live. Moreover, she added, Samira had finished the preparatory stage of education and was thus more "in demand," *ᶜalleeha il ᶜeen*, by many prospective grooms. As will be discussed in chapter nine, a girl's education is an avenue to increase a family's social mobility and status in the community, and increases a girl's marriageability. Women's options in resorting to an action such are *tatfiish* is thus partly shaped by other personal resources and qualities that a bride may possess, such as beauty or education.

This chapter has focused on premarital expectations and preparations for marriage in the study community. Menstruation and circumcision were discussed as "rites of passage" as well as gendering practices which serve to define male and female roles and bodies. The chapter has also discussed choice of spouse, highlighting some of the negotiations that go into that process. *Tatfiish* was presented as one covert way in which women may ward off a prospective spouse in whom they are not interested. The discussion in this chapter has set the stage for the next chapter, which will be focusing on marriage transactions and negotiations in more detail.

NOTES

1. *Ista⁻dil li bintak, wa la tista⁻dil li ibnak.* This popular local idiom, which will be discussed later in the chapter, was invoked by several of my respondents in the context of discussions about choice of spouse.

2. It is interesting to note in this context how gender roles and expectations vary by age, even within the span of a few years. While serving a brother's needs (such as fetching things for him, making him tea, washing his clothes and putting his shoes on) is an acceptable and expected role for young girls, it no longer reflects standard behavior at a slightly older age, as it is expected to be superseded by another role, that of a wife serving her husband.

3. As discussed in chapter four, the issue of "taking sides" was a constant source of anxiety throughout my fieldwork.

4. Premarital sexual relations took place in the community, but they were neither common nor socially endorsed. Attempts were made to conceal such affairs, through for example, hymen repair operations before marriage as will be discussed in chapter seven. Extramarital affairs were more common. Women normally blamed other women, not men, for such affairs. As one interviewee put it: "It is the woman who is shamed/blamed in such affairs, because nothing can shame a man." "A man is like a dog, if you give him a bone, he will come running to you, but if you ignore him, he will find a bone elsewhere," ventured another woman.

5. Economic pressures, the phenomenal rise in the cost of marriage and the increase in girls' education, have resulted in a rising age at marriage for females over the past decade (see Nawar et al. 1995). This is merely seen as a delay, however, and almost never as a permanent state of affairs.

6. I am referring here to awareness of the social implications of their gender, not their own personal identity or awareness of being female, which probably comes much earlier, but is not an area that I explored. The onset of menstruation, not circumcision, was identified as the critical turning point.

7. A woman's access to certain public spaces thus clearly depends on not just gender, but also her age and marital status. Married women with children have much freer access to a marketplace, for example, than unmarried girls who have reached puberty.

8. One of the arguments for the use of this term rather than female circumcision is that the latter incorrectly connotes that male and female circumcision have similar health implications, ignoring the significantly more adverse effects of female circumcision. See FGM Task Force Position Paper (1997).

9. The concerted and vocal campaign against female circumcision by Egyptian activists is a recent phenomenon which gained impetus with the United Nations ICPD conference in 1994.

10. Objections to the practice are based on the grounds of personal dignity and control over one's body, as well as on medical grounds. The possible immediate and long-term complications of circumcision, from the most severe such as death from uncontrollable bleeding to infections resulting in infertility, to long-term effects such as childbirth difficulties, urinary disturbances, and inability to fully enjoy sex, have been the subject of much debate and discussion, supported by some research.

11. Agarwal (1994) makes the important distinction between compliance and complicity. In the case of circumcision there was both compliance and complicity with the practice, unlike other practices as will be discussed later, where there was compliance, but varying degrees of complicity, and sometimes none at all.

12. Circumcision is practiced in a large number of mainly African countries, amongst both Muslims and non-Muslims. Tracing its origin in Egypt is fraught with speculation. The practice was either introduced from Africa, or is a Pharaonic practice that has survived and been more recently diffused to other parts of Africa. There is no historical evidence, however, that female circumcision originated or was even practiced by Muslims in Arabia, from where Islam spread

to other parts of the world. Female circumcision was also never practiced, and is not practiced today in many Arab Muslim countries such as Saudi Arabia, Iran, Syria, Lebanon, Jordan, Palestine, or any North African country other than Egypt (see Toubia 1995).

13. The issue of bathing after intercourse is heavily emphasized by women, and the term bathing, *istahamet*, is often used in conversations to mean that a woman or a man has had sex.

14. I wanted to follow up on this conversation with her husband to get his perspective on it, but I felt uncomfortable doing so. This was one instance where I feel my gender did inhibit me from following up on some issues with men. A study of male perceptions on circumcision, and sexuality more generally, would be an area well worth pursuing.

15. Given the importance of these findings, the Egyptian Fertility society, an Egyptian non-governmental association (NGO), in collaboration with the International Population Council, an international NGO carried out a follow up clinic-based study of FGM to investigate the types practiced in Egypt as well as assess the accuracy of the self-reporting. A total of 1,339 women selected at the outpatient services of eleven clinics providing gynecological or family planning services were interviewed. Following the interviews, gynecological examinations by specially trained physicians were conducted to collect data on the prevalence and range of severity of FGM. The findings of the study, which was funded by USAID, show that there was agreement between self-reporting and examination findings in 94 percent of the cases. In all, 93 percent of those examined were found to have some type of FGM. Unlike the 1995 sample, the population of the clinic-based survey was not a nationally representative sample. Care must thus be taken when interpreting its results. See Population Council (1996).

16. Male circumcision was also a universal practice in the community and was similarly referred to as *tahaara*. While I did not talk to people about it in as much detail, it is obvious from my limited discussions that no connection was made between the practice and sexual pleasure, or the goal of being more appealing to the opposite sex, as was the case with female circumcision. Although both forms of circumcision are referred to as purification rituals by community members, the meanings and the power relations underlying male and female circumcision are thus clearly quite different.

17. If the categories of "sex" or "body" are themselves gendered, and not a biological given, as the above analysis suggests, then this raises the complicated issue of the relationship between gender and sex. A critique of the binary categorization of sex/gender has been the focus of recent anthropological work, which has shown that in some societies, gender differences are not necessarily linked to binary sexed bodies. It is thus no longer as widely accepted that gender is determined by the obvious facts of biological sex differences, or that there is a one-to-one correspondence between sex and gender. As Moore argues: "We cannot afford to assume that binary exclusivity modeled on external genitals necessarily provides an appropriate model for understanding sexual difference and gender identity around the world" (Moore 1994: 45-46). See chapter one for a discussion of the genealogy of the concept of gender.

18. I personally do not approve of the practice. However, I am trying to link it more explicitly to power relations so as to better understand women's unquestioned acceptance of the practice and thus perhaps to address it more effectively, and in ways that go beyond legal measures. During my fieldwork, the success of the organized campaign by Egyptian feminists against female circumcision indirectly prompted the minister of health to issue a decree banning the performance of the operation in government hospitals. While I am not dismissing this as a major achievement in some respects, it is noteworthy the women in my sample completely dismissed and disregarded the decree. To them, it was not an achievement in any sense of the word. Most women currently have the operation performed in private clinics. Very few still resort to traditional midwives. The unintended consequences such a law could have in terms of making women less willing to go to doctors, and thus increasing their dependence on traditional midwives with the higher associated risks of infection, must be seriously considered as a possible backlash.

19. The Egyptian concepts of relatives, *araayib*, and family, *ᶜeela*, are broad and fluid ones, making it difficult to define what family or relatives are and leaving room for various individual meanings. The terms are expandable to include both nuclear and extended kin, and are sometimes extended to nonkin as well with whom one is bound through relations of mutual obligations (see Rugh 1984).

20. This reference to skin color is a euphemism for beauty.

6
MARRIAGE TRANSACTIONS
AND NEGOTIATIONS

"A man is to be trusted as much as a sieve is to be trusted with water" Arabic Proverb[1]

I was sitting on a plastic mat in the largest room of a two-story house, sharing a meal of lentils, molasses, dry bread and green onions with Om Sayed and some members of her extended family, her daughter, Om Mahmoud, and her grand-daughter Karima. As we casually talked about Karima's marriage, consummated four weeks ago, Om Mahmoud proudly recounted, for the third time, the particulars of the fight that took place over the value of Karima's marriage inventory, her *ayma*. Om Mahmoud explained how she insisted that the *ayma* be valued at four thousand Egyptian pounds,[2] listing in great detail the various items involved, whereas the groom's family, in particular his older sister, protested, insisting that the maximum value her brother would agree to sign for was two thousand pounds.

Om Mahmoud stood firm in her demands, however. After weeks of negotiations—during which the threat of canceling the wedding loomed—the groom succumbed and both he and his uncle, as guarantor, signed a four thousand pound *ayma*. The groom's sister, however, Om Mahmoud ends the story in a victorious, self-congratulatory tone, was so angry she did not even come to the wedding. Although I had heard this story three times by this point, its importance to my research had not yet quite sunk in. I had heard about the *ayma* before, but had largely dismissed it as a formality, and did not realize its centrality to marriage transactions. Munching on a piece of dry bread dipped in molasses, I casually asked the women whether the *ayma* was an important component of marriage negotiations in this community in general, or whether it assumed a significance in Karima's case for specific reasons. As I did not write an *ayma* myself when I got married eight years ago, I continued, I did not quite understand why Om Mahmoud made such a fuss about it, and I wondered if they could provide an explanation. The mixture of shock, pity and disbelief that my harmless question elicited from the three generations of women sitting around me was a turning point in my research. Om Mahmoud's reaction was the most severe:

> What! You did not have an *ayma*? How is this possible? Are you living in another world? ... Do you not know your rights as a woman? The *ayma* is the only way to protect a woman from men and from time, *il ayma tidman haᵓ il sit min il riggalla wiz-zaman*. When you get old, who will feed you? Your husband will find himself a pretty, fair new bride and kick you out of the house, *yizᶜutik*. Is there a house without an *ayma*? You were a fool. They sold you cheap ... ... If a woman does not have an *ayma* she is considered married for free, and people would belittle/humiliate her, *yiᶜayruuha* ... It is not your fault, maybe you were young and naive. (Om Sayed was clearly desperately groping for explanations for my disgraceful behavior, as in fact she knew from a previous discussion that I was married at twenty-eight, quite old by community standards.) But what about your parents, what is their excuse to throw you out like that, *nasik mish haraam ᶜaleehom yirmuuki*? You must go and make an *ayma* immediately. Give your husband some drugs, *birsham* (I presumed she meant to make him drowsy), and let him sign an *ayma* ... You must protect yourself by an *ayma*, an *ayma* secures a woman's rights, *il ayma bitsuun haᵓ il hurma*. Men are not to be trusted. A man is to be trusted as much as a sieve is to be trusted with water, *ya mᵓaamin lil riggal, ya mᵓaamin lil mayya fil ghurbaal.*

As I engaged in discussions in the community about marriage negotiations, probing more specifically into the issue of the *ayma*, this proverb was invoked by women many more times. It vividly illustrates the mistrust and suspicions that characterize gender relations specifically as they relate to marriage, which is the focus of this chapter. My aim is not to provide a comprehensive account of marriage negotiations in the community studied, capturing all the subtleties and complex dynamics that such relations entail. Rather, my aim is to focus on specific practices directly related to the main theoretical concerns of this book.

More general accounts of marriage in low-income communities in Cairo have been provided in several other studies (see for example Hoodfar 1997; Rugh 1984; Singerman 1995). The role of marriage in the Middle East as an arena for negotiating political and economic conflicts and the expression of competition in the wider society has also been well illustrated by several studies (Eickleman and Piscatori 1996; Rugh 1984; Tapper 1991). Much of the ethnographic data presented in this chapter, however, focuses specifically on some important practices through which women attempt to negotiate their impending conjugal contracts[3] in a context of poverty and high rates of male unemployment. I have chosen to focus specifically on two related practices which emerged as most salient in providing women in the study community with bargaining power in their marriages: the marriage inventory, the *ayma*, and the trousseau, the *gihaaz*.

Personal status laws in Egypt grant men a range of rights over women in marriage which expose wives to various sorts of vulnerabilities. These include men's rights to unilateral divorce, the right to marry up to four wives, and the right to forcefully return a wife to a marital home, the "house of obedience" law, *beet il taď a* (see Minces 1982; Zulficar 1993). As this chapter will demonstrate, however, these rights gain specific meanings and are contested differently in different socioeconomic and historical contexts. An elucidation of the practices of the *ayma* and *gihaaz* as objects of negotiation, as well as women's perspectives on them, illustrates how women consciously seek to expand their options and protect themselves, and their children, from the publicly acknowledged perils of men as husbands. They further illustrate how wives seek to increase their security financially in a context where men are either unwilling or unable to provide for them. The *ayma* and *gihaaz* are closely related to women's options in the informal labor market. As will be discussed in the chapter to follow, accumulating a sizeable *gihaaz* is one of the most important reasons why women seek paid employment.

An Overview of Marriage Protocols[4]

Marriage conventions and protocols in the community varied largely along religious lines. Among Muslims, who constituted the overwhelming majority, marriage negotiations typically underwent four stages, once an appropriate spouse was selected. The first stage, the formal declaration of intent, is signaled by both families getting together and reading the opening verse of the Quran, *iraayit il fat-ha.* This is considered an informal engagement, and is usually referred to as *khutu-uba,* engagement. The reading of the *fat-ha,* which usually takes place at the bride's residence, is often preceded by many negotiations regarding the timing of the following three stages: the formal engagement, *shabka,* the official religious ceremony, *katb il kitaab,* and the consummation of the marriage, *il dukhla.*[5] The financial commitments of both families are worked out, and agreed upon, at this stage, although they may remain the subjects of disagreements and renegotiations for many months afterwards.

The formal signature of the marriage contract and the religious ceremony, *katb il kitaab,* sometimes takes place at the same time as the *shabka,* the formal engagement party, and sometimes at the time of the consummation of the wedding, *leilit il dukhla.*[6] In situations where an engagement is expected to be long, there is a preference for signing the marriage contract at the time of the *shabka,* as this enables couples to associate more freely. Long engagements are becoming increasingly common, as families need time to amass the necessary "marriage capital," or want to wait for a girl to complete her education (see also Singerman 1995). The engagement party is usually paid for by the bride's family, and the wedding party by the groom's family, although families sometimes share the expenses of both events.

Discussions between families take on the tone of financial transactions, from the very first stage of marriage negotiations, with the usage of commercial terms like buying a bride, *bayī̄ha*, or selling a bride, *shariiha*, to express degrees of a prospective spouse's commitment to a marriage. The term "selling a bride" indicates that a groom and his family are not really committed to the marriage, whereas the term "buying a bride" suggests seriousness and willingness to invest financially in the marriage. Typically a groom must provide the marital home, and a present of gold, also referred to as a *shabka*, as well as the bedroom furnishings. The average value of an acceptable *shabka* in the community studied ranged between five and fifteen hundred pounds, and typically consisted of one or two 21-carat gold bracelets and a gold wedding band.

A particularly expensive type of *shabka*, and the unattainable dream of all the women I talked to, was known as *shabka shabah*, literally "ghost *shabka*," and consisted of two thick and elaborately decorated golden bracelets costing about LE1,2000 each. The use of the word ghost, "*shabah*" is particularly interesting to note. It refers to the nickname given by Egyptians to the top-of- the-line Mercedes automobile in Egypt, which costs over LE 600,000. A "ghost" Mercedes car, so named because of its speed, is the ultimate status, prestige and wealth symbol of the nouveau riche in Egypt. While acquiring a "ghost" Mercedes may be a sign of social mobility and a status marker for Egypt's upper classes, acquiring a "ghost" *shabka* is a sign of social mobility and a status symbol for the less privileged classes.

In addition to the *shabka*, the groom is typically expected to provide an apartment, or more commonly a room or two, as well as the bedroom furnishings, and the cotton filling for the upholstery of sofas and chairs, if there is a parlor or living room. The actual material for the upholstery is usually the responsibility of the bride. Securing a room or an apartment is not always possible, however, given the high cost of housing in Cairo, and new couples sometimes start the first years of their married lives in the parental household of the groom, or less commonly, in the parental household of the bride. The provision of the furniture for the rooms other than the bedroom and kitchen equipment is open to negotiation, but, as will be discussed later, is increasingly becoming the responsibility of the bride as part of her trousseau, *gihaaz*.

The dower, *mahr*, the payment of the groom's family of an agreed-upon sum of money, is part of marriage negotiations among Muslims in other communities in Egypt (see Rugh 1984; Singerman 1995). The *mahr* is an Islamic convention with a fixed meaning according to *sharīī̄a* laws which stipulate that a groom's father give the bride a cash payment. The *mahr* has accordingly been rigidly conceptualized as a "dower" in anthropological accounts. However, the *mahr* was not prevalent in the community I studied, suggesting that in practice it is a much more fluid and historically specific institution than is commonly portrayed.[7]

Marriage transactions, of which the *mahr* is a part, appear to have been adapted in response to broader socioeconomic changes, as will be discussed later. Only a few women, usually older ones who got married in rural areas, reported receiving a cash *mahr*. Many women explained that the *mahr* was part of the marriage negotiations of financially better-off people, *il naas il mabsuuta*, but it was not part of the practices of the very poor, *il naas il ghalaaba*, like themselves. The more common arrangement in the study community, already referred to, was that the groom (and/or his family), would directly purchase some of the furnishings and durable equipment for the marital home.

Financial arrangements varied, however, depending partly on the characteristics of a bride and groom, and the relationships between the families. In one instance, a very poor man agreed to marry the daughter of a merchant who was known to be slightly mentally retarded, on the condition that he would not pay anything and that the bride's family cover all marriage expenses. In another case, an illiterate man in his forties who had nonetheless amassed reasonable wealth as a construction worker in Saudi Arabia proposed to a nineteen-year-old old who had just obtained a high school diploma. Although both she and her family initially refused, they eventually agreed when the man suggested that he assume all the engagement and marriage costs.

For Copts, who constituted about 7 percent of my research sample, marriage negotiations typically include two stages: the formal engagement, *nus ikliil*, also referred to as *khutuuba*, and the signature of the marriage contract, *ikliil*. Both are religious contracts and ceremonies, and take place in church. For the *nus ikliil*, a formal contract is signed by the bride and groom, two witnesses and the priest. Breaking an engagement is thus more difficult for Copts than it is for Muslims, and requires formal procedures, including the signatures of the same two witnesses who signed the engagement contract as well as that of the priest on a new document. The formal engagement contract is the basis on which the church issues the permission for marriage.

The marriage contract, *ikliil*, is also signed by witnesses and a priest and normally kept in the church. Unlike Muslims, divorce is extremely difficult for Copts, and requires the written approval of the church. The only two acceptable grounds for a divorce are adultery, and conversion to another sect or religion. Because of the difficulty of divorce among Copts, several women told me that the church is now insisting that couples undergo blood tests to ensure freedom from major health problems before granting permission for a marriage.

There were many similarities in the financial arrangements of marriage transactions among Muslims and Copts. As with Muslims, a *shabka* is an essential component of the Coptic engagement. The value of the *shabka*, however, is written into the engagement contract, and gets automatically transferred to the marriage contract, unless the engagement is broken. Because a certain percentage of the value of the *shabka* goes to the church when it issues authorization for the marriage, most people do not declare its real value. As with Muslims, a Coptic husband is generally expected to provide the apartment, the difference being that women are expected to provide bedroom furnishings. Provision of other furniture and kitchen equipment is open to more flexible negotiation. Once formally engaged, *shabka* or *nus ikliil*, both Muslims and Copts are expected to present their fiancée and her family with occasional gifts of fruit, meat, and clothes.

The above accounts of marriage transactions, however, refer only to first time marriages. The remarriage of divorcees challenges some of the ideal marriage conventions described above. Marriage negotiations for a divorced woman deviate significantly from those of first-time "virgin" marriages. There were four divorcees in my sample of fifty-nine once married women. Two had remarried, and two were single. Of the single divorcees, one had gone back to live in her parent's home, which was in the same community. This was the most accepted practice particularly if a woman has younger children. The other divorcee lived on her own with her teenage son and daughter after physically dividing a two room flat with her ex-husband, who remarried. She was an older woman in her fifties and her parents were still living in upper Egypt. All four male divorcees had remarried.

When a divorced woman remarries she is generally expected to do so without making any financial demands on the groom; normally a groom is neither expected to provide a *shabka*, an apartment nor furniture. This was the case with the two divorcees in my sample who remarried. Community attitudes regarding divorcees and the expressed fear of divorce discussed in the previous chapter thus partly reflect material concerns. They are fears based on both loss of "honor" or bringing "shame" to a family as well as on economic calculations. Parents realize that in case of remarriage, a divorcee has very little power in future financial negotiations. No longer a virgin,[8] a woman loses an essential symbolic resource, virginity, which reduces her claims on her prospective husband. One of my interviewees explained why she does not want her daughter to marry a particular man who was known to be on drugs, "I cannot trust him, I am afraid he will take her a virgin and throw her out a non-virgin, *yitgawwizha bint, wa yirmiiha mara.*"

Moreover, divorced women and their children are expected to return and live in their natal home. This constitutes a financial burden on a woman's natal family leading to possible downward social mobility. Although husbands may continue to provide some financial support, all my accounts and observations suggest that a divorced women must supplement such support, through either drawing on her own natal family's resources, or working to generate an income herself.

The attitude of married and single women towards divorcees was often that of suspicion and caution, as Om Nasra's comments quoted earlier illustrate.[9] These attitudes, however, are I think less related to concerns about their reputations, and more to the fact that divorcees have little financial claims over prospective husbands. Divorced women are thus attractive candidates to take on as co-wives, particularly given the high cost of marriages.[10] One man, an impoverished thirty-year-old construction worker, told me that he would actually prefer to marry a divorced woman, particularly if she has everything on her *ayma* from a previous marriage, as there is no way he could amass the necessary capital for marrying a virgin.

Frictions in Marriage Negotiations: The "Materiality of Reputation"

Singerman (1995) highlights the importance of marriage in popular neighborhoods of Cairo, revealing the extent of financial and emotional capital that is committed to this process. She argues that the family in popular quarters of Cairo is a central institution that not only guarantees social security and access to resources, but that it fills a political vacuum as well. In the context of an authoritarian state which provides little opportunity for political participation in formal politics, the family provides an important avenue of participation in the public sphere. Her study provides a detailed description of the role that familial and informal networks play in advancing people's individual and collective interests, ranging from securing a good education, and finding a job, to gaining access to subsidized goods, or migrating.

Marriage was similarly a central concern in my study community, and negotiations, particularly over finances, extended over many months and were often fraught with tensions. Unresolved tensions sometimes caused conflicts and struggles between families that were remembered for years afterwards. Marriage negotiations are not individual matters, since what is at stake is the status, prestige and reputations of the two families concerned. When conflicts take place, disagreements quickly become public, with community members either taking sides or attempting to arbitrate. Such public disagreements are carefully orchestrated, however, as the reputation of both families are on the line. The following example of the frictions during a marriage negotiation illustrates the types of issues that arise during such conflicts. It also illustrates a more general theoretical point regarding reputation as a material resource among low-income groups, or what may be termed the "materiality of reputation."

Hoda, twenty-five years old, has been engaged to her neighbor for the past five years. Because they have not yet secured an apartment or any furniture, setting a date for the *katb il kitaab* has been delayed, much to the disappointment of Hoda and her parents. Hoda's father is a laborer in a local bakery and her mother works as a pieceworker sewing leather shoes for a nearby workshop. Hoda's parents were getting particularly anxious about the delay in the marriage because her fiancé visits regularly and they feared that people would start gossiping. Even though Hoda, pressured by her fiancé, had quit her job as a wage laborer in a jewelry workshop three years ago, she still had a problematic work history. She had had to go out of the community to work on a daily basis from the time she was thirteen years old and thus her reputation was particularly fragile.

On one of my many visits to Hoda's family, I found the entire extended family in terrible distress due to a fight that broke out in the street the previous night between Hoda's mother and her prospective mother-in-law. The fight was apparently triggered by a discussion between the two women, during which Hoda's mother-in-law announced, in a purposefully loud voice overheard by neighbors, that her son would be unable to provide Hoda with a separate apartment. If she wanted to go ahead with the marriage, Hoda would thus have to live in one of the rooms in their apartment. Moreover, she continued, in the same loud voice, they also could not afford to get the fancy, *makhsuus*, bedroom suite (which consists of three pieces and costs almost four thousand Egyptian pounds) and so Hoda would have to settle for the ordinary one (which costs only between fifteen and two thousand Egyptian pounds).

Hoda's mother could not contain her anger as this offer, announced so publicly, was "below their standard, value or status," *mish imitna*; it was insulting and offensive. Soon the two women were engaged in a screaming match in the street. Hoda's mother-in-law started smearing Hoda's reputation, insinuating that Hoda was not a virgin; she was "soiled merchandise," and her mother should have her checked out by a physician. Other members of both families, as well as neighbors, were soon dragged into the fight. Hoda's two unmarried sisters insisted that she break off the engagement immediately, as not doing so would mean that she accepted their accusations of not being a virgin, thus bringing shame to the entire family. Although enraged herself, Om Hoda, however, was not willing to break the engagement so easily:

> They are saying these things, so that we get angry and break off the engagement first, *nikrah*, and thus we have to return Hoda's *shabka*. I refuse to give them back the *shabka*. If they want to break the engagement, then they do it, because then they will have no claim over the *shabka*. I had an engagement party that cost eight hundred pounds and I paid for it from my own work. I insisted on having a big engagement party so that people know that my daughter is valuable, *imit-ha ⁿalya*. I made a detailed list of all the expenses incurred in the party, however in case a day like this might come. If they want the *shabka*, then they have to pay me back every piaster I paid on the engagement celebration.

Accusations and arbitration continued over two months, during which Hoda's marriage negotiations were the subject of much speculation and gossip. Eventually Om Hoda's family sent word that they no longer wanted the engagement, but that they were nonetheless keeping the *shabka*. This was not contested by the prospective groom's family, a critical fact that Om Hoda made sure that everyone knew, as it constituted a type of public apology. By keeping the *shabka*, even though they were the ones who broke the engagement, and by making this public, Om Hoda explained to me, she had ensured that her daughter's reputation, and thus her marriageability, had not been compromised by this nasty incident. Ten months later, the two families were still not on speaking terms. Hoda had sold the *shabka* and bought two rings and a golden pendant—which she conspicuously displayed to her neighbors—and had gone back to her job in the jewelry workshop.

The centrality, and more specifically, the materiality of reputation in the lives of the poor is well illustrated by this incident. "Poor people have nothing but their reputation", their *sumⁿa*, was a phrase I heard often during my fieldwork. Reputation in this community, however, is much more than a moral issue, as it may be in more middle—or upper-class communities. Protecting a family's reputation—in Hoda's case, publicly affirming her virginity and thus the honor of the family—is not only an individual issue or one of morality, but an issue of economic survival. Reputation is an essential symbolic resource that determines one's entire livelihood: getting a job, getting married, and being part of the community's networks that are critical to ensuring a decent livelihood.

A wide range of economic exchanges, such as getting a loan, buying on credit, finding a job, making a "good" marriage, accessing scarce food commodities from the black market, obtaining a ration or identity card, or registering a child in school, depends on reputation. For poor households, survival is based not just on the income of different members of the household, but on a much wider network of durable relationships of sharing, exchange and mutual help. "Survival in our world," explained one of my interviewees, "is based on reciprocal relations of lending and borrowing, *id-dunya salaf wi deen.*" The notion of "mutual indebtedness" as a concept underlying social relations in this community comes through clearly in this idiom. (See White 1994, for a discussion of a similar concept in urban working-class communities in Turkey.) Reputation is of particular relevance to women who actively seek to engage in informal networks of mutual assistance so as to secure their livelihoods and increase their ability to negotiate within the marital union, as will be discussed in chapter nine.

The strength of a household does not only depend on the economic capital its members possess, but on its "symbolic" capital as well (Bourdieu 1990). In a context of material deprivation, and in a situation where patronage ties mediate access to resources, and where dealings with the state bureaucracy require not only skill and money, but more importantly mediation through personal relations, *wasta*, the only possible form of accumulation becomes that of accumulating "symbolic capital."[11] Bordieu defines "symbolic capital" as material capital "misrecognized," i.e. assets like public acknowledgement, recognition, honor, and so forth. He argues that in many societies, "the interests at stake in the conducts of honor is one for which economism has no name and which has to be called symbolic, although it is such as to inspire actions that are very directly material. Conducts of honor, no longer seem as the product of obedience to rules of submission to values (which they also are since they are experienced as such), but as the product of a more or less conscious pursuit of the accumulation of symbolic capital" (Bourdieu 1990: 121). An appreciation of the materiality of reputation allows one to better understand the negotiations surrounding marriages in the study community.

The Marriage Inventory: "The *Ayma* Handcuffs a Man"

Within the context of marriage transactions and protocols described above, the *ayma*, marriage inventory, emerged as a critical component. As the anecdote at the beginning of this chapter reveals, the *ayma* is a practice that I stumbled upon in my discussions and I was unprepared to deal with how strongly women felt about its value. Indeed, the *ayma* has remained largely unexplored in anthropological accounts of the Egyptian family, including recent studies addressing marriage arrangements in Cairo in great detail (such as the Singerman study (1955) referred to earlier).

The *ayma*, which literally means inventory or list in Arabic, is used specifically to refer to a written document on which all items of furniture and equipment belonging to the new home are recorded and itemized, stipulating that these are the sole property of the bride. These items include the goods contributed by the bride, those contributed by the groom, and the items they receive jointly as gifts. The *ayma* is thus an inventory of marital property, which sometimes also includes the *shabka*.

Mutually agreed upon in advance, often after tough negotiations, the *ayma* is signed by the groom, before or on the day of the *katb il kitaab*, as well as by two witnesses who act as guarantors, in case he defaults on any commitments. The negotiations center on deciding on the monetary value of the *ayma*, with the bride's family usually attempting to inflate its value. By signing the *ayma*, a husband officially declares that he has received all these items for safekeeping. However, they remain the property of his wife, which she can claim back any time she wants during the marriage or in the event of a conflict, of widowhood or divorce. This stipulation is enforceable both legally and through informal community arbitration. Once signed, the *ayma* is carefully guarded by women, and is in safe-keeping with the bride's family, usually the mother, to ensure that the husband does not have access to it.

There is some variation in how an *ayma* is formalized and the types of items that are included in it. Variations appeared to be based on both the socio-economic standing and regional origin of the families involved. Most of the women in the community, tended to include equipment and furniture as well as the value of the gold of the *shabka*. Some women, particularly those who were relatively less well to do, also included breakable and exhaustible items like glasses, china sets, and bed linen, whereas others confined their *ayma* to durable items and furniture. Several women in the sample, who identified themselves as *masriyyiin*, not *fallahiin* or *Saᶜayda* of recent rural origin, emphasized that they would never include the value of the *shabka* into the *ayma* and that it was only the *fallahiin* who did that.

In most *ayma*(s), each item is detailed separately and is assigned a monetary value, which is often inflated. The value of all the items are then added up to make up the total value of the *ayma*. A few families preferred not to assign a monetary value to each item, but simply described the item in detail, noting such things as the type of wood used and the brand of the implement, explaining that this protected them against inflation. Once the *ayma* is acted upon in case of a marital dispute, a monetary value can be assigned to the items, based on current market prices.

The value of *ayma*(s) in the community varied tremendously, from a modest fifty Egyptian pounds to eight thousand Egyptian pounds. Some of this variation is, of course, a reflection of the date of the marriage, since I interviewed women who were married within a span of forty years. However, it is also important to note that the value of the *ayma* is not necessarily a good indicator of socioeconomic status, as in many cases some of the items included have not actually been provided, or their value has intentionally been inflated. For marriages which took place within the past two years, a typical *ayma,* which included a gold *shabka* of forty grams of gold, had a value of about 4000 pounds.

The *ayma* is usually formally negotiated by men, generally fathers, uncles or older brothers of the bride, but informally it is the women, generally mothers, aunts or older sisters of the bride, who decide on the items to be included and on their value. As Om Nasra put it:

When it comes to negotiations over an *ayma,* it is the women who needle and prompt, and the men who do the formal talking, *ilsitat bit wiz wil riggaala bititkallim.*

The *ayma* is not a stipulation of Islamic law, and although it has legal standing as will be seen later, it has no explicit basis in state legislation, but is based on customary law, ᶜ*urf.* The history of the *ayma,* in terms of when and how it was actually introduced, is difficult to trace. Although women were not aware of the origin of the *ayma,* many but not all of the older women I interviewed (in their sixties) recalled having an *ayma* in their marriages, but were not sure whether their own mothers also had one.

Although the importance of the *ayma* was uncontested among the women I interviewed, it appears to have taken on a new significance in more recent marriages in the community. As a central component of marriage negotiations, the *ayma* operates within the framework of specific rights and obligations enshrined by prevalent gender ideologies. Moore (1994) terms these local customary and standard understandings of the rights and needs of different types of people, local theories of entitlement. She argues that they are fluid, always subject to contestation, as well as "resources which are drawn up on in the process of negotiation" (Moore 1994: 104). Discussions with several generations of women in the study community suggest that "local theories of entitlement" may be changing, giving greater centrality to the *ayma,* partly in response to broader societal changes. Some of these changes, such as the dramatic increase in the cost of living which has been unmatched by increases in male wages and employment opportunities, are altering women's and men's relationship to, and expectations of, marriage.

The strong words that women used to convey why and how the *ayma* works to control and check male power, reveal that the *ayma* articulates a local discourse about female vulnerability in marriage. Amal, who is newly married, talks with great pride about her *ayma.*

111

My *ayma* was large, it was for seven thousand pounds. I have hand cuffed/tied up by husband with it, *katiftu biiha*. We put things in it that were not even there, like the television and a video. And he signed for them. This way he is restricted/controlled/ condemned, *mahkuum*, he cannot play with his tail, *yilab bideelu*, (This is an Arabic idiom generally implying illicit extramarital affairs), or get married and get cowife to live with me.

Karima, thirty-two years old and married and with three preschool-age children explains why her *ayma* is important:

> It is important so that he does not throw me out to my father's house after he takes what he wants from me, *ghiyyitu* (meaning sexual pleasure). I have a hold on him with an *ayma*, but without an *ayma* there is no rope with which I can tie him, *mafiih habl rabtaah biih*. Any time he can tell me to go out with my *galabiyya* (traditional dress for women in low-income areas). An *ayma* protects a woman's rights, *bitihfaz ħaɔ il sit*. Otherwise how can a woman ensure her rights, *tidman ħaɔaha izzaay?* Men, as a kind, cannot be trusted, *sanf el riggaala maluush aman.*

Shocked that I would even ask whether she had an *ayma*, Laila, whose parents migrated to Cairo from lower Egypt when she was a few months old, confirmed that she wrote an *ayma*, emphasized its role in protecting women's rights in marriage, and detailed some of its items:

> How can a girl marry without an *ayma*, if she does, she can be kicked out of the house any second. Her husband would have no incentive to try and get her back from her parent's house when there is a conflict and she is upset. The *ayma* is even more important than the deferred dower, *Muakhkhar*,[12] for safeguarding/ensuring a woman's rights, *damaan* ħaɔ *il sit*, to restrict/control a man, ɔ*alashan il ragil yibɔa mahkuum*. On my *ayma*, which was for thirty-five hundred pounds, I wrote all the things that both he and I got, from the bedroom, to the aluminum sets to the spice rack.

Laila then told me the story of her neighbor, Om Muhammed, whose husband divorced her without informing her, *ghiyaabi*, when she was in the village visiting her family. When she came back, she found that he had sold most of the furniture, had married someone else, and was now living with her in another community. She issued a complaint at the police station and her husband was eventually arrested. He returned some of the furniture, but was not able to provide the rest or to pay the remaining value of the LE 4000 *ayma*. He received a three-month prison term. While this only partly helped Om Mohamed, Laila continued emphatically, it nonetheless sent a strong message to other men in the community about how they should treat their wives.

The *ayma* appears to be used in various ways and gains different meanings in different marriage negotiations. It was sometimes used to screen potential grooms, or to improve a family's social status by showing off a daughter's value. The greater the value of the *ayma*, which is always public knowledge, the greater the status that the bride and her family acquire. Negotiations and transactions regarding the *ayma* thus seem to partly serve as a means for creating or reinforcing social ranking and distinctions amongst families. The possible role of the *ayma* as a form of insurance against women's vulnerability in marriage, however, is what is most relevant to my interests here. The next section will elaborate upon this argument.

The Ayma *in Practice: A Damage-Control Mechanism?*

The *ayma* is a local practice, which women appear to be using to safeguard their entitlement and rights within marriage, as they understand them, in a specific context of urban poverty where women's breadwinner status is becoming a fact of life. Realizing that they are disadvantaged in the marital union, women are taking explicit measures to "up the stakes" of being abandoned or mistreated. Some of the prerogatives of men that an *ayma* aims at restricting are the threat of divorce, the threat of being thrown out of the house, and the threat of being forced to accept a co-wife. The *ayma* can also be used to force a husband to take marital conflicts more seriously and attempt to resolve them, as well as to force a husband to divorce a woman, if she requests for it.

Reducing the husband's options in terms of taking on a second cohabitating wife was mentioned several times as one of the situations where an *ayma* can be invoked. Ostensibly, the main source of resentment was singled out as not that a husband could take another wife, but that the co-wife could be made to share the house. Om Samir explains:

> I do not care if he married someone else as long as she does not bring her here to use my *gihaaz*, the things on my *ayma*, and as long as my husband is making my life comfortable (meaning largely financially). With an *ayma*, it is more difficult for a man to remarry, because he can find himself penniless, ᶜ*ala ill balata*, if he has to get the furniture and equipment for another house.

On probing further, however, it became clear that in fact the *ayma* is used as a means to support women's desire to deter a husband from taking a second wife, cohabitating or otherwise. Women realize that finding another apartment or room, and furnishing it, is so expensive that a man can rarely marry a second wife unless his first wife accepts cohabitation. Women clearly believe the *ayma* serves as an important deterrent against polygyny. Although polygyny is legally allowed, in practice its rate is lower than 2 percent in Egypt. In my sample, there was only one polygynous marriage. Could these strategies be working after all?

The significance of the *ayma*, however, goes beyond ensuring a fair deal if divorce occurs, providing economic security for the future, or warding off the threat of a divorce or a co-wife. Perhaps just as importantly, it is used as a bargaining device, throughout the marriage. It enables women to monitor their husband's behavior and help ensure that they do not default on their main responsibilities as economic providers. A grandmother in her seventies, explains:

> The *ayma* is important not just to ensure a woman's rights if there is a divorce or a dispute, but it is also important to correct a man if he becomes deviant, *it̼awag* literally bent, or *mish maashy ̼alatuul*, (not walking straight).

On probing what *it̼awag* meant, it appeared to center on the man's responsibility to provide for his household. Mayada's husband's behavior was pointed out as an example of inappropriate behavior that reference to the *ayma* was able to address. Even though Mayada is newly married and pregnant with her first child, her husband, Ragab, has stopped providing for her and spends a lot of his time gambling and drinking. Mayada and her husband had a fight last month, during which he told her that if she did not like his behavior she could leave.

In response, Mayada's entire extended family intervened, insisting that she should divorce, because her husband's behavior was unacceptable, and demanding that he pay them the value of the *ayma*, estimated at LE 10,000, almost double the real value of the furniture and equipment listed. After a few days of negotiations and discussions, Mayada's husband came to his senses, *̼il*. He now gives Mayada money regularly and no longer spends all his wages on drinking. The family knew that Ragab had a reputation as a gambler, which is one of the reasons they had insisted on a large *ayma*. It is noteworthy, however, that part of the reason why the *ayma* was effective in this case is because Mayada and her husband were living with her extended family of fourteen people, and that the entire family was united in its decision.

Reda, a pieceworker originally from Tanta in lower Egypt, expressed deep sorrow for me because I did not have an *ayma*, since this implied that I had no security in my marriage. I was living *barakawi* (from *baraka*, meaning as a fatalist relying on good luck, with no strategies or plans for the future). This is the worst situation for a woman to be in, she emphasized. Reda views the *ayma* as a way to wear a man out, make his throat dry, *tinashif ri̼ il raagil*, so that divorce is not that easy for him. She was married two years ago and her *ayma* was valued at LE 6000. Although she has had no conflicts with her husband so far, so that the question of the *ayma* has never arisen between them, she explained that it was important to her sister Somaya who got married six years ago, whose husband divorced her last year because she was unable to conceive. She got back all the furniture and equipment, some of which he had provided.

Stressing how the *ayma* may protect some women, Mohsen, one of the few men I conducted in-depth interviews with and a relative of Mayada's, confirmed its importance as both a deterrent against a husband's misbehavior, as well as a negotiating tool in disagreements between spouses. He recounted the story of a woman who lives nearby and who wanted a divorce on the grounds that her husband was asking her to perform "improper" sexual acts, and was also forcing her to have anal sex. Her husband denied it, but she was adamant that a doctor examine her to confirm her complaints. After much arbitration by the elders of both families, an informal process of negotiations termed *taraadi*, her husband agreed to divorce her. They divided the items on the *ayma* between them, and she kept the *shabka*.

Amal, twenty-seven years old, and divorced last year, also recounts how the *ayma* enabled her to pressure her husband into divorcing her. She had signed her marriage contract two years ago, but the actual consummation of the marriage was scheduled for a year later. Her husband, however, had accepted a large *ayma*, detailed in Table 2, when they signed the marriage contract, although they had not yet provided most of the items listed. Amal explained that her mother insisted on an inflated *ayma* so as to secure Amal's future because her husband, who was from a different neighborhood, did not have a secure job and was of a lower socioeconomic background.

Six months after signing the marriage contract, Amal's husband began going out with another woman in public, no longer gave Amal any presents, and began maltreating and hitting her. The family insisted that he divorce Amal, but he refused unless he was paid one thousand Egyptian pounds in return. It was at this point that Amal and her mother went to a lawyer and issued a complaint in court, presented a copy of Amal's original *ayma*, and accused her husband of selling the items on it, a criminal offence known in the legal system as squandering movables, *tabdiid manqulaat*. Om Amal recalls:

> When he was unable to produce the items on the *ayma*, the judge sentenced him to six months imprisonment. He then entered into negotiations with us and we struck a deal, whereby we agreed to give up our rights, *nitnaazil*, if he divorced Amal immediately. This process took about six months and we paid two hundred pounds for the lawyer. If it were not for the *ayma*, we would have never been able to make him divorce Amal, and she would have remained at his mercy and miserable, *misaᵓiiha il dabaab*.

As I talked to more women and witnessed discussions about marriage arrangements, I began to realize that the *ayma* offered more than a local idiom for expressing women's views about power relations within marriage. It is also an important tool for women to secure their marriage, ward off the looming threat of divorce, and provide them with financial stability.

Nonetheless, a woman has to choose her battles carefully so as to decide strategically at which point the *ayma* may be invoked or used. Once the *ayma* is presented in court, the original document must be submitted (as will be discussed later). Once a settlement takes place, a woman loses recourse to her *ayma* for use in future marital negotiations, should she decide to continue with the marriage. Some women thus prefer to settle out of court. As an insurance policy for securing women's rights in the conjugal union—clearly perceived as an essential part of life, but nonetheless as a high-risk proposition—the *ayma* thus has some inherent limitations.

There are also other possible limitations to the *ayma* as a deterrent or damage-control mechanism. These are partly related to the possible breakdown and fragmentation of the normative pressures and moral community needed for the enforcement of the *ayma*. Although set in an urban context, most of my sample consisted of first-generation migrants to the city, who still maintained close knit relationships with relatives and had brought with them to Cairo many of their customary forms of conflict resolution. With the dispersion of the community over the years, however, some of these relationships and structures may become more fragmented and forms of customary pressure by family elders may break down. The possible challenges by emerging conservative forces to the legal standing of the *ayma*, as will be seen later in the chapter, may pose a further limitation to its effectiveness.

The *ayma* was only practiced among my Muslim respondents. Copts did not have an *ayma*, partly perhaps because divorce is generally not allowed by the Coptic church and marriage is a sacrament, rather than a contractual arrangement as is the case in Islam. Another reason may be that the underlying property regime in Coptic marriages is that of the joint property of spouses, whereas in Muslim marriages, the separation of property and goods, known as *zimma maaliyya munfasila*, is the underlying principle. This difference adds another layer of complexity to understanding women's options. It reveals how, even within similar socioeconomic locations, there is significant variation in men's and women's negotiating options due to variations in the marriage practices of different religious communities. Since the *ayma*'s value, however, goes far beyond deterring easy divorce and is used more generally to contest unacceptable actions by husbands throughout a marriage, more research is needed to investigate more carefully the corresponding marital strategies of Coptic women. The stipulations of the *ayma* are enforceable through both informal and formal mechanisms. In order to better understand how the *ayma* is enforced legally, I conducted interviews with two lawyers from the community, who had personally been involved in several cases related to the *ayma*.

Enforcing the Stipulations of the Ayma: *A Legal Debate*

Interestingly, my interviews indicated that legally the *ayma* falls under commercial transactions and contracts and thus is part of criminal law, rather than the personal status law which regulates marriage and divorce. Mr. Mahmoud, one of the lawyers explains:

> *Ayma* cases fall under the same category as defaulting on a commercial transaction such as writing invalid checks. Thus it is treated as both a criminal offense, which can

116

result in imprisonment, as well as a civil offense which results in a fine. This is unlike the deferred dower, *mu'akhkhar*, which is only a civil offence and thus does not entail imprisonment. Women can raise a complaint through two mechanisms: either issuing a written complaint at the police station, or a direct appeal in court. It is considered a misdemeanor, *gunha*, or squandering, *tabdiid amaana*. As a legal document, the *ayma* falls under safekeeping contracts, *'u'uud il amaana*, stipulated under clauses 340 and 341 in the criminal laws, and is thus considered a direct misdemeanor, *gunha mubashra*.

The second lawyer confirmed the legality of the *ayma*, as a commercial transaction, and, interestingly, expressed his sympathy for men, arguing that the *ayma* was a sword, *seif*, which married women dangle over their husbands' necks:

> I encounter many court cases related to *ayma* complaints. If problems occur in a marriage, it is common for a wife to say that her husband has squandered, *baddid*, the furniture, and a lot of times, what is written on the *ayma* is not actually there. Usually the courts respond by issuing a sentence for imprisonment (from six months to three years) if the husband does not produce the furniture or its value. The legal procedures are usually quick, and do not take more than two to three months. I usually sympathize with the men, however. If I was asked, I would say, ban the *ayma*, it is not a good custom, *'urf*. I usually sympathize with the men, because I know that many of the complaints raised by women are not real, they are fictitious, driven by ulterior motives and vengeance, *kaydiyya*.

This view was echoed in more subtle terms and couched in academic language, in the November 1996 issue of a widely read middle-class magazine published in Arabic, *Nus il Dunya*. In an article titled: "The *Ayma* Is a Useless Piece of Paper and the Law Is Clear" the writer, a male lawyer, probes into the legality of the *ayma* from an Islamic perspective, and from a legal point of view, using sophisticated legal language and resorting to examples from Islamic history and the Quran. After his extensive review, the writer concludes that the *ayma* has no basis in either Islamic *fiqh, law,* or in civil or criminal codes, and calls upon the courts to rethink its legality as it creates a lot of problems in marriages and is a burden on the court system. Although he does not articulate it outright, the writer was clearly arguing for a rejection of the *ayma*'s legal enforceability. His conclusions and recommendations are quite dangerous from the point of view of the women I talked to, for whom the *ayma* was indispensable both as an insurance policy and as a bargaining device in marital negotiations.

It is interesting to note, however, that this article did not elicit any reaction from women's rights activists in Egypt. This lack of response contrasts sharply with that concerning another recent newspaper article questioning the right of female professors to supervise academic dissertations by male students, on the presumed grounds that in Islam women have no right of supervision or guardianship, *wilayya*, over men. This latter article was the subject of several published responses by feminists, and the source of public debates amongst women's groups, some of whose members are academics or are in supervisory positions themselves, so that they were also directly threatened by the article. The article on the *ayma*, however, which is potentially more threatening to lower-class women, went unnoticed, possibly because this practice is more limited among the middle-and upper-classes. Since it is not part of their daily reality, the issues surrounding it were invisible to them.[13]

In fact, had I read the article on the *ayma* two years ago, before my fieldwork, I suspect it would not have attracted my attention either. This type of myopia is self-defeating and limiting. The possible erosion of the social and legal basis of the *ayma* actually offers a concrete issue, affecting the perceived interests of a broad segment of Egyptian women, around which participatory politics and mobilization of women can take place.

In summary, although ignored by both researchers and activists, the *ayma* is a central component of marriage negotiations, possibly found in many low-income communities, which protects women's self-defined entitlements in the marital union. Women's presentation of the rationale for the *ayma* using the same, seemingly unambiguous term for rights, *ḥaˀ*, is the same term used by women activists in Egypt and internationally, is significant. It illustrates how conceptions of rights and interests are socially and historically situated and are linked to both discursive elements as well as to constructions of meanings and identities (Fraser 1989; Molyneux 1998; Moore 1994). The use of the same terminology for rights and interests among different groups of women does not imply the same content and understandings of such interests. To elaborate this point further, it is necessary to make a small digression to illustrate the contrasting agendas and tactics of different constituencies of women in Egypt.

A Tale of Two Contracts: Toward a Situated Understanding of Women's Interests

"The *ayma* is like a contract, it regulates/has a hold on a groom," *il ayma zay il ˁaˀd, bitimsik il ˁariis*, was a phrase I heard repeatedly. The *ayma* was clearly seen and presented by women as a "contract," whose aim is to safeguard and ensure a "woman's rights", *ḥaˀ il mara* (including the right to request a divorce, ward off the threat of an unwanted divorce or ensure that a man does not default on his responsibilities). It is thus interesting to juxtapose it against the "new marriage contract" campaign, initiated by a prominent feminist lawyer in the early 1990s which gained impetus during the International Conference on Population and Development (ICPD) in 1994. An example of concerted action by several women's groups in Egypt, the campaign aimed at increasing women's leverage within their marriages by promoting the concept of marriage as a contractual arrangement, and emphasizing that as a contract between two parties, its terms, conditions, rights and obligations should thus be specified and agreed upon in advance.

118

The draft of an "ideal" marriage contract was drawn up and was discussed extensively in public forums, with a view to making it acceptable to the ministry of Justice as the basis of future marriage legislation for Muslims. The terms of the "new contract" reflected the legitimate priorities and anxieties of middle-and upper-class Muslim women in Egypt. It included new issues such as the right for married women to travel out of the country without the husband's approval (which currently is not allowed by law), the right to woman-initiated divorce, the right to work and the right to continue higher education after marriage. The contract stipulations may also be used to limit a husband's rights, as they exist in *shariᶜa* laws. For example one may stipulate that the marriage will be monogamous as one of the conditions.

The new contract was eventually rejected by the government, critiqued by the religious establishment, and failed to receive much support from the public, both men and women. The reasons varied, from charges that it "legitimizes the forbidden and forbids the legitimate," and is contrary to *shariᶜa*, to arguments that some of its stipulations, such as women's rights to work or travel abroad are harmful for the family, while others, such as the right to education, were not necessary since they are not questioned (Karam 1996). Other reasons, voiced in public seminars I attended, were that such a contract has overly materialistic undertones, threatening the harmony and symbolic meaning of marriage.

What is critical for my purposes here is that despite some obvious links between the marriage contract and the *ayma*, there was no reference to, or discussion of, the *ayma* at all during the campaign. Attempts to justify the "new marriage contract" to the public were largely based on excellent historical research. The research demonstrated that the idea of a contract with stipulations of rights and duties of husband and wife was not an alien concept and that it had historical precedent in the practices of Islamic dynasties in Turkey and Egypt. There was no attempt, however, to link it with current practices and marriage arrangements among the majority of women in Egypt, which have a clearly contractual basis as was described earlier in this chapter. In retrospect, I can now recognize that this made our campaign much weaker and prevented us from recognizing both similarities and differences across class boundaries, which could have strengthened the campaign by mobilizing a broader constituency of women.

A survey was conducted among low-income women to elicit their responses to the suggested contract, hoping to increase the campaign's base of support. However, none of the survey questions addressed lower-income women's actual concerns nor what their marriage negotiations actually entailed, so as to build on them and take them into account. The campaign had laudable aims and was a worthwhile effort. Nonetheless, its approach was a top-down and myopic one that did not allow for an understanding or appreciation of the diversity of women's perceptions of their interests and rights within marriage, their own idioms of articulating these interests, or their strategies for promoting their perceived interests.

This suggests, among other things, that the national identity of a researcher (or activist) is not automatically linked to the production of more "authentic" or "indigenous" knowledge. As Morsy et al. (1991) argue, emphasizing the impact of colonial domination and intellectual dependency, the production of knowledge

> is the output of people whose thought patterns reflect the "truths" of their social milieu. To the extent that indigenous anthropologists (and I would add women's rights activists) social milieus are not simply or purely "indigenous," neither are their thought patterns nor the "truths" of their scientific productions. (1991: 92)

As mentioned earlier, the language used in marriage negotiations in the study community was openly contractual and based on explicit material calculations and terms such as selling and buying. This language is considered quite "improper" among more upper-class Egyptians. In fact, in one of the many public discussions of the new marriage contract at a luxury hotel in the center of Cairo (at which I was present), one of the major criticisms voiced was that the contract was based on "Western," "materialistic" notions, and that it took out all the "love" and "emotion" out of marriage, relegating it instead to the domain of cold calculation and market transactions. This is not at all what marriage is about in traditional Egyptian culture, argued the speaker, an upper-class man in his mid fifties.[14]

An effective response, but one which was not voiced, would have been to point out the class bias inherent in this particular view of Egyptian marriage, by highlighting the largely material considerations and dispositions which characterize the marriage negotiations of a large proportion of families in Egypt. It would have been worth noting that the *ayma* is such an overtly financial arrangement that its stipulations fall under commercial laws. Clearly marriage acquires different meanings amongst different classes.

Azza Karam (1996) in her recent study of middle- and upper-class women activists in Egypt notes how the new marriage campaign was discredited. She argues that this was partly due to the lack of dialogue and alliance building between different groups of "feminists" (which she categorizes as "secularist," "Islamists," and "Muslim feminists") to safeguard women's rights. While I agree with Karam's call for horizontal coalition building, my data suggests that it may not be enough. Given the class and educational disparities in Egyptian society, which generate different, but possibly overlapping, perceptions of gender needs, rights and interests, it would seem crucial to strengthen campaigns not only through cultivating horizontal links, but also through forging more vertical coalitions, alliances and linkages, across class and educational lines.[15]

Such efforts would significantly enrich the current debates about priorities for change. It may also increase the chances for the success of some campaigns, by rallying more public support. Moreover, it could result in the politicization and mobilization of a broader and more diverse constituency of women and men, and carries the promise of encouraging the emergence of local leadership in different low-income communities, who could begin to articulate their own concerns more vocally and publicly. It seems to me that seeking actively to establish such shared platforms may be the only way to move from the largely individual "gender activisms"[16] of today to a social movement that is strong enough to challenge the many forces contributing to both gender and social inequality more generally in Egyptian society.

Bourdieu's stinging analysis of the possibilities of social change and his cynical view of the potential of organized resistance, while uncomfortable for many feminists, myself included, is nonetheless relevant in this context. Bourdieu "stresses the struggle among the privileged themselves and the relative inability of the oppressed even to enter into the 'dialogue' among more privileged groups" (Risseeuw 1991:177). This was clearly the case with the marriage contract that we were promoting presumably on behalf of all Egyptian women.

What this suggests, is that as middle and upper-class feminists in Egypt with privileges of class and education, we need to seriously consider the possibility that we may ourselves be perpetuating power inequalities. The unequal power relationship that we, as activists trying to challenge gender inequalities, have with other women on whose behalf we often speak, can perhaps be captured by Lukes' two-dimensional view of power discussed in chapter one. This is a form of power that operates and is exercised by "controlling the agenda, mobilizing the bias of the system, determining which issues are key issues, indeed which issues come up for decision and excluding those which threaten the interests of the powerful" (Lukes 1986: 9).

It seems to me that without necessarily intending it, we may be implicated in reproducing inequalities between women by privileging our own voices and discourses. By so doing, we may be not just marginalizing the priorities and discourses of other groups of women in Egypt, but we may also be blinded to understanding what shapes these alternative discourses. In the case of the *ayma*, what accounts for its importance is partly a context of general impoverishment for both men and women, in which women have few opportunities for financial security and ownership of economic assets. For most of the women in the study community, the items on the *ayma*, were the only property or economic asset that they owned, or could ever hope to own in the future. Incorporating these broader issues of poverty and economic vulnerability into our feminist theories and practice points the way forward to making social theory more relevant and addresses one of the identified sources of the "crisis" of social science in the Arab world, that is, "the missing link between societal problems and intellectual production" (Morsy et al. 1991: 85).

Closely related to the *ayma*, another important aspect of marriage negotiations in the study community centered on the marriage trousseau, *gihaaz*. Like the *ayma*, negotiations around the *gihaaz* reveal various ways in which women attempt to secure their futures financially in the face of declining male support, as well as increase their options of who to marry, where to live, and whether or not to work after marriage. It is with these issues that the next section is concerned.

The Trousseau: A Decent *Gihaaz* Increases a Woman's Status, *maᶜamha*[17]

On visiting Om Youssef one day, I found her carefully unpacking several large dusty cartons which had been piled on top of each other all the way to the ceiling of one room of her two-room apartment. She was displaying, with great pride, some of their contents: two sets of glasses (eight pieces each), plates, cutlery, kitchen utensils, and a china tea set richly decorated with pink roses, an electric blender, pots and pans, a rug, and four sets of bed sheets. Her audience was Om Sanna, a cheerful woman well known in the community for organizing *gamīᶜyya*(s) (informal rotating saving and credit societies). Om Youssef warmly called me to join in, explaining that her greatest items of pride were not in any of these cartons, but were located at the other corner of the room, covered with a red and white table cloth. With a dramatic gesture, she removed the cloth to reveal a brand-new washing machine and stove. These items were all part of her daughter's trousseau, which the family has been amassing for years, she proudly announced, detailing the cost and provenance of each item.

Later on, when we were alone, Om Youssef explained that she was intentionally showing off her daughter's amassed *gihaaz* so as to impress Om Sanna, and prod her into bragging about it to prospective families who were searching for brides for their sons. Om Sanaa, she elaborated, was not just known for organizing *gamᶜiyya*(s), but also for arranging marriages. A large *gihaaz* was an excellent way of finding a good husband these days and expanding a daughter's marriage options. Moreover, she added, a woman who goes into a marriage with a small *gihaaz*, risks degradation and loss of status both in her husband's family, as well as in the community at large, whereas a proper *gihaaz* increases a woman's status, worth and bargaining power with her husband.

In this section, I illustrate the use of the *gihaaz*, which includes all the material goods that the bride and her family provide for the new home, as another important element in marriage negotiations. Accumulating a *gihaaz* is a major financial undertaking, and young girls, and their mothers work hard at this task as their daughters approach puberty. Although fathers contribute to the *gihaaz*, it is a significantly higher on women's expenditure and savings priority for women than for men. The desire to accumulate a *gihaaz* is one of the main reasons why many women, particularly unmarried ones, defy community standards and seek paid work in workshops, a decision which will be discussed more fully in the following chapter.

The function of a *gihaaz* goes beyond its economic utility. It is much more than a material contribution by the bride, but has important symbolic value as well. The *gihaaz*, depending on its value and composition, is a public sign of either social status and success, or of failure and loss of prestige. The poorer a girl and her family is, the greater the social importance of her *gihaaz*. For a new bride, a large *gihaaz* is a critical resource for future marital negotiations, and is not a private affair, but an explicitly public one, as it is closely related to social mobility. Like other forms of consumption, it is a means through which families reaffirm their status in the community (see Fine 1992; Warde 1994). A "proper" *gihaaz* in the community studied is valued at a minimum of fifteen hundred Egyptian pounds, a major investment given the levels of income and women's wages in the community. Women, often with some assistance from men, put themselves out on a limb to amass the necessary capital.

Sabah, married recently, has been working for the past six years in an electronics assembly workshop to save for her *gihaaz*. She explains why amassing a large *gihaaz* was a high priority. Her reasons center on the *gihaaz* as a deterrent to possible abuse by her husband or mother-in-law, and were echoed by many other women:

A *gihaaz* enhances a girl's value and enables her to negotiate with her future husband and stand firm in front of him and her mother-in-law. It makes a woman able to answer back if they humiliate or insult her, *tekhali il sit ᶜeenha awiyya amam hamat-ha wi guzha, tiᵖdar tirud ᶜaleehum."* In addition to linen, towels and ten *galabiyya*(s), traditional Egyptian dress, my *gihaaz* also included electric equipment, such as a blender, a washing machine, and a television.

Similarly, Gamalat, a woman in her early thirties explains how entering a marriage with a "proper" *gihaaz* is a sign of prestige and status and a deterrent against potential spousal abuse. Her comments show how family honor, *sharaf*, is dependent in this case not on a woman's sexual behavior as is generally emphasized in the literature on "honor and shame," but also on a woman's ability to accumulate a large *gihaaz*.

A proper *gihaaz* is an honor to the family, *il gihaaz il hilw yisharaf il ahl*. A woman who does not have a proper *gihaaz* is considered a maid, *khaddaam*a, who has no family, *ahl*, and she can be abused by her husband, *yibahdilha*. If he gets angry, he can tell her go back to your parents, you did not bring anything valuable into this marriage.

There is an obvious link between the *gihaaz* and the *ayma* discussed earlier, since a large *gihaaz* will increase the overall monetary value of the *ayma*. Although both practices are part of the same cultural repertoire, they have different trajectories and may have evolved separately. However, I am arguing that in the spatial and temporal context of my research, there is a link between them as cultural resources that are drawn upon to improve a woman's bargaining power in her marriage. Om Ashraf's comments:

Before, gold was security enough for a woman but now the gold of the *shabka* is not enough, so a woman has to secure herself, *tᵓamin nafsaha*, with other items such as a refrigerator or a washing machine. All these (durable) items go into a woman's *ayma*. This embarrasses a man and forces him to provide a decent apartment and also to get more and better furniture, and to write this furniture into the *ayma* as well. A good *gihaaz* now would not cost less than four thousand pounds.

I was told that more unmarried girls in the community were currently part of the labor force than in the past. Discussions with older men and women, who confirmed that this trend has escalated since the early eighties, indicate that the main reasons are to enable a girl to acquire a respectable marriage trousseau. Hag Youssef, an older man who works as a guard in a community school, reflects:

> Girls have to pay a lot more now for marriage than in the past. A large *gihaaz* is critical as the items in the trousseau elevate a girl's status, *maᵓamit-ha*, improve her standing with her in-laws, and increase her marriage proposals in the community, *il haga bitaaᶜit il gihaaz bitshahilha*. If her parents cannot afford to purchase all the items of a *gihaaz*, then a girl must work for it.

One of the reasons a woman with a large *gihaaz* has a stronger standing with her husband and his family is that she shows him, and everyone else in the community, how she has reduced the financial burden on him. This creates a sense of indebtedness, and obligation is built into the relationship from the start. Moreover, as the *gihaaz* serves as a marker of status, a woman with a sizeable one increases the status of her husband and his family as well. This not only deepens their sense of indebtedness towards her, but also enables a bride to be more demanding in terms of choice of residence, such as refusing to live with her in-laws, or insisting on living close to her own mother.

The phenomenon of a bride's substantial contribution to her *gihaaz* appears to be relatively new. Interviews with older women reveal that expectations about the *gihaaz* and negotiations over it have changed dramatically over the past several decades. Whereas in the past, the groom was expected to provide everything, either through a *mahr*, or indirectly, a gradual change from a "dower" system to a "dowry" system appears to have occurred. In reflecting on these changes, Om Mustafa emphasizes the critical point that in the past it was not only unusual, but actually shameful, for a bride to contribute significantly to her *gihaaz*. A major contribution would imply that a girl's reputation was suspect, and that her family was thus eager to bribe a prospective husband so as to marry her off quickly:

> Now a *gihaaz* has to be complete, and so if the man cannot afford to get everything, the girl must get it herself. This way she can have some power, *ᶜeen*, with her husband and his family, and can talk to them eye-to-eye with her head raised. In the old days, however, the groom used to get everything, and a bride was not expected to bring anything into her marriage. In fact it was shameful for a woman to contribute to her

gihaaz, other than her personal things and clothes. If a family provided more than that people would suspect that they were trying to bribe the groom to marry their daughter because there was something wrong with her, *yiballasuu ᶜaleeha ᶜalashan yizᶜutuuha."*

Om Mohamed, seventy years old and married in upper Egypt when she was eleven years old recalls how the financial arrangements of her marriage were very different from that of her daughter's, who got married two years ago. Although a woman was expected to get a *gihaaz* in the "old days," both its composition, and symbolic meaning were very different.

My *mahr* was only seventy-five pounds. The only thing I provided was a wooden chest, *sanduᵓ,* with some clothes, soap, and a copper washing basin. It was so much simpler then. The groom would pay a *mahr* of a maximum of two to three hundred pounds and the father's bride would get everything with that money. People were not so materialistic then and things were much cheaper. The maximum that a woman got in terms of furniture was a bed. No fancy furniture, equipment or anything like that. Now, a girl cannot get married without these things. She would not be able to find a proper husband, *ᶜaleeh il iima.* For the past five years, I have been cutting down on daily expenses, joining several saving societies, and working in assembling washing pegs so as to get some of these things for my daughter. Her husband did not pay a *mahr,* but he built two separate rooms, with a bathroom for her on top of his father's house, and got a special bedroom. My daughter has also been working in a clothing factory for the past four years to complete her trousseau. We did not get everything we wanted, but we still managed to get a refrigerator, and a modern (meaning Western style) set of chairs and sofa made of wood.

Om Hussein, a sixty-year-old widow who runs a grocery shop comments similarly on how marriage related financial arrangements have changed:

Now, among the poor, the *mahr* is not very common, because things are so expensive. If a man pays a *mahr,* it will probably be too low to get all that is expected now and the woman will have to pay as much to get a proper *gihaaz.* So it is more common to ask the groom to provide some furniture instead. But women still have to provide much of the furniture themselves, not like in the old days, where they went into a marriage just with their *galabiyya*(s). In the old days, gold was more important than furniture. A groom had to get a lot of gold and the furniture was limited to a mattress, and, maybe a cupboard. In our days, if a girl's family got her what people are now getting for their daughters, her reputation would be suspect, as it would be as if they are helping the groom because they want to marry her off quickly to hide something.

Naema recounted how her sister's *gihaaz* was publicly displayed last year.[18] Her comments reveal an important relational concept, that of "*muᶜaayara,*" only partially translatable as belittle or humiliate, which underlies the emphasis on a large *gihaaz.* Her views found resonance in my discussions with many other women.

When Naema's sister was married, referred to as *kharagit* (literally went out of her parents' house), or *dakhalit* (literally entered, meaning entered her husband's house), she did so with five large cartons of clothes, and kitchen utensils, in addition to a washing machine and a stove, not a local one, she emphasized, but an imported one. Two days before her *dukhla* all these things were transported by truck from her father's to her husband's house in a public display.

> If we had not shown everybody what she is bringing to her marriage, people would have belittled/scorned her, and she would have started her marriage in a weak position vis-a-vis her husband.

Om Shaymaa, married in rural Asset, upper Egypt, forty years ago, also highlights the concept of *muuᶜayara* and elaborates on a specific custom that is no longer practiced.

> If a woman does not have a complete *gihaaz*, people would scorn her and she becomes the subject of gossip. This is so different than before … In the past, the man used to get not just a golden *shabka* and everything else, but also special china bracelets engraved with enamel from Assuit city, six of them, and the bride would wear them on the wedding night. When people came to visit them the next morning, they looked at the bracelets to ensure that they are broken. If a few are broken, that means that they did not have sex all the way, *makamiltuush lil aakhir*, but only flirted a little… My own bracelets were broken to pieces.

The Evolving Meaning of Marriage Practices

Understanding changes in marriage transactions requires a broader understanding of socioeconomic transformations. Two important interrelated changes have taken place in marriage negotiations over the past thirty years or so which require an explanation. The first is the change in the forms of exchange of marriage prestations, where women are now expected to contribute substantially to the setting up of a marital home. The second is the change in the composition of the specific commodities which are the subject of exchange, that is, changes in the composition of the *gihaaz*, moving increasingly in the direction of consumer durables, with less emphasis on items such as gold and copper, as was previously the case.

The first change may be related to the tremendous increase in the costs of marriage over the past thirty years, particularly in urban areas due primarily to an acute housing shortage, but also to the increased demand for more expensive furniture and equipment, which has not been matched by an increase in incomes. Securing a separate room or an apartment is a major financial undertaking in Cairo, and at the same time it has become an important expectation, tied to the

126

normative preference for an independent conjugal home, a preference that was clear in the study community.

Changes in family structure, normative expectations of marriage, residence patterns and material realities have made it imperative for both bride and groom to contribute to preparing the marital home. A man can no longer afford to provide both the physical dwelling as well as the furnishings and equipment that are now expected. For a woman, however, although an independent conjugal home is valued, it nonetheless carries its own risks, as it may increase a woman's dependence on the residence the husband provides (which would be invariably registered in his name), and thus her "fall back" position in case of marital conflicts may be weaker. Moreover, male under- and unemployment has meant that the ideal of the man providing for his family is seriously in question. Through the *gihaaz* and the *ayma*, women thus attempt to guarantee their material well-being over the long term.

The consumer durables that are part of the *gihaaz* are not simply consumption items. They also represent an important form of accumulating savings and assets. The high rate of inflation in Egypt, and the inaccessibility of banks, means that such savings actually make economic sense. Women can sell a television or a washing machine a few years after it is bought and not lose any money. In fact this form of buying consumer durables when money became available and selling the items when there was a financial crisis constituted a common survival strategy through which women in the study community managed their precarious living conditions (see also Hoodfar 1997).

The second type of change in the composition of the *gihaaz* must be understood within a broader context of the changing symbolic value of commodities as markers of social status, the politics of popular demand and consumption, and the cultural construction of value. As discussed in chapter two, Egypt's economic "open door policy" of the 1980s and the boom in labor migration to the Gulf countries, have ushered in a wave of consumerism with accompanying changes in systems of status and prestige. The demand for consumer durables, including imported items, has increased significantly, even among the less well-to-do. Consumer durables have acquired a new symbolic value as symbols of "modernity" and progress, *tattawur*, and as markers of social differentiation. They have in essence replaced the importance of traditional markers such as gold jewelry. Acquiring modern appliances and furniture has become an avenue of social mobility and prestige.

Appadurai's perspective on the circulation of commodities—which he defines as anything intended for exchange—is of relevance in this context for understanding changes in demand and consumer tastes. Arguing that things have a social life, he suggests that to understand changes in consumption patterns, we need to analytically focus on the "things" themselves that are the subject of demand, rather than on their forms of exchange. "The meaning of things are inscribed in their trajectories, uses and forms, … things in motion illuminate their human and social context" (Appadurai 1986: 5).

Such a focus, argues Appadurai, provides us with a better understanding of the changing nature of demand, and hence consumption, as constitutive of relations of privilege and prestige and as closely linked to the overall political economy of societies. He suggests that we regard consumption as social and relational, not as individual or private; consumption, and the demand it creates, is neither "bottomless" nor "culture-free," but is rather an effective mechanism for both sending as well as receiving social messages. Demand for consumer durables in particular "emerges as a function of a variety of social practices and classifications, rather than a mysterious emanation of human needs, a mechanical response to social manipulation or the narrowing down of a universal and voracious desire for objects or whatever happens to be available" (Appadurai 1986: 29; see also Warde 1994). It is within this analytical framework that changes in the composition of the *gihaaz* in the community studied, and its use by women in marital negotiations, are best comprehended.

The data presented in this chapter has demonstrated how women attempt to gain advantage and security in their marriages and limit the control and arbitrary exercise of power that they are aware that men, as husbands, may exert over them. The *ayma* and the *gihaaz* were presented as two practices that may be turned to such uses. The chapter presented a detailed examination of the *ayma* and *gihaaz* as transactions utilized by women to gain advantage, paying particular attention to the specific idioms underlying them, through which women express ideas like resentment, discontent, attempts at male disempowerment, and their own rightful entitlement. The arguments and idioms women used to make claims about men reveals a striking awareness amongst women of certain aspects of gender-based oppression. The literature on gender relations in Egypt is still heavily influenced by the image of the "corporate" family, where "male dominance is matched by female accommodation, male authority by female obedience" (Rugh 1984: 75), and undifferentiated family strategies (see B. Ibrahim 1985). Discovering a local, historically specific, and class-bound discourse about women's rights, entitlements, and perceived self-interest thus constitutes a significant finding.

The chapter has also illustrated how women's and men's interests are culturally and historically constituted, partly reflecting their specific social locations. Although existing within the same national "culture," women and men do not have a single "indigenous" view of marriage and marriage transactions, but several. Arguing for a more nuanced and situated understanding of women's interests, this chapter showed that, although women in the community studied used the same term for women's rights, *haˀ il mara*, as that used by more upper-class and intellectually inclined feminists, they often attached very different meanings to this term. A common gender thus does not imply common interests, even when similar terms for expressing these interests are used by different groups of women. Any claims about women's interests in Egypt thus need to be conceptualized very carefully. As Molyneux argues, women's interests are historically and culturally constituted, as well as related to specific socioeconomic locations.

Claims about women's interests need to be framed within specific historical contexts since processes of interest formation and articulation are clearly subject to cultural, historical and political variance and cannot be known in advance. (Molyneux 1997: 10)

A more situated understanding of women's negotiation strategies in marriage through microlevel, and context specific research can thus significantly enrich both feminist debates and activism.

The following chapter will shift the discussion from marriage negotiations to the conditions and consequences of women's participation in the informal labor market. The chapter will focus on two specific forms of employment, subcontracting and wage labor. The linkages between women's options and practices in their households and their choices and experiences in the market and workplace will be highlighted.

Notes

1. This is an Egyptian proverb often invoked during my discussions of marriage negotiations in the community.
2. One sterling pound in 1997 was equivalent to 5.6 Egyptian pounds.
3. The term ""conjugal contract" was first used by Whitehead (1981) to highlight the duties, roles and responsibilities that structures the relations between husband and wife.
4. Marriage conventions, negotiations, and prestations have long occupied a central place in anthropology. Discussions about the meanings of marriage payments, and the exchange functions of marriage, have been the subject of much debate and research. Some of the seminal works include Goody and Tambiah (1973) and Comaroff (1980). Because my research is not on marriage transactions and conventions per se, but rather more specifically on women's options and strategies within marriage arrangements, I do not review this literature here.
5. Sometimes these stages are condensed into three, with the *shabka* merged with either the *fatha*, or with the *katb il kitaab*.
6. The *dukhla* will be discussed in some detail in the following chapter.
7. See Moors (1991) for a comparison of the changing meanings of marriage and the *mahr* in a village in Palestine in the 1930s and the 1980s. Her study similarly points to the variability in the meaning of the *mahr*.
8. The rhetoric of female virginity occupies a central place in Egyptian culture in general. The hymen is sometimes referred to as *wish il bint*, the "face of the girl." This analogy with the face, which identifies a girl vividly, denotes the importance of female virginity. A girl without a face has no identity or place in the community (Khattab 1996). Issues surrounding proof of virginity in the study community will be discussed in the following chapter.
9. Unlike the cases of divorcees, there are no community expectations that widows will remarry, and thus they are less feared by other women.
10. The costs of marriages have skyrocketed over the past two decades, as a result of the dramatic increase in the cost of housing, as well as the cost of living generally as discussed in chapter two. Noting the large capital investments that marriages now require, Singerman concludes that: "the struggle to marry off children … is the single most concerted financial and social effort

that every family with children confronted" (1995: 109). Although Singerman's meticulous economic data suggests that her respondents were economically much better off than my sample, many of her observations are nonetheless relevant.

11. See Singerman (1995) for a detailed exposition of the role that informal networks and patronage play in Cairo's popular neighborhoods. The roles of some informal female networks will also be discussed in chapter nine.

12. The late payment is a sum of money that is written into the Muslim marriage contract and which the bride is entitled to in case of divorce.

13. Another study is needed to determine the prevalence of the *ayma* among the more middle and upper classes in Egypt. However, none of the women whom I know with this background had written an *ayma*. The six main feminist activists and researches who were involved in the campaign did not have an *ayma* themselves (personal communication with Hoda El-Sadda and Iman Bibars June, 1997).

14. This particular view of marriage in itself raises interesting questions about the middle-class "domestication" of women, the dependency of middle-class women on men, and the naturalization or "euphemization" of that dependency as "romantic love."

15. I am not underestimating the difficulty of such an effort since low-income women may not always have their own organizations and representatives to facilitate such linkages.

16. The term "gender activisms" comes from Margo Badran's work (1993,1995).

17. Although I use the terms interchangeably, the *gihaaz* is not exactly equivalent to the trousseau, which is defined in the dictionary as: "linen and clothes that a mother gives her daughter when she gets married" (see Fine 1992). The *gihaaz* in the study community, however, consists of not just the above items, but also includes furniture and equipment. Moreover, unmarried girls often work to provide some of these items themselves as will be discussed in the following chapter.

18. The ritual of publicly transporting and showing off a bride's trousseau is also a common practice in rural areas of Egypt.

7
DEFIANCE AND ACQUIESCENCE IN THE LABOR MARKET

"A man has one gall bladder, a woman has twenty four." Arabic Proverb

Om Azouz, a widow in her fifties, is squatting on the mud floor in her two-room rented flat staring at a low, round, wooden table normally used for eating, a *tabliyya*. Piled on the *tabliyya* are hundreds of aspirin-sized tin circles, each with a hole in the middle, a pile of two-centimeter-long pins, a short hammer-like instrument, and a round thick iron object the size of a saucer. Also sitting around the *tabliyya* is Om Azouz's daughter, a pretty but frail woman in her mid-twenties breastfeeding her youngest, and seventh, child. Om Azouz and Om Muhammed are about to start hammering the pins into the holes of the tin circles, a process called *talbiis shamaasi*. They will keep at this repetitive and tedious task for about ten hours, interspersing it with various household chores. This task is the second of a six-step process in the production of upholstery tacks. All other operations are carried out by men, on machines, in small-scale workshops in the community. Om Azouz describes her work as follows:

> I get twenty-five piasters per kilo (7 cents), but this is so little, *irshu daʕiif*, and my eyesight is not good, so I am slow. We get the unassembled tacks from Om Assem, who takes it from various workshops who want to help the poor, *yisaʕdu il ghalaaba*. It is hard work, *taʕab*, it breaks the back and results in finger injuries. The hammer often "bites", *biyʕud*, your finger. Look at my hands. But this is life. Women's work, *shughl il niswaan*, is like that, it causes heart aches and is tiring. My son, the one married to Om Muhammed, does not work, he is often drunk. He always fights with his wife and she gets angry and stays for months at her parents' house, leaving all the children to me.[1] How can I feed them? Sometimes they work with me, but it is dangerous. Samir stepped on a pin yesterday and his foot is now full of pus. The pharmacy prescribed a medicine but it cost LE 7. How can I afford it? My son does not help with this job. He

cannot. This is a job that requires sitting down for so long. It involves no *haraka*, movement, it is not a job a man can do. Men have no patience, *khuP*, for this kind of work. You see, a man has one gall bladder, *maraara*, a woman has twenty four.[2]

This chapter is concerned primarily with women's experiences in the "informal" labor market, and how these inform relations in both the household and the workplace. I highlight the inter-linkages and reciprocal influences between marriage negotiations and contestation in the labor market. The chapter discusses the role of gender in structuring skills, job opportunities, conditions of work and patterns of negotiation in the informal economy, focusing specifically on two forms of female employment, home-based piecework (subcontracting) and waged labor in small workshops.

Other forms of female employment exist in the community I studied, such as public sector work and self-employment (particularly, in retail). My focus on piecework and wage work, however, was intentional. First, both have been apparently on the increase over the past ten years. Yet they have remained virtually unexplored in the Egyptian context. Second, these two forms of work involved women at two different stages of their life cycle; married women with children were predominantly engaged in piecework, and unmarried adolescents in wage work. Given my interest in understanding how women cope with gender inequalities at work at different stages of life, these two patterns thus represented an obvious choice.

My fieldwork shows that women's negotiation options and their responses to the conditions of work vary significantly between these two types of employment, thus complicating any easy conclusions about women's resistance to unfavorable labor relations. As the data will illustrate, piecework tends to be generally "euphemized," or "mis-recognized" as forms of both charity and passing time. The labor relationships underlying piecework are not conceptualized by either the employers (all men) or the subcontractors (all women) as strictly financial transactions, but are presented as a form of charity. There is thus little attempt on women's part to challenge the terms or conditions of their work.

Women engaged in wage labor, on the other hand, have more individual and collective options for both covertly and overtly bargaining for better working conditions. As will be discussed below, this is partly due to the fact that women are excluded from the male-dominated apprenticeship systems characteristic of informal sector workshops which provide men with avenues of training and promotion. Female wage labor, in contrast, tends to be confined to dead-end jobs that have high turnover and require few skills. Women have much less of a vested interest than men in the workplace and little anticipation of upward mobility and better conditions. Their protest was thus often more open and confrontational than that of male wage workers with a stake in the enterprise.

It is widely acknowledged that information about women's labor participation in the informal economy is extremely sketchy in Egypt (Hoodfar 1997).[3]

Nonetheless, several scholars have contributed to an understanding of women's work, both in the formal and informal economy (for example B. Ibrahim 1985; Lobban 1996; Sullivan 1981; Shukry 1992; Zaalouk 1990; see also Fergany 1993 for an extended bibliography). Some more microlevel studies have also provided important insights into self-employment and income generating activities among poor women in the informal sector (see for example, Lynch and Fahmy 1984; and Rugh 1985). Most of these studies, however, have tended to be woman-centered, rather than gender-focused, without sufficient emphasis on analyzing the differences between men and women within the same sector.

Two areas that have not been addressed by any studies of the informal economy in Egypt, even those that deal specifically with women's work, are the examination of a potentially significant, and expanding female labor force in small-scale manufacturing, in both home-based piecework, and wage labor. This labor force is largely invisible. Pieceworkers are based at home, and are thus concealed from public view. Workshops that employ women are also often located on the second and third floor of buildings, and are not noticeable to casual visitors to these communities. Moreover, they often have a male "gate-keeper," in the literal sense, which makes it difficult for outsiders to even obtain access to these workshops. In what follows I will discuss both types of employment.

Acquiescence in The Labor Market: The Social Organization of Piecework

Unlike food vendors and grocers, home-based workers are a largely invisible labor force. I literally stumbled upon this type of work during my early months in the field, and it was only as I built more intimate relationships in the community, visited more households, and stayed for longer periods of time, that I began to realize how pervasive piecework, in fact, was. Over the course of a year, I carried out in-depth interviews with twenty-five women engaged in a range of subcontracting activities, as well as with middlewomen, and male workshop owners. Home-based piecework appeared to be largely dominated by a certain category of women at a particular point in their life cycle, namely women with younger children. These were both married women as well as divorcees, widows, and deserted women. The concentration of this category of women in home-based subcontracting illustrates how a female work force with specific age and marital trajectories is created (Heyzer 1981). As Beneria suggests: "Women, by means of their work trajectories and strategies, supply labor for different processes of capital expansion and proletarization according to the family cycle, a conditioning factor that does not pertain to men" (Beneria 1987:103).

The type of subcontracting observed in the communities I studied was all of the "vertical" type (Beneria 1987). These essentially involve assembly or production tasks for a certain enterprise following very specific instructions, with all raw materials, inputs, and design provided by the subcontractor. They included tasks such as polishing metal ornaments, sewing leather shoes, a process referred to in Arabic as *Shugl suruugi,* attaching hairpins to carton sheets, tying beads, known locally as *ladm,* assembling children's toys, assembling upholstery tacks, referred to as *talbiis shamasi,* removing extra pieces from plastic hangers and washing pegs, known as *tafsiis,* preparing lemons for pickling, and sewing ornaments on clothes and hair accessories.

All the subcontracting activities I observed, however, were geared to the national market rather than export. The subcontracting firms were themselves sometimes subcontracted by a larger firm, and ranged in size from three employees to larger ones of up to ten employees. Some were based in the same community, while others were located in different neighborhoods in Cairo, but had access to that specific community through the residence of the owner or his employees. I did not come across any subcontracting by multinational companies. Since I was primarily interested in women's work, I confined myself to the bottom of the subcontracting chain and did not investigate where these linkages would lead.[4]

Most of the subcontracting activity takes place inside the house, although in the heat of the summer, activities sometimes spill out onto the street. Women, usually from the same or neighboring households, often work collectively. All subcontracted tasks are repetitive, time-consuming, and require no, or very little, skill. Some, like assembling upholstery tacks, cause frequent finger injuries, back injuries and put a heavy toll on eyesight.

Moreover, home-based piecework is extremely low-paying, compared to the income levels in the informal sector as a whole. For example, eight hours of continuous work on assembling tacks earns a woman two Egyptian pounds (about forty English pence). Attaching one kilo of hairpins to carton sheets, which takes about twenty minutes, generates ten piasters (one English pence); an eight-hour day thus generates LE 2.40 (a little over forty English pence). Sewing shoes is slightly more lucrative. For one pair, which takes about twenty minutes to make, a woman could earn up to forty piasters; an eight-hour day, thus earns a woman a little over finve Egyptian pounds (almost one English pound).

The pay of home-based workers, who are exclusively women, is far below the minimum wage in Egypt, and much lower than average earnings in the informal sector. This becomes clear when the earnings indicated above are compared to the earnings indicated in the CAPMAS study of the informal economy in Egypt discussed in chapter two. When inflation and the irregular nature of home-based work are factored in, the meagerness of the income generated through subcontracting becomes even more apparent.

My oral histories indicate that piecework as a form of female employment has increased significantly over the past ten years. This increase is understandable in view of the increased levels of poverty and male unemployment as discussed in chapter two, as well as the casualization of employment generally. Given current trends of privatization and structural adjustment in Egypt, it is likely that sub-contracting arrangements will be intensified even more over the next few years, for reasons of both for demand and supply.

Women's income is becoming increasingly important for survival in low-income households, and at least eighteen percent of households are headed by women who are the sole breadwinners for their families (Fergany 1994b).[5] In my sample, of the fifty-nine once married women, twelve were de jure heads of households (eight were widowed and four were divorced). There were also five women who were deserted but not legally divorced. Many others reported not being fully supported by their husbands. As more poor women are driven into the labor market due to economic need, most have few options other than home-based piecework.

On the supply side, there are indications from many countries that the inter-national recession of the 1980s and the adoption of structural adjustment and labor deregulation policies have resulted in a global surge of new forms of flexi-ble labor relations, such as subcontracting, partly as a way for employers to keep production costs down (Baden 1993; Standing 1989). For employers, subcon-tracting ensures a risk-free, flexible[6] labor force that can be expanded or down-sized depending on the fluctuations of the business (Elson 1996).

Industrial subcontracting, geared to both international and domestic markets, has recently been recognized as an increasing trend in many parts of the world. Products are subcontracted from larger firms to smaller ones, and from those to home-based workers. Subcontracting is therefore not subject to regular labor laws or social security provisions. One of the main conclusions of the literature on sub-contracting follows Braverman's argument that subcontracting aims at the reduc-tion of labor costs, through changes in the division of labor. This is rendered possible by the fragmentation of the production process into simple tasks and the employment of workers associated with lower skill and lower wages (Beneria 1987).

It has been argued that this type of fragmentation of the labor force is often associated with "feminization."[7] One of the important findings of cross-cultural research on subcontracting is the overwhelming concentration of female labor in this new pattern of work, particularly at the lowest end of the subcontracting chain, i.e., as home-based workers. In both developed and developing countries, women seem to have been more affected by this trend than men (Beneria and Roldan 1987; Huws 1995; Mies 1982; Standing 1989; White 1994).

The association of female labor, in particular, with lower skills and wages, is the result of a complex alliance between gender and kinship ideologies that deter-mines the terms upon which women enter the labor market. Like men, women are bearers of not simply labor power, but also of gender attributes grounded in the prior division of labor enacted in specific family and household arrangements. "The terms upon which women may compete in the labor market are thus dictated by the social relations within which they operate as daughters, wives, mothers, widows, etc., and which impose ideological sanctions upon their identification as 'free labor'" (Standing quoted in Westwood 1988: 9). Thus, as Pearson (1994) argues, the automatic relationship often assumed between increases in female wage labor and women's empowerment must be substituted for a more careful empirical examination of changes in economic systems and their impact on women's roles.

In a groundbreaking study on industrial subcontracting in Mexico City, Beneria and Roldan (1987) illustrate how women are not part of an open labor market and do not have the same relationships to the means of production as men. Gender ideologies which identify women as possessing certain characteristics such as docility, being secondary earners and tolerance, and men with possessing attributes such as restlessness and impatience, mediate production relations to create a demand for specifically female or male labor. Along the same lines, a study of black and minority women working in family enterprises in Britain reveals that labor power is gendered and that this determines the conditions under which women and men sell their labor power. "Women's domestic roles in reproduction (servicing the household and family) are articulated with roles in social production that generate wages" (Westwood 1988: 4).

The Alliance Between Kinship and Gender Ideology

Kinship and community relationships and idioms played a significant role in accessing subcontracting work in the study community. Some tasks are subcontracted directly from a workshop to women. Many other tasks are allocated by a middlewoman, sometimes a relative of the workshop owner, who acts as a broker and gets a fee for her services. This reduces women's earnings. However, many of the women I interviewed emphasized the important role of a middlewoman revealing how daily survival requires the maintenance of membership in social relations and community networks and the continuous nourishing of a web of reciprocal arrangements. A form of "mutual indebtedness," noted by White (1994) in her study of Turkey, was also noticeable in the study community.

Karima, who is engaged in assembling upholstery tacks, comments on the important role of middlewomen. Her comments illustrate the patron-client relations operating in women's access to piecework:

> I now know the *warsha*, workshop, and I can go and get from it directly, but it is important to keep good relations with Om Hamid, the middlewoman. The production pace of this work is not regular and during times of scarcity, if I have a good relationship with her, I will be sure that she will keep giving me as much work as I can take and not reduce my quota, *tariiha*. The workshop owner, on the other hand, tries to be fair, and when production is slow, he reduces the amount given to everybody. You see, his aim is to help as many poor people as possible, but with Om Hamid, we have a special relationship, she also organizes *gam⁻iyya*(s), rotating saving associations, which my mother and I often join.

The owner/manager of one of the larger workshops producing upholstery tacks explained how and why he subcontracts to women.[8] His comments illustrate how socially constructed gender attributes are used in determining employment patterns and how once tasks are labeled feminine, they reinforce existing labor hierarchies. Piecework, in this case *talbiis shamaasi,* is defined as women's work because of the assumed feminine characteristics of patience, lack of mobility, ability to sit on the floor for long periods of time, endurance, and lack of responsibility for providing for their families. His comments also illustrate the current dependence of this type of manufacturing on cheap female labor, although this was apparently not always the case.[9]

> We subcontract only to women, not to men. A man would suffocate, *yitkhin?,* doing this kind of work with no movement, *haraka.* He has no *khu?* , patience. Also, it would be *ᶜeeb,* shameful, for a man to do a job that his wife is already doing or is known to be *shugl niswan,* women's work. Besides, what is twenty-five piasters a kilo. This cannot even pay for a man's cigarettes. A man works because he has major responsibilities … We subcontract to about one hundred women. Most are regulars and all are from the *hitta,* area or community. Women have always been engaged in this task, because there are no machines that can do it. It is only in the last ten years that production has increased to the point where hundreds of women are working. There are many workshops like us in the community. We try to distribute work fairly to women, to please them, *niradeehom.* Each gets about twenty kilos every three days. We subcontract women directly for twenty-five piasters a kilo, without a middlewoman.

Some of the subcontracted tasks have always been defined as women's work, such as polishing metal objects. Others, however, such as sewing shoes, *shughl suruugi,* have only recently become feminized. The production of shoes has historically been a male task requiring highly skilled craftsmen, *sanayᶜiyya,* who worked by hand. Sewing leather shoes was originally called *biyaz wi ibar* and involved a skilled process of piercing the leather on a wooden mould and simultaneously sewing it. As sewing machines which could sew leather were introduced in the 1950s, this production of hand-made shoes slowly died out,[10] and was replaced instead by two mechanized procedures. The first is piercing the leather, and the other is sewing the shoes. Both tasks were still defined as skilled male jobs, *a sanᶜa,* and were carried out in workshops by men.

Over the past eight years, however, the high wages of skilled male workers, and the increasing cost of machines induced workshop owners to cut down on costs by changing the division of labor, and shifting production from machine- to hand-sewn shoes. Shoes began to be subcontracted out to women to be hand-sewn at home, and the task, of *shughl suruugi* was redefined as an exclusively female job. Once this occurred, it became quickly naturalized and everyone seemed to forget that in the very recent past, it was a skilled male task. The historical development of this task demonstrates how "women's participation in a given labor process is affected not only by previously existent gender hierarchies and work histories, but it also reinforces these and creates new labor hierarchies based on gender" (Beneria 1987:14).

The manager of a workshop producing men's shoes explains why he subcontracts to women. The power of the ideology of domesticity, and of how kinship and charity idioms mediate work relations, come through clearly in his words:

> There is increasing demand now for hand-sewn shoes, but if we continued with the old practice of *biyaz wi ibar,* a shoe would cost two hundred pounds and no one would buy it. The way we do it now, it sells for about thirteen pounds. It would be too expensive for male workers to hand sew the shoes on the machines that imitate hand sewing. A *sanayᶜi* would demand 150 piasters per pair, whereas a woman will do it for only fifty piasters. Men have no *ruuh,* patience/spirit, for these types of jobs anyway.

A particularly significant aspect of gender ideology is its power to not only define certain areas as female as illustrated above, but more significantly its power to act retrospectively to create amnesia about the history of certain tasks. This comes through clearly in the following comments of another workshop manager. They reveal the increased poverty of the whole urban working class, women and men, again noting the crucial link between poverty, male unemployment or underemployment and female subcontracting.

> You see, *Shughl suruugi* is not really a skilled job, it is really similar to what women do at home. They sew clothes for their family don't they? Moreover, life is now very difficult and there are many poor women who have no support. This is a way we can help them, *nisaᶜd il ghalaaba.* I only give work to women in the community, who are like my family.

Research on export-based manufacturing in several Third World countries suggests similar findings about how gender ideology creates a loss of memory that results in rationalization of existing divisions of labor. Pearson illustrates how the redefinition of certain tasks in "world market" factories as women's work operates by likening such work to domestic skills that all women are presumed to have mastered. This "feminization" of chores is used to justify the preference for female labor in completely "non traditional" tasks, such as assembling electronic circuits under microscope magnification, or some forms of soldering and welding, which are likened to sewing or embroidery (Pearson 1994). However, as mentioned earlier, "feminization" may occur in certain jobs and under certain conditions, but it is not necessarily an inevitable global trend (see Elson 1996). Apart from the examples of hand-sewn shoes and upholstery tacks, in none of the other subcontracted activities that I witnessed was the labor of women substituted for formerly male labor.

Some subcontracted tasks are purely seasonal such as pickling lemon and assembling lanterns for Ramadan, the Islamic month of fasting. Others are more regular throughout the year. Some women switch from one type of subcontracting to the other, while others remain in the same type of work for many years. There are no opportunities for mobility or skill acquisition. The most that piece-workers can look forward to is a lateral move to a different and slightly more lucrative kind of subcontracting. Very few women are able to make the shift from home-based worker to middlewoman, and thus increase their earnings, and possibly also their skills, since being a middlewoman requires different types of skills and associations. The two women in my sample who were able to make this move were both relatives of workshop owners. Workshops, and middlewomen, sometimes keep written records of their subcontracting networks.

Workshops usually maintain a network of about thirty women, depending on the size of the workshop. Individual middlewomen usually have about ten women in their circle. Most women get to know about these opportunities by word of mouth, and existing kin and nonkin networks in the community. Home-based workers are usually not direct relatives of the middlewomen or the workshop owners. The relationships nonetheless take on kinship overtones, as will be discussed below. White suggests the use of the term "fictive kin" to denote such relationships (White 1994). Payment arrangements vary, but most women are paid on a weekly basis, either directly by the workshop, or through the middlewoman.

In the study community, there is more demand by women for piecework than the workshops can actually supply, even in the new lines of subcontracting like sewing shoes. This "crowding effect" means that manipulating social relations to ensure that one gets a steady supply of work under such conditions is thus an important feature of the organization of piece-work. Om Mahmoud, a married woman in her forties, comments on her work sewing shoes. Her comments reveal the complex alliances and extra-economic relations underlying the social organization of piecework in general, as well as the irregular nature of this specific task and its strict rules of completion given that it is one component of an entire production process:

> I have been doing this for two years only, together with my daughter. My husband's income from the water authority is not enough to cover our expenses any more and I need to buy the trousseau, *gihaaz*, for my daughter. Attiat, my neighbor who works as the *kummanda*, middlewoman, lives in the same street and she gives me work day by day. It is very difficult, because we have to finish the work the same day, regardless of when we receive it. For example, she gave me eight pairs last night at 12 P.M. and wanted them the next morning. I spent all night doing them. It takes me about twenty-five minutes to do one pair. We are paid every Saturday, thirty piasters per pair for our labor, *masnaᶜiyya*. But the work is not dependable. One week I make seven pounds, and one week I make twenty … the work is available year round, but the end of the summer is a particularly busy season. I first saw women engaged in this work about seven years ago, but there were few. There are so many more women now. I know personally about twenty, but I think more than half the women in this street do it. There are two middlewomen in this street. But the pay was higher before, women used to get fifty piasters a pair, now we get only thirty piasters. The middlewoman must be mak-

ing more money, but she is a resourceful, *milahlaha*, woman, a *dallala*, a door-to-door saleswoman, whom we have known for years. She is from upper Egypt, like us.

Further insights into the influence of middlewomen can also be gleaned from the comments of Om Aziza, the sister-in-law of a skilled shoemaker who owns a small workshop. Her explanation of how she herself became a middlewoman distributing shoes illustrates how women view piecework with mixed feelings. The fact that piecework is carried out at home and can be combined with domestic responsibilities[11] renders it attractive for some women. So does the limited range of acceptable job opportunities for women in the study community, particularly uneducated ones. Piecework and self-employment in primarily retail vending and marketing are the most culturally sanctioned forms of employment for uneducated women. Waged work is considered degrading and low-status as will be discussed later. So is domestic work, such as the occupation of cook and cleaner, for richer households. Om Aziza comments:

> When my husband went to prison on charges of drug dealing, I found a job as a seamstress in a workshop in Harit il Yahuud, but the hours were too long so I left. My sister's husband, who has a small shoemaking workshop, offered to give me some shoes to sew at home. It was a good job, because I could do it at home, be close to my kids, and no one can degrade me and say that I am a wage laborer in workshops, *bita͑t wirash* (the implications of such a label are discussed later in this chapter). This was three years ago. After a while, the load got too heavy so I started distributing to the women I knew and taught them how to do it. I take it from the *warsha* for fifty piasters per pair and pay the women twenty piasters per pair. `I distribute about three hundred pairs a day, to seven women and go down twice a day to the workshop to return and get work. It is important that we return the work the same day, so that the *sanay͑iyya* in the workshop can finish the shoe. I distribute to women who I know are in need, such as Om Youssef, whose husband does not work, so when I have some extra, I give them to her. But the demand from women is so great, I have to let many of them down. When work is slow, I give women who take from me permission to go take work from other middlewomen.

Subcontracted women do not have official leave or holidays and, for many of the tasks, are expected to work regularly and continuously as long as work is available. In other words the "flexibility" of piecework is often defined by the workshop owners, not by the women themselves. One of the criteria for middlewomen's choice of subcontractees in some types of tasks is thus their "dependability," defined as their ability to keep working on a regular basis with no breaks. In practice, this means choosing very poor women who are in dire need of cash with few alternative options for generating it.

One of the few acceptable reasons for not receiving the finished work on time is illness or personal circumstances, such as a family death. Possession by an alien spirit was sometimes mentioned as a type of "sickness" for which allowances for delays in work, or temporary halts, are made.[12] A middlewoman, whose usage of the pronoun, we, reveals that she identifies more with the male workshop owner than with the female workers, explains:

> The shoe workshop depends on these women, so I have to make sure that they are worthy of their trust. I select women who are in need, who are trustworthy, not women who will take this lightly, *yitdallaᶜu*, one day they work, and ten days not. We cannot make allowances for this. Of course if a woman is very sick, I understand. and distribute her work to someone else until she gets better. Take for example Om Samir, poor thing, she is possessed, *ᶜaleeha riih*, which has made her not herself for the past two weeks. She cannot eat, cannot even speak, so how can I ask her to work? I gave her allocation to someone else, until she gets better.

While piecework is an individual activity and each woman is paid individually for her work, it was common to see women working collectively in their homes. Often a neighbor would come in and join in the work for an hour or so and leave. What is important to note, however, is that not all the women who are working actually get paid. Some women, are thought of as really working, *biyishtaghalu*, and others as only helping, *biysaᶜdu*, or as passing time, *biyitsalu*. The women who are working are the only ones who get paid for the finished work. Others who are helping them do so out of social obligation and community expectations of cooperation and reciprocity. Women who are known to have no economic support from husbands such as divorcees or widows, or those whose husbands are not providing for them for a variety of reasons, were often "helped" in their subcontracting work by other women.

Women volunteer their labor and maintain such relations of cooperation, possibly because the pay for the work is so low and in anticipation of receiving the same kind of help from others, should they be in a similar situation of need. Given the precarious livelihoods of many of the families I studied such anticipation is not unfounded. Om Ashraf, a married woman living with her divorced sister-in-law and mother-in-law in the same household explains:

> The four of us, myself, my daughter, my sister-in-law and my mother-in-law work, together attaching pins to carton sheets. My sister-in-law is the one who goes and gets her quota from the workshop down the street. She gets maybe fifteen kilos or so a day. We all sit and do it together, but my daughter and I, we do not take any money from them. We are only helping them. My sister-in-law is unfortunate, her husband divorced her and left her with four children and no money. I am lucky, my husband is a skilled construction worker and makes good money ... So I try to help them ... Anyway it is *tasliya*, passing time, for us, it is only a few piasters.

Om Ashraf's comments also raise important questions about the extent to which women's time and money is more subject to appropriation in response to social demands than that of men.

"Symbolic Power" in Action: The Euphemization of Piecework

Although women saw some positive aspects of piecework, there was also a clear sense among all the women I interviewed that piecework is also low-paying and extremely tedious. They used strong terms to describe their work such as, *irshaha daᶜiif*, low- paying, *bitīᵗum il dahr*, breaks the back, *rabbina yikfiina sharaha*, God save us from it's evils, *taᶜab*, tiring, *ghulb*, misery, and bites the finger. This latter is a complaint I can personally relate to as I spent many hours engaged in subcontracting tasks with the women I interviewed. Although they appeared simple, in fact they required dexterity in holding the pliers or hammer in the right manner; even when one does, the hammer often slips and "bites" one's fingers.

Most women recognize these negative aspects of the work. However, this awareness did not appear to have been translated into a feeling of exploitation by either the middlewomen or the employers. At the same time that women sometimes complained about the middlewoman making too much of a profit, they are quick to emphasize how helpful and kind they also are, thus casting their relationships with them as essentially positive ones. Women's articulated grievances are thus not translated into any attempts to negotiate with middlewomen or organize action to change the terms of payment or conditions of work.

On the one hand, as illustrated, there was a high demand for piecework by poor community women partly due to the lack of alternative earning opportunities. Women thus fear that if they object to the terms of work, there will be many others who will take their place. It is noteworthy in this respect that the high demand for piecework by women is also due to the lack of financially adequate, accessible, and gender-sensitive social welfare policies by the government.[13]

The relative passivity of women vis-à-vis the middle women and their employers can also be explained in terms of the nature and workings of what Bourdieu terms symbolic power and symbolic violence, which results in a euphemization of social relations (Bourdieu 1977). In his study of the link between power, authority and patterns of reciprocity and exchange among the Kabyle peasants in Algeria, Bourdieu illustrates how relations of domination are construed as beneficial and constructive social relations. His work is an important addition to the discussions on the nature and mechanisms of power and hegemony as it highlights how power operates, not only as an external force that must be maintained through coercion and repression, but also through more subtle ideological forms. Domination is practiced and maintained through links and relationships that appear to be benign, or sometimes even positive. Bourdieu calls this process symbolic violence, "the gentle invisible form of violence which is never recognized and is not so much undergone as chosen, the violence of credit, confidence, obligation, personal loyalty, gifts, hospitality, piety—in short all the virtues honored by the code of honor" (1977: 192).

The relations underlying piecework in Cairo, which embody a complex alliance between gender, kinship and market ideologies, can best be understood within this framework.[14] Although acknowledging many of the negative aspects of their jobs, women generally saw them as an unfortunate, but inevitable part of their life and fate as poor women. My research suggests that the mystification of some aspects of the relationships underlying piecework works both ways, and is shared by both the women working as pieceworkers as well as those employing them. The workshop owners and middlewomen I interviewed did not appear to perceive of themselves as being exploitative, but rather as genuinely being chari-table, helping the poor, *musaᶜdit il ghalaaba*, and extending alms to the impov-erished, *sadaᵓa*, as good Muslims are expected to do.

This euphemization of piecework, by both employers and employees, as pass-ing time and helping the poor limits women's ability to contest their working conditions. Recasting piecework arrangements as benevolent and charitable, and as forging community solidarity, mutual help and reciprocity plays an important role in the lack of any active protest to such arrangements. Pieceworkers are regarded, and regard themselves, as unemployed women in need of charity, not as members of the labor force. The power of gender ideology to create a collective loss of memory about the history of the division of labor, to naturalize social rela-tions making them appear as what Bourdieu would term "doxa"—that is, com-monsensical and beyond the realm of the contestable—or to euphemize exploitative and unequal power relations, is vividly illustrated by the case of piece-workers in the community studied.

These arguments and findings support one of the few studies on home-based piecework in the Middle East (White 1994). In her pioneering study of ateliers and home-based workers in Istanbul, White finds that women's labor is closely linked to social and gender identity and to membership in social groups such as the family, and both kin and nonkin networks. "In Turkey, women's identity is largely expressed through complex sets of relations that involve giving and receiving labor. Exchanging labor and services in social groups, such as the fam-ily and neighborhood, is crucial for women's social and economic survival" (White 1994: 6). Women are under contradictory pressures. On the one hand they need to contribute to family income, and on the other hand, they should not work among strangers. Working as home-based pieceworkers allows women and men to resolve this contradiction: they can generate income for their families, without violating the expectations of the family and prevalent codes of "proper" female behavior.

White thus similarly concludes that the low wages, lack of security and tedious aspects of home-based piecework are naturalized, and "euphemized" as ones of kinship and expressions of community obligation and solidarity (White 1994). In the Egyptian case, however, I would argue that piecework also allows women and men to resolve another contradiction. It allows the community to fulfil its own expectations that needy women will be assisted offering them income-generating opportunities, while at the same time reinforcing gender hierarchies by keeping women out of areas of skilled wage work, reserving the latter for men.

143

Contesting Working Conditions: "Workshop Girls"

The conditions of piecework illustrate the power of gender and kinship ideologies which circumscribe women's ability to contest the terms of their employment. It would be premature, however, to draw any blanket conclusions on that basis about the strength of gender ideologies or the inability of women to bargain in the labor market. Another pattern of female employment that I discuss in this section illustrates that certain groups of women, at a particular stage of their life cycle, and under certain conditions of supply and demand, may deploy a range of public and private, collective and individual strategies to maximise their options, voice their discontent, and juggle the possible contradictions between marriage-ability and domesticity on the one hand and paid employment on the other.

My main argument in this section is that different forms of female employment—often corresponding to different points in women's life cycle—embody different forms of power relations and thus leads to different patterns and forms of resistance. Thus, unlike pieceworkers who represent a fragmented and docile labor force—despite their expression of discontent with piecework arrangements—wage laborers respond to their situation in a different way. Some appear to be engaged in a subtle process of negotiation that I characterize as "strategic trade-offs." Yet others may respond to their perceptions of unfair working conditions with an explicit, and gender specific form of revolt, termed *namrada* by workshop owners, which often takes collective forms.

My initial attempts to locate and gain access to workshops that employ women were frustrating. I was told by two of my key interviewees, that many girls were employed in such workshops, but that this would be a difficult area to explore in depth until I built stronger relationships in the community. Women do not admit to being employed by workshops, because wage labor is considered degrading, low-status work. Wage laborers are referred to as *banaat il wirash*, literally "workshop girls/daughters," which has a condescending connotation among community members.

Moreover, many of the workshops employing women are located on the upper floors of buildings and are thus difficult to identify. Workshop owners later told me that they "hide" their workers partly to "protect the girls" given the low status of such employment in the community. They also needed to protect themselves from government officials, particularly labor inspectors. Most such workshops are informal in the sense that they are unregistered or regulated by formal laws and do not insure their employees. In the few workshops that registered their employees for social insurance, women workers, in particular, were not insured as they were considered an unstable labor force with a high turnover rate. Workshop owners/managers are thus very careful not to reveal their female employees to strangers.

In contrast, although it is also illegal to hire children below the age of twelve, I was struck by the prevalence and visibility of child labor, mainly male, and by the lack of attempts to conceal it.[15] Women explained that if government officials come to check on workshops, it is easy to pretend that the boys are sons or relatives of workshop owners, "family" labor, which is outside of the domain of government regulation. It would also be easy to ask children to run into the streets away from the workshops if word goes around that an inspector is in the community. This would be more difficult to do with adult female labor.

Given this difficulty of gaining access to workshops, I decided to continue my research at the household level, until I was able to identify and build strong relations with women who are themselves employed in wage work. After several months in the field I was able to start exploring wage labor in greater detail. I visited seventeen workshops and interviewed twenty-six women wage laborers, and seven male workshop owners/managers. The workshops I observed ranged from those employing a minimum of two to a maximum of twelve people and produced diverse products: lollipops and candy, makeup, hair accessories, jewelery, furniture, electronic equipment, elastic bands, chalk, plastic utensils, socks, children's toys and ready-made clothes.

The women I interviewed ranged in age between thirteen and twenty-three years old., with only three older women who were either divorced or widowed. The predominance of an age-specific group—young, unmarried girls—in this particular type of employment contrasts sharply with the characteristics of those engaged in piecework, married women with young children. This confirms the point made earlier about age and marital trajectories having gender-specific implications in the labor market.

My interviews with workshop owners revealed a range of other gender-specific factors that affected female employment. Ragab Samir, who owns a workshop which produces costume jewellery, has been in this business for twenty-nine years, climbing the traditional male apprenticeship ladder from being a *sabi*, unskilled helper, to a *musaaᶜid*, semiskilled helper, to a *sanayᶜi*, skilled workman, to a *hirafi*, an even higher level of skilled workman. Ragab's workshop employs five men and four girls, between the ages of sixteen and twenty-one, none of whom are his relatives. This workshop represents an interesting case study of the role of gender in structuring several aspects of employment, so I will present it in some detail here.

As in many workshops, there is a clear segregation of tasks by gender in this particular workshop, which is a fairly large one consisting of three rooms on the third floor of a dilapidated building. The four girls are engaged in tasks referred to as finishing tasks, *tashtiib wi takmiil*. These include attaching the false gems to the metal backing, beading and packaging. The men, on the other hand, are engaged in the core of the work, namely, producing the different parts of the accessories and attaching the metal pieces. Ahmed explains why this gendered division of labor is essential:

> The girls are assigned the work which requires a lot of patience. If the boys do this kind of work, they would get fidgety and the cigarettes they would smoke would cost more

than what they would make. The men would not be able to sit quietly like this. They would start talking and make too much noise. The money that the men make for their tasks is much higher because men have obligations that are more important, and as a result they are naturally more skilled, *tabiᶜt-hum ahraf.* Girls will always remain the *subyan, subyan il hirfa,* the boys of the boys of the trade" (that is, positioned at the very lowest level of the skill).

The naturalization of skills and aptitudes is clear in this comment. Ragab's comment below also reveals an interesting similarity between the greater value assigned to male labor and the preference and value attached to giving birth to sons, who can bear the family name, in this community as well as Middle Eastern societies more generally. Ahmed explains:

> Girls are not as valuable to me as men. When a girl gets married, I have to ask her to leave the workshop, so I will be forgotten after a while. But a boy who is well trained will carry my name, as a highly skilled workman, *hirafi.* It will be known that he worked for me and was trained by me. He will always say my trainer was so and so, and my name will endure in the market, it will not disappear.

All the girls in the workshop are unmarried. This is not a coincidence, but a condition for the employment of women that does not apply to men. Ragab explains why he hires only single girls and does not allow them to continue to work after they get married. His arguments present a telling example of how "truths" are created to effectively check women's labor mobility and to keep them out of the skilled labor force. These truths become communal cultural standards to which women also subscribe.

> I started hiring girls only about seven years ago, but only unmarried girls. Once they get married, they have to leave. The boys can stay, but not the girls. You see, I have men and boys working here, and with married woman there could be greed, *tamaᶜ*, and problems, *mashaakil.* Once they get married, I can give them work to do at home on a subcontracting basis. I did that with several women who used to work with me as young girls.[16]

The use of space in Ragab's workshop is also vividly gendered. Similar to many other workshops I visited, there are significant variations in seating arrangements and space allocation based on gender. This partly reflects the low status of *banaat el wirash,* and is possibly related to the need to better control and monitor women's behavior. The four girls sat side by side on a long wooden bench, in the same room as the manager. They were all wearing a *higaab,* a scarf that covers their head and neck, referred to in the literature as the veil or the new veiling.[17] There was a cassette player on the manager's desk, which he switched on and off at will. The girls clearly did not have the right to do the same.

The male employees, on the other hand, had a separate, larger room of their own, with individual working tables and chairs and a cassette player over which they had control. In the hours I spent in the workshop during several visits, the men ordered tea, joked and talked loudly, walked around the workshop and had the cassette on, blasting music. The girls were not offered, and did not order tea, and did not once get up from their bench. I was intrigued that although Ragab admitted in his discussions with me that men talk more and are rowdier than girls, he still felt the need to monitor and supervise the work of the girls more closely, and as his comments below reveal, even whip them occasionally. On probing this issue, Ahmed explains:

> These girls have been entrusted to me by their parents, they are an *amaana,* for safe-keeping. So I have to make sure that they do not do anything improper like talk or joke with the men. The work of girls is sensitive, you always have to keep an eye on them. I insist that they have to cover their heads properly and I hit them with a whip lightly on their hands if I see them acting in an improper way or if I hear a dirty word. The girls eat together during lunchtime, and I eat with the men.

The terms and conditions of wage work clearly vary from workshop to workshop, but the above case illustrates some of the common features that have emerged from my fieldwork. Gender structures the terms and relations of employment in a variety of ways. First, there is a clear job segregation, with the skilled and mechanized tasks that offer job mobility being associated with men. In all the workshops I observed, certain tasks were clearly defined as female jobs and others as male jobs, with little exchange of tasks. A carpentry workshop manager explains why only men work on machines in his workshop, whereas women are involved in assembling furniture:

> Men prefer machines, it is much harder work. Men must feel they are sweating in their job. That is why they prefer to do the difficult jobs, not the light ones, *haagat il khafiifa,* like assembly. After all, men have a command over women, *il rigaal qawamuun ᶜala il nisaaᵓ* (this is a verse from the Quran that is open to several interpretations, but which is commonly used to justify male superiority over women).

Second, there are also marked wage differentials in unskilled jobs. An unskilled male worker can make up to seven Egyptian pounds (1.40 English pounds) a day, whereas an unskilled female worker would not make more than three Egyptian pounds (about sixty English pence) a day for the same job. Because female wage labor is so much cheaper, there is a high demand for it which is not matched by existing supply. This situation contrasts with the case of pieceworkers where demand far exceeds the supply of work. Partly as a result, wage laborers are better able to negotiate their terms of work than pieceworkers are, as will be discussed below.

Third, a common issue that emerged from my interviews relates to the existence of several forms of "sexual harassment" that both women and workshop owners were aware of. This is possibly because this type of employment is so looked down upon in the community. Forms of sexual harassment included complaints about offensive jokes, making passes, using dirty language, as well as actual physical molestation. Sexual harassment was one of the important reasons cited by several girls for quitting their jobs.

Zouba, a 45-year-old woman whose husband deserted her twenty years ago, has had extensive experience as a wage laborer in a range of workshops. She was one of the few once-married women working in a workshop and had a reputation for being tough and unintimidated by men. This was visibly reflected in what was considered her masculine-looking body and walk. Zouba currently works in a workshop producing plastic utensils, where she is engaged in removing the extra plastic pieces from hangers, a process called *tafsiis il rayish*. She is the only woman employed in the workshop, which has five other employees, all male, who work on the machines.

Zouba works squatting on the floor in one corner of a four by four meter room with practically no ventilation. I spent many hours over a period of two weeks squatting beside her and helping her with her task. Throughout, the smell of the burning plastic fumes was suffocating and by the end of the two weeks I had difficulty breathing. The noise of the four machines, which worked nonstop from 10 a.m. to 11 p.m. except for a short lunch break, was also deafening.

These intolerable conditions, however, did not deter Zouba from working at an incredible pace. Because she is paid by her production rate (seven piasters per kilo), she explained, every second counted, and every piaster counted as she was determined to ensure that her children could live a decent life and get the best education. On a bad day, she makes about fifty kilos (LE 3.5 , fifty pence), and on a good day she can make up to one hundred kilos (LE 7 , a little over one pound sterling). Zouba comments on the issue of sexual harassment in workshops:

> Women are tested in workshop, for two things: honesty and properness. Money is left lying around on purpose to see if a newly recruited woman will steal it. Men make sexual advances, in the form of dirty talk and looks, to see how the women will respond. The men want to see if the woman is a ^c*iP a*, sexually promiscuous or loose. It is up to the woman, however, to protect herself and prove to everyone that she is untouchable. The main rule is never to joke with the men. Once you do that you will no longer be able to keep the limits.

After I got to know her well, Zouba also volunteered information about her personal experience with harassment, as we were having lunch one day at a local cafeteria. She also explained how, many years ago, she decided to purposefully modify her own appearance to make herself look more masculine, *astargil*, in order to avoid harassment. She is not poorly groomed, her hands and palms are rough, she does not remove the hair on her arms or legs, and her gait is distinctly unfeminine by community standards. Zouba recalls:

> I was working in another plastic workshop three years ago. But I left because the men were bothering me, they were rude/dirty. I was once cleaning under one of the

machines and one of the men stuck his foot in my ass. I was furious and screamed at him, but he laughed and said, did you really feel anything, I thought you were cold/frigid. I complained to the workshop owner but he did not believe me and said that this is a man who prays and cannot do such a thing, so I must be lying to him. I asked for my pay and left. Workshop girls witness these kinds of problems all the time.

Amal, who is now married to a laborer in an upholstery shop and has two children, recalled with anger how she was harassed at her job in a workshop producing elastic bands when she was an adolescent. Her reactions are an excellent illustration of what Okely terms "moments of defiance" (Okely 1991).

One of the men who works in the workshop used to whistle to me all the time. Then one day he grabbed my breasts. I screamed at him and when I went back next day, I took a knife with me and made sure that I always kept it hidden in my sleeve … A week later he grabbed my breasts again and I stabbed his hand with the knife. It was bleeding and people gathered. I told the *usta* what happened, and he reprimanded the man, but did not fire him. He never came near me again.

The forth issue in workshops, as mentioned earlier, is that the utilization of space was also clearly gendered. Women were assigned less space and often worked on the floor, whereas the men would generally have chairs. Moreover, women's space was usually much more closely monitored and regulated than men's space. These arrangements were most obvious in the shoe, socks, electronics and plastic workshops. They were less obvious in the carpentry and candy-making workshops.

It is noteworthy, however, that only some of these aspects of gender discrimination, in particular wage levels and sexual harassment, were recognized as unfair and objected to by the women themselves. Others issues were identified by me, such as space allocation, regulation, control of dress and task segregation. Although I felt strongly about these issues, most of the women I talked to did not consider them as significant. This difference between my perception of gender-based discrimination and those of my interviewees is yet another example in support of one of the main arguments running throughout thisbook: prioritizing or contesting different parts of one's social reality is partly based on one's specific socioeconomic location and daily realities.

My interviews with workshop managers and my oral histories with older women in the community confirmed that female wage work has been increasing over the past five to ten years. A state of poverty and inflation, *il ghila*, on the one hand, and attempts by workshop owners to lower production costs, on the other, were the main reasons given for this increase. One workshop owner explains:

It is poverty that makes girls work in workshops, If a family is not in need why would they let her daughter work? People are squeezed, *mat-huuna*, and tired, *ta⁼baana*, it is not like before.

By emphasizing that women are working due to economic necessity, workshop owners, however, are simultaneously reinforcing gendered differences by confirming that women's work signals distress and is a sign not of progress, but of community deterioration and decay. In a context where masculinity and male worth are so closely linked to being providers, one way to maintain and reproduce gender hierarchies in a situation where men are less able to provide for their families is to reproduce such ideals. One workshop owner comments:

> Workshop work is no good. Would any girl opt to be known as *bint il wirash*, unless she has no choice. The fact that more girls are in workshops now is a sign of deterioration, *tadahwur*, not progress, *tattawur*.

The links between waged work and poverty, as well as its low status are also captured by Layla's shocked response to my question as to whether she has ever worked before she got married and had her two children. Looking offended, Layla whose father is a relatively well-off, *mabsuut*, wholesale fruit merchant says:

> Shame on you. Work? What work? You think I am one of those girls of the workshops! Of course I have never worked outside the house, ever. My father never made me want for anything, and when he died, my brothers continued to provide for us. They brought us a full marriage trousseau and married us off ...".
>
> Then, realizing that I myself work as I had told her about my previous work experience, she added: "Of course work is not bad. If one works like you with a degree and in a respectable place, that is fine. But if an uneducated woman works, (Layla left school when she was twelve), her eyes are opened to a lot of things and she becomes bold, *gariʾa*. If a woman is bold but ignorant, not educated, she becomes bad, *wihsha*, and can do wrong/improper things, *hagaat ghalat*. (She was referring to sexual behaviour in this context). No, thank God, we are not like other families. My father and brothers always provided for us and never made us in need of work.

A context of poverty, male underemployment and unemployment, and a rise in female-supported households provides the general framework for understanding the increase in female waged employment in this community. Within this context, the specific reasons that the working women themselves gave for working varied. An overwhelming number, however, cited preparations for marriage, in particular contributing to the costs of the trousseau, *gihaaz*, as the main reason. As discussed in the previous chapter, the *gihaaz*, and the related inventory of furniture and appliances, the *ayma*, play a critical role in enabling women to improve their status and that of their families, to increase their marriage options, and to gain leverage vis-à-vis their husbands and mothers-in-law.

Samah is a pretty seventeen-year-old who works in a carpentry workshop assembling washing pegs and furniture. Her parents got divorced when she was nine years old and since then both she and her mother have been working. Samah revealed her reasons for working, and her expectations of how working before

marriage may enable her to make a "better" marriage, meaning marriage to someone able to provide for her. She was aware that many married women, including
her mother who is a divorcee, are working to make ends meet, many of them as
pieceworkers, and she did not want to end up like that.

> I have been working in the same workshop for the past eight years. Even when I went
> to school I used to work during the vacations. I left school in 1st prep, when I was
> eleven years old, because we could no longer afford to pay for private lessons,[18] and I
> have been working full time here ever since, from 10 a.m. to 9 p.m. every day. I am
> paid by my production rate. In a bad week I make twenty pounds (less than three
> pounds sterling), and in a good week I can make thirty pounds (five pounds sterling).
> I usually give fifteen pounds or so a month to my mother to help with household
> expenses. The rest of the money I put in several saving societies, *gam^c iyya*(s),[19] so I can
> save for my marriage trousseau, *gihaaz* ... This is the main reason I am working. So far
> I have bought some of the "light" things, my set of "melamine"(plastic like set of cups
> and plates), and aluminium (washing basins, pots and pans), glasses and some sheets.
> But there are still other things like the refrigerator and gas oven that I want to buy. ...
> Once my *gihaaz* is completed, I will stop working. I do not want to continue working
> after I get married. I want to relax/rest. ... I hope that I will find a husband who will
> provide for me, appreciate me, *yi^Dadarni*, and compensate for the hard times I have
> seen, *yi^c awadni*. She then adds bitterly: "is it not enough that I have worked as a girl,
> will I also have to work when I get married? "

Aziza, a twenty-year-old who works in an electronics workshop echoed the
same sentiments.

> I used to work in a clothes workshop in another community, but I quit because I was
> harassed on the bus. Men used to come and stand very close to my back and I would
> hate that feeling, but could not say anything. I thus moved to this workshop which is
> near my house. I make about twenty pounds a week, which is less than I used to make
> at the other workshop, but at least I am not bothered in transportation. I give my
> mother five pounds to help with our expenses at home, and the rest goes into two
> *gam^c iyya*(s), one of which I am organizing. I am saving for my *gihaaz*. I bought many
> things and I will stop when I finish buying what I need and get married. It was my
> decision to work. But it is enough, I want to relax, *astirayyah*.

Aziza's comments also illustrate a more general finding that adolescent wage
laborers, particularly older ones, have some control over their income, and also
often make the decision to work themselves. Like Samah and others, some of
Aziza's wages go to her mother (it is predominantly the mother who has access to
the girl's wages, not the father, even when it is not a female-headed household).
Aziza manages, however, to keep about half of it to herself, to spend according to
her own priorities.[20]

Other reasons that women mentioned for working were paying for the education of a younger sister or brother, helping out with household expenses or pay-

ing the costs of a major medical operation. In most cases, however, unlike piece-workers who saw themselves engaged in these tasks indefinitely as a way to make ends meet, *banaat el wirash* were more goal-oriented and saw their jobs as terminating once they reached their goal. As mentioned earlier, the goal in most cases is preparing a marriage trousseau. Like Samah and Aziza, most of the girls I interviewed did not want to work after they got married.[21] There were very few exceptions. Nasra, a bubbly nineteen-year-old who works in a workshop that makes soap is one of them. Although she is also working primarily to complete her trousseau, she stressed that she enjoys her work and would continue working after marriage if her husband allowed it.

> I like my work. It makes me feel as if I am worthy and doing something meaning-ful, *liyya'iima.* I feel that I am alive when I go to work and talk to people. I want to keep working after I marry. Work is not shameful even if a woman is rich, *mabsuuta* and her husband provides for her, *mikafiiha.* (Nasra then quoted a popular Arabic rural proverb;) If you are poor work to help yourself, if your are rich work to get more gold (an investment for the future), *Ya fa'iira rudiih ͨala halik, ya ghaniyya ta'ili biih khulkhaalik.*

The previous section illustrated the role of gender in structuring the terms and conditions of waged labor and highlighted some of the areas around which women expressed their discontent. It also illustrated the contradictions and inter-relations between work and marriage choices. Female wage labor emerges as a low-status, disreputable job that could risk a girl's reputation (and that of her fam-ily) and affect her marriageability, a universal goal for women in the community and a critical component of their definition of womanhood. At the same time, the accumulation of a large *gihaaz,* one of the main reasons *banaat el wirash* work, also increases a girl's marriageability, and increases both her and her status and that of her family. One of the main problems that *banaat el wirash* have to con-tinuously confront is gossip in the community, *kalaam il naas.* When someone proposes to a wage laborer, there is a lot of talk, and her reputation may be ques-tioned. What is similarly being questioned, of course, is the economic standing of her family. Om Sanaa talks disdainfully about her son's plan to propose to a girl who works with him in a metal workshop:

> Can you believe it! He wants to get us one of those girls who grew up in workshops and who do not know right from wrong. These girls have poor manners, and who knows what they do with men all day long in the workshops. He can do as he pleases, but I warned him, she will not make him comfortable, *mish hatrayyahu.* He will not be able to control her, *yihkumha* (meaning both sexually and otherwise).

Given this common perception of wage work, how do women manage the risks involved, given that many have to work in order to acquire a *gihaaz*? How do women manage the risks of acquiring a poor reputation both for themselves and their families in a context where reputation is a critical resource for survival? How do they attempt to ward off the hazardous possibility of not being considered "marriageable" in a context where marriage is an unquestioned central part of identity? What options do women have for carving a space for themselves to work as wage laborers while at the same time ensuring their respectability? Given women's awareness of some of the unfavorable aspects of wage work, are they able to challenge employment terms and conditions, or are they, like pieceworkers, so constrained by the workings of gender and kinship ideologies that they are unable to protest?

My fieldwork suggests that due to a complex combination of socioeconomic, and personal factors, *banaat el wirash* are generally able to, and often do, contest some aspects of their situation or attempt to expand their options. The previous discussion illustrated some of these "moments" of defiance, such as temporarily covering one's hair or stabbing an intruder with a knife. The discussion that follows elucidates two further practices which in different ways, and at this specific point in time, act to mitigate the perils to reputation that waged work entails, or to challenge some of its perceived injustices. These are: public defloration ceremonies, *laf bil sharaf*, which literally means public display of a girl's honor, as well as the related hymen replacement operations; and a form of female rebellion, termed *namrada* by workshop owners, which connotes unjustified revolt, and is often of a collective nature. I discuss each in turn.

Managing the Risks of Wage Labor: "Strategic Trade-offs"

Defloration, or deflowering, refers to the process of rupturing the hymen of a virgin through intercourse. Because of the importance of virginity in Egyptian culture, it is customary, particularly among rural Egyptians, to deflower brides manually rather than through regular intercourse. This ritual, reportedly much less prevalent in urban areas, is performed by either the husband himself, or a traditional midwife, *a daaya*. There is practically no published research on this topic. Khattab's study of women's perceptions of sexuality, based on a sample of forty-two women in two villages in lower Egypt, provides one of the few studies which discusses this ritual (Khattab 1996). She describes the process as follows:

> The hymen is torn by inserting the forefinger enfolded in a white handkerchief into the outer vagina of the bride pushing hard until the hymen is ripped off and the blood oozes out on a handkerchief ... Guests wait quietly outside the house until one of the women assisting in the deflowering comes out with the handkerchief soaked with the blood evoked by tearing the hymen. Once the handkerchief is shown, cries of joy, *zaghariit*, are heard everywhere and the singing and dancing of female friends and relatives starts. (Khattab 1996:32)

What is the relevance of this practice in Cairo and how is it linked to women's work in the informal sector which is the concern of this section? This link was initially far from an obvious one. I only started perceiving a possible connection after I was invited to attend the deflowering ceremony of Samira, and started discussing this practice, its meaning and temporal development, with her and with other women in the community. Samira, who has been involved in wage work since she was thirteen, is a 23-year-old woman born in upper Egypt but raised in Cairo, with whom I became very close.

I was invited as an "honored guest" to attend Samira's defloration, which was carried out by her husband himself, not by a *daaya*. However, a *daaya*, Samira's mother, mother-in-law, a maternal aunt and I were also present in the room. Samira's intense fear and embarrassment showed on her heavily made up face, but she lay down submissively on the gilded bed without uttering a word. Her mother helped push the rented white wedding gown up to her knees and took her underpants off. The *daaya* and her mother-in-law then each held a leg and spread them apart, and her husband wrapped a white handkerchief around his forefinger and approached her.

I was standing in a corner at one end of the room, and turned around so as not to face them. I heard Samira screaming, then her mother-in-law shouting to her son: "push harder, and a little lower." More screams from Samira, and then quiet sobs. After what seemed like an eternity, but was actually only a few minutes, the *daaya* then shoved us all out of the room, except for Samira and her mother. Samira's husband and mother-in-law, faces beaming and holding the *mahaarim* (the white handkerchief soaked with fresh blood), came out of the room along with me, feeling quite sick to my stomach, to a crowd of people, mainly women, who started crying with joy. The crowd of over thirty people then left the house, one of them holding the *mahaarim* up high. They were joined by others, including more men, as they started walking in a procession through the streets beating drums and crying cries of joy, *zaghariit*. In a daze, I slowly walked back to my car which was parked at the entrance of the community.

I went to visit Samira a week later and found her with her mother, grandmother, and a number of other female relatives of different age groups. I initiated a conversation on defloration practices, asking how Samira was feeling. A lively discussion ensued. Although I had discussed defloration with women before, it was only through this encounter that I began to glimpse how public defloration may act to provide unmarried women with more choice in deciding to work in specific jobs. Samira admitted that it was a very painful and unpleasant experience, but was emphatic about its importance, even though her husband did not insist on it.

> I have been working for years, staying out till late and I do not want anyone to *yiᶜaayirny*, belittle/humiliate me. My work was important to me and I learned a lot about the market and made good money, but I have to prove to everyone that I am a respectable woman. .... Going around with my *sharaf* improves my family's reputation and affirms their honor and status, *shuhra lil ahl*. I know that Cairenes, *il masarwa*, do not do this like us, but people in this community do not all know each

other and there is a lot of gossip, so people need to know a good, *kiwayyisa* girl from a bad, *wihsha*, one. ... This is the price, *taman*, for my ability to work all these years before I got married.

I was quite struck by Samira's interpretation and the bluntness of her argument. I pursued this lead about perceiving public defloration as a price for waged work as I continued to acquire more information about defloration practices and experiences. Women often used less blunt and explicit terms than Samira, but I found that her interpretation, which seemed to imply the concept of a trade-off, found resonance and was echoed in different ways by many of the women I interviewed.

Defloration practices in the study community are defined as either *dukhla baladi*, inaccurately translated as traditional defloration, or *dukhla afrangi*, Western or foreign defloration.[22] The main difference between them is whether or not someone other than the bride and groom is present in the room when the deflowering takes place, and the manner of defloration, manually or through intercourse. In the baladi style, a *daaya* or female relatives are present, and one of them or the husband deflowers the bride manually. Both ceremonies, however, are usually followed by a festive, public ceremony to show off the honor, known as *laf bil sharaf.*

According to my oral histories, the public ceremonies to display the "honor" of a bride take on a much more elaborate and public form in Cairo than used to be the case in rural areas. This more elaborate form, however, appears to have become entrenched in the community as a new "tradition," *ᶜurf.* Such "re-invention" of tradition can possibly be conceptualized as a form of urban adaptation by rural migrants to the anonymity and changing conditions in urban areas which, among other things, requires single girls to work in waged work alongside unrelated males. In rural upper Egypt, the origin of the majority of my respondents, girls do not normally go out after puberty and it is known who belongs to which family, so there is less concern for public affirmation of honor, beyond the two immediate extended families.

The comparisons women provided between defloration practices in rural and urban areas, based on their own personal experiences, lends strength to this argument. Samira's grandmother recalls her own experience of defloration, which was a *baladi* one, but did not involve public display beyond the household.

El laf bil sharafᶜeeb fil Saᶜiid, public display of honor is shameful in upper Egypt. People know and trust each other and exaggerating the ceremony and importance of a *dukhla* means lack of trust. Also, this public display can cast a spell on the bride, *tishahirha.*[23] You see, if an infertile woman sees the *sharaf* of another woman, she can get pregnant, but at the same time she casts a spell on the woman whose *sharaf* was public and makes her infertile. This happened to one of our neighbors, *itkabasit fi dukhlit-ha*, who became infertile on her wedding night, and now will have to see the *sharaf* of another woman in order to become pregnant.

Om Mohammed, a relative of Samira who is in her fifties, reiterated this reasoning and emphasized how the *laf bil sharaf* has become much more elaborate since they migrated to Cairo.

> There was no *daaya* in my *dukhla* in Upper Egypt. It was just he and I, and then he went and showed the *sharaf* to our families. But when my daughter Magda got married, it was different. There were drums and people walked with her *sharaf* until dawn. Her brother even took a picture holding the *sharaf* (referring to the blood-stained handkerchief), which I still keep. Magda used to work in workshops outside this community. We have to cut people's tongues (stop gossip), *niksar kalaam il naas*.

Om Mohamed then told me about a woman who worked with her for six years in paper recycling workshops and who had gotten married recently. She was thirty-years old and still *bint binuut*, a virgin, when she left work to get married. Her family had a big *dukhla baladi* with a public ceremony and they took her *sharaf* and made a big celebration, *zaffa* in the community. A woman's *sharaf* is good, *hilw*, explained Om Mohamed. In response to my question as to whether this was in any way considered an unfair practice by community women or as humiliating to the bride, Om Ahmed replied:

> The most important thing is for a woman to find an opportunity to work and make money. This girl, God bless her, when she got married, was able to get a full *gihaaz* and four gold bracelets and a refrigerator. Her husband also got her two bracelets and the bedroom, but she got everything else for herself from her work. She will be like a queen in her house now.

Om Ahmed evaded a direct response to my question, but her comments are revealing as to what she considers as priorities for a woman, namely having a large *gihaaz* which plays an important role in increasing one's command in marriage as well as one's status and respect in the community. Because this can sometimes only be achieved through working, expanding one's options for respectable employment prior to marriage is thus critical. The status of families in the community and their honor is clearly negotiated and displayed by both a girl's virginity, but just as importantly, by the size of her *gihaaz*. Once again, the notion of a trade-off between these two status-conferring practices seems to be implied in Om Ahmed's comments.

Generally the type of ceremony is based on what the bride and her family want. The bride's family usually insists on an elaborate *dukhla baladi* with *laf*, if the bride has a history of working as a wage laborer, even if the groom does not want one. Attiyat, a forty-year-old woman who distributes shoes on a subcontracting basis to women told me that she was married in rural lower Egypt and a *daaya* deflowered her, but the *sharaf* was taken outside the bedroom and shown only to members of the two families, who were waiting outside the door. There was no public procession. Her younger sister, who was employed in workshops from the time they moved to Cairo, was also married last year in the village. They did not go around with her *sharaf* in the village but brought the *mahaarim* back to the neighborhood in Cairo where her sister lives and roamed the streets with it. Attiyat emphasized the extent to which workshop girls are criminalized by community standards:

> It is in Cairo, in the community where my sister grew up, worked and will continue to live that we must prove that she is innocent. It is exactly like a criminal who has to prove that he is innocent. The *dukhla baladi* and public ceremonies, preserve/protect a girl, *bitihfaz il bint*. If someone talks about her you can put your finger in her/his eye.

There are suspicions in the community, however, about the genuine nature of the results of the process of defloration. To remove any doubt, some women thus insist that the door be kept open when being deflowered. Om Sabah, who used to work in a workshop assembling boxes comments:

> My defloration was very painful, it was as if someone pierced my eye … But I am the one who insisted. We do not think this is against women's rights and things like that.[24] I am proud that I had it done this way and that I kept the door open. You see, we hear of people who do it *afrangi* and then they display blood that is not really the blood, you know pigeon blood and things like that … So keeping the door open is more proof, and is even more honorable for the family, *tisharaf wi titawil raᵓbit il ahl*. I also had a Christian woman in the room with me, she is a neighbor, so no one can say she is a direct relative and will cover up. My mother wrapped the *sharaf* around her head and went dancing in the streets with it.

It is worth mentioning at this point that religious discourse, largely articulated by men in the community, and which plays an increasingly important role in Egyptian culture, does not endorse the practice of *dukhla baladi* and the public display of *sharaf*. In fact, the *dukhla afrangi* was sometimes termed *dukhla Sunni*, meaning religiously sanctioned. The insistence of many women on performing an elaborate *dukhla baladi* must thus be appreciated as a palliative against possible family dishonor even though they know it is being increasingly condemned by religious authorities in the community, which many both fear and respect. The continuation of public defloration in this context shows how economic realities may override religious sanctions. It also illustrates how women can create, or undermine family honor and status not just through their sexual behaviour, which has been the main focus in studies of the Middle East, but also through material practices such as the *gihaaz*.

Om Sanna explains how she insisted that her working daughter undergoes a *dukhla baladi* with *laf* last year although her own experience in the village was different, and despite the disapproval of her son-in-law.

> In my case in the village, the man (read her husband) took my ᶜard (read deflowered her) himself and there was a pot of water to wash his hands in and that was that. No

laf. But my daughter's wedding night was different. I insisted that a *daaya* go in with them and that we go around with the *sharaf* in the streets … . My daughter worked in a sock factory for many years … We were able to provide her with a valuable/proper *gihaaz moᶜtabar*, but we have to cut people's tongues … My son-in-law is religious, he belongs to a *tariᴾa*, a Sufi order, and was very angry and said that this is not right and is against Islam. He even got me a sheikh to the house to convince me. But I insisted. This way she brought us honor, *tawwilit raᴾbitna*, with both her large *gihaaz* and her *sharaf* (i.e. public display of her virginity).

Om Ahmed, a 45-year-old widowed Cairene who works in the same sock factory as Om Sanna's daughter, is one of the few women in my sample who had a *dukhla afrangi* with no *laf.* Om Ahmed started working only eight years ago, several years before her husband passed away, to help pay for the education of her children. She had attended Om Sanna's daughter's wedding, and witnessed her public defloration ceremony. Her comments highlight the significance of regional origin, the possible role of defloration as a specific form of urban adaptation by recent rural migrants, and the relationship between Islamic sanctions and defloration.

Some women in Cairo now have a *dukhla afrangi*[25], even if they work before marriage. It is only the *Saᶜayda* who live in Cairo that still have the *dukhla baladi* because they are not used to women going out. … If they have worked in workshops, this is of course worse … But they now say the *dukhla baladi* is *haraam,* religiously forbidden. My brother-in-law lived in Saudi Arabia for seven years and he told us that it is religiously forbidden because it is *haraam* for anyone, even another woman to see any part of a woman above her knees.

To guarantee the smooth operation of the public rituals of defloration, however, mechanisms are in place to ensure that women who may not be virgins are protected in the process. Hymen replacement surgery, known as *tarᴾiᶜ* (literally patching), offers one such mechanism. Hymen replacement emerges as a largely urban phenomenon that is catering to the re-enforcement and entrenchment of public defloration rituals as an important "tradition" largely among recent migrants to the city. None of the older women recalled that this type of operation existed in their villages, although other forms of "cheating" were known to exist. Interviewees, however, were quick to tell me that they knew of several women in their community who underwent this operation. They generally made excuses for them and did not consider them as prostitutes, or necessarily disreputable. They had only made a "mistake," *ghalta.* What appeared important is not that they were not virgins, but that this fact, this *ghalta,* was not publicly recognized.

They make operations here to repair the hymen, *tarᴾiᶜ*, all the time. We hear and see a lot … If a doctor is clever, the *daaya* will not find out; but if he is not, it can be easily detected. In the village, there are none of these operations. If they hear a girl is like that they bury her alive.. Dr. Samir's nurse just told us about a woman who had the operation last week. She is getting married next month, and no one will find out.

I was directed to Dr. Samir, who performs these operations in one of the four neighborhoods I visited, but I was unable to identify, and thus interview, any of the women who actually underwent the operation. The following discussion is thus mainly based on my interviews with Dr. Samir and his nurse, Amina. My entry point to Dr. Samir's surgery was through his nurse, who one of my interviewees knew well. We first met in Amina's house for an informal chat, and then later met her at the clinic where we also had a quick discussion with the doctor. Because of the personal introduction, they were both quite open and frank with me, despite the obviously culturally illicit nature of their activities.

Dr. Samir, a general practitioner, has been operating a polyclinic in this neighborhood since 1985. He personally performs both abortions and hymen-replacement surgeries. The costs of hymen-replacement operations vary depending on their nature. The simplest one, which is performed on women who are getting married within a week or so, costs about two hundred Egyptian pounds. The more complicated one that can last for months costs about five hundred Egyptian pounds. Dr. Samir emphasized, however, that both were medically simple operations that take no more than half an hour. Women are given a mild form of general anesthesia and operated on in the clinic. They leave after a few hours. Last week, two operations were performed, one on a woman from outside the neighborhood.

Amina, born and bred in this particular neighborhood, provides Dr. Samir with access to the women who need the surgery. People trust her and she is known to be discreet. Amina sees herself as providing a service to women, who may have made a mistake, *ghalta*, or may have been drawn into a premarital relationship because they were naive and did not know any better.

> I am providing a service for women so that they are not found out and scandalized, *yit-fidhu*, on their wedding night, if anything is wrong. I do not ask any questions. It is not our business. The public *dukhla* is a big festival, *mahragaan*, in this community.[26]

One of the central questions that emerges from the previous discussion is why it is that the *dukhla baladi* remains so entrenched even though it is well known that female virginity can be faked. I argue that part of the reason is that the rhetoric and rituals of proving virginity are themselves gendering processes which reinforce the separateness and differentiation between men and women, publicly affirming male superiority and their authority and command over women. In the context of the study community, where men's masculinity is clearly threatened due to economic deprivation, as discussed earlier, the entrenchment of these rituals may thus also serve as "compensatory mechanisms" which reinforce gender hierarchies and male dominance.

What I have been suggesting so far is that women's insistence on an elaborate public defloration ceremony, despite its trauma, may be possibly interpreted as a trade-off, which enables some women to have greater mobility, more lucrative employment, and an ability to generate an income to purchase a significant *gihaaz*.

The *gihaaz*, in turn, and as discussed in the previous chapter, is an essential component of women's ability to negotiate in their future marriages, and to increase the status of their families. Clearly, I am not arguing for a direct or mechanical link between the presence of the *laf* in defloration, whether *afrangi* or *baladi*, and waged work. The situation is more complicated and there are many variables involved. Public defloration ceremonies are practices with multiple meanings, meanings which may evolve through time, and may be interpreted and appropriated in various ways by different women and men, based on individual, familial or regional variations.

For example, as discussed earlier, women (although only three, all of whom were originally from Cairo) did not practice this ritual even though they were employed by workshops prior to marriage. Moreover, waged work is by no means the only context in which public defloration ceremonies were considered desirable. My research shows that it was practised by other women who may not have worked as wage laborers, but who for various reasons were perceived to be exposed to possible perils which could compromise their reputation. Specifically, there were two other contexts where public ceremonies were deemed necessary. The first was in cases where a bride's father had been away for a long time and a girl had been brought up by her mother, without the continuous guardianship or control of a man. The second is when an engagement had been extended for several years, during which the groom has been known to frequently visit a bride and spend time alone with her.

While recognizing the multiple meanings and contexts of public defloration rituals, I suggest, nonetheless, that one possible and plausible interpretation of public defloration ceremonies is that they act as a type of what I have termed "strategic trade-off." As a trade-off, public defloration ceremonies allow women to pursue their choice to engage in wage work in order to achieve a certain material goal and yet affirm their respectability, honor and reputation, by submitting to certain practices that they may otherwise find traumatic or painful. Not only did I detect a discernible pattern suggestive of this link, but, perhaps more significantly, many women themselves explicitly articulated a perceived connection between wage work and this type of defloration. Women who did not engage in wage work before marriage definitely had more choice as to what type of *dukhla* they would have, whereas for those who did work, an elaborate public defloration ceremony was almost always a necessity. The main point to stress here is that for a certain group of women in Cairo, this was one way to create some areas of latitude to accommodate the contradictory demands of respectability on the one hand and more leverage in their marriages on the other, through the accumulation of a "proper" *gihaaz*.

It is possible to venture that the gendering practice of public defloration gains a specific meaning as the price women must pay to work in informal sector workshops. It acts as a culturally endorsed, and class-specific signifier of family "respectability," while addressing women's need to earn an income in the context of increasing economic pressures. In her study of the new veil among more middle class women in Cairo, Macleod (1992a; 1992b) suggests that the women she interviewed resorted to "traditional" signifiers, such as wearing the veil, to demonstrate their worthiness while allowing them to work, a process she terms "accommodating protest." The elaborate public rituals of displaying a bride's *sharaf* amongst the women I interviewed may not mean the same thing, and unlike veiling, it was challenged to some extent by conservative Islamic voices in the study community. It is nonetheless interesting to contemplate possible parallels between the two practices as responses, at this historical juncture, to the societal restrictions on women in a context where the material basis of male dominance is disintegrating, and where women's wages are becoming increasingly necessary for the survival of households.

While women engaged in wage labor may resort to a practice such as public defloration ceremonies as a means to work while maintaining their reputation (and that of their family), this tells us little about whether, and how, they are able to challenge the unfavorable working conditions in workshops. My data illustrates that workshop girls are often vocal about their concerns, and many take concrete steps to negotiate better terms, often in a collective manner. In what follows, I discuss one form of female protest, which is termed "*namrada*" by workshop owners, and which I came across in my research.

Overt Protest: *Namrada*

Namrada (which literally means rebellion or revolt, but also connotes unjustified, ungrateful behaviour), is the term used by several workshop managers to describe forms of female protest. It is clearly a gender-specific term. Men did not *yitnamradu*, they were considered more loyal to the workshops than women. Workshop owners often complained that women were ungrateful and had a higher rate of turnover than men. The areas of most vocal protest revolve around wage levels. Women overtly, and often collectively, articulate their desire for higher wages to the workshop owner. If he does not respond, a common strategy is to quit work in groups of two or three, without giving notice, so as to cause maximum disruption. This was contrasted with men's behavior, who even if dissatisfied, rarely quit en masse. A workshop manager recounts how three of his "best" women, whom he had trained for three years, quit without notice last week; Half jokingly he says "I had a coup d'etat, *inqilaab*, in my workshop last week." Then more seriously he adds: " One of the girls wanted a higher pay, *itnamradit*. I refused because I feel I am fair to her and what I am giving her is more than enough. She left last week, and was able to take with her two other girls. They were two of the best ones, whom I had trained for years, but they also *itnamradu*.

I later identified one of the girls and found that the three of them had moved to another workshop at the end of the same street where they had managed to negotiate slightly higher pay.

Samah, Aziza and Mervat, neighbors, have been working in a workshop manufacturing toys for three years after they left primary school, mainly to save for

161

their *gihaaz*. They voiced their dissatisfaction with pay levels, their decision to leave collectively, and their ability to negotiate for better terms:

> The owner used to delay payments, and sometimes reduce our weekly pay for no reason, *kan biyakulna fil abd*. He had also not given us a raise for three years. We were still paid fifteen piasters for each piece we finish, while other workshops give twenty and twenty-five piasters per piece. We asked for a raise, but he refused. So we agreed amongst ourselves not to go back after the feast holiday. We went to another workshop, but the people were rude and the *usta* used to insult us. We stayed there two months, and in the meantime, the owner of the old workshop convinced us to go back and promised to increase our pay. We agreed and we now take twenty piasters per piece.

Nehmedou, nineteen years old and her sixteen-year-old sister, both working in an electronics workshop (assembling recycled earphones), echoed this theme of female solidarity in their negotiations, highlighting the trade-off they made between sexual harassment and wage levels:

> My sister and I worked there for only two months. We were paid well, (thirty-five pounds a week, six pounds sterling) even after we took out the daily transportation expenses. But then we started hearing the men in the workshop making dirty jokes and giving us dirty looks, and did not feel comfortable. We both complained to the manager, but he said they are like your brothers, you are not to worry. Then one day, one of them asked me to go out with him, I told my sister this is it, we must leave the workshop, and we convinced another girl with whom we became friends there to leave with us. During the week, we went around to other workshops, this time in our own community, and the owner of an elastic-making workshop said he would hire us next week, the three of us. We stayed in the electronics workshop till the end of the week, took our pay and left without saying anything ... The pay is less here, but at least we do not get hassled, *mahadish biydayP'na*.

Several interrelated factors can explain why wage workers are more able and willing than pieceworkers to take concrete action to improve their working conditions. One reason is related to the low-status of wage work, which means that *banaat el wirash* have already broken a community norm, and so have become both bolder, but also less willing to settle for a wage level that does not make this trade-off worthwhile. Because they regard work as a way of gaining more security later in life, particularly in marriage, wage workers are more goal-oriented, and are thus willing and able to maneuver and persist to ensure that they reach this goal.

Supply and demand factors in the labor market also pay an important role in this equation. Unlike pieceworkers, there is a much higher demand for female wage workers than existing supply which improves women's bargaining position. In fact, several of my interviewees emphasized that workshop owners now prefer women to men, because they are cheaper, less noisy, do not smoke and they clean up the workshop after they finish work.

Recruitment patterns and the role that kinship plays in this process is also significant. Although still operative, kinship idioms play a much less significant role in the labor relations underlying waged work. Because transactions are much more overtly financial, it is more difficult for either the women or their employers to "euphemize" such work as "charity" or "community solidarity," as is the case with piecework. Moreover, partly because of the danger of sexual harassment at work, and because of the low status associated with wage work, workshop girls often seek jobs in groups of two or three, and are almost never recruited individually. This creates a form of solidarity that does not exist among pieceworkers, who constitute a much more fragmented labor force, or among male wage laborers, who are less in need of the type of protection that group recruitment offers.

Moreover, unlike the girls who are mostly in dead-end jobs and can only make lateral moves, boys and men have a much greater chance of upward mobility in the skill hierarchy. Because of their anticipation of higher wages, status, and power as they move up the ladder, boys and men have a greater stake in the system and thus may be less willing to openly defy workshop owners. This dynamic resembles the cyclical nature of women's power in the family, discussed in chapter one, which also affects women's ability and willingness to contest unfavorable relations within the household as discussed in earlier chapters.

My findings also suggest that associating covert action with women and overt action with men, a common association in the literature, must be challenged. Hart (1991) argues along similar lines. Her study shows how poor women's protest in a village in Malaysia was more direct than that of the men who are co-opted and entrapped into patron-client relations, the advantages of which they did not want to forego. The women, on the other hand, being largely excluded from this system, had greater latitude for more open confrontation.

This chapter explored how women respond to the conditions and terms of work in the informal labor market focusing on two specific forms of employment: piecework and wage labor. The role played by economic factors, gender, life cycle, and kinship idioms in structuring terms of work, earnings, labor relations and negotiation options within these two forms was illustrated. The different ways in which gender was implicated with kinship (see Loizos and Papataxiarchis 1991a) in these two work contexts were highlighted. The chapter also contextualized more general statements about women's passivity in the face of exploitative working conditions by examining how and why different forms of female work may result in different responses. These ranged from accommodation and acquiescence, to implicit trade-offs and reinvention of "traditions," to direct and open protest.

Having examined women's experiences and options as related to premarital negotiations in chapter six and to employment in the informal sector in this chapter, the following two chapters will explore gender arrangements and relationships within the marital union. Chapter eight will address conjugal relations and sexuality, while chapter nine will address intrahousehold decision making and how these are influenced by women's extrahousehold networks.

NOTES

1. Om Muhammed's case illustrates how the practice of the *ayma*, discussed in the previous chapter, is not always successful in deterring a husband from acts such as being drunk or defaulting on his role as economic provider. Om Muhammad had written an *ayma* when she got married ten years ago, but she had sold many of its items over the years to meet household expenses. Her husband, a day laborer in the construction trade, has been out of a regular job for many years. Moreover, asking for a divorce was not really an option for Om Muhammad. Her parents live in one small rented room, and it would be impossible for her and her six children to move in with them should she get a divorce. The alternative, living on her own, would not only be unacceptable by community standards, but would also be economically unfeasible given the high cost of housing.

2. This Arabic proverb vividly illustrates the role of gender in defining work patterns. Its underlying meaning is that women can endure and tolerate more stressful or unfavorable conditions. In Egyptian culture, one's gall bladder is thought to be highly affected by stress, anger or sadness, and susceptible to rupture under such conditions. Having more than one gall bladder thus denotes that a woman is more resilient and can be more tolerant of boring, tedious and frustrating situations. If one of her gall bladders is ruptured as a result, she has plenty more.

3. Based on official statistics, women's labor force participation in the Egyptian economy is estimated at between ten and twelve percent. This figure, however, is believed to be a gross underestimate as it refers only to the formal labor market. When the range of activities in the informal labor market are included, estimates of women's labor force participation reach 70 percent (Nassar 1996).

4. A study in one of the neighborhoods, carried out in 1980, indicates that many of the small informal enterprises supply finished or partly-finished products to formal sector firms (see Landor 1994).

5. This is probably a conservative estimate as it does not take into account de facto women-headed households, that is households where a husband may be physically available but where, for a variety of reasons, women may nonetheless be the main or only family providers. This estimate also does not take into account the households were women have been deserted, but are not legally divorced. In-depth community studies reveal that households headed by women reach to 30 percent of all households in some urban areas (El-Kholy 1990; see EQI 1987; Fergany 1994b).

6. Elson provides a useful analysis of how the term flexible is used to refer to three dimensions of the economic system: (a) the organizational structure of firms, whereby large firms subcontract to other firms and separate their workforce into a "core" and a more temporary "periphery"; (b) labor-market flexibility, referring to changes in regulations, contracts, etc., which facilitates employers' ability to hire and fire; and (c) flexibility in the pattern of production through rendering the division of labor less rigid, a process often labeled flexible specialization (see Elson 1996).

7. Elson (1996) cautions against an automatic link between feminization and flexibilization. She argues, based on a review of international comparative statistics on female shares of employment in the textile and electronics industries, that flexibility does not necessarily lead to female substitution in traditionally male jobs, and that the gender division of labor is often overridden by "flexibility". My data supports this cautionary note, as it illustrates how substitution did take place, but only in some forms of subcontracting activities.

8. See Landor 1994 for a detailed description of nail workshops in 1980 in one of the neighborhoods where I carried out my research. What is striking to note in Landor's account is that the process of *talbiis shamaasi* was then apparently carried out by men in these workshops and was not subcontracted to women. A process of feminization of the task of *talbiis shamaasi* had obviously taken place within the span of a decade.

9. It is critical to note, however, that this dependence on female labor cannot be understood only by reference to women's gender attributes, but must also be related to an understanding of changes that are occurring in the male labor force. As discussed earlier, one of the reason women are being driven into subcontracting work is due to the increase in male unemployment.

10. I was told that there were only two workshops in the four communities that still produce hand-made shoes. The one I visited had only two older male craftsmen, who confirmed that the old form of producing shoes has practically disappeared.

11. Such comments about women's desire for flexibility brings to the fore the ongoing debate about whether flexible work is inevitably detrimental to women's work. Elson makes the important point that flexibility must not be judged on previous standards of regular employment, which were more relevant to men anyway, but in relation to "the erosion of workers' rights and their ability to organize in defense of those rights" (1996:42).

12. Spirit possession is discussed in chapter eight.

13. The norms that limit women's earning opportunities in the community are reinforced by a patriarchal state ideology of the family that regards men as economic providers and women as financially dependent on them. For example, pensions to women heading their households, such as widows and divorcees, many of whom are engaged in home-based piecework, are extremely low. The assumption is that even if a husband is physically absent, a woman will be provided for by her male relatives, an assumption reminiscent of that of women as secondary income earners which thus justifies their lower wages. Moreover, many women find it difficult to access available social welfare benefits because of the complicated and intimidating bureaucratic procedures required (see El-Kholy 1996b).

14. Many of the ideas of this section were developed in an earlier paper presented at the Regional Arab Conference on Population and Development, December, 1996. See El-Kholy (1996a).

15. For a discussion of child labor in Egypt, see Azer and El-Adawy (1994); Abdalla (1988).

16. Within this community and specific work context, workshop owners argued that married women pose a greater threat than unmarried virgins. Unlike unmarried women, they have already tried sex, so would be more easily tempted by the men in the workshops, who would themselves be also more daring in making a pass at them. Because married women do not face the same risks of being publicly found out it they have sex, as unmarried virgins would, they are thus assumed to be more daring and promiscuous. They have less "symbolic capital" to protect (see previous chapter).

17. Naema, a seventeen-year-old girl who I knew well and whom I accompanied to this workshop, wears her scarf only when she goes to work. The rest of the time both at home and in the community, she does not wear it. Naema regarded the scarf as a uniform that she had to don when she goes to work, it was part of the deal, and she had not consciously thought about it. Macleod suggests that this "new veiling" in Cairo may be a form of "accommodating protest,", and Hoodfar argues that veiling in Cairo can be seen as a private strategy to venture into the public sphere (see Macleod 1990).

18. The costs of education, particularly, as it relates to intrahousehold decision making will be discussed in chapter nine.

19. The role of *gam⁼iyya*(s) as a socioeconomic support network for women is discussed in chapter nine.

20. This type of individual income retention and control is counterintuitive in the Egyptian context given the strong suggestions about family incomepooling, which emerge from the limited number of intrahousehold studied in Egypt. This finding is similar, however, to suggestions from Java, Indonesia, where research on factory-working daughters shows that they control a sizable amount of their income, and that much of their wages do not go into general household expenses, but are invested in rotating saving associations through which substantial sums of capital are accumulated (see Wolf 1990).

21. This finding contrasts sharply with Ibrahim's study of factory workers in the early 1980s where she finds that single girls acquired a deep sense of self-identity through their jobs and were likely to continue work after they got married (B.Ibrahim 1985). This difference is possibly related to the different nature of work conditions, labor relations, and status of jobs in the formal and informal sectors.

22. There are many permeations of the actual practice, which makes an easy distinction between *dukhla baladi* and *dukhla afrangi* difficult. My observations and discussions suggest at least four variations: *dukhla baladi* with public ceremony, *dukhla afrangi* with public ceremony, *dukhla baladi* without public ceremony, and *dukhla afrangi* without public ceremony.

23. *Mushaahara* is a widespread indigenous belief involving the casting of a curse or spell which makes women infertile or which reduces the milk of lactating mothers. For more on this concept and its relationships to perceptions of health. See Sholkamy (1996).

24. The reference to women's rights is I suspect, due to this woman's perception of my views on the subject and her depiction of me as an urban "Westernized" woman who probably viewed this practice as barbaric and a violation of women's rights. I say perception, because although I personally felt quite shocked by the practice, I actually did not discuss my feelings.

25. The data does suggest that recent rural migrants from upper Egypt tended to be more emphatic about the importance of the *dukhla baladi* and the *laf* if a girl has worked before marriage, than those originally from Cairo. However, most of the latter in my sample had also had public defloration processions.

26. I did not ask the doctor why and how he chose this particular community in which to open his practice. I also wanted to find out more about the women who seek out his clinic and his perception of changes in numbers over time, but was unfortunately not able to carry out another interview with him or the nurse.

8
CONJUGAL ARRANGEMENTS AND SEXUALITY

"A man is like a butcher, he likes a healthy cow." Arabic Proverb

Om Samir is in terrible distress. Her only married daughter, Nasra, who fell sick six months ago, is now unable to move. Her left leg is paralyzed, and she suffers from a debilitating headache. She can no longer cook or clean, nor can she earn money as a pieceworker stringing beads any more. Although Nasra has been to many doctors as well as specialized religious healers who have attempted to cure her by reading verses of the Quran,[1] her ailments have not gone away. Neighbors have advised Om Samir to take Nasra to a *hadra,* a public spirit possession ceremony, in a nearby community to find out whether an alien spirit is the cause of her illness. Om Samir is worried that Nasra's husband may get fed up with her daughter and demand that she and her two children leave the house and go back to her parents' house.

Om Samir, a widow, lives in two rented rooms with her married son and daughter-in-law. She has no other family in Cairo, her brothers and one sister still live in a village in upper Egypt. Om Samir's son has made it clear that there is no place for his sister Nasra in the two rooms they are renting, should her husband divorce her. Although Nasra had an *ayma* when she got married, in this case it would not be of much use as a deterrent either against divorce, or taking on a second wife. Om Samir explained. For one thing, they have no strong family support or connections in this community, no ͨizwa. All her family is still in the village. Moreover, Nasra's husband, an electrician from Cairo, would fight to ensure that he keeps many of the things on the *ayma.* He would receive support from others in the community, even from Nasra's brother, because Nasra is no longer fulfilling her husband's needs, and she has not been doing so for a long time. Om Samir explains:

167

A tired or sick woman is of no use to her husband, *matilzamuush,* he could throw her out, *yirmiiha,* and marry another wife, for she can neither satisfy his sexual needs, *tiᵓdi hagtu,* nor his household needs, *haagit beetu,* so what is her use. You see, a man is like a butcher, he likes a healthy cow, *il raagil zay il gazzaar, yihib il bihiima il ᶜaffiya.*[2]

Chapter six illustrated how unmarried women enter into marriage with widely shared expectations of their conjugal roles, and aware of at least some of the unequal aspects of power relations underlying marriage arrangements. It highlighted how men and women's relationships to marriage are evolving, and analyzed some of the means through which women attempt to increase their marriage choices and mitigate their relative vulnerability in marriage through practices such as the *ayma* and the *gihaaz.*

The current chapter moves the discussion of gender relations to power relations and contestation within the marital union. It discusses the nature of marital conflicts, and highlights attempts by women to voice their discontent. Spirit possession is presented as one such avenue. An analysis of women's spirit possession narratives leads me to suggest that spirit possession represents a cultural idiom which gives women, particularly married ones, access to a discursive space in which they can express their daily grievances. Spirit possession also sometimes allows women to negotiate roles that are at variance with social expectations and prevalent gender ideologies, as well as to develop new notions of personhood that go beyond those based on kinship. The two—seemingly unrelated—sites of contestation that were vividly articulated through spirit possession narratives, are responses to sexual demands by their husbands, and responses to the "islamization of everyday life."

Beyond Public Gender Ideologies: Spirit Possession as a "Subordinate Discourse"

As suggested in the chapter on theory, contestation implies that disadvantaged groups have some awareness that they are not getting what they want or deserve. Furthering our understanding of women's perceptions of their roles and situations, and the extent to which they have internalized dominant ideologies that disadvantage them, is thus a critical first step in understanding women's varied responses to inequalities. As several writers have pointed out, women's compliance with certain practices and the ideologies they embody does not necessarily mean they have internalized them, but may be due to lack of perceived alternatives or to fear. In other words, "compliance" does not necessarily imply "complicity" (Agarwal 1994).

Efforts to understand women's perceptions must thus entail not only listening to their formal statements, but also to the specific idioms and colloquialisms expressed in their daily lives. As Comaroff and Comaroff argue, consciousness is embodied not only in the overt and explicit statements of "common predicament on the part of a social group, but also in the implicit language of symbolic activity." Researchers interested in understanding the perceptions of subordinate groups will thus have to go beyond "formal institutions and statements and into the textures of the everyday" (Comaroff and Comaroff 1987: 192).

Several studies have sought to go beyond androcentric public ideologies and have focused on the identities, "conceptual systems," and narratives of women, expressed through activities such as women's oral poetry, carpet weaving, and women's religious rituals (Abu-Lughod 1986; Dwyer 1978b; Messick 1987). In her study of domestic weaving in North Africa, Messick offers the notion of "subordinate discourse" as a way of tapping alternative views of the world that may be articulated by women in subtle, nonpublic ways. She uses the practice of carpet weaving, an old craft of nonelite African women, as an example of such a subordinate discourse which is "distinguished by its coexistence with the dominant ideology of gender relations, and by its nonpublic, silent quality" (1987: 211). Weaving represents an elaborated body of specialized female knowledge, men are excluded from craft processes, and as a mode of expression, it offers alternative gender conceptions to those articulated by the more public patriarchal ideology (Messick 1987).

My forays into the routines of women's everyday life in low-income Cairo, has brought spirit possession to my attention, suggesting that it might be an example also off such a "subordinate discourse." I became aware that spirit possession is not a marginal, "exotic" ceremony in which a limited number of women are engaged, but that it may articulate a fairly pervasive and entrenched system of values, beliefs and practices among women in the study community. A close analysis of the narratives of fifteen possessed women in my community (thirteen of whom were married), in the context of a wider analysis of their livelihoods, leads me to suggest that spirit possession serves as a "subordinate discourse," or a "hidden transcript"(Scott 1990).[3] It is an avenue through which women express discontent, as well as articulate an increased awareness of their conflicting roles within their marriages and society at large.

Being possessed by a spirit results in multiple disabilities for women, in the form of symptoms such as headaches, paralysis, and listlessness. Nonetheless, possession also allows women to get entitlements (money, presents, etc.) from men, and more significantly, gives them new "voices" and identities. These voices address, often in contradictory and ambiguous ways, issues of concern to women, which may be ignored or avoided by men. Taqqu and March argue, based on their review of cross-cultural studies on spirit possession, that women's pursuit of "spiritual patrons" is primarily a "defensive" strategy aimed at self-protection and relief from the constraints placed upon them. However, spirit possession also has elements of assertiveness as it enables women to affirm themselves through articulation of alternative perspectives and notions of selfhood (March and Taqqu 1986).

169

The two recurring themes voiced through the narratives of spirit possession of the women I interviewed were two issues of very different orders; sexual relations, and responses to the "islamization" of everyday life. These two issues form the basis of the discussion to follow. A brief overview of the history and rituals of spirit possession in Egypt may, however, first be in order.

Spirit possession in Egypt has always been a predominantly, although not solely, female phenomenon. Its exact origin is still open to speculation. The belief systems and rituals involved were probably introduced into upper-class Egypt by African slaves in the eighteenth and nineteenth centuries (Fakhouri 1968; Nelson 1971), and gradually diffused to the rest of society where they were incorporated into existing beliefs and practices. The increasing revival of Islamism in Egypt, on the one hand, and the dismissal and ridicule of spirit possession by government officials, the media and professionals on the other, makes women's public admission of possession to outsiders rare. Nonetheless, my research suggests that the incidence of spirit possession and the rituals related to it may be still quite pervasive.

The basic components of spirit possession and rituals as embodied particularly in the *zaar* cult, have been partially described elsewhere (Fakhouri 1968; Kennedy 1967; Nelson 1971; Morsy 1978). The description below is based largely on my observations as a participant in these ceremonies, expanding on the accounts provided by others.

A possessed woman is referred to as *milammisa,* touched, or ᶜ*aleeha riih, gin,* or *asyaad.* The spirits are both male and female and have distinct names, personalities, nationalities, and religions. Anyone can be possessed, but there are some personal qualities, like vanity, ᶜ*ayᵓa,* and certain actions, like throwing hot water down a toilet or going to bed crying, that may make one more vulnerable. These qualities and actions are associated almost exclusively with women, which is one of the main reasons women are believed to be more susceptible to spirit possession than men.

Possession is manifested through a range of general symptoms. The most common of these are debilitating headaches, fatigue, irritability, feelings of suffocation, paralysis and obsessions. The spirits, depending on who they are, make both material and nonmaterial demands on the afflicted person. Once afflicted, women believe it is practically impossible to exorcise the spirits; they can only be appeased or placated by giving in to their demands and by participation in special spirit appeasing ceremonies.

There are two types of ceremonies, a public one referred to as *hadra,* and a private one referred to as *zaar,* which is by invitation only. The private ceremony, commissioned by a possessed woman in her own home, seems to be on the decline because it is much more costly, and is being replaced instead by public *hadra*(s), which are open to anyone. Both are fully ritualized events, but the *zaar* is much more elaborate, and appears to be less common. While I attended fourteen *hadra*(s), I attended only one *zaar.*

A *hadra* ceremony is orchestrated by an influential specialized broker usually an older woman, called a *kudya*, and often takes place in her house. The public *hadra*(s) I attended were held on a weekly basis, either on Mondays or on Fridays. Some began after the noon call to prayer and others after the sunset call to prayer. There were usually between ten and forty women present at any one time, sitting on the floor, exchanging experiences and narratives of possession, gossiping and sometimes also smoking cigarettes and drinking tea. Most of the women came from different quarters in the city, other than the one in which the *hadra* was taking place.

A band of usually male musicians comprising drums, flute and tambourine-played the different songs/beats, *da??a,* associated with the different spirits. The beats ranged from sombre ones to very joyful and festive ones. Each woman, according to the spirit(s) possessing her, had a special beat at the beginning of which she got up and danced, *tifa??r,* often with some cajoling from the lead musician. As the rhythm of the music picked up, some women went into a trance, from which they were revived through assistance from one of the other women by light hugs and strokes on the leg or back. The main objective of the ritual is to appease and satisfy the spirits so that they do not cause the symptoms from which the possessed women are suffering.

Not all the women who were at the *hadra(s)* were possessed, however. I learned that some women actually go to these ceremonies in an attempt to find out if they are possessed, which they do discover if they find themselves unable to resist dancing to a certain *da??a;* this serves as an initial diagnostic procedure. Other women go out of curiosity, or to have fun, *farfasha.*[4]

Two general approaches have characterized the anthropological study of spirit possession. Although the two approaches are not mutually exclusive and both have linked possession to asymmetrical power relations, there are important differences between them, both theoretically and methodologically. The first and predominant one has adopted a functionalist approach, arguing that possession beliefs are a traditional means by which women, and other deprived groups, temporarily alleviate the pressures resulting from their subordinate status. According to this approach, possession provides a culturally sanctioned "niche" enabling women to step out of their prescribed roles without facing public censure. The underlying assumption is that possession serves therapeutic and cathartic goals (Gomm 1975; Kennedy 1967; Lewis 1966; Morsy 1978).

The second approach questions the potential of a functionalist framework in fully appreciating a complex and multifaceted phenomenon such as spirit possession. Although not discounting the former approach, some scholars have argued for moving the debate beyond the culturally sanctioned function of spirit possession rituals, emphasizing the need to pay closer attention to the subtle messages and views inherent in the narratives and episodes of possession themselves (Boddy 1989). This requires developing a highly intimate relationship with possessed women, so as to carefully record their possession narratives.

Boddy goes so far as to argue that possession can best be understood as a "feminist discourse". Possession enables certain groups of women to not only articulate discontent, but also to express unconventional views on often taboo subjects, and in the process of doing so, to challenge taken for granted gendered identities and roles (Boddy 1989).

The narratives I was able to collect corroborated some of the insights of the latter approach. Possession did enable some of the women I interviewed to make demands that allowed them to temporarily suspend their prescribed roles, as mothers, wives, homemakers, and sexual providers. However, my discussions convinced me that possession cannot be explained away only as a traditional "outlet" or "catharsis" for deprived and powerless groups. By reflecting, sharing and discussing the grievances embodied in possession narratives, possessed women and others who are the audiences for their narratives, were able to reflect on their identities and social expectations in a way that I did not witness in other gatherings and discussions among women. This often had direct practical consequences for the way in which they negotiated with their husbands over sexual demands or in the type of dress they adopted, as will be discussed below.

My data suggests that spirit possession provides a meaningful account of women's subordinate place in a world of rapid social change. It is a dynamic discourse, whose text is closely related to a changing context. It is thus difficult to understand the text, the possession narratives, without understanding the context that shapes the material relations and daily livelihood struggles of the women I talked to. As will be discussed below, the construction of the possession narratives is a complex and contradictory process. Broader socioeconomic and political concerns find their way into the changing imagery and character of the spirits. Like other cultural forms, spirit possession episodes and imagery acquire new meanings and address new experiences as social relations and social boundaries are redefined during periods of social change. Women interpret and incorporate new circumstances in the wider society into their possession beliefs and rituals (Nelson 1971; Ong 1987).

I pursue the argument here that spirit possession is a subordinate cultural text that gives voice to women and allows them to subtly express a range of thoughts about their lives in general, and gender relations in particular, that they may not otherwise be able to overtly articulate. During both the *hadra*, and at other times when the spirits are manifest, *zahir*, women are able to make suggestions, challenge role expectations and gendered identities, and express daily concerns which in an everyday context may be inadmissible. These messages and suggestions are often contradictory. However, it is the very multivalence and obscurity of the messages transmitted through this idiom that contributes to their strength. Nonpossessed women, who are important audiences in such settings, can ponder these issues and possibly pursue suggested trains of thought and act upon them.

Boddy's work on spirit possession, based on fieldwork in a village in the Sudan, is perhaps the best illustration of the "articulatory potential" of possession. She argues that signals and messages women pick up from their own possession and from observing the episodes of possession in other women defy, challenge and rework conventional meanings of gender relations, opening up provocative, albeit ambiguous and opaque, directions of thought. "Messages communicated by women to both male and female villagers via the *zaar* often have subversive tones as well as supportive ones. Gender appropriate meanings emerge when individuals read these messages in light of their own experiences." Boddy concludes that: "possession can thus amplify a woman's double consciousness to the point where she is able to see her life, her society, her gender, from an altered perspective and a heightened sense of awareness" (1989:5).

In the following section, I attempt to illustrate how possession may enable some low-income women in Cairo to comment on and negotiate normative expectations of gender roles. I do so by examining the recurring "messages" that emerged spontaneously from my interviews and discussions. My relationships with possessed women began via an introduction to two possessed women in a Cairo neighborhood by a female street vendor with whom I had built a strong relationship early on in my fieldwork. They were her neighbors, and it is with them that I initially participated in *hadra*(s). They then introduced me to other possessed women whom they knew, and I got to know some others from my frequent visits to the *hadra*(s).

The spontaneity of the messages that emerged through women's narratives is critical to note. Unlike my interviews with other women in the community, where I often initiated specific themes to guide the discussions, my encounters with possessed women were totally unstructured. I focused on listening closely to their possession episodes and experiences and I had no clue as to what might emerge. The predominant themes in these narratives, perceptions of sexual relations and responses to the "islamization" of daily life were so compelling, however, that I decided to pursue them in more depth with more women in my sample than I had originally planned.

Negotiating Sexual Relations

Sexuality is a critical component in the construction of gender relations in the study community. This is consistent with several other studies on gender relations in the Middle East. Al-Messiri (978) notes that men's ability to keep their wives sexually satisfied, through "frequent and lengthy intercourse," is an essential element of both men's and women's notions of masculinity in low-income, *baladi*, Cairo. Moreover, *bint El Balad*, the traditional low-income urban woman, is assumed to be very aware of herself as a sexual, feminine being. This self-image is said to be reflected in the seductive way she wraps her *milaaya laf* (a traditional loose cover, to be distinguished from the current *higaab* and *khimaar*) around her hips and in her coquettish walk.

Insights into the importance of sexuality in the construction of gender identities can also be gleaned from Rosen's (1978) study in the city of Sefrou, Morocco. His research revealed that men differentiated themselves from women on the basis of fundamental differences in sexual nature. Women are viewed by men as possessing much more *nifs*, the thoughts and attributes that people have in common with animals such as lust and passion, than ᶜ*aql*, reason, rationality. Rosen's male informants argued that women's excessive sexual desire is what makes them referred to locally as *habl il Shitaan*, the rope of Satan, and necessitates that men, whom nature has equipped with much more ᶜ*aql*, systematically control women. The Moroccan woman, described by one of Rosen's male informants, is "like a Turkish bath without water, because she is always hot and without a man she has no way to slake the fire" (1978: 567).

Interestingly, however, women's commentary on their sexual relationships, revealed through possession narratives, were not in line with some of the above descriptions. The afflicted women I interviewed expressed not excessive sexual desire, but a consistent lack of interest in sexual encounters, at least in the context of their marital relations. The main issue I want to pursue, however, is that the spirit possession narratives on sex and sexual relations are not about women's enjoyment of sex or otherwise. They are primarily about power, subordination and negotiation within the specific rules of the games of their conjugal relationship. Women's narratives seem to be about their ability to control the circumstances under which sex is demanded of them, and the power and right to refuse intercourse.

The following excerpts from the narratives of possessed women illustrate the opaque and ambiguous commentary of women on their sexual lives. Om Youssef is an illiterate woman who works as a pieceworker and is married to a construction worker who spent several years in Kuwait in the early 1980s. She has three children. The following excerpt from her story is revealing:

> I have not been sleeping in the same bed with my husband for the past ten years and we have not had sex for as long as that. There is nothing I can do about it. The spirits do not allow me. When he comes near me I start kicking and screaming. One day I bit him so hard he bled. At first my husband used to get angry and to hit me, but now he understands that it is not up to me, *il asyaad* do not want it. I know it is *haraam* to deny my husband sex, and I have been to many doctors and I even made a *zaar* every year for the past three years, but the spirits still do not allow me, it is out of my control. I personally do not mind it however, I never enjoyed sex with him, it was always a duty. Sometimes he also hurt me.

Amal is more recently married to a fruit vendor and has two toddlers, a boy and a six-month-old baby girl. Amal was employed by a workshop before she was married and now assists her husband in his job. Amal's story is very similar to Om Youssef's although they do not know each other and actually reside in different neighborhoods. Amal recalls:

Mokhles, the spirit, has been with me for three years, before I got married, but I did not know it then. He made me refuse all marriage proposals. I got married in the end because Mokhles succumbed and let me get married. My eldest brother (I am the only girl among three brothers) insisted that I marry and beat me up for refusing. Mokhles did not want to see me beaten up so in the end he agreed and I got married to my current husband. Since I got married, however, I have had terrible headaches. I also hate sleeping with my husband. When he approaches me, I start screaming and I feel as if someone is strangling me. Mokhles manifested himself to me at a friend's *zaar* that I attended six months ago. He manifested himself as a tall pink-skinned giant with dark black hair. He told me he was in love with me and explained that he makes sex unbearable with my husband because he is jealous. Now I sometimes see Mokhles sleeping beside me on the bed, I can feel his breath on my neck.[5]

Most of the women related their narratives about what the spirits did or said retrospectively. However, I also witnessed two, rather unsettling, occasions when the spirit became manifest during the interview itself,[6] and started talking to me, and other women, directly. One of these spirits is Abdalla, a spirit possessing Om Ayman, who became manifest during an interview with her in the presence of some members of her family, and two neighbors. Abdalla's manifestation was preceded by a dramatic scene where Om Ayman started choking, gesturing wildly with her hands, and crying hysterically. After she calmed down and was offered a glass of water, Abdalla began to speak to me through her, but in an altered, hoarse, and slightly foreign voice. He expressed hatred for Om Ayman's husband, a wholesale grocery vendor, and his excessive and improper sexual demands:

He is a bull, ^c*igl*, and I despise him. He is trying to sleep with me and is asking me to do dirty things, *hagaat wiskha*. I love Amal (Om Ayman) and I do not want her to sleep with him, so every time he tries to sleep with her, I get in the middle of the bed and separate them and kick him. So one day, he said fine, if Amal does not want to sleep with me, then you sleep with me. I am a man, like him, but he is not ashamed to ask me to do these things. He is a very bad man.

One of the issues that emerged from many of the narratives and the discussions around them, is the explicit link that was made between female sexual services and male economic provision. This link was later confirmed by other nonpossessed women in my sample and, as will be illustrated later, provides a key to understanding gender roles and relations in the community. Om Youssef, newly married woman to a wholesale grocer and suspected of being possessed, makes this link as follows:

I get pain, *batwiga*, when I sleep with my husband. I do not enjoy it, *mafiih inbisaat*. I just wait for it to end. I am cold, *barda*. Samar told me that she had a similar situation and that someone advised her to see her *atar*.[7] She discovered that she was possessed by Yawer Bey. He is a very snobbish man and he hurts her when she has sex with her husband because he does not like her husband. You see her husband is not a respectable man. He does not give her enough money to buy proper clothes or house-hold items, even though he makes a lot. Samar suggested that maybe I am also pos-sessed. Maybe the spirit is angry with my husband too. He also does not provide for me. I will go with her to a *hadra* this week to find out.

What messages can one derive from the above narratives? What do they tell us, and just as importantly tell other women, about how women in the study com-munity view their own sexuality, their sexual relations with their husbands, their role as sexual partners, and the extent to which they have control over their sex-ual lives, that is, when, with whom, and how to have sex? While the messages are not clear and can be interpreted differently by women, several suggestions can be teased out: women do not enjoy sex with their husbands, their husbands make "improper" sexual demands, women's sexual submission is conditional on men's ability to provide for them. The list could go on.

However, more nuanced answers to these questions are only possible through analyzing and understanding the broader context which shapes these women's lives. This is a context where refusing sex is considered a religious sin, *haraam*, as will be discussed below, and which often results in wife beating. In a 1995 national survey that looked at the main reasons for wife beating in Egypt, women revealed that the single most important reason for being beaten up by their hus-bands was refusing to have sex (El-Zanaty et al. 1996).

To make sense of these findings, one also needs to situate them within broader understandings of gendered expectations within marriage.[8] As discussed in chap-ter five, the definition of manhood/masculinity, *ruguula,* in relation to a potential groom, generally coincided with the role of husband as economic provider, while definitions of womanhood/femininity corresponded to that of several specific roles for women: housewife, mother and provider of sexual services. A good woman/good bride, *il hurma il kiwayyisa,* is defined by the extent to which she is strong, healthy and can provide labor to the household, as well as sexual satisfac-tion, ᶜ*afiyya.* My own probing into intramarital negotiations, interestingly, revealed that women were not contesting each of these various expectations with equal vigor.

Married women did not typically protest about excessive child-care demands or household chores[9]. In fact many of the women I interviewed took great pride in showing off their clean and organized homes with cooked food available, and their children who were adequately fed, regardless of conflicts with their husbands. Women's roles as homemakers and mothers appeared as part and parcel of their self-definition as women. These are tasks they have been engaged in since they were young girls, caring for siblings and helping out with domestic chores. On the other hand, their provision of sexual services was not considered an absolute duty or indisputable part of their roles as wives, on the same footing as their maternal and housewifly duties. Taking my cues from the spirit possession data, I started dis-cussing women's sexual expectations and experiences in greater detail.

A word of caution is necessary, however, before presenting my analysis of women's narratives on sexuality and conjugal relations. Personal narratives as a tool for generating information, while powerful and revealing, nonetheless have inherent limitations, already alluded to in the chapter four. All narratives are self-serving and inevitably entail elements of self-justification. Hence they are not to be taken at face value. In discussions of marital relationships and conjugal conflicts—relations whose dynamics are complex and entangled in both emotions and material exchanges -, the problems of relying on women's narratives are compounded. When talking about relationships that are not going well, women may naturally want to present themselves as wronged, unfailingly blaming and condemning their husbands and providing justifications for their own actions. However, this does not detract from the importance of such narratives for focusing attention on the specific idiom and terms through which women choose to express marital discord and discontent. These, in turn, reveal important aspects of gendered expectations and gendered bases of power.

Sex, Power, and Economic Provision

Despite individual variations, four broad orientations and attitudes regarding sexual relations were discernible. The first was a general consensus among women that sex is a basic need for men, closely tied not only to concepts of maleness, but also to fundamental biological needs. Some women even emphasized that sex was the main reason why men seek marriage. On of my interviewees reflects:

> If it was not for sex, why would men get married?. If it was only for cooking and cleaning, their mothers could do that for them. Sex is the most important thing for a man.

Second, although in general men were expected to initiate sex, women could also occasionally take the initiative, but they had to modulate their demands carefully so as not to risk their reputations. Samira and Soad, neighbors and close friends in their early forties voiced similar views in a group discussion. Soad comments:

> We never initiate sex, we are respectable women, *muhtaramiin*, but of course there are other women who are vulgar/immodest, *bigha*, and they ask for it openly.

Om Sayeda, explains how she maneuvers when she wants to sleep with her husband:

> It is ^c*eeb* for a woman to ask her husband for sex, he would think her horny, *mish* ^ɔ*adra*, and would wonder if she was like that when he is away, she could sleep with any man. But a smart woman if she wants sex, she can ask for it indirectly, cajole a man and do things to make him demand it. This is what I do.

Third, although women could sometimes initiate sex, they had much less control over refusing it. Most of the women I interviewed said that an overt refusal of sex results either in coerced sex, verbal abuse, or physical violence. Although many unambiguously expressed their lack of interest in sex, refusal was generally not tolerated by husbands, so that many women reported engaging in sex against their wishes. This is a stark example of compliance with a certain type of behavior out of fear and not out of complicity.

A few women emphasized that their own husbands do not force them to engage in unwanted sex. They nonetheless viewed the provision of sexual services, essentially, as a duty. One woman explains:

> My husband is understanding, and if I have my period or am tired, he does not insist. Most husbands are not so understanding and force it on their wives. But it is not always a man's fault. A man must feel free at home (free to have sex on demand), otherwise he will seek it outside. For women sex is a responsibility, a duty and a religious obligation, *mas⊃uuliyya, wi wagib, wi fard.*

Many other women, especially those who reported conflicts with their husbands over household finances, were particularly negative about their sexual relations. They also felt they had some legitimate rights to refuse sex. Om Adel, a pieceworker married to a street sweeper, responded very directly to my question as to how she views her sexual relationship with her husband:

> I do it against my wishes, *di haaga ghasb* ᶜ*an il wahid.* It is difficult for a woman to get out of this. Everything else can be refused except for this. The maximum you can do is say you are tired or have your period and hope that your husband will not insist. But you can only do this for a day or two, not all the time. Sex is the most important thing for a man. He demands it, he is the one who comes and asks for it, he sleeps with me every other day. If I do not sleep with him, he can go and marry someone else.

Stronger expressions of resentment are voiced by the following three interviewees to describe their feelings towards their sexual obligations:

> Every time we have sex it is a fight. When he asks me, it is like I have a terrible job to do. Sex to me is like a sad/sorrowful event, *karab.* If I say no, he hits me and gets angry. Men take no excuses when it comes to sex even if a woman is tired.

> I hate/cannot stand, *mabat⊃ish,* having sex with my husband. He sleeps with me when I am fast asleep, I am a heavy sleeper and he takes advantage of that. He is disgusting. I wake up in the process and start screaming and slapping my face, *altum.* Sometimes even my period does not deter him, he uses a condom, ᶜ*azil,* to sleep with me when I have my period (I later probed whether he also used a condom as a birth control method, and Om Aya said no, she uses the pill).

> When my husband wants to have sex, *y⊃idi maslahtu* (literally satisfy his desire), and I say no, he drags me in front of my children as if I am a cow, a *bihiima.* I have no dignity, *karaama.* These things are supposed to be private, not public in front of the kids.

Fourth, and very significantly, women's propensity to reject or resist sexual demands seems to be directly related to their perception that their husbands are defaulting on their roles as economic providers. Clearly, marriage for these women may have been about much more than material exchanges. However, many inevitably use the maintenance argument when they wanted to default on sex. They complain that their husbands are not providing for them adequately,[10] and use this as a way of challenging their obligations as sexual providers. Om Adel explains quite bluntly:

> He does not even approach me for sex anymore. He understands that I will not sleep with him. Why should I? Does he feed me?

None of the women made a link between the fact that they are circumcised and their lack of interest in sexual encounters with their husbands. Om Yehia, married to a construction worker, emphasizes that female circumcision does not impede a woman's sexual enjoyment. She was one of the few women who said that she had found sex pleasurable at some point. She comments:

> I am circumcised and I used to like to sleep with my husband. He made me comfortable and provided for his household. Five years ago, however, he reduced the *masruuf* he was giving me and stopped getting anything for the house … He still approaches me for sex, but I no longer want it or enjoy it.

She then went on to reflect bitterly on the more general plight of women who can no longer depend financially on their husbands:

> A man is a man by how much he spends on his house, *il Raagil raagil fi masrufaatu*. There are no men any more. Men have become irresponsible, *il rigaala khaⁱa*. If a man economically provides for his wife, *misatit miraatu* (literally makes her a woman, *sit*) then he has a right to control her, *lih haᵓ yithakkim*, and sleep with her two or more times a day if he wants. But there are no men these days.

This link between breadwinner status and sexual rights has already been alluded to in a few anthropological studies of Egypt. In her study of the self-images of *bint El Balad*, Al-Messiri (1978) shows how women's notions of masculinity center mainly on the ability of the husband to earn an income and provide for his family. A man who does not fulfill this expectation is referred to as a *mara*, a degrading slang term meaning woman, but which when used only in reference to men implies a "loss of masculinity." As a *mara*, a man loses culturally sanctioned prerogatives over his wife, and his unrestricted access to her sexual services. The close link between notions of masculinity and provider status has also been noted in other Egyptian ethnographies (Hoodfar 1990; Rugh, 1984). These cultural ideals do not necessarily reflect reality as discussed in chapter two, but are further reinforced by state laws that define the man as breadwinner and the woman as a housewife, or at most a secondary earner.[11]

The study by Shahla Haeri (1989) of temporary marriage, *muťa*, in Iran, although highly specific to *Shiťa* doctrine, is nonetheless relevant in this regard. Her study brings to light the underlying premises of marriage in Islam in general and its associated doctrinal presumptions and conceptualizations of men and women. Haeri highlights how, despite their differences, all schools of Islamic law consider marriage as a contract, *ťaqd*, between two transacting parties. Legally, religiously and socially, a contractual transaction lies at the core of Muslim marriage, whereby men gain an exclusive right over women's sexual services, in return for payment of money or valuables, traditionally in the form of a bride price, *mahr* (Haeri 1989).

Haeri's interviews with women, men, and religious scholars in Iran in the 1980s, as well as her historical research, reveals the embeddedness of the concept of "contract" in Iranian beliefs and its significance as a discourse underlying Muslim marriage. Iranian women were in essence either "leasing the womb," in the case of temporary marriage, or "selling it," in the case of permanent marriages. Haeri writes:

> [A]s with other forms of social exchange, a contract of marriage is at once a legal, religious, economic and symbolic transaction. In the context of Iranian society, the all prevailing concept of contract functions as a "root paradigm" informing people's consciousness and orienting their behaviour in their daily interactions and transactions (Haeri 1989: 29)

The underlying logic of the very crudely put phrase, "sex for maintenance," that came through in many of my own interviews can similarly be understood with reference to the underlying normative understanding of the terms of the Islamic marriage "contract." Such a contract, which governs the majority of the marriages of my interviewees, stipulates that women be available for sex on demand for husbands who meet their maintenance obligations.[12]

The concept of *nushuuz*, which is derived from Islamic thought and denotes female disobedience, is also of relevance on this point. Although not mentioned explicitly by my interviewees, the notion may have an implicit influence on their perceptions of gendered roles. According to Mernissi (1987), the concept of *nushuuz*, mentioned in a verse in the Quran, is interpreted by Muslim commentators to mean a serious offence and rebellion by women indicated by their refusal to obey a husband's requests, particularly for sex.

Mernissi argues that the verse on *nushuuz*, which has been interpreted by some as sanctioning the right of men to hit their wives, is taken by religious authorities today as a way of authorizing violence against women.[13] This perception that denial of sex is a grave offence, and that fulfilling a husband's sexual demands is a religious duty for a woman was clear from my interviews. Women did not generally think they had the right to refuse sex, except perhaps if their husbands had lost their conjugal entitlements by not providing for them. As discussed in chapter three, this may become an increasing problem in light of rising poverty and male unemployment. If a woman perceived her husband as having defaulted on his material obligations, then she was generally less willing to honor her part of the bargain or "contract." As the above section illustrates, this unwillingness is occasionally voiced overtly, but more often is articulated more covertly, sometimes through the idiom of spirit possession.

In addition to sex, the other recurrent theme revealed through the spirit possession narratives revolved around women's commentary on religious practices and expectations. Clearly this is an issue of a very different order than sex and sexuality. The arena of sexuality relates directly to daily interactions between men and women, and therefore any grievances in this regard are directly felt, and articulating discontent is relatively straightforward. However, the influence of religion on women's daily lives, and its manifestations at the community level, is much more diffuse and would be expected to result in contradictory and dispersed responses. The following section explores the theme of religious expectations as they emerged in the possession narratives and attempts to analyze them within the broader context of the "islamization of everyday life" which is taking place in the study community.

Responses to the "Islamization" of Everyday Life

In the four neighborhoods I visited, there was much evidence of what may be termed the "islamization" of everyday life, already noted in previous chapters. In all four neighborhoods local mosques and Islamic charitable associations were playing an active role in providing a range of services, particularly in health care, cash handouts for orphans and widows, religious instruction and interest-free credit. One of the most visible and popular services was the orphans' support program, *kafaalit il yatiim*. Regular handouts of money, clothes and sometimes school uniforms are distributed through this program which is administered on a monthly basis by several fully veiled women, *munaqqabaat*, from outside the community. There were four hundred women, divorcees or widows, registered to receive this service at one of the mosques in one of the neighborhoods.

In all four neighborhoods, local mosques appeared to play an active role in the articulation of appropriate roles for women. The Friday sermon, *khutba*, regularly made reference to family values and the need for women to demonstrate modesty, *hishma*, and to fulfill their obligations to their husband and children. One of the mosques where I attended Friday prayers was distributing, free of charge, tapes of Quranic recitations and lectures on Islamic morals. These were circulating widely in the community.[14]

A recent study of a low-income neighborhood in the north of Cairo similarly documents the increasing influence of Islamist discourse on women's everyday lives, and the role played in particular by local mosques in this process. Ghanem (1996) argues that the role of the mosque, which is a highly gendered space, seems to reinforce power relationships in the family. Major parts of the discourses circulated there call for the total and absolute right of men over women, who should always obey their husbands, fathers and mothers. ... The mosque manifests and shapes the ways in which gender is constructed. Inside the mosque, women are spatially separated from men, their access to the mosque is conditional on the absence of the menstrual period, and within its confines they are required to wear a long and loose dress and to totally cover the hair and chest. (1996: 194).

Ghanem describes the increasing involvement of religious leaders, both male and female, in the arbitration of family conflicts. She also shows increasing attempts to open up the mosque for women and increase their participation, by investing in setting up separate sections, arguing that this represents an attempt to counter other spaces to which women have begun to have access, such as the work place. These features were also visible in my study community. The point to stress is that unlike the workshops, which as discussed in chapter seven, which are a stigmatized public space, or the *hadra*(s), which are tolerated but generally discouraged, the mosque is a space that women are consciously encouraged to frequent.

Segregated religious classes were an important feature in several of the local mosques in the study community. I attended several sessions, which usually followed either the Friday noon prayers or the sunset prayer and lasted for about an hour. None of the women in my sample were regular attendees, except during the fasting month of Ramadan, but all had attended at some point during the past few months. Most classes were led by educated women from outside of the communities, all of whom were affiliated with il *Gam⁻iyya il Shar⁻iyya*, one of the most prominent Islamic charitable organizations in Egypt. At one of the classes I attended, white T-shirts were distributed free of charge to the women who were attending the classes. These were a present for their children explained the "teacher," and they should let other women in the community know that they too could get T-shirts if they attended the classes.

The majority of the women in these classes were wearing a headscarf; a few donned a *khimaar*. There were many more younger, unmarried women, some with a degree of formal education in these classes, than in the *hadra*(s). In fact, the type of audience, the dress formality, dress code and the strict atmosphere in the classes contrasted sharply with the relaxed and informal atmosphere of the *hadra*(s) I attended. Much of the discussion during those classes revolved around the need for women to be more pious, to wear the *khimaar*, to renounce worldly pleasures and anticipate death, and to fear God and their husbands, *khushu⁻*. Informal meetings amongst women, such as those of the *hadra*(s) were denounced as *haraam*, and a waste of time in gossip, *namiima*, time that should be spent in devotion to one's family and to god. In her study of what appears to be similar religious classes in one low-income Egyptian community in the 1980s Guenena also finds that "the discussion of Islam was used to encourage behavior changes such as wearing Islamic dress and to stop women from using contraceptives which are considered harmful to the future of the nation" (Guenena 1986).

Local mosques also played an important role in providing health care. Clinics attached to two of the mosques in the community provided some of the best-quality, friendliest and most affordable services in the area according to the women I interviewed. I did not spend any time in the various "Islamic clinics" in the community, but Hatem (1994) suggests that the many clinics which have spread in neighborhoods in Cairo over the past decade are often used as a base for spreading a conservative interpretation of Islam. Health-care professionals often encourage patients to participate in the increasingly common phenomenon of segregated religious study groups for both men and women discussed earlier.

A process of "islamization" of everyday life was therefore evident in the study community. The following section explores responses by some women to this process and to perceived pressures on them to conform to "Islamic" modes of behavior. I only discuss, however, the type of responses to such pressures that were revealed through an analysis of women's spirit possession narratives. Such pressures must be located within the broader context, discussed in chapter two, of a rising Islamist discourse which has been gaining momentum since the early 1970s in Egypt.

These pressures on women do not come directly, or only, from their husbands, but also from other members of the family as well as from the broader community of neighbors, relatives, and local leaders. The lack of conformity to certain types of behavior affects the reputation of the entire family and its status vis-a-vis others in the community. For example, the pressure on one of the possessed women, Om Naema, to cover her hair, *tit-hagib,* came directly from one of her unmarried daughters, who herself had donned the *higaab,* and who feared that her mother's refusal to do so and her other "un-Islamic behavior" could seriously jeopardize her own marriage options. Husbands were also under the same kinds of pressure to ensure that their wives submitted to interpretations of proper Islamic behavior, such as wearing the *higaab* and/or *khimaar,* spending more time listening to the Quran and religious tapes than to popular music, and being more obedient toward them, including sexually. While clearly the implications of religious indoctrination goes beyond the conjugal relationship, it also has a direct impact on marital affairs which is why it is relevant to the concerns of this chapter.

One of the striking features of the spirit possession narratives of the fifteen possessed women I interviewed in depth was the fact that most of the women were possessed by Christian spirits. I had not seen a reference to this in the literature and was therefore quite puzzled. The prevalence of Christian spirits was confirmed during the *hadra*(s) I attended. One of the beats repeated often and to which people danced was called the monastery beat, *Daʾit il diir,* which is requested by Christian spirits. Christian spirits made a series of demands on the women. These included purchasing silver pendants with a cross and Christ on them, going to church, drinking beer, refusing to perform Muslim prayers, refusing to wear two types of dress interpreted by some as proper Islamic dress, the *higaab,* the scarf that covers the head and neck, and the *khimaar,* which covers the face and entire body.

All the Muslim women I interviewed defined themselves as good practicing Muslims, and being Muslim was an important part of their self-identity. Their observances of Islamic practices varied greatly, but most generally fasted during Ramadan and some prayed, although not necessarily on a regular basis. Some attended prayers and religious classes in local mosques, particularly during Ramadan. The ultimate aspiration of many was to make the pilgrimage to Mecca, the *hig.*

The women possessed by Christian spirits, however, could not live—up to their self-image as "good Muslims". Many could not stand to hear the Quran, or the call for prayer, or to pray themselves. Om Samia, a forty-year-old married woman who sells bread and has two daughters, comments:

> I know I am possessed by a Christian spirit because I saw him several years ago, I still feel him sleeping beside me when I go to bed. He is a priest and is tall, white and good-looking. He asked me to buy a silver cross and I got one and have been wearing it ever since. I have always prayed regularly and read the Quran, but he does not like it. Now, when I pray, I feel like someone is choking me and I fall down.

Echoing what appears like a desire to dispense with the imposition of certain religious practices, Om Naema, married with two sons and two daughters, talks about her experience of possession. Om Naema is married to a guard who runs a small grocery shop in the afternoons. She does not earn a cash income herself. One of her daughters is married and living in Saudi Arabia, and the other is a seventeen-year-old who left school when she was twelve and voluntarily took up the *higaab* three years ago. She has been trying to convince her mother to do the same. Om Naema's comments reveal an interesting perception of identity and of the Christian as the "other" as she conflates Christians and foreigners, referring to both as *Khawaaga*(s), foreigners. This may be a reflection of increasing interfaith tensions in Egypt. It is also possibly related to the attempts of a rising Islamist discourse, as discussed earlier, to cast Copts in Egypt as the "other within" (see Shukralla 1994). Om Naema talks about her experiences:

> I stopped praying and insisted on getting a dog. People told me this was bad because a dog in a house makes the angels go away. But I was very attached to this dog. I used to walk like a madwoman in the street and then suddenly I would fall down unconscious in the form of a cross, *atsallib.* I went to many doctors, but they could not heal me. My neighbor suggested that I go and see my *atar,* and I did. The *kudya* told me that I am possessed by a Christian spirit who is in love with me, *ᶜaashiᵓ*, and wants me to make him a *zaar.* I made him a *zaar* and I got all the things that Christian spirits like, you know they are like *il Khawagaat,* foreigners. I had a large buffet with cheese, *gibna ruumy,* olives, and beer. I invited many friends. I felt much better afterwards, but every now and then the symptoms come back … Just last week my daughters found me tearing my clothes as a tape reciting the Quran was on.

Several of Om Naema's neighbors and her daughter confirmed her narratives and recalled several instances when she would fall down in the street in the form of a cross. Her daughter also confirmed how hysterical Om Naema becomes when she hears Quranic tapes, and confessed that she was worried that such behavior by her mother may affect her own reputation and marriageability.

Sannaa is a 19-year-old woman finishing a high school diploma in nursing. She is one of the highest educated women in my sample and is also one of the two unmarried women among the group of possessed women. She comments on her possession by Christian spirits:

> I am possessed by two Christian spirits, Girguis and Mary. My beat is the monastery beat, *Daᵓit il diir.* I just find myself pulled when I hear it and I keep dancing. But I also like to dance to the beat of the Prophet, *madiih il Nabi.* Mary and Girguis are young and they want me to wear shorter skirts and trousers and not to pray. When I hear the call to prayer, I keep screaming and have to close my ears. I want to wear the *higaab,* but they do not allow me. I tried once and I had a continuous headache for two weeks. I had to stay in a dark room and tie my head from the pain. My mother took me to many doctors but nothing worked.

When I asked women why so many of the spirits were Christian, and whether this was a recent phenomenon, one of my interviewees, an older woman who has been possessed for many years, explained that there are many more Christian spirits nowadays than in the past. "I heard that this is because the priest in the nearby community, Father Samaan, has asked the Christian spirits to spread to our community, *sarahhum ᶜaleena.*" Another woman ventured a similar conspiracy theory, but at a more global level: "It is because the Grand Pope in America, the head of the Christians, has asked the spirits to go to the Muslim world and possess Muslim women. They want us to be *nasaara,* Christians, like them."

Amal, a married woman who has been possessed by two Christian spirits for the past five years had a different interpretation:

> The spirits are not really Christian. They are all Muslim and they are good. We just say they are Christian because Christian spirits are stronger, they are more difficult to get out when the sheikhs come and read Quran. Muslim spirits may respond to the sheikhs' use of Quran, but Christian ones do not and so the Quran cannot get them out. The maximum that a sheikh can do is to make them become Muslims.

I was told of several cases when a sheikh could not get the spirit out, but at least managed to convert him or her to Islam. According to the women I interviewed, however, resorting to sheikhs to get the spirits out, and more particularly attempting to convert spirits to Islam, has become widespread only in the past ten years.

The above accounts point to the complex ways in which spirit possession narratives are constructed by selectively incorporating elements of everyday life, resulting in a "bricolage" of themes picked up from daily practices as well as from broader commentary on socioeconomic and political life articulated through the media. The women I interviewed generally saw themselves as good Muslims. The fact that so many spirits are Christians, and have specific "anti-Islamic" demands could possibly be interpreted as a reflection of some subconscious resistance to increasing attempts to regulate women's lives that are justified in the name of Islam.

The Islamic establishment is against *zaar*[15] Possessed women are considered to be lacking in faith, *imanhum Dảiif.* The predominant response from local religious leaders, as well as husbands, to women's possession is to persuade and pressure them to become more pious, to take the *higaab* or *khimaar*, to pray, to read the Quran regularly, and to join the religious classes in the mosques rather than participate in the spirit possession circles. Given this broader context, possession, specifically through the manifestation of Christian spirits, may be articulating a "counterhegemonic" cultural text. Such a text would allow women to deal with their desires to conform to their own self-perceptions as good Muslims, without succumbing to the recent pressures on them to display certain behavior that is being defined by others as "proper" Islamic behavior.

Some of the demands of Christian spirits, such as wearing short skirts and trousers, and their assumed link with foreigners and the West (two of my interviewees mentioned America specifically) are also of interest. This may reflect the mixed signals about "modernity" and the "West" (which is identified with America in popular thinking) that are portrayed through the media. This is a "West" whose ideas and products are often sought after (see for example the *gihaaz* items discussed in chapter six), but whose influence is also feared as promoting moral decadence. For example, satellite television and Western cinema and video films were regularly referred to in Friday prayers by one religious leader in a local mosque as "satanic transmissions," *beth shaytani,* that all good Muslims should avoid.

The above interpretations and arguments suggest one plausible explanation for the specific imagery of the spirits at this specific point in time and allude to the historical specificity of the subordinate discourse of spirit possession. They also allude to the ways in which spirit possession challenges gender relations and may alter relations in concrete and tangible ways in women's and men's daily lives.

The Potentials and Limitations of "Subordinate Discourses"

I have been arguing that the spirit possession idiom, widely shared by women, is a powerful communicative mechanism that enables women to both express discontent, as well as negotiate gender expectations and identities in their daily lives. In the process, everyday assumptions and expectations about gender roles and relations may be challenged. The significance of spirit possession goes beyond the acts of individual women. It constitutes a discursive space as well as a complex and diffuse cultural repertoire, that is not based on written text, but on a consensual recognition of signs and symptoms of possession.

An indication of the potential threat represented by this discourse may be seen in the relentless, and increasing, attempts by male Sunni healers [16] to not only discredit spirit possession, as they also attempt to discourage other forms of vernacular beliefs and practices, such as *muulids* or visits to saints' shrines, but also to specifically target and combat it. Part of the reason behind this apparent targeting of spirit possession may be directly related not only to its form, but to its content, that is, the narratives it generates particularly those regarding sexual relations and religious observance. The messages that community members receive from women who actually refuse to have sex with their husbands, or who insist on not wearing a certain type of dress, can be rather unsettling of prevalent gender ideologies. Spirit possession could be particularly worrisome for men because of its potential to lead to the much debated, and feared, female disobedience called *nushuuz* mentioned earlier.

What gives spirit possession its resilience and the ability to withstand such pressures is the degree of overlap that exists between spirit possession beliefs expressed by women and those of "religious" healers alike; both believe that humans can be possessed by *gin*(s). The difference, however, is that whereas women believe you can only appease the spirits through traditional *zaar*(s) or *hadra*(s), *Sunni* healers attempt to exorcise the spirits. The attempt at converting the spirits, however, is suggestive of the failure of exorcising them and thus a testimony to the strength of the discourse of spirit possession.

Mahmoud, an engineer who has recently become known in the community as a religious healer, explained to me how he became a healer, referred to as either *Sunni,* or more specifically as a Quranic healer, *yi^caalig bil Quran.* Dismissing possession and *zaar* as heresy and irrational behavior when he was young, Mahmoud was reintroduced to it when he was working in Saudi Arabia when he listened to the complaints of a colleague. The nature of those complaints is of interest since they correspond to some of the themes appearing in women's possession narratives discussed earlier. Mahmoud's colleague was in distress because his wife, who was subsequently diagnosed as possessed, used to respond with bouts of shrieking whenever he approached her sexually during his vacations in Cairo and refused to sleep with him.

Although intrigued, Mahmoud still dismissed the issue of possession as trivial until he returned to Cairo a few years ago, after six years of work in Saudi Arabia,[17] and became an active volunteer member on the board of a local mosque. In the mosque, stories were circulating about community women possessed by Christian spirits. There were other stories about women possessed by spirits who were inflicting upon them a range of ailments, including the inability to have sex with their husbands. There were also reports that these women were resorting to churches and priests to appease the spirits. Mahmoud, and a group of young men he got to know through the mosque, became quite concerned and decided to do something about this phenomenon.

Seeking out a specialized sheikh for advice, Mahmoud and his colleagues began learning the "methods" of Quranic healing so as to counter what they perceived as the shameful phenomenon of Muslim women (our women, *sitattna,* is how he referred to them) going to church as well as resorting to heretical, traditional spirit possession ceremonies. Mahmoud read extensively on the topic, and joined the healing sessions of a well-known sheikh for a few months as an apprentice to gain practical experience. Now a self proclaimed "religious" healer, Mahmoud emphasized that he cures patients of spirit possession afflictions, mostly women, for free.[18]

Two of the possessed women I interviewed, who were cousins, had asked Mahmoud to visit them for a healing session, after reportedly being pressured by their husbands. One of the women also said that she felt compelled to see a *Sunni* in response to demands by her eighteen-year-old daughter who held a preparatory school degree and was a frequent participant in the women's religious classes at a local mosque. Thus an important point to stress at this point is thus that "religious healing" may be urged upon possessed women not only by men, but also by a certain group of women, perhaps the more educated and younger ones.

Over a course of four sessions, Mahmoud was unable to exorcise the spirits, but managed to convert one of them. Both women, however, continued their visits to the *hadra*(s) at the same time as they were being "treated" by Mahmoud.[19] Both said that the involuntary shrieking that came upon them whenever their husbands approached them sexually, or when they heard the Quranic tapes, did not go away. I later probed into this issue with the husband of one of the women, who confirmed that he is still unable to approach his wife sexually because of the fits which overtake her when he tries to do so.

Thus, despite these alternative efforts to deal with possessed women, there appears to be a fair degree of resistance on the part of women to counter this encroachment into their space and to hold on to their more traditional practices of *zaar* and *hadra*(s). Women's attempts to hold on to their modes of dealing with spirit possession are reflected both in their use of an Islamic idiom to justify their actions (many stressed that spirits are mentioned in the Quran and that their practices are thus religiously sanctioned), but also possibly through the unconscious or conscious manipulation of the imagery and demands of the spirits. A separate study would be required to establish changes over time. However, many of my interviewees stressed that they know more possessed women now than in the past, that many more spirits are Christians, and that while the incidence of the *zaar,* the more elaborate private ceremony, has decreased, the *hadra*(s) are still a widespread and important feature in the lives of many low-income-women in Cairo.

Despite attempts to undermine it, possession thus appears to have survived as a powerful idiom that enables women to voice some of their everyday concerns and "latent grievances," in response to a "latent power" (see Lukes 1986). This covert discourse, however, does not completely escape the categories of formal dominant discourses and is thus limited by them. As argued in chapter one, in the search for the "infra-politics" of disadvantaged groups, there is a danger of over estimating the potential of everyday forms of resistance to radically change power relations.

In this instance, the danger of exaggerating the ability of possession to challenge power relations is illustrated graphically by an inadequately publicized murder case. This was published in Egypt's foremost Arabic newspaper, *Al Ahram*, in June, 1995, under the title: "Possessed Girl Beaten to Death by her Father To Get the Spirits Out of her Body." The reported story goes as follows. On June 3rd, 1995, Sahar Emad El Din Youssef, a thirteen year-old girl who lives in the lower Egyptian town of Mansura, was found dead in her room. The death was due to repeated beatings with a plastic hose.

Investigations revealed that the girl's parents, both engineers had taken up what was termed "Islamic dress," *il ziy il Islami,* the previous year, meaning the *khimaar* for the wife and an ankle-length white *galabiyya* for the husband. They quit their work and started pressuring their daughter to also take up the *khimaar*. She refused, apparently because she was possessed by spirits who forbade her to do so. After several months of pressure, her parents kept her home from school, locked her in a room and started beating her with a plastic hose to get the spirits out. Sahar's spirits of resistance were defeated. She died. What messages or conclusions members of her community, including her schoolmates, derived from this episode is difficult to judge.

The previous sections have attempted to shed light on some aspects of power relations within the conjugal union and ways in which women may voice their discontent through "subordinate discourses." Spirit possession was presented as one such avenue. Spirit possession, a complex phenomena with multiple referents, appears to play an important role as a cultural idiom which gives women, particularly married ones, access to a discursive space in which they can express ideas, and sometimes actually negotiate relations at variance with social expectations and prevalent gender identities. The two recurring themes which emerged most vividly through the spirit possession narratives relate to women's responses to sexual demands from their husbands and to the "islamization" of their everyday life. The following chapter will discuss other areas, such as the education of daughters and budgetary allocations, which also emerged as subjects of contestation between men and women within the household.

NOTES

1. Quranic healing, ᶜ*ilag bil Quran*, is an apparently widely spread alternative medical system in Cairo which will be discussed later in the chapter. The healers are generally men, and the patients often women. I was told by both healers and community members that this was an increasing phenomenon in their communities.
2. Healthy does not do justice to the word ᶜ*affiya*, which is a more complex concept implying sexual maturity, radiance and physical strength. It is a gender-specific term. I have never heard it used to describe a man.
3. There is a great degree of similarity between Messick's notion of the "subordinate discourse," and James Scott's "hidden transcript," which he defines as "a discourse that takes place offstage, beyond the direct observation of the dominant groups" (Scott 1990). The difference is that Scott developed the notion in the context of agrarian class relations and was not particularly sensitive to gender issues, whereas Messick's term applies specifically to an analysis of gender relations and ideologies.
4. It is only by appreciating the dreariness and difficulties which characterize some aspects of the daily lives of low-income women in Cairo and their limited access to "recreational facilities," that one can appreciate the importance of the concept of *farfasha*.
5. This reference to pale skin is a euphemism for physical beauty. As was evident from women's comments in earlier chapters, shades of skin color were important markers of beauty and identity in the study community. It is also interesting to note in Amal's comments how the spirits are viewed not as intruders, but as protectors.
6. This was both an unnerving and bemusing situation. As discussed in chapter four, part of me did not believe what was going on and wanted to dismiss it as a charade, a form of female theater, a show put on for my benefit. It was hard for me to come to terms with the fact, as I eventually did, that everyone around me seemed to really believe that the spirits can become manifest and can speak to us. This raises the issue of symptoms as cultural texts and forms of cultural communication and expression. I was initially shut off from a linguistic universe, knowledge of which is taught and culturally acquired. The women around me were reading and decoding signs and symptoms, which I could not access.
7. *Atar* is the term used for a type of diagnosis that is made by a specialist person to find out the type of spirit and what his or her demands are.
8. As discussed earlier, there are variations in gender role expectations according to life cycle and marital status: a good adolescent girl, a good bride, a good wife, a divorcee, etc.
9. For houses with no sewage facilities, disposal of waste water was pointed out as one of the most onerous household chores. While women often complained of it, however, they did not contest that it was part of their duty and roles as women, or more commonly the role of younger girls in the household. Complaints about certain tasks are not necessarily contestation of roles. This of course raises the difficult issue of consent discussed in the chapter on theory.
10. Whether this was the case or not, is of course difficult to ascertain, since I did not talk to their husbands, and did not get their views on the reasons for marital discord, or how the cycle of conflict started. It may be that a woman's initial coldness towards a husband and her reluctance to have sex with him has produced disinterest or unwillingness on his part to provide for her, which in turn increases her resentment towards him and strengthens her unwillingness to engage in sexual relations.
11. As discussed briefly in earlier chapters, these gender constructs are clearly reflected in government employment policies, and in social security and social assistance systems.
12. I do not want to imply that women reduce marriage into a simple exchange of sex for money devoid of any sentiment or to simplify the complex layers of interdependence and emotions inherent in any conjugal arrangement. However, this connection is one that did come through clearly in my interviews, and is thus difficult to ignore. This prevailing conception of marriage

may not be the view of the Islamic religious establishment. This is, however, outside the scope of my interest as I was concentrating on the perceptions of a specific group of women and how these informed their actions and practices. I did not interview any religious scholars on this issue. Moreover, it is probable that this normative understanding of marriage may not find resonance amongst the upper-class sections of Egyptian society as was discussed in chapter six.

13. Mernissi discusses the great difficulties scholars encounter in interpreting this verse and the difference of opinion and lack of clarity that surround it. She notes that one established Muslim scholar devoted twenty-seven pages of his commentary to it and provided not less than two hundred contradictory opinions on its meaning.

14. A content analysis of such tapes would be a fascinating undertaking, but one which was unfortunately outside the scope of this study.

15. The Islamic establishment, as embodied in state institutions and public discourses, has always tried, to varying degrees depending on the context, to discourage practices it considers "unorthodox," popular, or folk customs. These have included not just spirit possession ceremonies, but also visitation of saints' shrines, *muulid*s, and so forth.

16. *Sunni* is a generic term that was used to describe extremely religious men who wear white *galabiyya*(s) and grow long beards in the tradition of the Prophet. Sunni healers are those who attempt to cure illness through "Quranic methods."

17. The link with Saudi Arabia is noteworthy and indicative of *wahabi* influence which is strictly against all forms of innovations, *bidaᶜ*. This influence, an aspect of "globalization," was infused into Egyptian society partly through the waves of regional migration that took place in the 1970s as discussed in chapter three.

18. Mahmoud explained that although he does this task on the side "to serve God," some of his other colleagues have left their jobs and have taken up religious healing as their main profession. Although Mahmoud stressed that he does not get paid for his services, he admitted that professional healers do, which, he argued, is legitimate in Islam according to a saying, *hadith*, by the Prophet.

19. Mahmoud's methods, like that of other healers, involve writing certain Quranic verses on paper using saffron, *zaᶜfaraan*, which produces a reddish/orange liquid when mixed with water. Patients are then asked to dip the paper in a glass or basin of water and then either drink it or bathe with it. Other methods included reading Quranic verses in the ear of the afflicted patient, and sometimes, slapping them or hitting them with a stick. The latter device is meant to frighten the spirit, explained Mahmoud, but the afflicted person does not feel any pain.

9

INTRAHOUSEHOLD DECISIONS
AND EXTRAHOUSEHOLD
NETWORKS

ಿಲೆಸಿ

"I would sell my clothes to keep my daughter in school."[1]

With a focus on intrahousehold decision making and relations, this chapter elaborates on some key areas of disagreements and conflicts between husbands and wives and discusses how they are resolved. Decisions regarding the education of daughters emerged as a particularly important issue over which women's and men's priorities, aspirations and strategies diverged. A significant part of the chapter is thus devoted to a discussion of this issue.

Women's resources, and hence their relative bargaining power, is not solely determined by their familial context, but is also influenced by their access to extrahousehold options (Harris 1981; Agarwal 1997). Thus the chapter also discusses the role of women's informal networks, highlighting in particular how they may serve to enhance women's choices and latitude of decision making within their households. Several studies have highlighted the crucial role of informal networks in Cairo's neighborhoods (Hoodfar 1997; Nadim 1985; Rugh 1979; Singerman 1995; Wikan 1980). My own discussion will focus more specifically on three types of female networks which are instrumental in supporting women's attempts to gain an advantage in their marriages. These are: spirits possession ceremonies, *hadra*(s), female run grocery shops, *bᵓaala*(s), and rotating credit associations, *gamᶜiyya*(s).

In the past scholarship on families and household arrangements has emphasized the existence of "household strategies" (Bruce and Dwyer 1988; Guyer and Peters 1987; Hart 1995). The household was conceptualized as an income-pooling unit, with an assumption of harmony and consensus between household members. Studies in Third World settings have further stressed the centrality of

192

the family unit as a resource for the survival of the poor, ethnic minorities and rural-to-urban migrants (Glenn 1987). Early research on family dynamics in Egypt was heavily influenced by this approach. "Adaptive family strategies," and decision making as a "family calculus" were highlighted as explanations for the behavior of individuals within the household (B. Ibrahim 1985; Rugh 1984).

Feminist critiques beginning in the early 1980s, however, have challenged the idealized, normative view of households as necessarily harmonious, undifferentiated units whose members pursue common strategies. Such strategies, it was argued, are often assumed, rather than historically and empirically investigated. More recent research has led to an increasing recognition of divergences of interests within households, thus paving the way for a more nuanced understanding of household dynamics. This alternative approach to the household recognizes power differentials between genders and generations, and possible conflicts over interests, needs and priorities (Bruce and Dwyer 1988; Folbre 1986,1988; Guyer and Peters 1987; Harris 1981; Hart 1995; Sen 1990; Whitehead 1981; Wolf 1990).

Within this context, several studies have highlighted how power and conflict within households are most clearly manifested in the area of budgetary allocations and decisions regarding spending, savings and investments (Bruce and Dwyer 1988; Pahl 1989). As a result of her work with female pieceworkers in Mexico City, Roldan (1988) found that "money constitutes an important base of power." She thus argues that "the analysis of allocational forms should contribute substantially to our understanding of how gender hierarchies are imposed and reproduced within households, as well as to the existence of points of resistance to such inequality" (1988: 229).

These findings are similar to suggestions from research in the Egyptian context. Al-Messiri's study of intrahousehold relations in Cairo reveals several types of financial arrangements and different levels of economic complementarity between husband and wife that are based on both regional origin and men's occupation. She concludes that there is "a close association between money and power in the husband-wife relationship. The partner who has access to financial resources of the family, has more to say in terms of decision making and is more dominant" (1985:219). In her study of low-income households in Cairo, Hoodfar (1988, 1997) similarly finds that men and women had divergent priorities in cash disposal and expenditures, and recognizes that control of cash flow is closely related to power relations between husbands and wives.

By the early 1990s, more recent conceptualizations of the household (without denying the importance of economic factors) also emphasized the role of ideology in decision making. The outcome of negotiation between household members was seen to be determined not only by economic factors such as access to material resources, but also by how "social identities," are defined, that is, by specific views about the rights, responsibilities and needs of different household members (Folbre 1992; Moore 1994; Hart 1995). As Moore argues: "Bargaining is about definitions and interpretations, it is both symbolic and material. What is needed is a clear understanding of how gendered identities are implicated in the determination of discourses about the rights and needs of specific sorts of individuals" (Moore 1994: 10). My own data supports this view. Budgetary issues were a major area of conflict between married couples whose expenditure priorities often diverged. "All our problems are over money/expenses, *il masariif*, was a phrase I heard often in my discussions. Nonetheless, conflicts also revolved around interpretations of rights and needs, such as whether a girl needs to be educated, for example.

Understanding the nature of decision making within households was a challenge, given that I spent much of my time exclusively with women. My data thus depends on women's accounts, as well as on the fights and disagreements between married couples that I witnessed firsthand. Unravelling the intricate processes of decision making was further complicated by the fact that it was not always easy to achieve a straightforward and clear cut understanding of who made decisions -husband, wife, or other family members. Patterns of decision making and negotiations did not emerge easily. These patterns were also not set, but changed according to the nature of the decision, men's and women's stage in the life cycle, their earning capacity and their specific budgetary arrangements.[2]

Some areas of decision making nonetheless appeared to be gendered in a fairly straightforward manner. For instance, decisions regarding daughter's circumcision and defloration ceremonies were largely recognized as female prerogatives with decisions made openly without consultation with men, and sometimes despite male disapproval. Other decisions, such as decisions to have an abortion or a hymen repair operation were similarly made by women, without prior consultation with men. Unlike those concerning defloration and circumcision, however, these were decisions made secretly.[3]

Men generally had greater latitude in decisions concerning issues of physical mobility, such as in visiting parents or friends or spending the night or week out of the house. Taking on a co-wife was clearly also a male decision, although, as discussed earlier, one which women attempted to actively influence through practices such as the *ayma*. Other areas like decisions regarding birth control or choice of a spouse allowed more room for negotiation and a consultative decision-making process between husband and wife. Male opinion was often formally deferred to in case of disagreement, though sometimes secretly defied.

One important area of disagreement between men and women, which emerged early on in my fieldwork, relates to decisions regarding the education of daughters. This was an issue where disagreements between spouses were often evident and an area where women's resourceful attempts to circumvent their husband's authority were most manifest. Wives were generally more adamant about educating their daughters than their husbands and they actively sought ways to achieve this objective.

The discovery that women struggle to educate their daughters caught my attention as a counterintuitive finding in the Egyptian context. The common assumption, based on observations and studies in rural areas, suggests that it is women who pull their children out of school to receive help with domestic chores. I thus decided to investigate this issue in greater depth.

The issue of girls' education is also of particular interest because as will be shown below, it has a direct bearing upon women's aspirations and ability to avoid abuse both in the marital union and in the labor market. It is also of interest because it may constitute an example of a longer term and more proactive strategy by women for enhancing their options and improving their livelihoods, one that could result in an intergenerational change in the favor of women. In this sense, it is in contrast to some of the other short-and medium-term protective practices such as driving a prospective spouse away, *tatfiish*, the marriage inventory, *ayma*, the marriage trousseau, *gihaaz*, and public defloration ceremonies, *laf bil sharaf*, which were discussed in earlier chapters.

"I Would Sell My Clothes To Keep My Daughter in School": Investing in the Future

The education of girls was often a subject of disagreement between husband and wife. Disagreements revolved around both the initial decision regarding a daughter's enrollment as well as that of continuing her schooling. The high costs of education, largely due to the necessity of investing in informal private lessons[4], increase markedly after the first five years of schooling. According to estimates by various people in the study community, private lessons cost a total of LE 25 to LE35 a month for all subjects during the first five years of elementary schooling. Once in preparatory school, however, the cost for each subject is LE10 per month. Assuming that a child takes private lessons in an average of five subjects, this means a fixed cost of LE 50 per month. In addition to the costs of private lessons, other significant costs of schooling include uniforms, books, and snacks during the school day. Thus, for poor households, education, especially beyond elementary school, becomes a significant financial burden that must be balanced against other family needs (for an excellent and extensive survey of these costs see El- Baradei 1996; Fergany 1994a).

While the education of daughters was one of the sources of conflicts between husband and wife, sometimes resulting in beatings by the husband, the education of sons appeared to be less contested. Husbands and wives generally felt equally ambivalent about the education of a son beyond elementary school. On the one hand they viewed a boy's education as a source of social mobility for the family. On the other hand, it reduced the possibility of getting a steady apprenticeship in a small-scale workshop that could both earn the family an immediate income, as well as secure him a skilled job in the same trade in the future. With girls, however, there was a clearer difference of opinion.

The reasons for men's ambivalence, and sometimes reluctance to educate their daughters, appears to be partly related to poverty and the need to balance limited income with a range of household expenses. Part of the reason, however, is also related to different interpretations of the value of educating girls. Female education appears to be towards the bottom of men's list of expenditure priorities, whereas for women it is a crucial item.[5]

Women's defiance sometimes took the traditional form of getting angry and leaving the house to go stay with their parents, *ghadbana*, discussed in chapter five. Fatma, a thirty-year-old woman with one daughter in fourth grade of primary school says:

> I wanted to give my daughter private lessons immediately after school started, but my husband wanted to delay them for a few months. I knew if my daughter does not start lessons at the beginning of the year, the teachers will persecute her, *yistaᵓsaduuha*, and will fail her even if she does well. I insisted and we had a big fight. I left the house, *ghidibt*, and stayed in my mother's room next door for a week. Then he came and made up with me and said he will pay for the lessons. He has paid for this month, but I know this will be a continuous fight every month.

Another woman also *ghidbit* like Fatma, but she stayed in her parents' house for two months to pressure her husband into continuing to pay for the private lessons of his two eldest daughters. This strategy worked partly, and a compromise was reached whereby the husband agreed to pay half the costs. The woman agreed to pay the other half, which she managed to save from both her income as a home-based subcontractor, and from the daily food allowance, *masruuf*, that her husband gives her.

I also observed more subtle responses to men's reluctance to invest in educating their daughters. Three women I interviewed kept their daughters in school for several months without the knowledge of their husbands. Om Ahmed, a frail 34-year-old woman married to a day laborer in a carton-recycling workshop is one of them:

> My husband thinks it is unimportant to educate a girl, but I told him she must not grow up to be ignorant, *gahla*, like me. He still refused, so I sent her anyway without telling him. He found out by chance six months later, when he met her in her uniform coming back home … He beat me up and swore to divorce me if I do not take her out, *hilifᶜalaya bil talaᵓ*. My brother and my neighbors intervened, calmed him down, and gradually convinced him that he should let her continue, that education is a good thing and that I will contribute towards the costs from the money I make selling bread … He finally agreed, and my daughter now is in sixth primary. My dream is that my daughter can continue to secondary school.

Samiha, a feisty woman aged twenty-six who has been engaged in sewing on a subcontracting basis for the past eight years (including the two years since she got married), comments bitterly that if it was not for the money she earns from her work, her children would not be in school.

I pay for most of their expenses. My husband would rather put his money in a video. I am the one who made a decision to educate them, took them to get photographed, I applied, I arranged for lessons with their teachers, and paid for everything. If the school asks for a parent, I am the one who goes. He does not even know where the school is. If I cannot educate all of them, then Aya, my daughter, is my priority. If a girl is educated, she has dignity/pride, *karaama*, her husband cannot control her, *yisaytar ᶜalleeha*. She would also be able to marry an educated man. I cannot subject my daughter to the hard work and humiliation, *bahdala, marmata*, that I saw as an ignorant woman. I cannot let my girl grow up like that. If I do not educate all my children, at least I have to educate my daughter Aya.

When a husband refuses to meet education costs, some women use escalating tactics. Initial tussles often result in arguments, getting angry, seeking family and community support, refusing to have sex, or leaving the house. If all this fails, it is common for a woman to try to pay for the cost herself. Seeking paid employment, usually in menial and low-paying jobs, saving from housekeeping allocation, the *masruuf*, and joining rotating credit societies, *gamᶜiyya*(s) (which will be discussed below) are three of the most common methods that women deploy to keep their daughters in school.

Om Yehia, a co-wife in her forties who runs a grocery, has put five of her six girls and one boy through school. Her husband, a semiskilled worker in the construction trade, used to give her a weekly allowance, but has stopped doing so for the past few years. She thinks he is having an affair with a woman from a neighboring community, and is visibly upset about both his affair and the fact that he no longer gives her an additional allowance. Om Yehia comments:

My husband thinks educating the girls is useless. They will marry someone and go away, he would say. I ignored him, however, and I sent them all, but he did not pay a piaster for it. Through the profit from the *bꝑaala*, and through saving from the *masruuf*, I am able to make ends meet, but it is so expensive … God willing, I will continue their education. Education is critical for a girl so that if her husband dies, if she gets divorced, or if he stops providing for her, she can respectably support herself, not become miserable, *titwikis*, like what happened to me. She can also get a respectable job, *wazeefa muhtarama*. An educated woman will also not take an ignorant man, *gahil*. With an education she will marry better.

Amina, an uneducated woman in her early thirties with a son and a daughter, assembles upholstery pins on a subcontracting basis. Her husband is a driver, but does not have a regular job. Her comments reveal that boys have better access than girls to income earning opportunities through learning a skill through an apprenticeship in a workshop, an option that is not available for girls. This is why she prefers to use the earnings from her work to pay for her daughter's education. She comments:

I am engaged in this job that breaks the back, mainly to keep my children in school, particularly my daughter. My son can work in a workshop in the afternoons and make some money towards his school expenses, but my daughter cannot. I do not want any-one to say that she is a workshop girl, *bint wirash*.[6] Their father does not have a regu-lar job. He will not pay for education and after many fights he said he will pay only for the private lessons of the boy, not the girl. If I wanted to keep the girl in school also, I would have to pay for it myself.

Om Ahmed, a 48-year-old woman, took up a job as a wage laborer in an infor-mal factory producing socks, so as to provide for the education of her children beyond the preparatory stage. Her comments point to a critical issue, raised by other women, regarding the conditions of employment which women aspire to:

I was adamant/insistent, *musirra*, that they finish their education. It is particularly important for me to educate my daughter, because I was not educated, an education enables one to work, *il taᶜaleem ᶜalleeh ᶜamal*. There is work and work. The work of educated people is different. Am I like a *muwazafa*, a government employee? If I were educated would I work in a job like this one? Yes I may earn more here, but the minute the owner tells me I do not want you, it is finished, I have to leave. If I work for twenty years, I will also never get a pension. Education for a girl is also important nowadays because when a good man proposes, he would always asks: What degree does the girl have?

An interesting issue that emerged from my data is the link that some women made between education and the goal of minimizing household violence against women. Om Sahar is an uneducated woman with two daughters and one son. Her husband told her last year that he cannot afford to continue paying for school expenses, particularly the regular monthly costs of private lessons. Om Sahar comments:

I told him that my children must get an education, my son can quit school, but not my daughter. I would sell my clothes to educate my daughter. If my daughter has a degree, her husband would not dare beat her up the way you beat me. If I was educated, you would not be able to lay a hand on me. I would be a respectable *muwazafa*, and I would have married someone who appreciates me, *biyᵖaddarni*, and has a clean tongue, *lisaano nidiif*.

Other women also made this link between domestic violence and the educa-tion of girls. Attiyat, a 30-year-old middle woman who distributes shoes to com-munity women to sew at home and has four children, comments:

The education of a girl is a treasure, *ᶜalaam il bint kinz*. An educated girl would be able to marry a decent/respectable man, who will treat her well, *yiᶜamilha kowayes*, and would not scream at her or hit her for no reason. An ignorant woman has no dignity, and is powerless, *malhaash hiila*, but an educated woman would not tolerate what we tolerate from our husbands. Education is more important for a girl than for a boy. A boy has many job options when he grows up, even if he is not educated. But for a girl, education will assure her the best job. It is better than putting money aside for her. What would she do with the money? Open a workshop?

Such comments suggest that the often-cited proverb indicating that women do not mind being beaten, "being beaten by a lover is like eating raisins, *darb il habiib zay akl il zibiib,*" must not be taken at face value as a portrayal of all women's world views on this issue. In fact, women's views on violence were quite complex and sometimes ambiguous, representing an excellent example of how the consciousness of subordinate groups in "hegemonic relationships" is a mix of contradictory views and values. Some of these views reflect the values of the dominant groups, and some emerge more directly from practical experience (Eagleton 1991).

In my discussions, two categories of violence which I term "justified violence" and "unjustified violence" were evoked by women at different times, referring to both the reasons sparking the violence and the degree of abuse. Women sometimes regarded violence—wife beating and verbal abuse—as a nondesirable practice, unjust, wrong, and generally "unjustified." In some cases, however, violence, was also regarded as "justified." These were cases where a woman was believed to have breached deeply ingrained expectations, such as flirting publicly with another man. As discussed earlier, refusal to have sex was sometimes considered an offense serious enough for a woman to deserve beating and at other times was not. In the long term, women appear to be addressing the issue of violence through educating their daughters.[7]

In contrast to the many women I interviewed for whom a girl's education was high on their list of priorities, I only encountered one case where when a woman said that her husband wanted their daughters to stay in school, but she disagreed and felt it would be a waste of money. There were many more cases, on the other hand, where the wife would insist that her daughter stay in school but her husband would not agree, would not take the required bureaucratic steps to register his daughter, or would be unwilling to pay for it. I also encountered several cases when a woman decided, on her own, to take her daughter out of school. Om Tamer explains why she took her daughter out:

> I took her out when she was fourteen because she was very pretty and I wanted to protect her, I was afraid that she would be harassed by the male youth in the streets and by her male teachers.

Om Tamer's husband did not go against her decision nor argue about it. It was clearly his wife's decision.

Of course, women's aspirations and attempts to keep their daughters in school do not always work. There were many cases when women had to take their daughters out of school because, despite all their efforts, they could still not find the necessary resources, were unable to find paid employment, had to make trade-offs between education costs and other important costs such as that of the *gihaaz,* or could not convince their daughters to remain in school. Of the fifty-nine once married women in my sample, ten reported that they were unable to pursue their struggles to educate their daughters. One of these women is Om Zeinab. In resignation she recalls:

> My husband, who works in a coffee shop, refused to buy Magda a new uniform at the beginning of the school year. She had to wear the old one and she was ashamed and said that people made fun of her, so she decided not to go anymore. What could I have done, I am helpless and have no money, *mabil yad hiila.* If I had money, it may have been different.

Neama, a fifteen-year-old, talks about her reasons for quitting school, despite her mother's initial insistence. The trade-offs between investing in education or accumulating a *gihaaz* (discussed in chapter six) as two status-enhancing mechanisms for girls is evident in her remarks:

> If my mother keeps working to pay for the costs of my education, she will not be able to start saving for my *gihaaz.* So I decided to leave school and start working to help complete my *gihaaz.* My mother was upset and said what about your future, but I told her that this(meaning ensuring a good marriage through a proper *gihaaz*) is my future too. She agreed and I have been working now for three years and have already bought an aluminium set, sheets, and a refrigerator.

The suggestions emerging from my data that there may be a difference between men and women in the value put on girls' education and in the efforts pursued to secure schooling is noteworthy in view of the demonstrated link between female education and "empowerment" worldwide (see for example El-Hamamsy 1994; Jejeebhoy 1996). The mothers who insist on educating their daughters may neither be feminists nor possess a consciousness of their oppression as women in the way it is commonly understood. After all these are the same mothers who insisted on circumcising their daughters or on public displays of their virginity, as discussed in chapters five and seven. Nonetheless, the reasons women offered for keeping their daughters in school also indicate an awareness of women's vulnerability to injustice and abuse in both their marital relations and in their working environment.

The two reasons most often cited for insisting that daughters complete their education are: finding a respectable job, *waziifa muhtarama,* and finding a *muhtaram,* respectful, and educated husband with assurance of a regular income, thus avoiding abuse both at work and at home. What is striking is that both reasons center on a search for respect, and are closely related to some aspects of these women's own self-identity and including unpleasant memories and demeaning practical life experiences in both marriage and employment. Bourdieu's notion of the *habitus* is illuminating in this respect. The habitus, argues

Bourdieu, "as a product of history, produces individual and collective practices, ensures the active presence of past experiences deposited in the form of schemes of perception, thought and action." Women's aspirations and behaviour can be considered 'anticipations of the habitus' ... "those practical hypotheses based on past experiences and which give disproportionate weight to early experiences" (Bourdieu 1990:55).

An educated woman could, in the eyes of the women I interviewed, avoid the menial and low-paying jobs that many of them are now engaged in, such as piece-work or waged work in workshops, discussed previously. Such work is considered both degrading and low-paying. Anxious that their daughters may need to seek paid employment in the future, and aware of links between securing financial independence and increasing their leverage for decision making within their household, mothers attempt to enhance their daughter's future opportunities for finding "respectable" jobs. These would be jobs with better work conditions, regular working hours which can accommodate their domestic roles, social security benefits, and a decent and assured income at the end of the month—unlike the jobs they themselves are currently engaged in.

Given the high level of graduate unemployment in Egypt (see Fergany 1995), it is difficult to judge how realistic these dreams are. Nonetheless, there were several "models" of upward mobility, success stories pointed out to me and circulating in the community of certain women who through their education were able to find jobs, with local offices of the ministry of social affairs, with local NGOs, and, in two cases, with private sector firms outside the community.

Education was also seen as a way to expand marriage options and to reduce the possibility of marital violence. Women reasoned that education elevated the status and prestige of a woman (and her family's) in the community and enabled her to better contest and defy domestic violence. This may partly be because investing in a daughter's education suggests to members of the community that she is valued by her family. Some women argued, again sometimes through specific examples, that an educated woman is likely to have more choices of who she would marry. She is also more likely to marry an educated man who they believed would be more inclined to treat her well. What all of this suggests is that at least some women appear to be actively seeking ways of addressing the issue of marital abuse, including violence.[8] Women's insistence on educating their daughters thus appear to be fulfilling both practical gender interests, interests derived from the practical daily needs and realities of women and which may imply a complicity with existing gender hierarchies, as well as strategic gender interests, those which consciously challenge the premises underlying current gender relations and thus have trans-formatory potential[9] (Molyneux 1985, 1998). The suggestion that women in low-income areas of Cairo are particularly eager to educate their daughters is at variance with most studies and observations regarding girls' education in rural Egypt Existing studies refer to general "family" pressures and objections, arguing that parents are more reluctant to invest in their daughters because they eventually "marry out" (see for example El-Baradei 1996). I was able to identify only one recent study in rural Egypt that hints, albeit in passing, to a gender difference in decisions regarding education, in the other direction. In her field study of the sociocultural context of early marriage in two villages in Egypt, El-Hamamsy (1994) addresses the reasons why many of the women married over the past ten years did not get a formal education. Her study finds that "some 49 percent of the women reported that they did not attend school because parents, particularly the father, did not believe in girls' education and thought it was useless or socially shameful" (El-Hamamsy 1994:22). Other studies, observations, and conventional wisdom however claim that one of the main obstacles to girls' education is women's burdensome household chores in rural areas, and thus suggest that it is primarily mothers who pull their daughters out of school so that they can help out with domestic chores, such as cooking, fetching water and caring for younger siblings, as well as assist in agriculture related activities, animal husbandry and dairy production.[10]

Rural and Urban Differences: Some Hypotheseses

A number of hypotheseses regarding urban-rural differences[11] in attitudes and practices regarding girls' education may be entertained. The first hypothesis is related to the different nature of domestic chores and unpaid family labor in urban and rural areas. Women's household chores in urban areas are generally less time-consuming. For example, two of the most time-consuming activities in rural areas which require the assistance of girls, namely baking bread and fetching water, are much less relevant in urban areas where many women buy ready-made bread and have easier access to tap water, inside or outside the house. Other time-consuming activities, like food processing and dairy production, are also largely replaced in urban areas by cash purchases. Child-care responsibilities may also be less demanding in urban areas due to a smaller family size. The women I interviewed were very aware of these differences between their own domestic chores and those of rural areas, and expressed them in their reluctance to let their daughters marry into rural households.

The second hypothesis is related to urban women's personal experience of paid employment. Unlike rural women, many poor urban women have first-hand experience in paid employment in the informal sector. Not all informal sector work is necessarily low-paying. However, as mentioned earlier, many women in the community studied were engaged in two forms of informal sector employment: home-based piecework, which is irregular, tedious and poorly paid, and wage labor, which pays better, but offers no security, provides limited opportunities for job mobility, entails the risk of sexual harassment, and is considered a highly "unrespectable" job for girls.

With male unemployment steadily rising over the past decade, and being more deeply tied into an inflationary cash economy, poor urban women also recognize, more than their counterparts in rural areas, that their daughters may need to seek paid employment in the future. Education becomes not just an avenue for social mobility and respect, but also a hedge against future insecurities. By educating their daughters, urban mothers believe they can secure them more "respectable"—not necessarily higher paying—jobs, jobs with better terms and conditions than the ones they have themselves experienced.

Finally, I venture a hypothesis about the changing nature of family structures in urban areas that affect residence patterns, household dynamics, intergenerational flows and support systems, as well as normative expectations from female kin. The centrality of women in urban kinship systems, a phenomena termed interchangeably "matrifocality," "matrilateral asymmetry," "matrilateral bias," and "gynefocality," has been suggested by several studies in Western industrialized countries (Yanagisako 1978). This phenomenon characterizes both intra-and intergenerational relationships, and has been observed in residence patterns, flows of mutual aid and exchange, frequency of visitation, and in sentiments of closeness (Vatuk 1971).

One explanation for this phenomenon is related to the differentiation in male occupational roles accompanying industrialization, which has meant that the household is no longer a central economic production unit and thus that relations between men have lost some of their strength. Other explanations have centered on families' desire to cope with the conflicting pressures of a commitment to an independent nuclear family and conjugal unit, on the one hand, and the need to maintain mutual dependence and extrahousehold ties and solidarity, on the other. Yanagisako (1977) argues, based on her research among Japanese-American families in Seattle in the U.S., that because female ties were viewed by her interviewees as less economically and politically demanding, and as based more on sentiment than on "instrumentality," female interpersonal networks were less threatening to ideologies of conjugal independence .

One of the few attempts to test the "matrilateral hypothesis" is provided by Vatuk's study of first-generation urban migrants in two neighborhoods in North India. She finds that while kinship systems were still predominantly patrilineal both structurally and normatively, there was an increasing trend towards matrilateral kin. This was reflected in more visits and interaction between a married woman and her sisters in the urban setting and the acceptance of a broader range of roles for a wife's relatives as opposed to those formerly deemed appropriate only for the relatives of the husband (Vatuk 1971).

In my study community, there were similarly some indications of strong relations between female kin, particularly between mother and daughter. As mentioned in chapter seven, working adolescent daughters normally gave a portion of their wages to their mothers, not their fathers. Older unmarried sons, on the other hand, generally retained most of their income. Moreover, there was a strong preference for women to live close to their own mothers when married, and as discussed earlier, one of the issues prospective brides actively negotiated was choice of residence. Once married, visits between mother and daughter were undoubtedly much more frequent than those between a son and his mother. Of the few extended households in the community, three were based on a groom living in his wife's parents household, an unconventional residential structure in the Egyptian context. Community members did not express any negative sentiments regarding this residential pattern.

It is plausible to argue that at a more general level in the Egyptian urban context, a trend towards matrifocality may be in the making. Mothers' expectations of daughters may be changing with respect to old-age security and support. In an urban nuclear family context, daughters may acquire more importance as a source of future support. Whereas in a rural family, an older woman could count on the services of her coresident daughter-in-law, this is less likely in urban areas where most families are nuclear. In such a context, it may be that mothers increasingly rely on their daughter(s) to support them in their old age, as well as to help them in coping with the complexities of urban life such as dealings with the bureaucracy.[12] Women know from practical experience that literacy is a particular advantage for survival in the urban context, and thus arguably resolve to invest in their daughter's education.

Several women recalled their experiences of having to go to a doctor, or a government office, and their frustrations at not knowing how to read the bus numbers, directions, or instructions. "I always take my (educated) daughter with me when I go to get my pension," ventured one woman. My observations suggest that it was daughters, more often than sons, who were called upon in such situations. These observations and tentative hypotheseses clearly require further investigation as to exactly how family relationships may be changing due to the demands put on women and men by urban life.

The implications of the above suggestions are multiple, both at the theoretical and policy levels. One implication is that attempts to close the gender gap in education in Egypt will not simply be realized through the efforts of governments and donors to build more "girl-friendly" schools and the laudable activities of the government and NGOs to introduce literacy classes. Perhaps just as importantly, these goals will be realized through the daily struggles and aspirations of thousands of illiterate women to enroll, and keep, their daughters in school. These struggles are both material, necessitating efforts to find the necessary means to cover education costs, but also symbolic and ideological in that they may defy male authority with respect to decisions in this area. Of course, women's efforts do not always achieve their intended consequences.[13] What is critical to note here, however, is that failure, in this specific instance, is often due to women's inability to generate the necessary financial resources to pursue their aim. Household poverty in general, and women's lack of an independent and adequate income, in particular, emerge as important reasons why women's attempts in this arena sometimes meet with failure. This supports Agarwal's argument, in her critique of Sen's (1990) overemphasis on women's lack of perception of their self interest, that the issue at stake is often not sharpening women's perceptions of their self-interest, but improving their ability to overcome the external constraints that prevent them from pursuing these interests (Agarwal 1994). In the Egyptian context, policies that can assist with the financial costs of the education of girls in poor urban areas, either directly in the form of scholarships, or indirectly through providing women with access to more lucrative income-earning opportunities, can significantly improve women's "fallback" positions, and are clearly called for.

Theoretically, my data challenges some of the still pervasive notions of women's false consciousness which pervades much feminist writing, and which casts women as passive beings who internalize their subordination and perpetuate their own oppression. Despite increasing data that questions these notions, and although several scholars are moving away from this simplistic, and ahistorical approach, as Agarwal points out in a recent book, it is still: "a longstanding view which continues to hold sway" (Agarwal 1994: 422). The comments by Sahar El-Mogy, an Egyptian feminist and writer, in her review of a recent study on reproductive health in rural Egypt in an important Arabic-language journal on women's studies, are an excellent example of this prevalent view in Egypt. Emphasizing how the study reveals various forms of oppression from which rural women suffer, she argues that the main problem is as follows:

> [T]hey (meaning poor rural women) are not able to alleviate their oppression or challenge it, because they are not aware that they are being oppressed in the first place. Society has made women into spokes in a wheel, into dolls that have learned how to perform certain roles and who have neither the consciousness nor education that can enable them to begin to question and challenge their surroundings. The first question that must be tackled before improvements in women's position can be made is: How can we make women realize the nature and severity of their oppression. (Hagar 1994 226, translated from Arabic)

Focusing on decisions regarding the education of girls, this section has illustrated that women and men in the same household may have divergent interests and priorities. These are often reflected in conflicts over budgetary allocations and serve to complicate decision-making processes within households. The above discussion has illustrated that an examination of intrahousehold relations is thus critical for understanding power in gender relations and the ways in which women may seek to gain leverage to pursue their own priorities. However, women's resources, and hence their relative power, are not solely determined by their familial context but are also influenced by their access to extrahousehold options. An analysis of relations, strategies and networks that go beyond the household is thus also crucial. This forms the focus of the following section.

Beyond the Household: Extrafamilial Networks

A number of feminist writers have argued that the household is an inadequate unit of analysis, as intrahousehold power relations and hierarchies are shaped not only by household dynamics, but by socioeconomic and ideological forces beyond it (Harris 1981; Moore 1988). Others have cautioned that an overemphasis on the household also leads to misleading conceptualizations of the household as an autonomous unit where marital arrangements are given priority over other types of social arrangements in defining relations between men and women (Whitehead 1984, quoted in Moore 1988).

Women's multiple roles in extrahousehold kin and nonkin networks have long been ignored in the analysis of kinship and power structures in anthropology. This "invisibility" of women has, however, been challenged by several feminist anthropologists who have pointed to the diverse forms of cooperation between women, and their relevance to women's ability to improve their bargaining positions. Several writers have suggested that women who are not well integrated into durable and lasting support networks often have less independent decision-making powers and are more subject to male authority within households (Chaplain and Bujra 1982; March and Taqqu 1986; Moore 1988).

Women's networks have, as a result, received increasing attention in cross-cultural research over the past ten years. Using ethnographic data, from diverse societies in the developing world, March and Taqqu (1986) argue that some women's informal networks have transformatory potential, and can be effective "catalysts for change." They show how extrahousehold social networks, mostly informal loosely structured groupings, play a critical role in mediating women's access to many kinds of material and emotional resources, services, and information. These networks can have considerable legitimacy and power, often enabling women to better voice their concerns and perspectives, widen their options, and enhance their solidarity and spheres of influence (March and Taqqu 1986).

Many studies of Middle Eastern societies similarly stress the importance of women's networks. Joseph's study of an urban working class community in Lebanon demonstrates the vitality and intensity of street-based networks, which are primarily the domain of women. Her study highlights the role of the neighborhood street, *Zaruub*, as a boundary marker of a social unit, and as the site of intricate and deep relations of reciprocity and sharing that transcend family and kinship (Joseph 1978). In the Sudan, the cult of *zaar*, has been pinpointed as a specifically female extrafamilial network that enables new migrants to adapt to urban life (Constantinides 1978). Hale (1993), also drawing on research in the Sudan, goes further in emphasizing the potentially political nature of *zaar* gatherings and networks and interprets them as "protest ceremonies," during which issues of concern to women, ignored or avoided by other groups, are raised.

Although I started out with an awareness of such networks and was prepared to explore linkages and forms of cooperation between households, my early discussions with women on these topics were frustrating, as mentioned in chapter four. As I spent more time in the community, however, I began to observe the range of networks of mutual help that did exist. For example, washing clothes involved a common form of cooperation between women in different households. Women with access to a roof usually offered others use of roof space, washing pegs and washing ropes. Since four or five families could need to use the roof of the same house, a system of rotation was usually agreed upon in advance to avoid problems and to accommodate everyone's needs. The timing of the weekly wash was based on the husband's day off, and thus on his occupation. For a government employee that day was Friday, and thus a family who had men working in the government would normally do the weekly wash on Thursday. The day off for workers in the informal sector was Sundays, and such families would thus wash on Saturdays.[14]

I observed and participated in several networks. These served as important avenues for providing women with access to financial resources and information, emotional support, recreation, and space for the articulation of discontent. In this section, I analyze three such networks: spirit possession circles, female-run grocery shops, and rotating credit associations. There are important difference in their bases for membership, their structures and their purposes. However, all three networks can be described as leader centered—that is, revolving around a single female leader. They also incorporate both "active" and "defensive" strategies,[15] and have a predominantly, but not exclusively, female membership.

Women-centered Networks: Hadra(s), Bꟼaala(s) and Gamᶜiyya(s)

Spirit possession as a communicative mechanism has been discussed extensively in chapter eight. Spirit possession circles, *hadra*(s*)*, however, not only provide a discursive space for the emergence of an alternate "language" to express discontent and negotiate social expectations, but, as in the Sudan, they also provide an important physical space for some low-income Cairene women to socialize freely. The *hadra*(s*)* ceremonies provide one of the few nonkin, non-neighborhood-based female networks in low-income Cairo. They thus carve out an important and separate physical and social space for women where they can forge new relationships outside the confines of their daily lives, relationships which supplement kinship relations. During the breaks between the dancing, women often discussed common problems, and exchanged advice about marriage, health, children, employment and other areas of concern. *Hadra*(s) thus provide a context for the emergence of new notions of personhood, notions based on same-sex friendships, but not on the dominant principles of domestic kinship, such as mothers, daughters, wives, aunts and so forth, which play a central part in defining female identity. The *hadra*(s) thus provide an interesting example of how, as Loizos and Papataxiarchis argue, in specific contexts kinship may be "implicated in the construction of gender identity" in a manner that is quite different than the way it is in the dominant conjugal model of gender, which informs much of ethnographic analysis (1991a).

The *hadra*(s*)* is female dominated and are led and managed, to a large extent, by women.[16] The role of the *kudya*, on which a *hadra*(s*)* is dependent, is an exclusively female occupation with considerable prestige, status and influence. It is an achieved role that does not derive from association with men (as husbands, brothers, or fathers), but is earned through successfully orchestrating spirit possession ceremonies over many years. It is noteworthy, that only a woman who has been previously possessed, or is currently afflicted, can become a *kudya*. The role of the *kudya* is often passed on from possessed mother to possessed daughter.

As I learned when I asked the *kudya* at one of the ceremonies to make a diagnosis, *atar*, for me, matriarchal concepts are central to the diagnostic procedures related to spirit possession. To find out their *atar*, a woman (or man) has to provide the *kudya* with a piece of personal clothing (I provided a T-shirt, although the *kudya* had insisted that I provide a more personal item). Then a woman or a man writes their first name, and that of their mother only, on a piece of paper. When the *kudya* asked me to write my mother's name, I could not help but contrast this with the request for my father's name on all official papers and documents in Egypt, and I must admit to a certain sense of pleasure. "In our world," explained the *kudya*, "mothers are more important than fathers." Several studies have similarly highlighted how women's rituals often honor specifically female roles. As Tapper (1983) and Sorabji (1994) show, a significant portion of women's gatherings around *muulids*, celebrations of the birth of the Prophet, in both Turkish towns and the city of Sarajevo, revolves around the celebration of the nativity and motherhood of the Prophet's mother.[17]

What strengthens the potential power of a *hadra*(s) as independent female space is that it is not exclusively a women's network. Afflicted men sometimes participate, but they are usually very limited in number. This is probably one of the few instances where women mix with men in the same confined space, but where men represent a minority. At the *hadra*(s) I attended, the number of women at any one time ranged between ten to forty; the number of men never exceeded three, and they looked terribly intimidated and uncomfortable. In most of the *hadra*(s) I attended, there were no men present at all.[18]

Some women go to the *hadra*(s) on a regular basis and a familiarity quickly develops amongst the "regulars," which a *kudya* assured me does not happen with the men. After I had been to the same *hadra*(s) for several consecutive times, I started recognizing faces and felt much more relaxed, familiar, and like I belonged to a group. From the way some women greeted me, I also suspect that they had started to recognize me as a "regular." Women of all ages participate in spirit possession networks, even those who are not necessarily possessed, as mentioned earlier. In the ones I attended, however, there was a predominance of married women in their middle years. Some relationships established during a *hadra*, may be followed up and developed outside its physical confines. I was unfortunately unable to probe into this aspect as much as I would have liked, however, partly because of time constraints, and partly because there seemed to be reluctance among the women to admit to keeping in touch with those they met in *hadra*(s). This reluctance indicates that *hadra*(s), while tolerated, do not have full public legitimacy and sanction.

Another common network in the study community is focused around small female managed grocery stores, *bꞮaala*(s), which are often home-based. These serve as a place for meetings and exchanges between women. Running a grocery, is not an exclusively female role as is the case of the *kudya* mentioned above, or the *gamᶜiyya* leader, whose role will be discussed below. Many are run by women, but there are also *bꞮaala*(s) run by men. However the latter tend to be larger, better stocked, and, at least as far as the women are concerned, they do not provide the same support network.[19]

Most of these *bꞮaala*(s) have a relatively steady clientele[20] of approximately twenty to fifty women who, over time, develop intimate relations with each other and use the grocery shop as a locale for sharing a wide range of information regarding jobs, health, marriage opportunities, marital problems, and the like. The relationships between the grocer and other women are based on more than mere financial transactions, but also incorporate many elements of patron-client ties, partly because of the control that the grocer has over much-valued, and often scarce, subsidized goods, such as rice and sugar. The relationship is further complicated because many *bꞮaala*(s) are illegal and unregulated. Thus when word goes around that a government official is checking the area, word is quickly sent to the grocer, often by one of her regular clients, and the shop is promptly closed. A grocer thus conducts her relationships with clients carefully, since there is always the threat that an angry client could expose her to government officials.

The profitability, size and sphere of influence of *a bꞮaala* varies, growing or decreasing partly depending on the charisma and resourcefulness of its manager. Some of the women running these *bꞮaala*(s), also manage to become organizers of saving associations, *gamᶜiyya*(s), which will be discussed below. This constitutes an example of how starting a micro-enterprise such as a *bꞮaala* can grow from merely a way of increasing one's income to make ends meet to becoming a strategy for exerting substantial influence in the distribution of resources and gaining prestige in the community. Clients are tied to these groceries by a daily or weekly credit system of *shukuk,* buying on credit, and it is through checking out a woman's "credit history," that a grocery owner can determine who is trustworthy and reliable enough to incorporate into a *gamᶜiyya*. This minimizes repayment problems and also helps to secure her own reputation in the community as a successful *gamᶜiyya* leader.

My observations support findings in one low-income community in Cairo which suggests that women value these interactions around *bꞮaala*(s) so much that they purposefully spread their purchases throughout the day (Shorter et al. 1994). It is important to note, however, that *bꞮaala*(s), are more valuable in this respect for women at a certain point in their life cycle. These are unmarried older adolescents, or recently married women whose mobility is usually more restricted than older women and younger girls. While the latter group also uses the *bꞮaala*(s), they also have more access to retail or wholesale markets outside their neighborhoods.

A third, pervasive type of network in the community is the *gam^ciyya,* an informal rotating credit and savings association. The importance of rotating credit
associations as both a financial and social support system has been highlighted by
several researchers and in societies as diverse as India, Mexico, Malaysia, China,
Barbados, Jamaica, Nigeria, and the Cameroon (Taqqu and March 1986).
Despite cross-cultural variations, a feature they share in common is their disproportionate representation of women.

Several studies in Egypt have highlighted the role of *gam^ciyya*(s) (Hoodfar
1997; Nadim 1985; Singerman 1995; Wikan 1980). *Gam^ciyya*(s) are formed by
a group of people who are interested in saving money for a specific purpose. Each
member contributes a similar and agreed-upon sum of money into a common
fund on a regular basis, weekly, monthly or daily. Each member is then given the
whole amount of money in the fund based on the agreed upon system of rotation.

Singerman's study in Cairo neighborhoods is perhaps the most detailed one highlighting the prevalence of *gam^ciyya*(s). She shows how they provide a critical informal mechanism for financing marriage expenses in particular, in a context where
marriage expenses are extremely high and where people have no access to the formal
banking system. Singerman estimates that a large portion of national gross domestic savings may in fact be circulating in informal savings, and argues that the "savings ethic" in the country is no doubt much stronger than official estimates would
lead one to expect. Since *gam^ciyya*(s) are predominantly organized by women, she
further argues that women are the real "bankers" in Egypt (Singerman 1995).

Gam^ciyya(s) were common in the community studied. The *gam^ciyya*(s) I
observed and participated in were based on either residence or place of employment, were all managed by women, and had a disproportionate female membership. A *gam^ciyya* is initiated by one person, who gathers a group from ten to
thrity people, mainly women, who may be interested in joining. The members of
the group may not themselves know each other, but are linked through the person who initiated the *gam^ciyya* and who becomes its leader and manages the common fund. Some members contribute more than one share. The personal
circumstances of the different members are taken into account when deciding on
collection rotations, and the *gam^ciyya* leaders play a crucial role in this process of
decision making. Rotation periods vary, but most were on a weekly basis, with a
single payment ranging from three pounds to fifteen pounds a week.

While many women were involved in *gam^ciyya*(s), it is important to note that
they were not an option for all women. Very poor women were often excluded
from these networks. Some told me that they have never joined a savings society,
because they had neither the luxury of a steady income themselves, however meager, nor a husband with a steady income that would ensure the regular repay-
ments. In fact not joining a *gam^ciyya* is often a good indication of the level of
poverty of a woman and her household.

As I found out when I was asked to join a *gam^ciyya* myself, its organizers wel-
come new members, even if they are from outside the community. In fact,

gam^ciyya(s) often act as a way of integrating a newcomer into community networks. New members, however, are checked out as carefully as possible, but more importantly, they get their payment at the end of the cycle. After demonstrating their trustworthiness, they can then be allocated progressively earlier rotations. In the four *gam^ciyya*(s) I participated in during my fieldwork, I was allocated either the last rotation or the one before last. I think in my case, however, it had less to do with trust, and more to do with my being perceived as a resource, someone who could afford to add to the capital without benefiting from early returns. Being paid last, however, was not necessarily perceived as a disadvantage. Some women said they like to be paid at the end of a cycle as they did not want to be in debt. In their case, their motives for joining a *gam^ciyya* were those of not getting advance payments, but were more related to ensuring that the money they are able to save every month was not spent and was protected from possible diversion into household expenses.

Unlike that of the grocer and the *kudya*, the role of a *gam^ciyya* leader is not as specialized as a profession or activity, but is usually combined with other roles. Grocers, as mentioned earlier, and door to door saleswomen, *dallala,* often organize *gam^ciyya*(s) capitalizing on their extensive networks of clients. Although theoretically anybody can start a *gam^ciyya*, some women in the community had a particular fame as g*am^ciyya* organizers and others had bad reputations and were to be avoided.

Conflicts often occurred in *gam^ciyya*(s), due to a member defaulting on a rotation, or another demanding an earlier turn in the midst of rotation due to an emergency situation. Reallocating turns and making allowances for these kinds of emergencies, without alienating other members, as well deciding when to put pressure on defaulting members to honor their agreement, requires skill and intimate knowledge of the circumstances and character of each member. A good *gam^ciyya* leader was thus considered one who ensures that members takes their turns on time, resolves conflicts in a fair manner, taking people's personal circumstances into account (such as a sudden death or illness), is flexible about turns if necessary, and ensures the privacy of the individual women involved in the *gam^ciyya*(s).

Usually, but not necessarily, the organizer of a *gam^ciyya* takes the first turn. Other turns rotate subject to negotiation with the organizer and tailored to the demands and circumstances of individual women, such as an impending birth, marriage, or the beginning of the school year. Once a woman has committed herself to a *gam^ciyya*, she must honor it to the end of a rotation. It is highly frowned upon if she quits in midcycle. Unless there is a 'cas de force majeure', she is not entitled to take back the money she has deposited into the *gam^ciyya* until the very end of the cycle. Exceptions are made, however, as in the case of a widow whose room caught fire destroying most of her meager belongings. She had already been allocated the total amount of the *gam^ciyya*, but had three installments with a total of fifteen pounds left. The *gam^ciyya* leader paid them herself.

Unlike the *hadra*(s), and *bɔaala*(s), where some women know each other and often meet, *gamᶜiyya*(s) are not networks in the physical or personal sense. *Gamᶜiyya(s)* are more "anonymous" networks, where members may not know each other, or may only know some of the other members. Sometimes the only direct link between the members is the organizer herself, who usually knows the members on a personal basis. In fact, it is important that people do not know who else is in a *gamᶜiyya*, Om Nagi, the leader of one of the *gamᶜiyya*(s) I joined explained to me, because a *gamᶜiyya* could be cursed by the evil eye, *titnizer.*

Another *gamᶜiyya* organizer said that this secrecy is necessary because sometimes women, particularly those who have an independent source of income, join a *gamᶜiyya* without the knowledge of their husbands as they may want to spend the money on something of which the husband disapproves (such as educating a daughter or having an abortion for example), or may want to protect their incomes from possible demands by a husband. My observations and discussions actually confirmed that some women are quite careful not to tell their husbands when they have joined a *gamᶜiyya*. A good *gamᶜiyya* leader thus does not leak out information out about who is in her network so that these women do not get into trouble with their husbands.

As with the two networks discussed above, *gamᶜiyya*(s) are a predominantly, but not exclusively, female network. Some *gamᶜiyya*(s) are all female, some are all male, and some are mixed. The majority would seem to fall in the first and third categories. It is interesting to note, however, that even the all male *gamᶜiyya(s) are* organized by women. As mentioned earlier, not every woman can become a successful *gamᶜiyya* organizer. A *gamiᶜiyya* leader must possess a diversity of skills to manage these networks well and successful organizers acquire significant influence and status in the community. However, the reasons given as to why *gamᶜiyya* leadership is a specifically female role did not always reflect an awareness of the considerable skills required by this job. "Women organize *gamᶜiyya*(s), not men," one woman told me, "because they are the ones who are staying at home and have empty heads, *mukhkhuhum faadi.*" Other community members were more cognizant that women possess special qualities which enable them to mobilize people, in a way that men cannot: "Men cannot organize *gamᶜiyya*(s)," ventured Sayeda, "because they cannot gather people together around them, *yillimu il naas,* like women can."

Gamᶜiyya(s) play an important role in enabling individual women to gain more control and decision-making power within their marriage, partly by providing them with an avenue for obtaining financial assistance, and thus relative financial independence. By getting advance payments or saving money through joining a *gamᶜiyya*, a woman may be able to start small income-generating ventures—such as vending, or recycling activities—to put a daughter through school, or to buy items for her *gihaaz.* Many women are able to join *gamᶜiyya*(s) through shrewd savings from the daily or weekly housekeeping allocation that their husbands provide, taking particular care to cut down on expenses in a manner that cannot be detected by their husbands.

One of the particularly interesting findings that emerged from my observations of *gamᶜiyya*(s), but which so far has not been noted in the literature, is that some women use the *gamᶜiyya* as a way of diverting male income, which they believe rightfully belongs to them. This was particularly the case in better-off households where a husband was making a reasonable income but not spending it according to the priorities of his wife. Om Muhammed, who generates an income of about LE3 a day, through selling *belila* (a popular dessert dish made from wheat, milk and sugar) and sweets at the corner of her street, and is married to a semiskilled worker in an electrical workshop, explains her reasons for joining *gamᶜiyya*(s). I quote her extensively below, because the use of *gamᶜiyya*(s) as a way of rerouting male earnings, invoked by a few other women, comes through very clearly in her comments.

Gamᶜiyya(s) are complex social arrangements with multiple facets and purposes that clearly cannot be reduced to a single purpose. Not all women viewed *gamᶜiyya*(s) in the same light as Om Muhammed. Nonetheless, I highlight Om Muhammed's reasoning because it adds an interesting nuance to our understanding of how some women may deploy *gamᶜiyya*(s) as strategies to gain what they perceived to be their rightful entitlement from their husbands. Om Muhammed comments:

I found that joining a *gamᶜiyya* is the best way to get money out of my husband. You see, he makes a lot of money, but his hand is loose, *ᵓidu sayba*, and he has bad habits. He spends most of it on cigarettes and even hash. He wants a son, and when he gets angry with me, he threatens to marry another woman who can bear him a son. I do not care if he takes another wife as long as he does not reduce the little that he is already paying for us; at least if he has another wife, he may be less willing to keep on asking me for money. You see, he is also always asking me for more money, all the time, and twice he hit me for not giving him any. Would God approve of this? It is a good thing he does not know how much money I make. I never leave my money in the house. I put as much as I can in the *gamᶜiyya* every week. Not only that, but I also use the *gamᶜiyya* as a way of *aᶜsuru*, squeeze, i.e. to squeeze money from him. I demand two or three pounds from him every now and then and say that it is for my share in the *gamᶜiyya*. Not paying your turn in is very shameful around here and would jeopardize our relationships and reputation in the community. What else do poor people have but their reputation, *sumᶜa*? So he always, although reluctantly, gives me the money for the *gamᶜiyya*. I have to be clever, however and not demand it too often. It was my neighbor who gave me this clever idea. She is a really *nas-ha*, savvy/smart woman. I think I have taken more money from my husband since I started joining *gamᶜiyya*(s) this year than I have ever before. Mind you, this is money rightfully owed to me and my children, it is our right, *haᵓi wi haᵓ ᶜiyaali*.

This chapter has focused on intrahousehold decisions and extrahousehold relations and discussed possible links between the two. In particular, the role of extrahousehold networks in increasing women's leverage and bargaining power vis-a- vis their husband's was emphasized. The education of daughters was presented as one site of contestation between husbands and wives and an area where women deployed a range of tactics to pursue their priorities and aspirations. Some of the resources they drew on in this process lay outside their immediate household. The chapter has thus also discussed the role of extrahousehold informal networks. The focus has been on three specific networks which emerged as crucial in supporting women's attempts to improve their lives. These are: spirits possession ceremonies, *hadra*(s), female run grocery shops, *bi'aala*(s), and rotating credit associations, *gam'iyya*(s).

NOTES

1. This is a quote from one of my respondents.
2. I did not investigate budget arrangements in any depth. For more on this area, see Hoodfar (1988) and Nadim (1985).
3. Abortion is illegal in Egypt. Women nonetheless talked to me openly about their decision to abort as a way of avoiding another child. Women commonly used traditional, and often unsafe, methods such as drinking loads of boiled onion peel, or inserting sticks of *Mulukhiyya* (a traditional green vegetable with a long stem) in their wombs. Less commonly, if they could amass the LE150 pounds required, some women resorted to a private clinic. Men were never consulted in such decisions, and women made every effort to ensure that they did not find out.
4. The very low salaries of school teachers in Egypt has resulted in the emergence of the "private lesson" phenomenon as a strategy for teachers to supplement their salaries. Although officially discouraged by the ministry of education, it is currently a common reality, and a real cost of a theoretically free educational system. It is expected practice in all schools that teachers organize after-school-hours private lessons for groups of students. This phenomenon, which has increased markedly since the mid-1980s, is so ingrained in the current educational system that students who refuse to take private lessons run the serious risk of being failed in their exams, regardless of their performance. Because of its illegal and informal nature, it has been difficult to capture the national scale of this trend. One estimate, however, is that private tutors in Egypt earned around US$ 2 billion during the school year 1994-95 (Kossaifi 1996).
5. While the provision of the *gihaaz*, discussed in chapter six appeared to be more of a priority for wives than for husbands, the differences were not of the same magnitude as those concerning decisions about the education of daughters. It is also noteworthy that while women gave a high priority to both the *gihaaz* and education, they often have to make "trade-offs" as to whether they should allocate more of their limited resources for one or the other. These decisions are shaped by many factors including the number of wage earners in the family, the number of daughters, and how well a daughter performs at school.
6. *Banaat el wirash*, as discussed in the previous chapter, is a term with degrading connotations used for girls who work in wage labor in informal sector workshops, either in the community or outside it.
7. In the more immediate and short term, women addressed marital abuse through resorting to community pressure. One common way was for the woman who had been subjected to violence to complain, dramatically and in a voice loud enough for her neighbors to hear, about her husband's actions. These monologues were a common, culturally endorsed form of communi-

cation that aims at what I would term "publicizing the private." By doing so a woman ensures that domestic violence, and the behavior of her husband, is somewhat checked as it becomes a community affair subject to public arbitration and judgment.

8. Domestic violence from the perspective of women I interviewed, and that which they contest, is defined narrowly to include beating and insults. It did not include female circumcision, which is included in the broader definitions of domestic violence by some feminist organizations in Egypt and abroad.

9. See the chapter on theory for a more detailed discussion of gender interests, rights and needs.

10. I am grateful to Dr. Malak Zaalouk for drawing my attention to this point. As an expert working on girls' education programs with UNICEF in rural Egypt for many years, her initial reaction to my findings were those of extreme surprise.

11. I do not want to imply that rural and urban are homogenous categories, and I appreciate the differentiation within both categories. Fergany (1994a) presents important differentiation in attitudes and services within urban communities. Nonetheless, I think for the purposes of the specific hypothesis I am developing, one can still talk broadly about differences between rural and urban settings.

12. The bureaucracy in Egypt is notorious for its complexity. Even simple dealings, such as issuing a birth certificate or accessing a pension, take time, effort and connections.

13. A recent study of primary enrollment, based on World Bank estimates, indicates that in Egypt in 1960, enrollment rates in primary education were higher than the average for middle-income countries. After twenty-five years, this rate is lower than the average for low-income countries. The main difference relates to female education. The same study estimates female enrolment rates has decreased in poor urban communities (Fergany 1994a).

14. Another form of extrahousehold cooperation was organising community decorations during the fasting month of Ramadan. Women collect payments from households, usually on a street-by-street basis, and children gather to cut small colored pieces of paper and tie them to string. These, together with plastic and paper lanterns are hung up from balcony to balcony. The result is a beautiful array of decorations that give a festive and colorful touch to what is otherwise a dusty and dreary looking community. The decorations are not taken down at the end of the month, but are left to be blown away by the wind over the months.

15. March and Taqqu distinguish conceptually between "defensive" associations which are based on women's exclusion from male society, and where women thus unite due to "shared adversity" or in response to a crisis or constraint beyond their control, and "active" associations, which not only provide emergency support and protection, but may also amass significant resources, enabling women to expand their choices. These are not mutually exclusive categories (March and Taqqu 1986).

16. I say to a large extent, because as mentioned earlier some of the lead people in the ceremony, namely the musicians, are men. Moreover, in seeking a "voice," it is interesting to note that women may be appropriating male images of power, since many of the spirits possessing women, and who give them a voice and sometimes protect them as well, are in fact men. Although certainly not a rule, my impression is that women are usually possessed by male spirits, and men, by female spirits.

17. In her excellent analysis of *muulids* in a politically turbulent Sarajevo in 1990, Sorabji provides an important contrast to the prevalent view of women's rituals as specifically female, "counter-hegemonic" models to dominant male ideologies which thus enable women to contest their gender roles. Unlike the situation in the 1980s, *muulid* participants in Sarajevo in 1990 actually had "mixed motives." *Muulids* had become a forum for expressing both solidarity, and conflicting views between different groups of women over the nature and basis of that solidarity. While *muulid* participants viewed themselves as religiously motivated, their perceptions of the implication of Islam and its relationship to Muslim and national identity vis a vis the Serbs and Croats varied. "At the *muulids* of 1990, open disagreements between Muslims lay only mil-

limetres beneath the skin of ritual unity and was perceived as a threat both to personal integrity and to Muslim unity" (1994: 113). Sorabiji's observations emphasize the point made earlier about the historical specificity of spirit possession narratives.

18. I did not interview or talk to any of the possessed men in *hadra* (s). Several women, and one *kudya,* however, told me that men who attend are often homosexuals-which they referred to interestingly, not in the degrading terms of *khawal,* nor that of *mara* mentioned earlier, but in the more neutral one of *mukhanas.* Some of the men were also newly married men who are impotent, referred to as tied, *marbuut,* (meaning the penis is tied). The *hadra*(s) thus provide a context for the emergence of forms of "subordinate masculinities" that challenge "hegemonic" notions of masculinity (See Lindisfarne and Cornwall 1994), and enable the articulation of "de-sexed forms of personhood" (see Loizos and Papataxiarchis 1991b).

19. I say female run, not owned because female run *bꞮaala*(s) are sometimes co-financed or owned by a husband, who may also sell himself in the evenings, as an additional job. This does not reduce the importance of *bꞮaala(s)* as support networks, however, as women adjust their shopping times to fit those of the wife's availability.

20. Grocers explained that there are two types of clientele: steady, *zubuuna dayma,* and one off, *zubuuna tayyaary.* The *bꞮaala* serves as a network only for the steady clients.

CONCLUSION: TOWARD AN "ORGANIC FEMINISM"

This book began with a seemingly straightforward question: how do a particular group of women in low-income neighborhoods in Cairo perceive and respond to gender relations and hierarchies, both in their households and in their workplace? Over two hundred pages later, the answers seem anything but straightforward. If one can draw any tentative conclusions, it is that women's perceptions and responses are complex, contradictory, and in continuous flux as they interact with broader socioeconomic conjunctures. Whether in their families or in the labor force, women's perceptions of inequity, and their responses to their conditions varied significantly. These variations partly depended on the type of employment they were engaged in, the phase of their life cycles, and the availability (or perception of the availability) of alternative options. Thus any single conclusion about women's willingness and ability to challenge existing gender arrangements and any assumptions of homogeneity of motives, perceptions and strategies would be erroneous. It also follows that any attempts by activists and policymakers to advance women's interests are bound to be varied and complex.

The book demonstrates, with certainty, however, that neither narrow Marxist approaches to resistance and consciousness, nor the ahistorical, universal usage of the notion of patriarchy, both of which imply a sense of fixity and emphasize the "false consciousness" of subordinate groups, are adequate frameworks for understanding women's options and responses to gender hierarchies in their daily lives. At the other extreme, my data also suggests that an approach that almost glorifies and romanticizes poor women's strategies, by depicting low-income women as strong, resourceful, and knowing actors, able to successfully manipulate custom and conventional gender arrangements to their advantage, is also far too simplistic.

The women in my study display both defiance and compliance, both lack of articulated awareness of their self-interest and positions of relative subordination, and high levels of awareness of some of the injustices against them as women. Sometimes their actions are pragmatic, seeking immediate relief. At other times, they seek more medium-term or longer-term gains. Both a "culture of silent endurance"[1] and a culture of what I would term "silent defiance" exist simultaneously.

My data demonstrates that in some contexts, women are both willing, and able to dispute existing gender arrangements, and to successfully influence the outcome of negotiations to their advantage. For example, as shown in chapter seven, workshop girls, *banaat il wirash*, who are usually unmarried, are often able to negotiate for better wages. Moreover, as discussed in chapter nine, many women, through deploying a range of tactics such as temporarily deserting the marital home, *ghadbana*, joining *gam⊂iyya(s)* and engaging in paid employment, were also able to pursue their aspirations to educate their daughters, often against the wishes of their husbands.

In other instances, women articulate discontent and resentment in strong terms, but seek damage limitation rather than radical change. These attempts were clear in the practice of the *ayma*, the marriage inventory, discussed in chapter six. An examination of women's views on the *ayma* reveals a local, class-bound discourse about women's rights and interests which demonstrates a striking awareness amongst women of their relative disadvantage in marriage. The *ayma*, whose stipulations are enforced both legally and through informal mechanisms, *taradii*, was used by women as a means to settle marital conflict in their favor, to ward off the looming threat of a divorce or having a co-wife imposed, and to provide them with some degree of financial stability. Although aware of their vulnerability in marriage, by insisting on a large *ayma* women are not directly attempting to challenge their subordinate position within marriage, but rather to limit the damage that could result from such a position.

In other contexts, women are both aware of injustices, and willing to challenge them, but unable to pursue their aspirations due to external constraints, such as fear of physical violence, the inability to generate an income, or the difficulty of accessing social security benefits. For example, as discussed in chapter eight, some women expressed sexual disinterest, and, sometimes, outright revulsion towards their husbands. Yet many reported submitting unwillingly to their husbands' demands for sex, partly due to fear of being beaten up, being thrown out of the house, or being divorced.

Other women, as seen in chapter nine, are unable to pursue their priority of keeping their daughters in school due to their inability to harness the necessary resources. Yet they clearly value girls' education, more so than their husbands, as an avenue both for ensuring a respectable job for women, *wazeefa muhtarama*, and for reducing the possibilities of physical and verbal abuse by a future husband. These are good examples of instances where women's responses are not necessarily related to their lack of perception of self-interest, but rather are due to external circumstances which constrain their ability to pursue these interests. The women in the above examples demonstrate compliance, but not complicity (see Agarwal 1994).

Yet in other contexts, women are both compliant and complicit with certain practices, which ostensibly seemed to perpetuate their positions of disadvantage, but which they do not perceive or articulate as such. These are cases where women appeared to have themselves internalized existing gender norms and ideologies. The case of female circumcision discussed in chapter five, is a case in point. Circumcision was not viewed as a form of genital mutilation, as it is viewed by middle-class feminists, but as a form of bodily purification that makes a woman more feminine and sexually appealing to a husband. It is both a "rite of passage" for women, and a gendering practice closely tied to constructions of men and women's worth and roles in the community, as well as to constructions of male and female bodies.

By a gendering practice, I mean one that serves as a public reminder of the power differentials between men and women and of women's subordinate position in society. Decisions regarding circumcision are primarily women's decisions, in which men are generally not consulted. Although many women recalled how painful their circumcision was, they are also emphatic about its importance. I did not encounter any questioning of the practice at all. This is a case of apparent complicity with the gender order, which may indicate women's unquestioning acceptance of certain aspects of their lives.

My data further illustrates that some women accepted certain practices, partly due to their internalization of gender norms as is the case with circumcision, but they responded in a manner that cannot be neatly described as either complicity or compliance (which connotes some degree of force, physical or moral). Their response can more aptly be described as a form of acquiescence. This form of acquiescence is particularly evident among pieceworkers, discussed in chapter seven.

Pieceworkers acknowledge the low-paying, tedious, and hazardous working conditions under which they labor using strong words such as back-breaking, *biti\tum il dahr,* low-paying, *irshaha daᶜiif,* and God save us from its evils, *rabinna yikfina sharaha.* However, they do not view it as reflecting any injustice against them as women or as workers, but rather as part of their fate as poor women. The labor relations underlying piecework are not conceptualized by either workshop owners (all men) or pieceworkers (all women), as strictly financial transactions. Rather they are presented as a form of charity and extending alms to the poor, *sadaqa.* Women thus take no steps to try and challenge the conditions of piecework or bargain for better terms.

However, in other forms of work, such as wage labor, mainly performed by single female adolescents, women are much more aware of several aspects of gender discrimination, particularly unequal pay and sexual harassment. Unlike pieceworkers, workshop girls, *banaat il wirash,* are both willing, and sometimes able, to contest some of the unfavorable aspects of their work. Some engaged in practices directly aimed at deterring sexual harassment, through individual and momentary protest, such as stabbing an intruding male coworker with a knife, or manipulating their bodies to look more masculine. Others engage in more collective attempts to negotiate for better wages, often successfully, through *nam-*

rada, a gender-specific term that implies unjustified rebellion. As shown in chapter seven, women in groups of two or three quit work without notice so as to cause maximum disruption, in search of better wages or terms of work.

The different responses by *banaat il wirash* and pieceworkers to their working conditions are due to a different conjuncture of a number of economic, personal and cultural factors. These include market factors of supply and demand (unlike the case of pieceworkers, there was much more demand than supply for women's waged work, partly due to the community's negative view towards this form of work), the different role played by kinship idioms, and the marital trajectory and phase of women's life cycles. These contingent responses confirm the difficulties of making any blanket statements about women's ability to negotiate in the workplace.

By exposing the various ways in which women respond to gender hierarchies, the book has shed light on the mechanisms and modalities of power, and how these may operate at the microlevel, both in the home and in the labor market. One mechanism is that of "euphemization," that is, recasting exploitative relationships as positive ones, as Bourdieu (1977, 1980) suggests (see chapter seven). The power of euphemization was very clear in the case of sub-contracting. Both pieceworkers and middlewomen "misrecognized" or obfuscated the relations underlying piecework as passing time, *taslia,* and as forms of charity and community solidarity. The example of pieceworkers further highlights an important aspect of power, that is, the power of gender ideologies to create a collective loss of memory about the history of certain labor processes. As the example of hand-sewn shoes illustrated, gender ideologies acted retrospectively to naturalize certain tasks as women's work, even though they were exclusively male tasks only a few years earlier.

Drawing on Foucault's analysis of power (see chapter one), the book also illustrated how unequal gender relations are maintained and reproduced by creating and sustaining certain commonsensical or self-evident "truths" about men and women's roles. In a context where families are increasingly dependent on female wages, female employment has become inevitable. However, by constructing the meaning and implications of female employment in certain ways (for example, "proper girls do not work," "the work of women is a sign of deterioration not progress," "only the desperate would allow their girls to be called "*banaat wirash*," "married women in workshops promote male greed"), women are simultaneously able to enter into wage labor, and yet are kept out of its more lucrative and skilled areas, which are reserved exclusively for men.

Moreover, my data illustrates how myths with religious references are creatively invented to legitimate gender hierarchies. For example the anecdote regarding the assumed excessive sexual demands of the daughter of the Prophet, recounted in chapter five and which has no factual historical basis, is nonetheless widely circulated and believed. This myth serves to reinforce certain understandings about how a female body should look and appropriate behavior towards a husband, and thus serves to sanction circumcision. As suggested in chapter five, the universality of female circumcision in the community and women's strong adherence to the practice, occurs in the context of reluctance by official religious institutions, such as il Azhar, to unequivocally endorse it as religiously sanctioned. Religious myths are nonetheless created to legitimize it.

One of the findings that emerged from the data relates to the interlinkage between women's household and workplace options, confirming similar conclusions from other studies (see for example, Afshar 1993; Rugh 1985). As discussed in chapter seven, *banaat il wirash* were essentially participating in the labor force in order to gain more leverage and widen their options in their future marriages, by accumulating a large *gihaaz*. The triangular relationship between the *gihaaz* (which links directly with the *ayma*), public defloration ceremonies, and women's waged work is of particular interest. It is not only testimony to the complex relationships between work and family options, but also illustrates how women's choices are affected by broader socioeconomic changes, and how women attempt to manipulate conventional arrangements in order to expand their choices. The *ayma* and the *gihaaz,* as essential items of marriage negotiations appear to have gained a particular importance over the past twenty years.

The conditions and consequences of women's employment in the informal economy revealed in this study make any simple link between women's ability to participate in the labor market and their empowerment questionable. Pieceworkers were integrated into the labor market, albeit intermittently and under precarious working conditions. Given current economic recession, labor deregulation and the effects of structural adjustment in (see chapter two), casual work in general and home-based piecework in the informal sector, in particular, is likely to increase. At the same time, policy and research interest in the resilience and growth potential of the informal sector in Egypt for creating jobs is mounting.

The crucial question that still remains to be answered however is to what extent will this growth will incorporate the labor of women? To what extent will the success of the informal sector be based upon the existence of a pool of cheap female labor with no prospects for mobility or job security? Given projections for the growth of the informal sector and its increasing role in export-oriented industrialization, will the gender composition of skilled waged employment change, and will women become skilled workers, *sanaf-iyya?* Or will they simply increase the ranks of unskilled home-based workers doing industrial piecework and accept unfavorable working conditions, low pay and lack of social security and mobility, as in the case of Turkey (see Berik and Cagatay 1994)) and Mexico (see Beneria and Roldan 1987)?

Women working for wages in small informal workshops are better paid than pieceworkers, although they also have limited avenues for mobility and skill acquisition. *Banaat il wirash* have managed to creatively resolve some of the immediate contradictions posed by working outside the home, by manipulating and recrafting traditional practices, such as public defloration ceremonies, *laf bil sharaf,* discussed in chapter seven. By saving and accumulating a large *gihaaz,* they are also able to gain leverage in their future marriages, mitigate their vulnerability against divorce and maltreatment, and secure themselves financially.

So, in many respects, it can be argued that wage work in the informal sector enhances women's bargaining power in their households. Again, however, the question is, at what cost? While venturing into a new "public space" and gaining leverage in their marriages, *banaat il wirash* may simultaneously be reinforcing normative gender expectations, through public defloration ceremonies, and the self-confessedly traumatic experience of the *dukhla baladi.* In addition to the emotional cost to the individual women involved, these practices also serve to perpetuate the ideal of female chastity, and sanction gender inequalities and the pressures put upon women.

Certainly access to cash generated through employment is an important bargaining tool for women. For example, it enables some women to pursue their long-term aspirations, such as educating their daughters, which may result in intergenerational mobility for women. It allows others to realize their medium-term priorities of accumulating a *gihaaz,* thus expanding their choices of who to marry and where to live, as well as strengthening their bargaining positions vis-a-vis both their future husbands and mothers-in-law. However, the conditions of women's paid work described in this study, and the trade-offs that women make in the process of juggling such work in the context of a certain gender ideology, also emerge as important considerations when making connections between women's labor force participation and their empowerment.

My data also suggests that the neat distinctions between overt and covert practices and actions, which permeates most of the literature on resistance, is inadequate to describe the range of practices that women engage in. The assumption that women's protest tends to be covert, uncoordinated, and individual, whereas men's protest is more open and collective, needs further examination. For example, women employed in wage work engaged in a gender-specific form of collective, open revolt, *namrada.* Workshop girls were often even more vocal and open about their discontent than male workers. Because they are excluded from the male-dominated apprenticeship system characteristic of informal sector workshops, which provides men with avenues for training and promotion, women could afford to be more confrontational than male workers with a stake in the enterprise.

Moreover, my data shows that, contrary to prevalent assumptions in the literature, covert action is not necessarily individual, and collective action is not synonymous with open protest. Sometimes women acted individually, attempting to resolve conflicts to their advantage or defy current expectations. Attempts at *tatfiish,* discussed in chapter five, used by unmarried women to discourage uninteresting marriage suitors by leading them to refuse the match, is an example of a covert, nonconfrontational, individual attempt to pursue one's options. Temporarily deserting the marital home, *ghadbana,* or stabbing a rude coworker with a knife are other examples of individual attempts at resolving a disagreement, but which are both confrontational ones and represent more open statements of discontent.

Other coping responses and practices observed in the course of my fieldwork were both collective and overt, such as *gam^ciyya*(s), rotating credit and savings societies. While they played an important role in enabling individual women to widen their choices in their households, they do not represent forms of collective protest. As discussed in chapter nine, however, these networks enabled women to increase their material resources and thus pursue certain priorities, such as accumulating a large *gihaaz*, having an abortion or undergoing a hymen repair surgery. Moreover, *gam^ciyya*(s) also supported some women in engaging in individual subversive actions, such as diverting a husband's income.

Spirit possession circles, *hadra*(s), are another collective, informal network which offers women a social and discursive space to indirectly express their grievances and defy some of the restrictions on their behavior, mobility and dress. As argued in chapter eight, spirit possession is a widely shared cultural idiom, a form of "subordinate discourse," through which women seek to express discontent, negotiate gender expectations and develop new notions of selfhood that are not based on kinship. An exploration of women's spirit possession narratives suggested two recurring themes of discontent, the lack of control over their sexuality, and the current pressures concerning their dress and mobility in the name of Islamic modesty.

A process of "islamization of everyday life" was evident in the study community (see chapters two, three and eight). Spirit possession may be partly interpreted as a response to such a process. Many women reported being possessed by Christian spirits, who demanded that they refuse to wear the *higaab* or *khimaar*, stop praying, stop attending religious classes or listening to the Quran and religious tapes. Possessed women often yielded to these demands, and their behavior was tolerated to a certain extent. As seen in chapter eight, the apparently increasing attempts to undermine spirit possession rituals through recourse to an alternative, male-dominated, "religious" curing system, *ilag bil Quran*, is testimony to the strength of spirit possession practices.

"Veiling," or donning the *higaab*, has been widely discussed as one visible response by middle-class women to the increasing islamization of everyday life in Egypt (see for example Macleod 1992a; 1992b). As suggested in chapter eight, however, refusal to take up the *higaab* by some women because they are possessed may be another response, but one that is articulated and enacted much more covertly and subtly and amongst women of a different socioeconomic location. However, responses articulated through the idiom of spirit possession have their limitations in terms of challenging power relations, and may come at a tremendous personal cost. The case of the fourteen-year-old possessed girl who was beaten to death by her parents because she refused to wear the *khimaar* in response to the demands made by the spirits, is a sad, but vivid, illustration of these limitations.

My data also reveals a response by women to the contradictions in their daily lives that does not fit neatly in the overt/covert dichotomy. I have termed this response "strategic trade-offs." This is a response that enabled women to deal with the contradictory demands on them to both generate an income, lucrative enough to cover the costs of their *gihaaz*, and yet retain their respectability and central identity as wives and mothers. Women's insistence on a traumatic *dukhla baladi,* public defloration ceremony, sometimes despite the disapproval of their husbands and with the knowledge that it is not religiously sanctioned, in order to venture into waged work, is an excellent example of such a strategic trade-off. Another example of a strategic trade-off is that which mothers sometimes are forced to make between investing in a daughter's *gihaaz* versus investing in her education, as discussed in chapter nine.

Given these findings and observations about the varied and complex negotiations surrounding gendered roles, what conclusions may be drawn for future agendas of research and policy? Clearly, this study has barely scratched the surface on many issues, about which our stock of knowledge is still very limited; much more needs to be done. One of the aims of this book was is to offer new insights, which can form the basis for informed hypotheseses that merit further research.

A central perspective, largely absent from this book, is that of men and how they perceive the gender order of which they are a part. How do they view sex and sexuality? What are their responses to circumcision? What are their perspectives on women's education and employment? How do they define masculinity and femininity? How are they coping with their increasing inability to fulfill their central role as breadwinners and to what extent is this tied to their perceptions of masculinity?

However, as explained in chapter four, I have made a "strategic trade-off" myself, which enabled me to access women's worlds in an intimate way that I am convinced would not have been possible had I attempted to spend as much time with men. I am also doubtful that men would have been willing to openly share with me their views on some of these questions. My focus on women enabled me to provide a rich perspective on their experiences in negotiating gender hierarchies and on their views on important, sensitive, and not easily observable issues, such as the conditions and consequences of subcontracting and wage work, the *ayma*, the practice of defloration and sexual attitudes. None of these issues have been studied to any satisfactory extent in the Egyptian context.

One of the central themes revealed by the book, which merits further attention, is the existence of major discrepancies between the approaches and agendas of middle-class feminist activists in Egypt, and the practices, priorities and perceptions of the low-income women I studied. Yet there are also points of overlap and communality. This was illustrated in some detail in chapter six, by juxtaposing the *ayma* against the "new marriage contract" campaign, which was initiated by Egyptian feminists in 1994. Both the *ayma* and the proposed contract were viewed by different groups of women as critical vehicles for increasing women's leverage in marriage and furthering women's interests. Although the definition of these rights and interests varied, there were also obvious links and points of overlap. For example, both the *ayma* and the new contract attempt, in different ways, to address the risks and injustices of unilateral divorce and polygyny.

However, despite these connections, there was no reference to, or discussion of, the *ayma* at all during the campaign for a new marriage contract. A survey was conducted among low-income women to elicit their responses to the suggested contract in an attempt to increase the campaign's base of support. However none of the survey questions addressed low-income women's actual marriage negotiations or probed into their strategies for dealing with their perceived interests. The campaign had laudable aims and was a worthwhile effort, but it was a top-down and myopic one, which may have been one of the reasons why the new marriage contract was eventually rejected by both the government and the public.

A main question that emerges is thus how can we bridge the gaps between diverse, often class-bound, gender interests and priorities? Is it possible to find common ground and thus move beyond limited "gender activisms" and towards slowly building a process that would result in a broad-based and sustainable social movement? I have been trying to argue, that the largely "top-down" approach, which has characterized Egyptian feminist activism over the past decade, clearly has limitations, and may even result in backlashes. Moreover, as argued in chapter six, in the name of gender equality, such an approach may actually result in perpetuating inequalities amongst women. By controlling the agenda and deciding on the key issues, are more privileged women not in fact exercising a form of power over other women? This is power in the sense that it results in marginalizing the voices and priorities of certain categories of women, deterring them from entering into the dialogue as equal partners, and reinforcing the hegemony of middle-class priorities and discourses.

The existence of such discrepancies clearly has implications for development and feminist activism, not just in terms of pointing out past mistakes, but also by suggesting possibilities for alliances. For example, current attempts to change personal status laws in Egypt could be strengthened significantly by mobilizing women around issues of concern to them such as the *ayma*, which links easily with broader demands for changes in laws affecting marriage, divorce and domestic violence. The possible erosion of the legal basis of the *ayma*, due to pressures from conservative forces, as discussed in chapter six, also emerges as an important priority for feminist activism. Moreover, the lack of women's control over their sexual lives and their financial vulnerability are concerns strongly voiced by many of the women in my sample. These issues need to be pursued further, and could serve as key concerns around which mobilization of a broader constituency of women could occur.

Women's daily struggles may not result in radical outcomes or in altering power relations between men and women in and of themselves. Nonetheless they provide a store of issues, ideas and priorities to better inform feminist debates and agendas, as well as development policies. Perhaps more importantly, an understanding of women's daily concerns and struggles is a first step towards paving the way for dialogue amongst women of different classes, which may suggest areas around which broader constituencies of women could be mobilized and politicized. Such dialogue also offers a chance for the emergence of local leadership around issues of direct relevance to a larger number of women, who can themselves begin to intervene at the level of setting the feminist agenda and discourse.

My data also suggests that the prevalent state of male unemployment, the increasing number of female-headed households, and women's perspectives on this state of affairs poses an important "contradiction" in prevailing gender ideologies which could serve as a "branching point" or "lever of change" (see Lukes 1986). The socioeconomic context discussed in chapter two, while constraining for women in many ways, may also offer an excellent opportunity to begin articulating "countertruths" which could serve to unsettle current gender arrangements. These are only some possible avenues of further inquiry and action suggested by my exploratory study amongst a limited number of women in several communities in Cairo. Further microlevel research on women's daily struggles and practices in different settings in Egypt is clearly needed.

Theoretically, the approach suggested in this study can further our understanding of how certain aspects of social reality are more contestable than others, and how women in different socioeconomic and historical contexts have different layers of apprehension of social reality. Such apprehension is not static, but changes with changing circumstances. Some of the important questions thus become when, and at what point, are different aspects of social reality perceived as unjust? When, and at what points, do aspects of social reality appear as natural, as what Bourdieu would term "doxa", and thus become incontestable? (See also Kandiyoti 1998.) What makes the accessible so inaccessible? Finally, what does this tell us about how power relations operate, the ways in they are perpetuated, and the ways in which they could be transformed?

In an attempt to combine my theoretical concerns with my more practical activist goals, I want to offer a new concept which may provide a way forward in thinking about, and challenging gender inequalities. This is the concept of "organic feminism," a concept that I have coined, borrowing from Gramsci. Although Gramsci developed the concept of the "organic intellectual" in a different context,[2] I think it may nonetheless be interesting to think of a parallel concept with regard to feminist activism. I do not propose to use it in exactly the same way, as I am not talking about "organic feminists" (focusing on the actors). Rather I aim to pursue the articulation of an "organic feminism," or "organic feminist agendas," i.e., focusing on the issues.

The term "organic feminism" seems to me a much better one than that of the class-and context-free term of "indigenous" feminism, which is used to denote activism and scholarship in Third World countries. For example, as seen in chapter six, there is not one "indigenous" view of women's interests within marriage in Egypt, but several; not one response to cope with women's subordinate positions and vulnerability in marriage, but many. The public discussion regarding the new marriage contract referred to in chapter six, and the findings regarding the *ayma* put into question the usefulness of the homogenizing term, "indigenous", as they reveal that the meaning of marriage itself varies significantly between women of different classes, and even amongst the middle classes themselves. A concept such as organic feminism also allows us to get away from the dichotomies and essentialism of concepts such as "Western" versus "indigenous," which have plagued feminist scholarship for so long. Organic feminism suggests that within any context, a sustainable and effective way to mobilize a broad constituency of women and thus to advance the goals of challenging gender inequalities and socioeconomic injustices may be to invest more time and effort in making agendas of social change more "organic."

By "organic," I mean more than "bottom-up," as it is now used in development discourse. Rather, I use the term in the Gramscian sense to refer to a dialectical and evolving process of dialogue and interaction amongst different groups of women in different locations, all of whom may have legitimate priorities and concerns. This is not a linear process, as the term "bottom up" implies, but rather a self-questioning, contradictory and dialectical one that acknowledges the inherent power inequalities amongst the different actors, is open to learning about their different perspectives, and is committed to seeking possible common grounds for action. Such a process would eventually result in the articulation of an agenda that is shaped by a more diverse set of concerns which reflect the shifting realities of women's daily lives in different socioeconomic contexts; an agenda which does not, a priori, disregard or marginalize the concerns of any group. As the data shows, women's priorities, agendas, and strategies for change in Egypt may vary significantly on some issues and may overlap on others. An "organic feminism" does not dismiss the important role of intellectual feminists, nor disregard their ideas, but argues that their roles need to shift to that of learners, catalysts and mobilizers, rather than agenda setters.

My preference for a concept such as "organic feminism," rather than that of "participatory" or "bottom up" feminism, is thus partly because the latter concepts do not adequately capture the dialogue and dialectical process implied in the concept of "organic feminism." Moreover, because a concept such as "organic feminism" is a more overtly political one, it may not be as easily appropriated by institutions across the political spectrum (as is currently the case with the concept of "participatory development," for example), and thus become abused or devoid of its content. Rather, the concept of "organic feminism" can remain one that is espoused by organizations which have an explicit interest in addressing gender inequalities, and unequal power structures more generally.

Moreover, such a concept can reach out to a broader segment of feminist intellectuals, whose professional background is not in development work, and who are thus often unaware or skeptical of concepts such as "bottom-up" or "participatory" which emerge from development discourse. This is certainly the case with many of the key actors in the "women's movement" in Egypt—who, despite their common middle-class affiliation—come from diverse educational and political backgrounds, such as social development work, law, and human rights activism. In some ways, the concept of "organic feminism" is a more inclusive one, which could facilitate the forging of both horizontal and vertical alliances amongst women.

Promoting such a concept, however, will be no easy task. Developing anything organic implies first a total decomposition.[3] It requires that as middle—and upper-class, intellectual feminists, we are ready to completely 'decompose,' that is, to take apart and radically rethink our current ideas and approaches to addressing gender inequalities, to be open to experimentation and conscious social learning, and to allow new visions to start evolving based on a much stronger dialogue with women in diverse social locations.[4] A further challenge is that there may be few popular organizations representative of different groups of women, through which such a transformatory dialogue can begin to take place. Nonetheless, women's formal and informal institutions and networks do exist, and while many may be neither representative or strong, some may nonetheless present possible platforms for engagement.

Clearly I offer this concept in a speculative, probing and searching mode. I realize that it will require more theoretical work to develop it further. Perhaps "organic feminism" may not be a workable concept. Perhaps it is impossible to develop a feminist agenda broad enough to accommodate diversity without losing its basic principles of human rights and justice, an agenda that is "diverse," but not so "fragmented" that it loses any possibilities for action, or lends itself to easy manipulation by those in power. As Goetz argues:

> [T]here is a fine divide between diversity and fragmentation, and it is a divide that can be widened by development planners who feel unwilling to accommodate women's concerns. The apparatus of domination has always been able to benefit from maximum differentiation. It can accommodate—and has done, as the history of WID has shown—separate spaces for potentially divisive differences much more easily than it can stomach a genuine inclusion of difference. (1991: 146)

While remaining aware of these difficulties, an approach that furthers the concept of "organic feminism," may nonetheless be worth a chance. The data presented in this work gives us some reason for optimism as it demonstrates that despite differences amongst women in Egypt, there are also important areas of possible overlap. These could provide a practical springboard towards the adoption of a theoretical and strategic approach informed by the concept of "organic feminism."

NOTES

1. This term comes out of Khattab's study (1992) on reproductive health in two villages in Egypt.
2. Gramsci developed the concept in the context of his thinking about the relationship between civil society and the state. He argued that the transformation of civil society must precede a socialist seizure of state power. Gramsci argued that it would be erroneous to set up hierarchical, centralized structures that are not in touch with the everyday realities of the masses and that are alienated from historically evolving grass-roots organizations. While the popular classes may not espouse a pure revolutionary consciousness, they could be transformed though the organic dialectical interaction with "organic" intellectuals. For Gramsci, the concept of the organic intellectual thus linked the intellectual sphere with popular consciousness. He argued that it is only through the mediating role of organic intellectuals, intellectuals who are an organic part of the daily realities of a community, and who are able to articulate new visions within the shared symbols of a larger culture, that Marxism could be truly become a "counterhegemonic" force (see Boggs 1976).
3. I am grateful to my Ph.D. colleague from the Philippines, Albert Alejo for making this point when I was trying out the concept on him a few years ago.
4. Although arguing for respecting diversity amongst women, I am clearly taking a position that departs from that adopted by both so-called "cultural feminists" or "deconstructionists," for whom the issue of "difference" is also of paramount importance. Rather, I agree with Goetz who has argued that despite the diversity of women's interests, accounts and identities, "some accounts are vitally more true than others," and that, as feminists, we must strive for establishing "some minimalist, but objective, grounds on which to distinguish between the truth and falsity of divergent interpretations of the world" (Goetz 1991: 149).

Table (1) Population of Egypt, 1937-1995

Population of Egypt and the percentage living in rural and urban areas,
1937-1995

Year	Total Population in millions	Percent Urban	Percent Rural
1937	15,921	28.2	71.8
1947	18,967	33.5	66.5
1960	26,085	38.2	61.8
1966	30,076	40.0	58.8
1976	36,626	43.8	56.2
1986	48,254	44.0	56.0
1995	58,978	U	U

U = Unknown

Table (2) An Example of an *Ayma*

Amal's *ayma* (Married in 1996 and divorced in 1996)

Serial	Number	Description of Item	Value (LE)
1	5	2 bracelets, 21 K gold, 40 grams; 1 gold wedding band, 2 grams	
2	1	bedroom with cubboard, 8 pieces made of wood	4,500
3	1	"modern" parlor, 3 pieces	1,000
4	1	wooden cubboard	350
5	1	set of plastic plates and tea cups il-Sherif brand	140
6	1	set of aluminum pots and pans, 14 pieces	80
7	1	small electric heater, Olympic brand	50
8	1	small electric mixer, Molynex make*	150
9	1	6 foot refrigerator, Ideal brand**	650
10	1	oven with four torches, United Manufacturers brand**	750
11	1	Washing machine, Ideal brand**	450
Total	16	16 items that cost LE 8,470 exclusive of the gold items	8,470

*　This is an imported item
**　These are subsidized products, manufactured locally

Map 1
**Cairo: Expansion of Built-up Area
1947 to 1986**
Drawn by David Sims
Copyright © 1989 The American University in Cairo Press

Some uncontrolled areas

1 Manshiet Nasser
2 Ezbat al-Hagana
3 Shubra al-Khayma
4 Munira Gadida / Imbaba
5 Zenin
6 Bulaq al-Dakrur
7 al-Ahram
8 Dar al-Salam
9 Arab Rashad

built by 1947

1947 to 1986
planned
and controlled

uncontrolled
on private land

uncontrolled
on state land

historical limit
of watered (agricultural) land

Qalyubia Gov.

Heliopolis

Nasr City

Cairo Gov.

Gamaliya

Tahrir
Square

Sayyida
Zeinab

Giza Gov.

AIRPORT

PYRAMIDS

Maadi

Helwan

0   5

Appendix (1)

Description of Study Population

Number of households visited: 46
Number of women interviewed: 88
Number of men interviewed: 12
Number of workshops visited: 17

Marital Status of Female Population*

Status	Frequency
Married	42
Engaged**	11
Single	18
Widow	8
Abandoned (not legally divorced)	5
Divorced	4
Total	**88**

*   All the men in my sample were married
** This figure includes those who are informally engaged, as well as those who have read the *fat-ha,* but who have not yet had a formal engagement party, *shabka*

Occupational Status of Female Population

Occupational Category	Frequency
Pieceworker	25
Middlewoman (for piecework)	5
Wage labourer	26
Self-employed: vendors, grocers, recycling	14
Student	2
Not Working for an income	9
Government Employees	2
Local clerical jobs (with local clinics, pharmacies, mosques, and NGOs)	5
Total	88

Occupational Status of Male Population

Occupational Category	Frequency
Skilled workshop owner	6
Unskilled worker	3
Lawyer	2
"Religious Healer"	1
Total	12

Educational Status of Female Population

Educational Category	Frequency
Illiterate	63
Completed 6th grade*	12
Completed Prepatory School	6
Completed Secondary School	7
Total	88

* Either through the formal school system or through certified literacy classes

Educational Status of Male Population

Educational Category	Frequency
Illiterate	5
Primary School Degree	2
Secondary School Degree	2
University Degree	3
Total	12

Sample Population by Type of Household

Type of Household	Men	Women
Nuclear	7	63
Extended	4	25
Total	12	88

Appendix (2)
Guiding Research Questions

Three sets of issues guided my discussions and in-depth interviews. First, there was a set of issues related to women and men's roles and behavior. This included questions such as; what are the distinct roles and responsibilities of women and men, at different phases in their life cycle, both in the household and in the workplace? How are different household responsibilities divided and negotiated? How do women's roles as paid workers, interact with, and affect, their roles as mothers, wives and daughters?

Second, there was a set of issues related to beliefs and expectations. Some of the questions included: What does the widely quoted Arabic idiom: *Il sit wa il raagil* (a man is a man and a woman is a woman) currently mean to both men and women? What are the prevailing beliefs and norms about maleness and femaleness and to what extent are these shared by both men and women? How does this vary by age? How are these beliefs related to actual behavior? How are discrepancies between commonly held beliefs and observed/actual behavior explained?

Third, there was a set of questions related to patterns of negotiation and bargaining. Some of the questions included: What kinds of constraints are currently operating on women? How do different women perceive those constraints? How does this differ according to age, life cycle and pattern of employment? To what extent and in what ways are women attempting to shape, create, negotiate, accommodate, resist, or challenge the current gender arrangements? What are the specific symbols and contents of women's and men's power? What are the various bases, sources and usage of this power? What are the symbols and contents of women and men's subordination? How do women seek to influence or control men, or other women in the process of negotiating relations? What types of community networks for women currently exist? What role do they play in mediating and negotiating gender relations and expectations? Are new possibilities for resistance opening up for women? Who are the women who are more likely to engage in such resistance? Who are the men who are likely to be sought out as allies?

For each set of arrangements that I proposed to investigate, I also formulated some more specific guiding questions. With regards to marriage and the conjugal contract, questions related to pre-marital standards and expectations, marital conflicts, and resource allocation. With regards to the first component, pre-marital standards and expectations, questions included: How are decisions about marriage taken? To what extent are women involved in the choice of spouse? Why do women get married? What are the implications of not getting married? Who is involved in negotiating marriages? What are the terms of the marriage contract? Do defloration ceremonies take place? What are their implications? Are women circumcised? Why? Why not? How are decisions regarding circumcision negotiated?

With regards to the second component, marital conflicts and sexuality, questions included: What are the expectations of men and women regarding the initiation and frequency of sexual relations? How common are extramarital relations and how are these perceived by men and women? How is polygamy viewed? To what extent do women perceive it as a threat? Is wife beating prevalent? accepted? Under what conditions is it justified? Under what conditions is it not accepted? How is it resisted? What are the mains causes of marital conflicts? How does the construction of femininity and masculinity mediate the way in which such conflicts are perceived, negotiated and resolved?

With regards to the third component, resource allocation and budgetary control, the questions included: Who pays for what and how is this determined or negotiated? What happens when household expenses cannot be met? What is the extent of intra-household cooperation or conflicts regarding resource allocation? How are items, and individuals prioritized? How are decisions regarding savings, investments and expenditures taken? To what extent is masculinity related to the concept of breadwinner and provider? What are the implications of men not being able to provide for their families? what are the implications of women being the main breadwinners? What forms of extra-household forms of financial cooperation and support that exist? What roles do women and men play in such networks and how does their participation affect their ability to negotiate within the household?

With regards to the second set of arrangements that I proposed to investigate, that is gender relations in the informal labor market, questions included: why are women working? Who took the decision to work? How do women find out job opportunities? Through their husbands? Other women? What is considered proper women's work and what is the role of gender in defining pay levels and terms of employment? How are wages negotiated? How are earnings spent and invested? What problems are women currently facing as paid workers? How are they trying to address these problems? If they had a choice, would women still be working? Would they want their daughters to work? In the same type of job as themselves? Why? Why not?

BIBLIOGRAPHY

Abaza, M. 1987. "The Changing Image of Women in Rural Egypt." *Cairo Papers in the Social Sciences*. no.10, Cairo: American University of Cairo Press.

Abdalla, A. 1988. "Child Labour in Egypt: Leather Tanning in Cairo." In *Combating Child Labour,* ed. A. Bequele and J. Boyden. Geneva: International Labour Organisation.

Abdel-Fadil, M. 1983. "Informal Sector Employment in Egypt.*" Technical Paper No. 1 of the International Labour Organisation (ILO) Comprehensive Employment Strategy Mission to Egypt.* Geneva: ILO.

Abt Associates and the General Organisation for Housing, Building Planning and Research. 1981. "Informal Housing in Egypt." *Report to the U.S. Agency for International Development.* Cairo: USAID

Abu-Lughod, J. 1985. "Migrant Adjustment to City Life : the Egyptian Case." in *Arab Society: Social Science Perspectives,* ed. S. Ibrahim and N. Hopkins. Cairo. American University in Cairo Press.

_____. 1971. *Cairo: 1001 Years of the City Victorious.* Princeton: Princeton University Press.

Abu-Lughod, L. 1995. "The Objects of Soap Opera." In *World's Apart: Modernity Through the Prism of the Local,* ed. Daniel Miller. London: Routledge.

_____. 1993. *Writing Women's Worlds: Bedouin Stories.* California: University of California Press.

_____1991. "Writing Against Culture" in *Recapturing Anthropology: Working in the Present,* ed. R.G. Fox. Santa Fe: School of American Research Press.

_____1990a. "The Romance of Resistance: Tracing Transformations of Power through Bedouin Women." *American Ethnologist* 17:41-55.

_____1990b. "Can there be a Feminist Ethnography?" *Women and Performance.* 5 (1):7-27.

_____1988. "Fieldwork of a Dutiful Daughter." In *Arab Women in the Field: Studying Your Own Society*, ed. S. AlTorki and C. El-Solh. New York: Columbia University Press.

_____1986. *Veiled Sentiments: Honour and Poetry in a Bedouin Society.* Berkeley and Los Angeles: University of California Press.

Acker, J., K. Barry, and J. Esseveld. 1983. "Objectivity and Truth: Problems in Doing Feminist Research." *Women's Studies International Forum.* 6 (4): 423-435.

Afshar, H., ed. 1993. *Women in the Middle East: Perception, Realities and Struggles of Liberation.* London: Macmillan.

Afshar, H. and C. Dennis, eds. 1992. *Women, Recession and Adjustment in the Third World.* New York: St. Martin's Press.

Agarwal, B. 1997. "'Bargaining' and Gender Relations: Within and Beyond the Household." *Feminist Economics.* 3 (1):1-51.

_____1994. *A Field of One's Own: Gender and Land Rights in South Asia.* Cambridge: Cambridge University Press.

Ahmed, L. 1992. *Women and Gender in Islam: Historical Roots of a Modern Debate.* New Haven: Yale University Press.

_____1982. "Western Ethnocentrism and Perceptions of the Harem." *Feminist Studies* 8:521-534.

Al-Ali, N. 1997. "Feminism and Contemporary Debates in Egypt." In *Organising Women: Formal and Informal Women's Groups in the Middle East*, ed. by D. Chatty and A. Rabo. Berg: Oxford University Press.

Al-Messiri, S. 1978. "Self Images of Traditional Urban Women in Cairo." In *Women in the Muslim World*, ed. N. Keddie and L. Beck. Cambridge: Harvard University Press.

AlTorki, S. 1986. *Women in Saudi Arabia: Ideology and Behaviour Among the Elite.* New York: Columbia University Press.

AlTorki, S. and C. Fawzi El-Solh, eds. 1988. *Arab Women in the Field: Studying Your Own Society.* New York: Syracuse University Press.

_____1988. "Introduction." In *Arab Women in the Field: Studying Your Own Society.* Ed. S. AlTorki and C. Solh. New York: Syracuse University Press.

Amin, G. 1989. "Migration, Inflation and Social Mobility: A Sociological Interpretation of Egypt's Current Economic and Political Crisis." In *Egypt Under Mubarek*, ed. R. Owen and C. Tripp. London: Routledge.

Amin, G. and E. Awni Taylor. 1984. *International Migration of Egyptian Labour: A Review of the State of the Art.* Ottawa and Cairo: International Development Research Centre.

Anderson, K. and D. Jack. 1991. "Learning to Listen: Interview Techniques and Analyses." In *Women's Words: The Feminist Practice of Oral History*, ed. S. Gluck and D. Patai. London: Routledge.

Appadurai, A. 1986. "Introduction: Commodities and the Politics of Value." In *The Social Life of Things: Commodities in Cultural Perspective*, ed. by A. Appadurai. Cambridge: Cambridge University Press.

_____. 1990. "Disjuncture and Difference in the Global Cultural Economy. *Public Culture: Bulletin of the Centre for Transnational Cultural Studies.* 2:2:1-24.

Assad, M. 1980. "Female Circumcision in Egypt: Social Implications, Current Research and Prospects for Change." *Studies in Family Planning* 11 (1): 3-16.

Assad, T. 1986. "The Concept of Cultural Translation in British Social Anthropology." In *Writing Culture: the Poetics and Politics of Ethnography,* edited by J. Clifford and G. Marcus. Berkeley: University of California Press.

Aswad, B. 1978. "Women, Class and Power: Examples from the Hatay in Turkey." In *Women in the Muslim World* ed. N. Keddie and L. Beck. Cambridge: Harvard University Press.

Auybi, N. 1995. "Rethinking the Public/Private Dichotomy: Radical Islamism and Civil Society in the Middle East." *Contention* 4, no. 3:79-105.

Azer, A. and M. El-Adawy. 1994. *Towards the Implementation of the Convention on the Rights of the Child in Egypt.* Cairo: UNICEF.

Baden, S. 1993. "The Impact of Recession and Structural Adjustment on Women's Work in Developing and Developed Countries." *Working Paper.* Geneva: International Labour Organisation.

Badran, M. 1995. *Feminists, Islam and the Nation: Gender and the Making of Modern Egypt.* Princeton: Princeton University Press.

_____1993. "Independent Women: More Than a Century of Feminism in Egypt." In *Arab Women: Old Boundaries, New Frontiers,* ed. Judith Tucker. Bloomingdale: Indiana University Press.

Bahie El-Din, A. 1993. "Equality Before the Law: Women and Men in the Criminal Laws of Egypt." *Report presented to the Gender Task Force in Preparation for the 1994 International Conference on Population and Development.* Cairo: National Gender Task Force (in Arabic.)

Barakat, H. 1993. *The Arab World: Society, Culture and State.* Berkeley: University of California Press.

Batrach, P. and M. Baratz. 1970. *Poverty and Power: Theory and Practice.* New York: Oxford University Press.

Beechey, V. 1979. "On Patriarchy." *Feminist Review* 3:66-82.

Beneria, L. 1992. "Accounting for Women's Work: The Progress of Two Decades." *World Development* 20, no. 11:1547-1560.

Beneria, L. and S. Feldman, eds. 1992. *Unequal Burden: Economic Crisis, Persistent Poverty and Women's Work.* San Francisco: Westview Press.

Beneria, L. and M. Roldan. 1987. *The Crossroads of Class and Gender: Industrial Homework, Subcontracting and Household Dynamics in Mexico City.* Chicago: University of Chicago Press.

Berik, G. and N. Cagatay. 1994. "What has Export-oriented Manufacturing Meant for Turkish Women?" In *Mortgaging Women's Lives: Feminist Critiques of Structural Adjustment*, ed. P. Sparr. London: Zed Books Ltd.

Boddy, J. 1989. *Wombs and Alien Spirits: Women, Men, and the Zaar Cult in Northern Sudan*. Madison: University of Wisconsin Press.

Boggs, C. 1976. *Gramsci's Marxism*. London: Pluto Press Limited.

Bolak, H. 1990. "Women Breadwinners and the Construction of Gender: A Study of Urban Working-Class Households in Turkey." Ph.D. diss., University of California, Santa Cruz.

Bourdieu, P. 1990. *The Logic of Practice*. Translated by Richard Nice. New York: Polity Press.

_____1977. *Outline of a Theory of Practice*. Oxford: Oxford University Press.

Borland, K. 1991. "That is Not What I Said: Interpretative Conflict in Oral Narrative Research." In *Women's Words: The Feminist Practice of Oral History*, ed. S. Gluck and D. Patai. London: Routledge.

Bott, E. 1971. *Family and Social Network*. 2nd ed. London: Tavistock.

Bruce, J. 1989. "Homes Divided." *World Development* 17, no. 7:979-991.

Bruce, J. and D. Dwyer, eds. 1988. *A Home Divided: Women and Income in the Third World*. Stanford: Stanford University Press.

Bryceson, D., ed. 1995. *Women Wielding the Hoe*. Oxford and Washington: Berg Publishers.

Butler, J. 1992. "Contingent Foundations: Feminism and the Question of Post-Modernism." In *Feminists Theorize the Political*, ed. J. Butler and Joan Scott. London: Routledge.

Butler, J. and J. Scott, eds. 1992. *Feminists Theorize the Political*. London: Routledge.

Buvinic, M. 1989. "Investing in Poor Women: The Psychology of Donor Support." *World Development* 17, no. 7:1045-1057.

Buvinic, M. and N. Youssef. 1978. "Women-Headed Households: The Ignored Factor in Development Planning." Unpublished Report Submitted to Agency for International Development/Women In Development Programme. Washington: International Centre for Research on Women.

Campo, Juan Eduardo. 1995. "The End of Fundamentalism: Hegemonic Discourse and the Islamic Question in Egypt." *Contention*, 4, no.3.

Caplan, P. 1988. "Engendering Knowledge: The Politics of Ethnography." *Anthropology Today* 4, no. 5:8-12; no. 6:14-17.

Caplan, P. and D. Bujra, eds. 1982. *Women United, Women Divided: Comparative Studies of Ten Contemporary Cultures*. Bloomington: Indiana University Press.

Castells, M. and A. Portes. 1989. "The World Underneath: The Origins, Dynamics, and Effects of the Informal Economy." In *The Informal Economy: Studies in Advanced and Less Developed Countries*, ed. A. Portes, M. Castells and L.A. Benston. Baltimore: John Hopkins University Press.

Central Agency for Public Mobilisation and Statistics (CAPMAS). 1985. *The Labour Market in Egypt: The Informal Sector.* Cairo: CAPMAS (In Arabic).
_____.1995. *Statistical Year Book 1992-1994.* Cairo: CAPMAS.

Chant, S. ed. 1997. *Women-headed Households: Diversity and Dynamics in the Developing World.* London: Macmillan Press.
_____1991. *Women and Survival in Mexican Cities: Perspectives on Gender, Labour Markets and Low-income Households.* Manchester: Manchester University Press.

Clifford, J. and G. Marcus, eds. 1986. *Writing Culture: the Poetics and Politics of Ethnography.* Berkeley: University of California Press.

Cohen, J.M. and W. Uphoff. 1980. "Participation's Place in Rural Development: Seeking Clarity through Specificity." *World Development* 8, no. 3:213-236.

Collier, J. and S. Yanagisako, eds. 1987. *Gender and Kinship: Essays Towards a Unified Analysis.* Stanford: Stanford University Press.

Comaroff, J. 1980. "Introduction." In *The Meaning of Marriage Payments,* ed. by J. L. Comaroff. London: Academic Press Inc.

Comaroff, J. and J. Comaroff. 1987. "The Madman and the Migrant: Work and Labour in the Historical Consciousness of a South African People." *American Ethnologist* 14, no. 2:191-209.

Cornwall, A. 1996. "For Money, Children and Peace: Everyday Struggles in Changing Times in Ado-odo, Southern Nigeria." Ph.D. thesis, School of Oriental and African Studies. University of London.

Constantinides, P. 1982. "Women's Spirit Possession and Urban Adaptation in the Muslim Northern Sudan." In *Women United, Women Divided: Comparative Studies of Ten Contemporary Cultures,* ed. P. Caplan and D. Bujra. Bloomington: Indiana University Press.

Davis, K., M. Leijenaar, and J. Oldersma, eds. 1991. *The Gender of Power.* London: Sage Publications.

Davis, K. 1991. "Critical Sociology and Gender Relations." In *The Gender of Power* ed. by K. Davies et al. London: Sage Publications.

Delsing, R. 1991. "Sovereign and Disciplinary Power: A Foucaultian Analysis of the Chilean Women's Movement." In *The Gender of Power,* edited by K. Davis et al. London: Sage Publications.

De Soto, H. 1986. *El Otro Sendero.* Lima: Editorial El Barranco.

Doan, R. M. and L. Bisharat 1990. "Female Autonomy and Child Nutritional Status: The Extended-family Residential Unit in Amman, Jordan." *Social Science and Medicine* 31, no.7:783-89.

Dorkenoo, E. 1994. *Cutting the Rose:Female Genital Mutilation, the Practice, and its Prevention.* London: Minority Groups Publications.

Dwyer, D. 1978a. "Ideologies of Sexual Inequalities and Strategies for Change in Male / Female Relations." *American Ethnologist* 5, no. 2:227-240.

_____.1978b. *Images and Self Images: Male and Female in Morocco.* New York: Columbia University Press.

Dwyer, K. 1982. *Moroccan Dialogues: Anthropology in Question.* Baltimore: Johns Hopkins University Press.

Eagleton, T. 1991. *Ideology: An Introduction.* London: Verso.

Early, E. 1993a. *Baladi Women in Cairo: Playing with an Egg and a Stone.* London: I.B. Tauris.

_____. 1993b. "Getting It Together: Baladi Egyptian Businesswomen. In *Arab Women: Old Boundaries, New Frontiers,* ed. by J. Tucker. Bloomington: Indiana University Press.

United Nations Development Programme. 1997. *Egypt Human Development Report.* Cairo: United Nations Development Program.

National Gender Task Force. 1994. *Egyptian NGO Platform of Action.* Prepared for the United Nations Conference on Population and Development (ICPD. Cairo: National Gender Task Force (in Arabic).

National Gender Task Force. 1995. *Egyptian NGO Platform of Action.* Prepared for the United Nations Conference on Women. Cairo: National Gender Task Force (in Arabic).

Eickleman, D. 1989. *The Middle East: An Anthropological Approach.* New Jersey: Prentice Hall.

Eickleman, D. and J. Piscatori. 1996. *Muslim Politics.* New Jersey: Princeton University Press.

El-Baradei, M. 1996. "The Educational Status of Women in Egypt." Paper presented at a conference titled: "Enhancing the Socioeconomic Status of Women in Egypt." American University in Cairo, 1996.

El-Guindy, F. 1981. "Veiling *Infitah* with Muslim Ethics: Egypt's Contemporary Islamic Movement." *Social Problems.* 8:464-485.

El-Hamamsy, L. 1994. "Early Marriage and Reproduction in Two Villages in Egypt." *Occasional Paper.* Cairo: Population Council Regional Office for West Asia and North Africa.

El-Kholy, H. 1998a. "A Tale of Two Contracts: Towards a Situated Understanding of Women's Interests in Egypt." In *Situating Globalizations: Voices from Egypt,* ed. C. Nelson and S. Rouse. Germany: Transcript Publishers.

_____.1998b. "I Do Not Want to Have Sex With My Husband: Spirit Possession as a Discourse of Protest Among Low-Income Women in Cairo." Paper presented at the Conference on Middle Eastern Studies, Irbid, Jordan, 1996.

_____.1998c. The Feminisation of Poverty or Expanding Employment Opportunities for Women: A Case Study of a Street Sweeper in Cairo. Unpublished paper. SOAS, 1997.

_____.1997. "The Education of a Girl is a Treasure: Gender Politics in Low Income Egypt." *Occasional paper.* Cairo: The Population Council's Regional Office for West Asia and North Africa.

_____.1996a. "The Alliance Between Gender and Kinship Ideologies: Female Sub-Contractors in Cairo's 'Informal Economy'" In Proceedings of the Regional Arab Conference on Population and Development. Cairo and Brussels: International Union for the Scientific Study of Population (IUSSP).

_____.1996b. "Poverty Alleviation Programs: An NGO Perspective." Paper presented to the United Nations Development Programme Arab Regional Conference on Poverty Alleviation in the Arab World, February 1996, Syria.

_____ .1990. "Towards a Typology of Women-Headed Households: Some Suggestions from Field Research in Cairo, Egypt." Paper presented to the Population Council Workshop on Family Resources and the Household, June 1990, Istanbul, Turkey.

El-Kholy, H. and N. Al-Ali. 1998. "Inside/Outside: The 'Native' and the 'Halfie' Unsettled" In *The Social Sciences in Egypt: Emerging Voices. Cairo Papers in the Social Sciences.* Ed. L. Herrera and S. Shami. Cairo: American University in Cairo Press.

El-Rehimy, O. 1996. "The A*yma* Is of No Value and the Law is Clear." *Nus El Dunya Magazine.* Year 4, Issue 339,11 August. (In Arabic).

El-Sadawy, N. 1980. *The Hidden Face of Eve.* London: Zed Press.

El-Solh, C. F. and J. Mabro, eds. 1994. *Muslim Women's Choices: Religious Belief and Social Reality.* Oxford: Berg Publishers.

El-Wafd. 15 October 1997. "One Quarter of Egypt's Population is Supported By a Woman (In Arabic).

El-Waly, M. 1993. *The Residents of Shacks and Informal Settlements: A Population Map of the Governorates of Egypt.* Cairo: Engineers Syndicate Publications. (In Arabic)

El-Zanaty, F. E. M. Hussein, G. A. Shawky, A. Way and S. Kishor. 1996. *Egypt Demographic and Health Survey, 1995.* Maryland and Cairo: National Population Council (EGYPT) and Macro International Inc.

Elson, D. 1996. "Appraising Recent Developments in the World Market for Nimble Fingers: Accumulation, Regulation, Organisation." In *Confronting State, Capital and Patriarchy,* ed A. Chhachhi and R. Pittin. New York: St. Martin's Press.

_____ .1992. From Survival Strategies to Transformation Strategies: Women's Needs and Structural Adjustment. In *Unequal Burden: Economic Crisis, Persistent Poverty and Women's Work* edited by L. Beneria and S. Feldman. San Francisco: Westview Press.

_____ .ed. 1991. *Male Bias in the Development Process.* Manchester: Manchester University Press.

_____.1989. "The Impact of Structural Adjustment on Women: Concepts and Issues." In *The IMF, the World Bank and the African Debt, Vol. II, The Social and Political Impact,* ed B. Onimode. London: Zed Books.

Environmental Quality International (EQI). 1987. *Income Generating Project for Women-Headed Households: Final Report.* Final project report presented to OXFAM and the Ford Foundation. Cairo: EQI.

Fakhouri, H. 1968. "The Zaar Cult in an Egyptian Village." *Anthropological Quarterly* 41, no. 2:49-77.

Farah, N. 1996. "Regional Trends in the Poverty Alleviation MENA Region: The Urban-Focused Area-Based Development Approach." Paper prepared for UNICEF. Cairo: Cairo Centre for Development Studies.

Fardon, R., ed. 1995. *Counterworks: Managing the Diversity of Knowledge.* London: Routledge.

Fergany, Nader 1997. "Government Biased for the Rich and Does Not Care About the Poor." *Rosalyousef.* 11 (August) 3609: 64-66 (In Arabic).

_____.1995. *Strategic Issues of Education and Employment in Egypt.* Cairo: Al Mishkat.

_____.1993. *Urban Women, Work and Poverty Alleviation in Egypt: A Literature Review.* Cairo: Al Mishkat.

_____. 1994a. *Study of Primary Enrolment and Acquisition of Basic Literacy and Numeracy Skills: A Field Survey in Three Governorates.* Cairo: Al Mishkat. (In Arabic).

_____.1994b. *Women-Headed Households in Egypt.* Cairo: AlMishkat.

Ferguson, J. 1990. *The Anti-politics Machine: 'Development', De-politicisation and Bureaucratic Power in Lesotho.* Cambridge: Cambridge University Press.

Female Genital Mutilation Task Force (FGM). 1997. *FGM Task Force Position Paper.* Cairo: FGM Task Force.

Fierlbeck, K. 1997. "Getting Representation Right for Women in Development: Accountability, Consent and the Articulation of Women's Interests." In *Getting Institutions Right for Women in Development* ,ed A. M. Goetz. London and New York: Zed Books.

Fines, A. 1992. "A Consideration of the Trousseau: A Feminine Culture?" In *Women's History,* ed M. Perot. Translated by Felicia Pheasant. Oxford: Basil Blackwell.

Folbre, Nancy, ed. 1992. *Women's Work in the World Economy.* Hong Kong: Macmillan.

_____.1991. "Women on Their Own: Global Patterns of Female Headship". *Women and International Development Annual* 2:1989-126.

_____.1988. "The Black Four of Hearts: Towards a New Paradigm of Household Economics." In *A Home Divided: Women and Income in the Third World,* ed. J. Bruce and D. Dwyer. Stanford: Stanford University Press.

_____.1986. "Cleaning House: New Perspectives on Households and Economic Development." *Journal of Development Economics* 22:5-40.

Foucault, M. 1986. "Disciplinary Power and Subjection." In *Power,* ed. S. Lukes. Oxford: Basil Blackwell.

_____. 1983. "Afterward: The Subject and Power." In *Michel Foucault: Beyond Structuralism and Hermeneutics,* ed H. Dreyfus and P. Rainbow. Chicago: University of Chicago Press.

_____. 1981. *History of Sexuality. Vol. 1: An Introduction.* Translated by Robert Hurley. London: Penguin Books

_____. 1980 .*Power/Knowledge: Selected Interviews and Other Writings, 1972-1977,* ed C. Gordon. New York: Pantheon Books.

Fraser, N. 1989. *Unruly Practices: Power, Discourse and Gender in Contemporary Social Theory.* London: Polity Press.

Geertz, C. 1988. *Works and Lives: The Anthropologist as Author.* Stanford: Stanford University Press.

Geiger, S. 1990. "What's So Feminist About Women's Oral History?" *Journal of Women's History* 2, no.1.

Ghanem, F. 1996. "Globalisation and the Struggle Over the Public Sphere: Negotiating Power Relationships in the Family in a Low-income Neighbourhood in Cairo." Proceedings of the Regional Arab Conference on Population and Development. Cairo and Brussels: International Union for the Scientific Study of Population (IUSSP).

Gittens, D. 1985. *The Family in Question: Changing Households and Familiar Ideologies.* London: Macmillan.

Glenn, E. N. 1987. "Gender and the Family." In *Analysing Gender: A Handbook of Social Science Research,* ed B. Hess and M.M. Ferree. Newbury Park: Sage Publications.

Gluck, S. B. and D. Patai, eds. 1991. *Women's Words: The Feminist Practice of Oral History.* London: Routledge.

Goetz, A. M. and R. S. Gupta. 1996. "Who takes the Credit? Gender, Power and Control over Loan Use in Rural Credit Programmes in Bangladesh. " *World Development* 24, no.1: 45-63.

Goetz, A. M. 1991. "Feminism and the Claim to Know: Contradictions in Feminist Approaches to Women in Development." In *Gender and International Relations* edited by R. Grant and K. Newland. Milton Keynes: Open University Press.

Goody, J. and S.J. Tambiah. 1973. *Bridewealth and Dowry.* Cambridge: Cambridge University Press.

Gorelick, S. 1991. "Contradictions of Feminist Methodology." *Gender and Society* 5, no. 4:459-477.

Greely, M. 1983. "Patriarchy and Poverty: A Bangladesh Case Study." *South Asia Research.* No. 3: 35-55.

Grown, C. and J. Sebstad. 1989. "Introduction: Towards a Wider Perspective on Women's Employment. " *World Development* 17, no. 7:937-952.

Guenena, N. 1986. *"The Jihad: An Islamic Alternative in Egypt."* Cairo Papers in the Social Sciences 9, no. 2. Cairo: American University in Cairo Press.

Guyer, J. 1988. "Dynamic Approaches to Domestic Budgeting: Cases and Methods from Africa." In *A Home Divided Women and Income in the Third World*, ed J. Bruce and D. Dwyer. Stanford: Stanford University Press.

Guyer, J. and P. E. Peters. 1987. "Introduction to Conceptualising the Household: Issues of Theory and Policy in Africa." *Development and Change*, no. 18:197-213.

Gomm, R. 1975. "Bargaining from Weakness: Spirit Possession on the South Kenya Coast." *Man* 4, no. 10:530-43.

Haddad, Y. 1987. "Islamic 'Awakening' in Egypt." *Arabic Studies Quarterly* 9: 234-236.

Haddad, L, L. R. Brown, A. Richer and L. Smith. 1995. "The Gender Dimensions of Economic Adjustment Policies: Potential Interactions and Evidence to Date." *World Development* 23, no. 6:881-896.

Haeri, S. 1989. *Law of Desire: Temporary Marriage in* Shiiᶜa *Iran.* Syracuse: Syracuse University Press.

Hoda El-Sadda and Salwa Bakr (1995). *Hagar: On Women's Issues.* Book 2. Cairo: Dar Sinai Publishing House. (In Arabic).

Hale, S. 1993. "Transforming Culture or Fostering Second-Hand Consciousness? Women's Front Organisations and Revolutionary Parties— the Sudan Case." In *Arab Women: Old Boundaries, New Frontiers*, edited by J. Tucker. Bloomington: Indiana University Press.

Hancock, G. 1989. *Lords of Poverty: The Power, Prestige, and Corruption of the International AID Business.* New York: Atlantic Monthly Press.

Handousa, H. and G. Potter, eds. 1991. *Employment and Structural Adjustment in Egypt in the 1990s.* Cairo: American University in Cairo Press.

Handousa, H. 1991. "Crisis and Challenge: Prospects for the 1990s." In *Employment and Structural Adjustment in Egypt in the 1990s*, ed. by H. Handousa and G. Potter. Cairo: American University in Cairo Press.

Hanna, M. 1985. "Real Estate Rights in Urban Egypt: The Changing Sociopolitical Winds." In *Property, Social Structure and Law in the Modern Middle East*, ed by Anne Elizabeth Mayer. Albany: State University of New York Press.

Harding, S. ed. 1987. *Feminism and Methodology: Social Science Issues.* Milton Keynes: Open University Press.

Harris, K. M. 1993. "Work and Welfare Among Single Mothers in Poverty." *American Journal of Sociology* 99, no. 2:317-52.

Harris, O. 1981. "Households as Natural Units". In *Of Marriage and the Market: Women's Suboridnation Internationally and its Lessons*, ed. K. Young and R. McCullagh. London: Routledge.

Hart, G. 1995. "Gender and Household Dynamics: Recent Theories and their Implications." In *Critical Issues in Asian Development* ed. M.G. Quibria. Hong Kong: Oxford University Press.

_____.1991. "Gendering Everyday Resistance: Gender, Patronage and Production Politics in Rural Malaysia." *Journal of Peasant Studies* 19, no.1:93-121.

Hartsock, N. 1987. "The Feminist Standpoint: Developing the Ground for a Specifically Feminist Historical Materialism." In *Feminism and Methodology: Social Science Issues,* ed. S. Harding. Milton Keynes: Open University.

Hartman, H. 1979. "The Unhappy Marriage Between Marxism and Feminism." *Capital and Class* 3:1-33.

Hastrup, K. 1992. "Writing Ethnography: State of the Art." In *Anthropology and Autobiography*, ed. J. Okely and H. Callaway. London: Routledge.

Hatem, M. 1994. "Privatisation and the Demise of State Feminism in Egypt." In *Mortgaging Women's Lives: Feminist Critiques of Structural Adjustment,* ed. P. Sparr. London: Zed Books.

_____.1992. "Economic and Political Liberation in Egypt and the Demise of State Feminism." *Journal of Middle Eastern Studies.* no. 24:231-251.

_____.1987. "Class and Patriarchy as Competing Paradigms for the Study of Middle Eastern Women." *Comparative Studies in Society and History* 29, no. 4:811-818.

_____.1983. "Women and Work in the Middle East: The Regional Impact of Migration to the Oil Producing States." Paper Presented at the Conference on Women and Work in the Third World, 1983. University of California, Berkeley.

Haynes, D. and G. Prakash, eds. 1991. *Contesting Power: Resistance and Everyday Social Relations in South Asia.* Delhi: Oxford University Press.

Hoare, Q. and G. Nowell Smith, eds. 1971. *Antonio Gramsci: Selections from the Prison Notebooks.* New York: International Publishers.

Hobart, M., ed. 1993. *An Anthropological Critique of Development: The Growth of Ignorance.* London: Routledge.

Heyzer, N. 1981. "Towards a Framework of Analysis." *In Women and the Informal Sector, IDS Bulletin*, ed. C. Moser and K. Young. Brighton: Institute of Development Studies.

Holub, R. 1992. *Antonio Gramsci: Beyond Marxism and Post Modernism.* London and New York: Routledge.

Hoodfar, H. 1997. *Between Marriage and the Market: Intimate Politics and Survival in Cairo.* Los Angeles: University of California Press.

_____. 1990. "Survival Strategies in Low-income Households in Cairo." *Journal of South Asian and Middle East Studies* 14, no.4:22-41.

_____.1988. "Household Budgeting and Financial Management in a Lower-income Cairo Neighbourhood." In *A Home Divided: Women and Income in the Third World* ed. by J. Bruce and D. Dwyer. Stanford: Stanford University Press.

Hoodfar, H., and D. Singerman, eds. 1996. *Development, Change and Gender in Cairo: A View from the Household.* Bloomington: Indiana University Press.

Hopkins, N. 1991. "Informal Sector in Egypt" *Cairo Papers in Social Sciences.* 14, no. 4.

Huws, U. 1995. *Action Programmes for the Protection of Home-workers: Ten Case Studies from Around the World.* Geneva: International Labour Organisation.

Ibrahim, B. 1985. "Family Strategies: A Perspective on Women's Entry to the Labour Force in Egypt." In *Arab Society: Social Science Perspectives,* ed. S. Ibrahim and N. Hopkins. Cairo: American University in Cairo Press.

Ibrahim, S. 1985a. Egypt's Islamic Militants. In *Arab Society: Social Science Perspectives,* edited by S. Ibrahim and N. Hopkins. Cairo: American University in Cairo.

_____.1985b. "Urbanisation in the Arab World: The Need for an Urban Strategy." In *Arab Society: Social Science Perspectives,* ed. S. Ibrahim and N. Hopkins. Cairo: American University in Cairo.

Ibrahim, S. and N. Hopkins, eds. 985. *Arab Society: Social Science Perspectives.* Cairo: American University Of Cairo Press.

Ilbaz, S. 1997. "The Impact of Social and Economic Factors on Women's Group Formation in Egypt." In *Organising Women: Formal and Informal Women's Groups in the Middle East,* ed by Dawn Chatty and Annika Rabo. Oxford: Berg.

Issawi, C. 1982. *An Economic History of the Middle East and North Africa.* New York: Columbia University Press.

Jejeebhoy, S. 1995. *Women's Education, Autonomy and Reproductive Behaviour: Experience from Developing Countries.* Oxford: Oxford University Press.

Jones, C. 1986. "Intra Household Bargaining in Response to the Introduction of New Crops: A Case from North Cameroon." In *Understanding Africa's Rural Households and Farming Systems,* ed. by J. Moock. Boulder: Westview Press.

Joseph, S. 1993. "Gender and Relationality Among Arab Families in Lebanon." *Feminist Studies* 19, no. 3:465-486.

_____ .1978. "Women and the Neighbourhood Street in Borj Hammoud, Lebanon." In *Women in the Muslim World,* ed. N. Keddie and L. Beck. Cambridge: Harvard University Press.

Kabeer, N. 1994. *Reversed Realities.* London: Veroso.

Kandiyoti, D. 1998. "Gender, Power and Contestation: Rethinking Bargaining with Patriarch." In *Divided We Stand: Gender Analysis and Development Issues,* edited by R. Pearson and C. Sacks. London: Routledge.

_____, ed. 1996. *Gendering the Middle East: Alternative Perspectives.* London: I.B. Tauris.

_____.1995. "Reflections on the Politics of Gender in Muslim Societies: From Nairobi to Beijing." In *Faith and Freedom: Women's Human Rights in the Muslim World,* ed. L M. Afkami. London: I.B. Tauris

_____.1991. "Islam and Patriarchy: A Comparative Perspective." In *Women in Middle Eastern History: Shifting Boundaries in Sex and Gender,* ed. Keddie and B. Baron. New Haven: Yale University Press.

_____. 1988. "Bargaining with patriarchy." *Gender and Society* 2, no. 3:274-290.

Keddie, N. 1979. "The Problems of Writing about Middle Eastern Women." *International Journal of Middle Eastern Studies* 10, no. 2:226-227.

Keddie, N. and B. Baron, eds. 1991. *Women in Middle Eastern History: Shifting Boundaries in Sex and Gender.* New Haven: Yale University Press.

Keddie, N. and L. Beck, eds. 1978. *Women in the Muslim World.* Cambridge: Harvard University Press.

Kennedy, J. 1967. "Nubian Zar Ceremonies as Psychotherapy." *Human Organisation* 26, no. 4:185-94.

Kepel, G. 1992. "God Strikes Back: Re-Islamization Movements in Contemporary History." *Contention* 2, no. 1:153-159.

Khafagy, F. 1984. "Women and Labour Migration." *MERIP Reports* 14, no. 124:17-21.

Khattab, H. 1996. "Women's Perceptions of Sexuality in Rural Giza." *Monograph in Reproductive Health*, no. 1, Reproductive Health Working Group. Cairo: The Population Council Regional Office for West Asia and North Africa.

Khattab, H. 1992. *The Silent Endurance.* Amman and Cairo: UNICEF and the Population Council Regional Office for West Asia and North Africa.

Khattab, H. and S. El Daeif. 1982. *The Impact on Male Migration of the Structure of the Family and Roles of Women in Egypt.* Cairo: The Population Council.

Kompter, Aafke. 1991. "Gender, Power and Feminist Theory." In *The Gender of Power,* ed. K. Davis and J. Oldersma. London: Sage Publications.

Korayem, K. 1987. *The Impact of Economic Adjustment Policies on the Vulnerable Families and Children in Egypt.* Cairo: Third World Forum and UNICEF.

Kossaifi, G. 1996. "Sociopolitical Dimensions of Poverty in the Arab World." Paper presented to the UNDP Arab Regional Conference on the Eradication of Poverty. February 1996 in Damascus, Syria.

Landor, J. 1994. "Poverty and the Urban Labour Market: An Anthropological Study of a Peripheral Slum in Cairo." Ph.D. thesis. London School of Economics. University of London.

LaTowsky, R. 1995. "PVO Assistance: Direct AID to the Poor." *Report number 2, Egypt PVO Sector Study Prepared for the World Bank.* Cairo: World Bank.

_____.1984. "Egyptian Labour Abroad: Mass Participation and Modest returns." *MERIP Reports* 14, no.123:11-18.

Lewis, I. 1966. "Spirit Possession and Deprivation Cults." *Man* 1, no. 3:307-329.

Lindisfarne, N. and A. Cornwall, eds. 1994. *Dislocating Masculinity: Comparative Ethnographies.* London: Routledge.

Lobban, R., ed. 1996. *Middle East Women in the "Invisible" Economy.* Gainesville: University Press of Florida.

Loizos , P. and E. Papataxiarchis, eds. 1991. *Contested Identities: Gender and Kinship in Modern Greece.* Princeton: Princeton University Press.

_____.1991a. "Gender and Kinship in Marriage and Alternative Contexts." In *Contested Identities: Gender and Kinship in Modern Greece,* ed. P. Loizos and E. Papataxiarchis. Princeton: Princeton University Press.

_____.1991b. "Gender, Sexuality and the Person in Greek Culture." In *Contested Identities: Gender and Kinship in Modern Greece,* ed. P. Loizos and E. Papataxiarchis. Princeton: Princeton University Press.

Lukes, S. 1974. *Power: A Radical View.* London: Macmillan.

_____.ed. 1986. *Power.* Oxford: Basil Blackwell.

Lynch, P. and H. Fahmy. 1984. *Craftswoman in Kerdassa, Egypt: Household Production and Reproduction.* Geneva: International Labour Office.

Macleod, A. E. 1992a. "Hegemonic Relations and Gender Resistance: The New Veiling as Accommodating Protest in Cairo." *Signs: Journal of Women in Culture and Society* 17, no. 31:533-557.

_____.1992b. *Accommodating Protest: Working Women, the New Veiling, and Change in Cairo.* Cairo: The American University in Cairo Press.

_____ .1986. "Hegemony and Women: Working and Re-veiling in Cairo, Egypt." Paper presented at the Northeastern Political Science Association Annual Meeting, November.

March, K. S. and R. L. Taqqu. 1986. *Women's Informal Associations in Developing Countries: Catalysts for Change?* Boulder: Westview Press.

Marcus, G. and M. Fischer. 1986. *Anthropology as Cultural Critique: An Experimental Moment in the Human Sciences.* Chicago: Chicago University Press.

Marcus, G. and D. Cushman. 1982. "Ethnographies as Text." *Annual Review of Anthropology* 11: 25-69.

Mayoux, L. 1995. "Beyond Naivety: Women, Gender Inequality and Participatory Development." *Development and Change* 26:235-258.

Meyer, J. 1991. "Power and Love: Conflicting Conceptual Schemata." In *The Gender of Power,* ed. K. Davis and J. Oldersma. London: Sage Publications.

Mbilinyi, M. 1989. "I Should Have Been a Man: Politics and Labour Process in Producing Personal Narratives." In *Interpreting Women's Lives,* ed. Personal Narratives Group. Bloomington: Indiana University Press.

McDonald, G. W. 1980. "Family Power: The Assessment of a Decade of Theory and Research, 1970-1979." *Journal of Marriage and the Family* no. 42:841-854.

McLellan, D. 1973. *Karl Marx: His Life and Thought.* London: Macmillan Press.

McNay, L. 1992. *Foucault and Feminism.* Cambridge: Polity Press.

Mernissi, F. 1987. *The Veil and the Male Elite.* Addison -Wesley Publishing Company.

_____ .1988. *Doing Daily Battle: Interviews with Moroccan Women.* London: The Women's Press.

_____.1975. *Beyond the Veil.* New York: John Wiley and Sons.

Merrick, T. and M. Schmink. 1983. "Households Headed by Women and Urban Poverty in Brazil." In *Women in the Third World,* ed. M. Buvinic, M. Lycette and W.P. McGreevy. Baltimore: John Hopkins University Press.

Messick, B. 1987. "Subordinate Discourse: Women, Weaving and Gender Relations in North Africa." *American Ethnologist* 14, no. 2:210-25

Middleton, D. 1992. "Development, Household Clusters and Work-Wealth in Manta." *City and Society* 5, no. 6:137-153.

Mies, M. 1982. *The Lace Makers of Narsapur: Indian Housewives Produce for the World Market.* London: Zed Press.

Miller, D. 1995. *Worlds Apart: Modernity Through the Prism of the Local.* London: Routledge.

Millet, K. 1969. *Sexual Politics.* London: Abacus.

Minces, J. 1982. *The Home of Obedience.* London: Zed Books.

Mitchell, T. 1990. "Everyday Metaphors of Power." *Theory and Society,* 19:545-77.

Mohanty, C. 1988. "Under Western Eyes: Feminist Scholarship and Colonial Discourses." *Feminist Review,* no. 30: 65-88.

Molyneux, M. 1998. "Analysing Women's Movements." In *Divided We Stand: Gender Analysis and Development Issues,* ed. R. Pearson and C. Sacks. London: Routledge.

_____.1985. "Mobilisation Without Emancipation? Women's Interests, the State and Revolution in Nicaragua." *Feminist Studies* 11, no. 2:227-254.

Moore, H ed. 1996. *The Future of Anthropological Knowledge.* ASA Decennial Conference Series. London: Routledge.

_____.1994a. *A Passion for Difference.* Cambridge: Polity Press.

_____.1994b. "Divided we Stand: Sex, Gender and Sexual Difference." *Feminist Review,* no.47:78-95.

_____.1988, *Feminism and Anthropology.* Cambridge: Polity Press.

Moors, A. 1991. "Gender, Property and Power: *Mahr* and Marriage in a Palestinian Village." In *The Gender of Power,* ed. K. Davis, K.M. Leijenaar and J. Olersma. London: Sage Publications.

Morsy, S., C. Nelson, R. Saad and H. Sholkamy 1991. "Anthropology and the Call for the Indigenization of Social Science in the Arab World." In *Contemporary Studies of the Arab World,* ed E. Sullivan and J.S. Ismail. Edmonton: University of Alberta Press.

Morsy, S. 1978. "Sex Differences and Folk Illness in an Egyptian Village."In *Women in the Muslim World*, ed. N. Keddie and L. Beck. New Haven: Yale University Press.

_____.1988. "Fieldwork in my Egyptian Homeland: Towards the Demise of Anthropology's Distinctive Other." In *Arab Women in the Field: Studying Your Own Society*, edited by S. AlTorki and C. El-Solh.

Moser, C. 1989. "The Impact of Recession and Adjustment Policies at the Micro-level: Low-income Women and their Households in Guayaguil, Ecuador." In *The Invisible Adjustment: Poor Women and the Economic Crisis*. The Americas and Caribbean Regional Office: UNICEF.

_____.1993. *Gender Planning in Development Theory: Practice and Training*. London and New York: Routledge.

Moser, C. and K. Young. 1981. "Women and the Informal Sector."*In Institute of Development Studies Bulletin* 12, no. 3. Brighton.

Morcoss, W. 1988. *Sukan Misr*. Cairo: Research Centre for Arab Studies. (In Arabic).

Murray, C. 1987. "Class, Gender and the Household: The Development Cycle in Southern Africa." *Development and Change*, no. 18:235-250.

Nadim, N. Al-Messiri. 1985. Family Relationships in a *harah* in Cairo". In *Arab Society: Social Science Perspectives*, ed. S. Ibrahim and N. Hopkins. Cairo: American University Press.

Nassar, H. 1996. "The Employment Status of Women in Egypt." Paper presented at the conference entitled "Enhancing the Socioeconomic Status of Women in Egypt", March, 1996. American University in Cairo.

Nawar, L., C. Lloyd and B. Ibrahim. 1995. "Women's Autonomy and Gender Roles in Egyptian Families" In *Family, Gender and Population in the Middle East: Policies in Context*, ed. C. Obermeyer. Cairo: American University in Cairo Press.

Nelson, C. 1974. "Public and Private Politics: Women in the Middle Eastern World." *American Ethnologist* 1, no. 3:551-63.

_____.1971. "Self, Spirit Possession and World View: An Illustration from Egypt." *International Journal of Social Psychiatry* Vol. 17:194-209.

Nelson, N. and S. Wright, eds. 1994. *Power and Participatory Development: Theory and Practice*. London: Intermediate Technology Publications.

Netting, R., R. Wilk and E. Arnould, eds. 1984. *Households: Comparative and Historical Studies of the Domestic Groups*. California: University of California Press.

Nicholson, L. 1994. "Interpreting Gender."*Signs*, 20, no. 1:79-105.

Nussbaum, M. 1995. "Human Capabilities, Female Human Beings." In *Women, Culture and Development*, ed. J. Glover and M.C. Nussbaum. Oxford: Clarendon Press.

O'Hanlon, R. 1991. "Issues of Widowhood: Gender and Resistance in Colonial Western India." In *Contesting Power: Resistance and Everyday Social Relations in South Asia*, ed. D. Haynes and G. Prakash. Delhi: Oxford University Press.

O'Hanlon, R. 1988. "Recovering the Subject: Subaltern Studies and Histories of Resistance in Colonial South Asia." *Modern Asian Studies* 22, No. 1:189-224.

Okely, J. 1991. "Defiant Moments: Gender, Resistance and Individuals." *Man,* no. 26:189-224.

Okely, J. and H. Callaway, eds. 1992. *Anthropology and Autobiography.* London: Routledge.

Oldersma, J. and K. Davis. 1991. "Introduction." In *The Gender of Power,* ed. by K. Davis, M. Leijenaar and J. Oldersma. London: Sage Publications.

Oldham, L., H. El- Hadidi and H. Tamaa. 1987. "Informal Communities in Cairo: The Basis of a Typology." *Cairo Papers in the Social Sciences* 10, no.4, Cairo: American University in Cairo Press.

Olson, K. and L. Shopes. 1991. "Crossing Boundaries, Building Bridges: Doing Oral History Among Working-class Women and Men." In *Women's Word: The Feminist Practice of Oral History,* ed. S. Gluck and D. Patai. London: Routledge.

Oncu, A., C. Keyder and S. Ibrahim, eds. 1994. *Developmentalism and Beyond: Society and Politics in Egypt and Turkey.* Cairo: The American University in Cairo Press.

Ong, A. 1987. *Spirits of Resistance and Capitalist Discipline. Factory Women in Malaysia.* New York: State University of New York Press.

Pahl, J. 1989. *Money and Marriage.* London: Macmillan Press.

Papps, I. 1992. "Women, Work and Well-being in the Middle East: An Outline of the Relevant Literature."*Journal of Development Studies* 28, no. 4:595-615.

Patai, D. 1987. "Ethical Problems of Personal Narratives, or Who Should Eat the Last Piece of the Cake?" *International Journal of Oral History* 8, no. 1:5-27.

Pearson, R. and C. Sacks, eds. 1998. *Divided We Stand: Gender Analysis and Development Issues.* London: Routledge.

Pearson, R. 1994. "Gender Relations, Capitalism and Third World Industrialisation." In *Capitalist Development,* ed. by Leslie Sklar. London: Routledge.

Personal Narratives Group, eds. 1989. *Interpreting Women's Lives.* Bloomington: Indiana University Press.

Population Council. 1996. "Clinical-Based Investigation of the Typology and Self Reporting of FGM in Egypt." *Final Report, Asia and Near East Operations Research and Technical Assistance Project.* Cairo: The Population Council Regional Office for West Asia and North Africa.

Pun, N. 1996. "Searching for a Feminist Genealogy: Gender, Sex and Body." Ph.D. research seminar. Department of Anthropology and Sociology. School of Oriental and African Studies. London.

Rabinow, P. 1977. *Reflections on Field Work in Morocco.* Berkeley: University of California Press.

Ramazanglu, C. 1989. *Feminism and the Contradictions of Oppression.* London: Routledge.

Rassam, A. 1980. "Women and Domestic Power in Morocco." *International Journal of Middle East Studies* 12:171-179.

Raymond, W. 1977 *Marxism and Literature.* London: Oxford University Press.

Reinharz, S. 1992. *Feminist Methods in Social Research.* Oxford: Oxford University Press.

Risseeuw, C. 1991. "Bourdieu, Power and Resistance: Gender Transformation in SriLanka." In *The Gender of Power,* ed. K. Davis, M. Leijenaar and J. Oldersma. London: Sage Publications.

Rizk, S. 1991. "The Structure and Operation of the Informal Sector in Egypt." In *Employment and Structural Adjustment in Egypt in the 1990s,* ed. H. Handousa and G. Potter. Cairo: American University in Cairo Press.

Roldan, M. 1988. "Renegotiating the 'Marital Contract': Intra-Household Allocation Patterns of Money Allocation and Women's Subordination Among Domestic Out-workers in Mexico City." In *A Home Divided: Women and Income in the Third World,* ed. J. Bruce and D. Dwyer. Stanford: Stanford University Press.

Rosaldo, M. and L. Lamphere, eds. 1974. *Women, Culture and Society.* Stanford: Stanford University Press.

Rosen, L. 1984. *Bargaining with Reality: The Social Construction of Social Relations in a Muslim Community.* Chicago: University of Chicago Press.

_____.1978. "The Negotiation of Reality: Male and Female Relations in Sefrou, Morocco." In *Women in the Muslim World,* ed. N. Keddie and L. Beck. Cambridge: Harvard University Press.

Rosenhouse, S. 1989. "Identifying the Poor: Is Headship a Useful Concept?" LSMS Working Paper No. 28, Washington DC: World Bank.

Rowbotham, S. 1981. "The Trouble with Patriarchy." In *People's History and Socialist Theory,* ed. R. Samuel. London: Routledge and Kegan.

Rugh, Andrea. 1985. "Women and Work: Strategies and Choices in a Lower-Class Quarter of Cairo." In *Women and the Family in the Middle East,* ed. E. Fernea. Texas: University of Texas Press.

Rugh, Andrea. 1984. *The Family in Contemporary Egypt.* New York: Syracuse University Press.

_____.1979. "Coping with Poverty in a Cairo Community." *Cairo Papers in the Social Sciences* 2, no. 1. Cairo: American University in Cairo.

Sayigh, R. 1996. "Researching Gender in a Palestinian Camp: Political, Theoretical and Methodological Issues." In *Gendering the Middle East: Alternative Perspectives,* ed. D. Kandiyoti. London: I.B. Tauris.

Scott, A. M. 1991. "Informal Sector or Female Sector? Gender Bias in Urban Labour Market Models." In *Male Bias in the Development Process*, ed. D. Elson. Manchester: Manchester University Press.

Scott, J. 1992. "Experience." In *Feminists Theorize the Political*, ed. J. Butler and J. Scott. London: Routledge.

Scott, J. 1990. *Domination and the Arts of Resistance: Hidden Transcripts*. New Haven and London: Yale University Press.

_____.1986. "Everyday Forms of Resistance." *Journal of Peasant Studies* 13, no. 2:5-35.

_____ .1985. *Weapons of the Weak: EveryDay Forms of Resistance*. New Haven: Yale University Press.

Sen, A. 1990. "Gender and Co-operative Conflicts." In *Persistent Inequalities: Women and World Development*, ed. Irene Tinker. New York: Oxford University Press.

Shanti, K. 1996. "Economic and Social Status of Female Heads of Households: Need for Intervention Under New Economic Policy." *The Indian Journal of Social Works* 57, no. 2: 309-326.

Sharabi, H. 1992. "Modernity and Islamic Revival: The Critical Task of Arab Intellectuals." *Contention* 2, no. 1:127-138.

Sholkamy, H. M. 1996. "Women's Perceptions: A Necessary Approach to Understanding Health and Well-being." *Monograph in Reproductive Health, No.2, Reproductive Health Working Group*. Cairo: The Population Council Regional Office for West Asia and North Africa.

Shorter, F., L. Oldham and B. Tecke. 1994. *A Place to Live: Households, Families and Child Health*. Cairo: American University in Cairo Press.

Shorter, F. 1989. "Cairo's Leap Forward: People, Households and Dwelling Space." *Cairo Paper in the Social Sciences. Vol. 12, No.1*. Cairo: American University in Cairo.

Shukralla, H. 1994. "The Impact of the Islamic Movement in Egypt." *Feminist Review*, no. 47:15-32.

Shukralla, H. 1989. "Political Crisis / Conflict in Post-1967 Egypt." In *Egypt Under Mubarak*, ed. R. Owen and C. Tripp. London: Routledge.

Shukry, A. 1988. *Women in Rural and Urban Areas: A Study of their Life and Work. Contemporary Sociology Series*. Cairo: Dar El-Ma^rifa El Gaame^iya (In Arabic).

Singerman, D. 1995. *Avenues of Participation: Family, Politics and Networks in Urban Quarters of Cairo*. Princeton: Princeton University Press.

_____.1990. "Politics at the Household Level in a Popular Quarter of Cairo. " *Journal of South Asian and Middle East Studies* 13, no. 4:3-21.

Sorabji, C. 1994. "Mixed Motives: Islam, Nationalisms and *Mevluds* in an Unstable Yugoslavia." In *Muslim Women's Choices: Religious Belief and Social Reality*, ed. C. El-Solh and J. Mabro. Oxford: Berg Associates.

Standing, G. 1989. "Global Feminisation Through Flexible Labour." *World Development* 17, no.7:1077-1095.

National Committee for the Preparation for the 1995 United Nations International Women's Conference. "Status of Women in Egypt 1994." Draft Report Submitted by the National Committee. (In Arabic.)

Strathern, M. 1987a. "Out of Context: The Persuasive Fictions of Anthropology." *Current Anthropology* 28, no. 3:1-77.

_____.1987b. "An Awkward Relationship: The Case of Feminism and Anthropology." *Signs 2*, no. 21:276-292.

_____.1988. *The Gender of the Gift: Problems with Women and Problems with Society in Melanesia.* Berkeley: University of California Press.

Stauth, G. 1991. "Gamaliya: Informal Economy and Social Life in a Popular Quarter of Cairo.*" Cairo Papers in the Social Sciences* 14, no. 4, Cairo: American University in Cairo Press.

Sparr, P. ed. 1994. *Mortgaging Women's Lives: Feminist Critiques of Structural Adjustment.* London: Zed Books Ltd.

Sullivan, E. L. 1981. "Women and Work in Egypt." *Cairo Paper in the Social Sciences* 4, no. 1. Cairo: American University in Cairo Press.

Sullivan, D. 1994. *Private and Voluntary Organisations in Egypt: Islamic Development, Private Industries, State Control.* Gainesville: University Press of Florida.

Taher, N. 1986. "Social Identity and Class in a Cairo Neighbourhood." *Cairo Papers in the Social Sciences* 9, no.4. Cairo: American University in Cairo Press.

Tapper, N. 1991. *Battered Brides: Politics, Gender and Marriage in an Afghan Tribal Society.* Cambridge Studies in Social and Cultural Anthropology. Cambridge: Cambridge University Press.

_____ .1983. "Gender and Religion in a Turkish Town: A Comparison of Two Types of Formal Women's Gatherings." In *Women's Religious Experiences: Cross-cultural Perspectives.* London and Canberra: Croom Helm.

_____.1979. "Mysteries of the Harem: An Anthropological Perspective on Recent Studies on Women in the Middle East." *Women's Studies International Quarterly* 2:481-487.

Taylor Awni, E. 1984. Egyptian Migration and Peasant Wives. *Middle East Research and Information Project (MERIP) Reports* 14, no. 124:3-10.

Tinker, I., ed. 1990. *Persistent Inequalities: Women and World Development.* New York: Oxford University Press.

Toubia, N. 1995. *Female Genital Mutilation: A Call for An International Campaign.* New York: Rainbow.

Tucker, J., ed. 1993. *Arab Women: Old Boundaries, New Frontiers.* Bloomington: Indiana University Press.

Turton, A. 1986. "Patrolling the Middle Ground: Methodological Perspectives on Everyday Peasant Resistance." *Journal of Peasant Studies* 13, no. 2:36-48.

United Nations Children's Fund (UNICEF). 1989. *The Invisible Adjustment: Poor Women and the Economic Crisis.* Santiago: UNICEF-The Americas and Caribbean Regional Office.

United Nations Development Program (UNDP) 1995. *Human Development Report.* New York: Oxford University Press.

United Nations Development Program (UNDP). 1997. *Human Development Report.* New York: Oxford University Press.

Vatuk, S. 1971. "Trends in North Indian Urban Kinship: the 'Matrilateral Asymmetry' Hypothesis." *Southwestern Journal of Anthropology* 27: 287-307.

Vickers, J. 1991. *Women and the World Economic Crisis.* London and New York: Zed Books Ltd.

Visweswaran, K. 1994. *Fictions of Feminist Ethnography.* Minneapolis and London: University of Minnesota Press.

Warde, A. 1994. "Consumption, Identity Formation and Uncertainty." *Sociology* 28: 877-899.

Watson, H. 1994. "Separation and Reconciliation: Marital Conflict Among the Muslim Poor in Cairo." In *Muslim Women's Choices: Religious Belief and Social Reality,* ed. C. El-Solh and J. Mabro. Oxford: Berg Publishers.

Webster, S. K. 1982. "Women, Sex and Marriage in Moroccan Proverbs." *International Journal of Middle East Studies* 14:173-184.

Westwood, S. and P. Bhachu, eds. 1988. *Enterprising Women: Ethnicity, Economy and Gender Relations.* London: Routledge.

White, C. P. 1986. "Everyday Resistance, Socialist Revolution and Rural Development: The Vietnamese Case." *Journal of Peasant Studies* 13, no. 2: 49-63.

White, J. B. 1994. *Money Makes Us Relatives: Women's Labour in Urban Turkey.* Texas: University of Texas Press.

Whitehead, A. 1981. "I'm Hungry Mom: The Politics of Domestic Budgeting." In *Of Marriage and the Market: Women's Subordination Internationally and its Lessons,* ed. K. Young, C. Wolkowitz, and R. McCullagh. London: Routledge.

_____ .1979. "Some Preliminary Notes on the Subordination of Women." *IDS Bulletin* 10, no. 3. Brighton: Institute of Development Studies.

Wieringa, S. 1994. "Women's Interests and Empowerment: Gender Planning Reconsidered." *Development and Change* 25:829-848.

Wikan, U. 1980. *Living Among the Poor in Cairo.* Translated by A. Henning. London: Tavistock Publications.

Wolf, D. 1990. "Daughters, Decisions and Domination: An Empirical and Conceptual Critique of Household Strategies." *Development and Change* 21:43-74.

Association for the Development and Enhancement of Women (ADEW)), 1994. Women-headed Households in Egypt: A Panel Discussion."

Organized by ADEW at the ICPD NGO Forum 1994. Cairo: Association for the Development and Enhancement of Women (ADEW).

World Bank. 1995. "Workers in an Integrated World." *World Development Report.* New York: Oxford University Press.

Wright, S., ed. 1994. *Anthropology of Organisations.* London: Routledge.

Yanagisako, S. 1979. "Family and Household: The Analysis of Domestic Groups." *Annual Review of Anthropology* 8:161-205.

_____ .1977. "Women-Centered Kin Networks in Urban Bilateral Kinship." *American Ethnologist* 4:207-226.

Young, K., C. Wolkowitz, and R. McCullagh, eds. 1981. *Of Marriage and the Market: Women's Subordination Internationally and its Lessons.* London: Routledge.

Zaalouk, M. 1990. *Labour Information System Project: Women.* Preliminary Report 1. Cairo: CAPMAS.

Zurayek, H. and F. Shorter. 1988. "The Social Composition of Households in Arab Cities and Settlements: Cairo, Beirut and Amman." *Regional Papers.* Cairo: The Population Council. Regional Office for West Asia and North Africa.

Zulficar, M. 1993. *Women in Development in Egypt: A Legal Study.* Cairo: UNICEF.

INDEX

꧁꧂

A

Abdel-Fadil, M., 35
abortion, 212, 214n.3
Abu-Lughod, J., 23, 49
Abu-Lughod, L., 26, 63
Acker, J., 82
Agarwal, B., 27, 204-205
age in structural position of women, 25
Al-Messiri, S., 75, 173, 179, 193
Anderson, K., 78
Appadurai, A., 127-128
Association for the Development and
    Enhancement of Women (ADEW), 4, 5,
    64, 65
ᶜawaanis (spinsters), 85
ayma (marriage inventory). See marriage
    transactions and negotiations
aytaam (orphans), 56-57, 58

B

baahitha (researcher), 65
bargaining, 26
Beneria, L., 133, 136
birth control, 178, 194
Boddy, J., 172-173
Borland, K., 81
Bourdieu, P., 18, 63, 92, 109, 121, 142, 200-
    201, 220, 226

C

Cairo
        ᶜashwaᵓ iyyat settlements, 46, 48-49
        female street sweepers in, 40
        "first-step migration," 48

Gamaliya, 51, 53, 55
haara (social and political division;
    narrow alleyway), 46, 47, 49, 50,
    60n.1
il-Azhar, 51
il Ghouriyya, 51
il masriyyiin or masarwa (original
    dwellers), 58, 110
ᶜizbet il safih (hamlet of steel), 53
Khan il Khalili, 51
Manshiet Nasser community, 46-47,
    51-55, 58
mosaic of subcultures, 50
Muqattam, 1
Qayet Bey cemetery, 51
Sayeda Aisha, 52
Sayeda Zeinab, 54-55
"study community," description of,
    55-60
"urbanites," types of, 50, 51
water and sanitation, 54
CAPMAS, 35, 134
Comaroff, J., 168-169
conjugal arrangements and sexuality
        "articulatory potential" of spirit
            possession, 172-173
        Christian spirit possession of women,
            183-186
        female sexual services and male
            economic provisions, 175
        hadra ceremony, 167, 170-171, 188,
            223
        haraam (religious sin for refusing sex),
            176

259

"Islamization" of everyday life and
spirit possession, 181-186, 223
negotiating sexual relations, 173-177
sex, power and economic provision,
177-181
spirit possession as subordinate
discourse, 168-186
subordinate discourses, potential and
limitations of, 186-189
wife abuse in Egypt, 176, 178
zaar cult and spirit possession, 170,
188

D

daaya (traditional midwife), 89
dakhalit dunya (getting married), 85
dardasha (informal discussions), 77
Davis, K., 28-29
defiance, for education of daughters, 196
defiance and acquiescence in the labor
market
alliance between kinship and gender
ideology, 136-141
child labor *versus* "family" labor,
144-145
deflowering ceremonies, role of,
153-161, 195, 221-222, 224
female wage labor, 132
"feminization" of labor tasks and labor
force, 135, 138
gendered division of labor, 145-153
hymen replacement surgery, 158-159
middlewoman, 136, 139-141
"mutual indebtedness," 136
overt protest: *namrada,* 161-163,
219-220, 222
piecework, "euphemization" of, 132,
142-143, 219, 220
"proper" female behavior and
working, 143
risks of wage labor, 153-161
sexual harassment in workshops, 147-
149, 219
social organization of piecework, 133-
136
"strategic trade-offs" and wage work,
160-161, 224
"workshop girls" (*banaat il wirash*),
144-153, 218, 220, 221
deflowering ceremony, 153-161, 195,
221-222, 224

domestic abuse, 39
duktuura (Ph.D.), 65
Dwyer, D., 79-80

E

education
of daughters in a household, 194,
195-205, 218
rural and urban differences in
educating daughters, 202-205
Egypt
Bedouin communities in, 26
domestic violence link with cost of
living, 39, 199
economic liberalization and structural
adjustment, 38-41
family arrangements, 34
impact of male out-migration, 37
increase in consumerism, 37-38
"informal economic sector," 35
Islamic discourses, rise of, 41-44
migration, regional and internal, 36-
38
national democratic party (NDP), 52
"open door" (*el infitaah*) policies, 38,
43, 50, 127
poverty levels in, 34-35
socioeconomic profile of, 34-35
"state feminism," 38-39
state support of health and education,
41
structural adjustment policies (SAPs),
39-41, 50
unemployment rates of females and
males, 40
urbanization, rates of, 36, 230
women-headed households, 34
Egyptian Demographic and Health Survey
(EDHS), 92
Eickleman, D., 3
ElAli, N., 71
El-Hamamsy, L., 202
El-Mogy, S., 205
ethnography
analytical approach and research
questions, 74-77, 236-237
"angle of vision," 63, 82
Arabic proverbs and colloquialisms,
79-80
communities in study, 46-47
familiarity and distance, 70-74

education of daughters, 194, 195-
205, 218
and families, 75-76, 83n.5
sites for gender relations, 76
as unit of analysis, 75-76
See also intrahousehold decisions and
extrahousehold networks
hymen replacement surgery, 158-159

I

Ibrahim, S., 50
identity cards *(bitaqa shaksia)*, 5, 67, 69
ikhtaaru (spouse), 94
il kheir dakhal gismaha (good enters a girl's
body), 85
infitaah ("open door policies"), 38, 43
International Conference on Population and
Development (ICPD), 118
International Monetary Fund, 39
intrahousehold decisions and extrahousehold
networks
diverting male income to *gam*⊂*iyya,*
213
extrafamilial networks, 205-214
female run grocery stores *(bi*ᵓ *aala),*
209
gam⊂*iyya* (rotating credit or savings
associations), 210-213
hadra ceremonies in female networks,
207-208, 223
patterns of decision making, 194
rural and urban differences in
educating daughters, 202-205
Iran
temporary marriage in, 180
war with Iraq, 36
Iraq
Egyptian migration to, 36
war with Iran, 36
irhabiyyiin ("terrorists"), 49
Islam
*Ashira il Muhammadiyya (private
voluntary organization), 52
conservative movement in Egypt, 41-
44
"fundamentalism," 42
il Gam⊂*iyya il Shar*⊂*iyya* (private
voluntary organization), 52, 182
"Islamic dress," 189
"Islamist" movement, 42

islamization of everyday life, 44, 170,
181-186, 223
kafaalit il yatiim (orphan support
program), 52, 57, 181
local mosque health clinics, 44, 183
marriage protocols in, 103-106, 180
"political Islam" movement, 42
private voluntary organizations
(PVOs), 52
Ramadan, 73, 182
response to spirit possession in
women, 186
segregated religious classes for women,
182
stereotypes by religion, 59, 60
"true" Muslim family, 42
Israel, 36

J

Jack, D., 78
Jordan, Egyptian migration to, 36
Joseph, S., 25, 206

K

Kandiyoti, D., 27, 29, 42
Karam, A., 120
key-money, 43
Khattab, H., 86, 87
khawagaaya (foreign woman), 71, 72
khimaar (cover of entire face and body), 182,
183, 184, 186, 189, 223
kinship
alliance between kinship and gender
ideology, 136-141
relationship to gender, 24-25
role in subcontracting work, 136-141
kudya (female broker for a *hadra*), 171, 188,
192, 208
Kuwait
Egyptian migrant workers to, 36
Iraqi invasion of, 38

L

Landor, J., 38
Lebanon, dynamics of Arab families, 25
Libya, Egyptian migration to, 36
Loizos, P., 207
Lukes, Steven, 18-20, 22

A BEDOUIN CENTURY
Education and Development among the Negev Tribes in the Twentieth Century

Aref Abu-Rabia

The Bedouin in the Negev region have undergone a remarkable change of life style in the course of the 20th century: within a few generations they changed from being nomads to an almost sedentary and highly educated population. The author, who is a Bedouin himself and has worked in the Israeli Ministry of Education and Culture as Superintendent of the Bedouin Educational Schools in the Negev for many years, offers the first in-depth study of the development of Bedouin society, using the educational system as his focus.

From the contents: Introduction; Ottoman Education; Bedouin under British Mandate; Education during British Mandate; Negev Bedouin Education: 1948–1998; Negev Clans and Tribes: Sheikhs and Notables; Bedouin Education in Arab Countries

Aref Abu-Rabia teaches in the Department of Middle East Studies at the Ben-Gurion University of the Negev.

2001, 224 pages, 3 maps, 8 tables, 15 halftones, bibliog., index
ISBN 1-57181-832-4 hardback

WOMEN AND THE POLITICS OF MILITARY CONFRONTATION

Palestinian and Israeli Gendered Narratives of Dislocation

Edited by **Nahla Abdo** and **Ronit Lentin**

"This is a brave and fractured book that bears the marks (and wounds) of conflictual histories and contemporary confrontations in Palestine/Israel... This unique book opens up new [meaning] of what Zionism and Israel have meant for Jews and Palestinians."
—**Lila Abu-Lughod,** Professor of Anthropology and Gender Studies, Columbia University

"History and biography converge in this stunning collection of personal narratives. [The book] is testament to the urgency of dialogue between Palestinian and Israeli women. These essays probe the searing pain of life under Israeli military occupation and the complex sorrow of dislocation and exile. They push us to examine the limits of nationalisms, the moral scaffolding of the state of Israel, and the legacy of the Sho'ah. I know of no other work that so deftly expresses the tenacity of surviving, the daring of resistance, and the will to forge a just peace."
—**R. Ruth Linden,** Lecturer, University of California, San Francisco

"Powerful, moving, and revealing.... This book is a must for anyone who is interested in the Israeli/Palestinian conflict and in issues of national and gender construction."
—**Tamar Mayer,** Professor of Geography, Middlebury College

Nahla Abdo is Professor of Sociology at Carleton University, Ottawa. **Ronit Lentin** is course co-ordinator of the MPhil in Ethnic Studies at the Department of Sociology, Trinity College Dublin.

2002. 336 pages, bibliog., index
ISBN 1-57181-458-2 hardback
ISBN 1-57181-459-0 paperback

www.berghahnbooks.com

Related Titles by *Berghahn Books*

ENGENDERING FORCED MIGRATION
Theory and Practice

Edited by **Doreen Indra**

"A rich collection...written from a wide range of disciplinary perspectives."
—**Asian and Pacific Migration Journal**

At the turn of the new millenium, war, political oppression, desperate poverty, environmental degradation and disasters, and economic underdevelopment are sharply increasing the ranks of the world's twenty million forced migrants. In this volume, eighteen scholars provide a wide-ranging, interdisciplinary look beyond the statistics at the experiences of the women, men, girls, and boys who comprise this global flow, and at the highly gendered forces that frame and affect them. In theorizing gender and forced migration, these authors present a set of descriptively rich, gendered case studies drawn from around the world on topics ranging from international human rights, to the culture of aid, to the complex ways in which women and men envision displacement and resettlement.

Doreen Indra is Associate Professor of Anthropology at the University of Lethbridge, Alberta. Her most recent work has been on environmentally forced migrants in Bangladesh and the social construction and culture of disasters. She is the co-author of *Continuous Journey: Social History of South Asians in Canada*, co-editor and author of two volumes on refugees in Canada and is author of many academic journal articles in the field of forced migration.

1998. 400 pages, bibliog., index
ISBN 1-57181-134-6 hardback
ISBN 1-57181-135-4 paperback
Volume 5, *Studies in Forced Migration*

www.berghahnbooks.com